McDougal Littell
CLASSZONE ▶

Visit **classzone.com** and get connected.

ClassZone resources provide instruction, practice and learning support for students and parents.

Help with the Math

- @Home Tutor enables students to focus on the math and be more prepared for class, using animated examples and instruction.
- Extra examples similar to those in the book provide additional support.
- Hints and Homework Help offers assistance solving select homework exercises.

Practice, Practice, Practice

- eWorkbook includes interactive worksheets with additional practice problems.
- Problem of the Week features a new problem to solve every week.

Games and Activities

- Crossword puzzles, memory games, and other activities help students connect to essential math concepts.
- Math Vocabulary Flipcards are a fun way to learn math terminology.

Animated Math

- Engaging activities with animated problem-solving graphics support each lesson.

Access the online version of your textbook at **classzone.com**

Your complete text is available for immediate use!

McDougal Littell
Where Great Lessons Begin

McDougal Littell

Math*Thematics*

NEW EDITION

Senior Authors

Rick Billstein
Jim Williamson

The STEM Project

SUCCESS THROUGH EXPLORING MATHEMATICS

BOOK 1

Photography Acknowledgments
Cover: *Coral in Soma Bay, Gorgonian Fan* © Settimio Cipriani/Grand Tour/Corbis; *Maze at Hampton Court* © Skyscan Photolibrary/Alamy; *Diplodocus Dinosaur and Human Skeletons* © Louie Psihoyos/Corbis.

Table of Contents: iv © Settimio Cipriani/Grand Tour/Corbis; **v** © Skyscan Photolibrary/Alamy; **vi** © Phil Schermeister/Corbis; **vii** © Frans Lanting/Minden Pictures; **viii** © Jim West/The Image Works; **ix** © Louie Psihoyos/Corbis; **x** © Jose Fuste Raga/Corbis; **xi** © Chuck Place/Alamy.

Scavenger Hunt: xxi Jorge Alban/McDougal Littell/Houghton Mifflin Co.

Further acknowledgments for copyrighted material can be found at the end of the book and constitute an extension of this page.

THE STEM PROJECT   *McDougal Littell Math Thematics®* is based on the field-test versions of The STEM Project curriculum. The STEM Project was supported in part by the

 NATIONAL SCIENCE FOUNDATION

under Grant No. ESI-0137682. Opinions expressed in *McDougal Littell Math Thematics®* are those of the authors and not necessarily those of the National Science Foundation.

ISBN-13: 978-0-618-65605-9
ISBN-10: 0-618-65605-7

456789 0914 11 10 09

Internet Web Site: http://www.mcdougallittell.com

McDOUGAL LITTELL
MATH*Jhematics*
Book 1

SENIOR AUTHORS

Rick Billstein   Department of Mathematical Sciences, The University of Montana, Missoula, Montana

Jim Williamson   Department of Mathematical Sciences, The University of Montana, Missoula, Montana

REVISION WRITERS

Lyle Andersen, Jean Howard, Deb Johnson, Bonnie Spence

MATHEMATICS CONSULTANTS

Dr. Ira Papick   The University of Missouri, Columbia, Missouri

Dr. David Barker   Illinois State University, Normal, Illinois

PROJECT EVALUATOR

Dr. Ted Hodgson   Montana State University, Bozeman, Montana

CONSULTING AUTHORS

Perry Montoya, Jacqueline Lowery, Dianne Williams

STEM WRITERS

Mary Buck, Clay Burkett, Lynn Churchill, Chris Clouse, Roslyn Denny, William Derrick, Sue Dolezal, Doug Galarus, Paul Kennedy, Pat Lamphere, Nancy Merrill, Perry Montoya, Sallie Morse, Marjorie Petit, Patrick Runkel, Thomas Sanders-Garrett, Richard T. Seitz, Bonnie Spence, Becky Sowders, Chris Tuckerman, Ken Wenger, Joanne Wilkie, Cheryl Wilson, Bente Winston

STEM TEACHER CONSULTANTS

Melanie Charlson, Polly Fite, Jean Howard, Tony Navarro, Paul Sowden, Linda Tetley, Marsha Vick, Patricia Zepp

MODULE 1

PATTERNS and PROBLEM SOLVING

Connecting the Theme *From tiles to quilts to kites, designers use numbers and geometry to make products sturdy,
speedy, or less expensive. You'll discover how patterns in
mathematics can be more than just pretty.*

MATH DETECTIVES

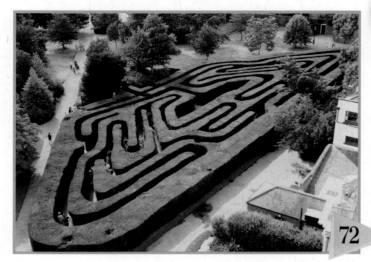

72

Connecting the Theme *Detectives use factual information, patterns, past experiences, and different strategies to solve problems. You will see how mathematics can be a tool for solving a variety of problems.*

Module Features

MODULE PROJECT
Pop-Up Art, pp. 73 and 124–125

STUDENT RESOURCE
Student Self-Assessment Scales, p. 87
Using a Protractor, p. 117

EXTENSION
Applying Experimental Probability, p. 83

Assessment Options

PORTFOLIO ASSESSMENT
   EXTENDED EXPLORATION (E²):
   Pattern Block Angles, p. 123
   REFLECTING ON THE SECTION:
   pp. 83, 95, 110, and 121

ONGOING ASSESSMENT
   CHECKPOINTS: pp. 76, 78, 88, 89, 91, 99, 102, 104, 114, 115, and 117
   KEY CONCEPTS QUESTIONS:
   pp. 80, 92, 106, 107, and 119
   STANDARDIZED TESTING:
   pp. 96 and 111

MODULE ASSESSMENT
   REVIEW AND ASSESSMENT:
   pp. 126–127
   REFLECTING ON THE MODULE:
   p. 127

MODULE 3

MIND GAMES

128

Connecting the Theme *Most games involve a mix of chance and strategy. How can you develop a strategy for winning? You'll play number games, invent puzzles, and run experiments to find the winning edge.*

Module Features

MODULE PROJECT
Puzzle Making, pp. 129 and 194–195

CAREER CONNECTION
Choreographer and Dancer, p. 170

EXTENSION
Extending Decimal Place Value, p. 146
Products in Lowest Terms, p. 182

Assessment Options

PORTFOLIO ASSESSMENT
EXTENDED EXPLORATION (E²):
The Cleaning Crew, p. 164
REFLECTING ON THE SECTION:
pp. 136, 146, 162, 169, 182, and 192

ONGOING ASSESSMENT
CHECKPOINTS: pp. 132, 133, 140, 142, 149, 150, 151, 153, 156, 166, 167, 174, 175, 177, 178, and 187
KEY CONCEPTS QUESTIONS:
pp. 134, 143, 158, 168, 178, and 190
STANDARDIZED TESTING:
pp. 137, 147, 163, 171, 183, and 193

MODULE ASSESSMENT
REVIEW AND ASSESSMENT:
pp. 196–197
REFLECTING ON THE MODULE:
p. 197

STATISTICAL SAFARI

MODULE **4**

198

Connecting the Theme *In the field, a biologist watches an animal's movements and records the data. Counting, classifying, and comparing animals can help protect a species. You'll find out how mathematics helps in studying animals.*

MODULE 5

CREATING THINGS

280

Connecting the Theme *Designers give an artistic flair to every type of creation. You'll see how people use mathematics to create everyday objects. You'll also give your personal touch to some creations.*

COMPARISONS and PREDICTIONS

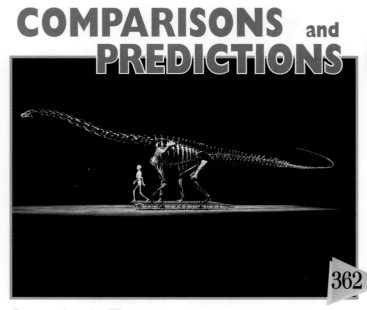

362 ▶

Connecting the Theme *In news, sports, or weather, reporters like to compare the fastest, strongest, greatest, and longest. You'll see how artists use scale, and how scientists make predictions.*

Module Features

MODULE PROJECT
Mystery Tracks, pp. 362 and 433–435

STUDENT RESOURCE
How to Measure, p. 384

CAREER CONNECTION
Oceanographer, p. 417

EXTENSION
A Doubling Rate, p. 379

Assessment Options

PORTFOLIO ASSESSMENT
  EXTENDED EXPLORATION (E²):
  The Ideal Chair, p. 395

  REFLECTING ON THE SECTION:
  pp. 371, 379, 393, 404, and 431

ONGOING ASSESSMENT
  CHECKPOINTS: pp. 366, 367, 375, 376, 383, 386, 388, 398, 400, 409, 411, 412, 420, 421, 422, 423, and 427
  KEY CONCEPTS QUESTIONS:
  pp. 368, 377, 389, 401, 402, 413, 416, 427, and 428
  STANDARDIZED TESTING:
  pp. 380, 394, 405, 418, and 432

MODULE ASSESSMENT
  REVIEW AND ASSESSMENT:
  pp. 436–437

  REFLECTING ON THE MODULE:
  p. 437

WONDERS of the WORLD

438

Connecting the Theme *Behind the world's greatest construction projects lie legends of love, fame, competition, and glory. You'll look across centuries and continents to see how engineers use mathematics to build a better marvel.*

MATH-THEMATICAL
MIX

498

Connecting the Theme *In this module, you will connect and expand mathematical topics you studied in earlier modules. You will use mathematics to find and compare measurements.*

THEMATIC APPROACH

ORGANIZATION OF THE BOOK

This book contains eight modules. To get an overview of the modules and their themes, look at the Table of Contents starting on p. iv.

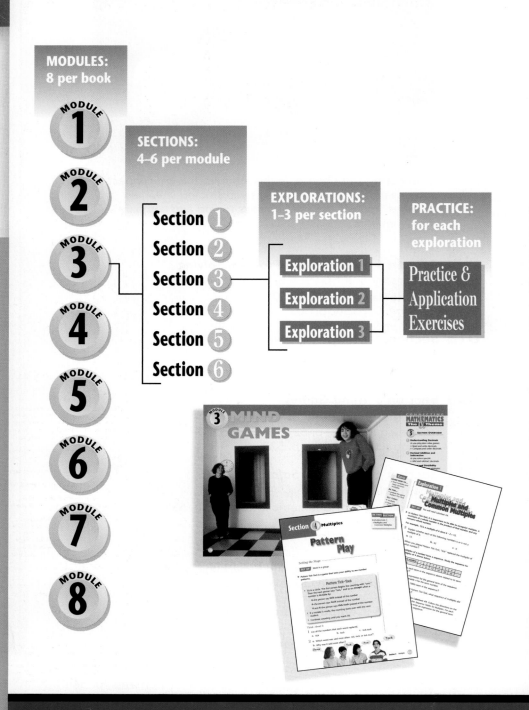

MODULES:
8 per book

MODULE **1**

MODULE **2**

MODULE **3**

MODULE **4**

MODULE **5**

MODULE **6**

MODULE **7**

MODULE **8**

SECTIONS:
4–6 per module

Section **1**
Section **2**
Section **3**
Section **4**
Section **5**
Section **6**

EXPLORATIONS:
1–3 per section

Exploration 1
Exploration 2
Exploration 3

PRACTICE:
for each exploration

Practice & Application Exercises

MODULE THEME & PROJECT

Each module's theme connects the mathematics you are learning to the real world. *Mind Games* is the theme of Module 3. At the end of each module is a Module Project that relates to the module theme.

The Module Project
As you learn new math skills, you can apply them to your work on the Module Project. By the end of the module, you'll be able to complete the project and to present your results.

MODULE 3 MIND GAMES

CONNECTING MATHEMATICS The & Theme

3 SECTION OVERVIEW

1. **Understanding Decimals**
   As you play place value games:
   * Read and write decimals.
   * Compare and order decimals.

2. **Decimal Addition and Subtraction**
   As you solve a puzzle:
   * Add and subtract decimals.

3. **Factors and Divisibility**
   As you develop game strategies:
   * Use divisibility tests.
   * Find factors and greatest common factors.
   * Find prime factorizations.
   * Explore powers of a number.

4. **Multiples**
   As you explore patterns in a game:
   * Find multiples and least common multiples.

5. **Fraction and Mixed Number Multiplication**
   As you solve a story puzzle:
   * Multiply fractions.

The Module Project

Puzzle Making

Story and number puzzles can be fun to solve and fun to create. You will explore how to solve several different types of puzzles. Then you will use the mathematics you have learned in this module to create your own puzzle. At the end of the project you will combine your puzzle with those of your classmates in a *Class Puzzle Book*.

Divisibility The puzzle on the notebook includes clues that involve divisibility.

1. Solve the puzzle. Is there more than one possible answer?

2. How can you combine the two divisibility clues?

3. Suppose the fourth clue had been, "It is an even number." What would the solution be?

4. **Create Your Own** Write a number puzzle that has 5 clues. At least one clue must involve divisibility.

What's the number?
* It has two digits.
* It is divisible by 5.
* It is divisible by 3.
* It is an odd number.
* It is greater than 70.

Cross Number Puzzles Cross Number Puzzles can be created by writing problems so that answers in overlapping squares of the puzzle have the same digits. Unused squares are filled in gray.

5. Use the clues to answer *3 down* and *7 across.*

Across	Down
1. $11.4 \cdot 0.4$	1. $12.8 - 7.9$
5. one and four thousandths	2. $0.05 \cdot 0.03$
6. numerator of $32\frac{2}{9}$ when written as a fraction.	3. $22 + 28.2$
	4. 8^2
7. a multiple of 25	5.
9.	8. a prime between 50 and 60
10. GCF of 27 and 18	

Parts of this puzzle were created by working backwards, first filling in answers on the cross number grid and then writing the clues.

6. Clues for *9 across* and *5 down* have not yet been written. Write a clue for each that will produce the answers shown in the corresponding numbered boxes of the cross number puzzle.

SECTION OVERVIEW

SECTION ORGANIZATION

The diagram below illustrates the organization of a section:

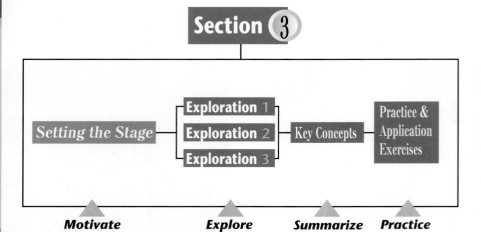

Section **3**

Setting the Stage → Exploration 1 / Exploration 2 / Exploration 3 → Key Concepts → Practice & Application Exercises

Motivate   **Explore**   **Summarize**   **Practice**

Section **3** **Factors and Divisibility**

IN THIS SECTION
EXPLORATION 1
♦ Testing for Divisibility
EXPLORATION 2
♦ Prime Factors
EXPLORATION 3
♦ Powers of Numbers

Paper Clip Products

Section Title and Mathematics Focus
The title of Section 3 is *Paper Clip Products*. Its math focus is *Factors and Divisibility*.

Setting the Stage
begins with a reading, graph, activity, or game to introduce the section.

Setting the Stage

SET UP Work with a partner. You will n̶
• 2 paper clips • 10 each of tw̶

Paper Clip Products is a strategy game involving multiplication.

Paper Clip Products

♦ Player 1 starts. Place the paper clips on numbers in the factor list. They may both be on the same factor. Multiply the numbers and place a chip on the product on the game board. (Player 2 will use a different color chip.)

♦ Player 1 and Player 2 alternate turns. On a turn, leave one paper clip where it is, and move the other clip to any factor. Cover the new product with a chip.

♦ A turn ends when a player covers a product or if a product is not on the game board or is already covered.

♦ A player wins by covering three adjacent products horizontally, vertically, or diagonally.

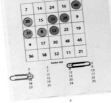

Use Labsheet 3A. Play *Paper Clip Products* twice.

Think About It

1 If you are Player 1, where might you want to place the first two paper clips? Why?

2 What kind of moves did you avoid? Why?

EXPLORATIONS & KEY CONCEPTS

In the explorations you'll be actively involved in investigating mathematics concepts, learning mathematics skills, and solving problems.

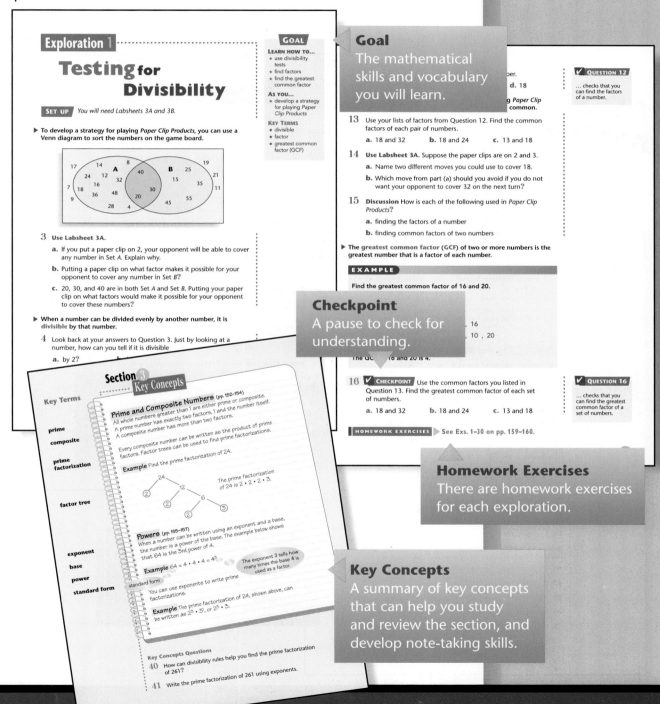

Exploration 1

Testing for Divisibility

SET UP You will need Labsheets 3A and 3B.

▶ To develop a strategy for playing *Paper Clip Products*, you can use a Venn diagram to sort the numbers on the game board.

GOAL

LEARN HOW TO...
• use divisibility tests
• find factors
• find the greatest common factor

AS YOU...
• develop a strategy for playing *Paper Clip Products*

KEY TERMS
• divisible
• factor
• greatest common factor (GCF)

Goal
The mathematical skills and vocabulary you will learn.

3 **Use Labsheet 3A.**

a. If you put a paper clip on 2, your opponent will be able to cover any number in Set *A*. Explain why.

b. Putting a paper clip on what factor makes it possible for your opponent to cover any number in Set *B*?

c. 20, 30, and 40 are in both Set *A* and Set *B*. Putting your paper clip on what factors would make it possible for your opponent to cover these numbers?

▶ When a number can be divided evenly by another number, it is **divisible** by that number.

4 Look back at your answers to Question 3. Just by looking at a number, how can you tell if it is divisible

a. by 2?

d. 18

...g *Paper Clip* common.

13 Use your lists of factors from Question 12. Find the common factors of each pair of numbers.

a. 18 and 32   b. 18 and 24   c. 13 and 18

14 **Use Labsheet 3A.** Suppose the paper clips are on 2 and 3.

a. Name two different moves you could use to cover 18.

b. Which move from part (a) should you avoid if you do not want your opponent to cover 32 on the next turn?

15 **Discussion** How is each of the following used in *Paper Clip Products*?

a. finding the factors of a number

b. finding common factors of two numbers

▶ The **greatest common factor (GCF)** of two or more numbers is the greatest number that is a factor of each number.

EXAMPLE

Find the greatest common factor of 16 and 20.

✔ QUESTION 12
... checks that you can find the factors of a number.

Checkpoint
A pause to check for understanding.

, 16

, 10 , 20

The GC... 18 and 20 is 4.

16 **✔ CHECKPOINT** Use the common factors you listed in Question 13. Find the greatest common factor of each set of numbers.

a. 18 and 32   b. 18 and 24   c. 13 and 18

HOMEWORK EXERCISES ▶ See Exs. 1–30 on pp. 159–160.

✔ QUESTION 16
... checks that you can find the greatest common factor of a set of numbers.

Homework Exercises
There are homework exercises for each exploration.

Section 3
Key Concepts

Key Terms

prime

composite

prime factorization

factor tree

Prime and Composite Numbers (pp. 152–154)
All whole numbers greater than 1 are either prime or composite.
A prime number has exactly two factors, 1 and the number itself.
A composite number has more than two factors.

Every composite number can be written as the product of prime factors. Factor trees can be used to find prime factorizations.

Example Find the prime factorization of 24.

The prime factorization of 24 is 2 · 2 · 2 · 3.

exponent

base

power

standard form

Powers (pp. 155–157)
When a number can be written using an exponent and a base, the number is a power of the base. The example below shows that 64 is the 3rd power of 4.

Example 64 = 4 · 4 · 4 = 4³

standard form

The exponent tells how many times the base 4 is used as a factor.

You can use exponents to write prime factorizations.

Example The prime factorization of 24, shown above, can be written as 2³ · 3¹, or 2³ · 3.

Key Concepts
A summary of key concepts that can help you study and review the section, and develop note-taking skills.

Key Concepts Questions

40 How can divisibility rules help you find the prime factorization of 261?

41 Write the prime factorization of 261 using exponents.

SECTION OVERVIEW ▶

PRACTICE & APPLICATION

Practice and Application Exercises will give you a chance to practice the skills and concepts in the explorations and apply them in solving many types of problems.

VARIED PRACTICE

Balanced Practice

These exercises develop algebra, geometry, numerical, and problem solving skills and help you communicate mathematical ideas.

Section 3

Practice & Application Exercises

YOU WILL NEED

For Ex. 28:
◆ Labsheet 3A

Test each number for divisibility by 2, 3, 5, 9, and 10.

1. 168   2. 53   3. 499   4. 66,780

5. 4326   6. 75   7. 1011   8. 50,436

9. a. If a number is divisible by 9, is it divisible by 3? Explain.

   b. If a number is divisible by 3, is it divisible by 9? Explain.

List all the factors of each number.

10. 28   11. 51   12. 64   13. 72   14. 80

Find the greatest common factor of each set of numbers.

15. 14 and 28   16. 12 and 17   17. 21 and 51

18. 43 and 69   19. 54, 36, and 72   20. 22, 64, and 80

Greatest Common Factors can be used to write fractions in lowest terms.

Example: Write $\frac{12}{30}$ in lowest terms.

$$\frac{12}{30} = \frac{2 \cdot 6}{5 \cdot 6}$$ Use the GCF to write the numerator and denominator as products.

$$= \frac{2 \cdot \cancel{6}^{1}}{5 \cdot \cancel{6}}$$ Divide the numerator and denominator by the GCF.

$$= \frac{2}{5}$$ lowest terms

Use the greatest common factor of the numerator and denominator to write each fraction in lowest terms.

21. $\frac{12}{32}$ 22. $\frac{25}{35}$ 23. $\frac{36}{54}$ 24. $\frac{27}{63}$

Mental Math Show how to find each product using mental math. Use what you know about factors and compatible numbers.

FOR ◀ HELP

with *writing fractions in lowest terms,* see **MODULE 1, p. 61**

Section 3 Factors and Divisibility **159**

Reflecting on the Section

exercises help you communicate ideas through oral reports, journal writing, visual thinking, research, and discussion.

$2^5 = 32$
$2^4 = 16$
$2^3 = 8$
$2^2 = 4$
$2^1 = 2$

60. a. What mathematical operation is used to go from 32 to 16? from 16 to 8? Does this pattern continue throughout the sequence 32, 16, 8, 4, 2?

   b. Based on the pattern, what is the value of 2^0?

   c. How does this compare with the number of sections after 0 folds in the paper-folding pattern in Exploration 3 on page 155? Explain.

Oral Report

Exercise 61 checks that you can apply your understanding of divisibility and prime factorization.

Reflecting ◀▶ on the Section

Be prepared to discuss your answer to Exercise 61 in class.

61. a. Write the prime factorization of each number in the table.

   b. What do you notice about the prime factors of the numbers that are divisible by 6?

   c. Use your results from part (b) and the divisibility tests you know. Write a divisibility test for 6.

Divisible by 6	Not Divisible by 6
72	44
30	39
114	175
24	63
138	70

Spiral ◀▶ Review

62. A bag contains 1 red marble, 2 yellow marbles, and 7 blue marbles. What is the theoretical probability of drawing a red marble from the bag? a green marble? (Module 2, p. 80)

63. If possible, sketch a triangle that is both obtuse and scalene. (Module 2, pp. 106–107)

Decide if the given lengths will form a triangle. (Module 2, p. 106)

64. 3 in., 2 in., 6 in.   65. 4 ft, 22 ft, 25 ft

Write an equation for each word sentence in Exercises 66–69. Use *t* for the term and *n* for the term number. (Module 1, p. 21)

66. The term is three more than the term number.

67. The term is four times the term number.

68. The term is two more than three times the term number.

69. The term is the term number to the third power.

70. Use your equations from Exercises 66–69 to find the first 4 terms of each sequence.

 162   Module 3   Mind Games

Spiral Review

exercises help you maintain skills by revisiting material from previous sections in the book.

ADDITIONAL PRACTICE

At the end of every section, you will find Extra Skill Practice. If needed, you can use these exercises for extra practice on important skills before you begin the next section.

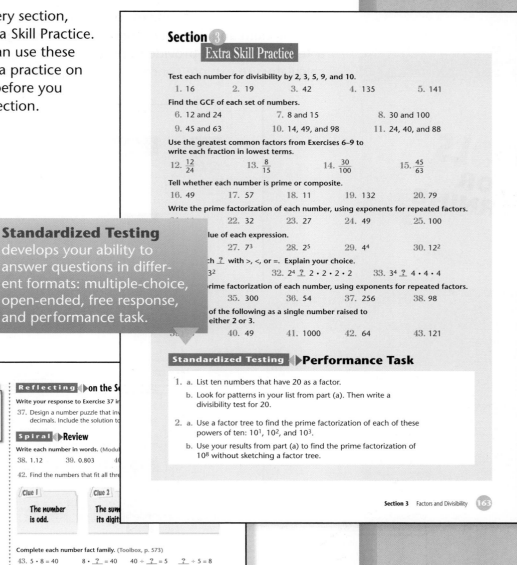

Section 3
Extra Skill Practice

Test each number for divisibility by 2, 3, 5, 9, and 10.
1. 16   2. 19   3. 42   4. 135   5. 141

Find the GCF of each set of numbers.
6. 12 and 24   7. 8 and 15   8. 30 and 100
9. 45 and 63   10. 14, 49, and 98   11. 24, 40, and 88

Use the greatest common factors from Exercises 6–9 to write each fraction in lowest terms.
12. $\frac{12}{24}$ 13. $\frac{8}{15}$ 14. $\frac{30}{100}$ 15. $\frac{45}{63}$

Tell whether each number is prime or composite.
16. 49   17. 57   18. 11   19. 132   20. 79

Write the prime factorization of each number, using exponents for repeated factors.
22. 32   23. 27   24. 49   25. 100

value of each expression.
27. 7^3 28. 2^5 29. 4^4 30. 12^2

h ? with >, <, or =. Explain your choice.
3^2 32. 2^4 ? $2 \cdot 2 \cdot 2 \cdot 2$ 33. 3^4 ? $4 \cdot 4 \cdot 4$

rime factorization of each number, using exponents for repeated factors.
35. 300   36. 54   37. 256   38. 98

of the following as a single number raised to
either 2 or 3.
40. 49   41. 1000   42. 64   43. 121

Standardized Testing ◀▶ Performance Task

1. a. List ten numbers that have 20 as a factor.
   b. Look for patterns in your list from part (a). Then write a divisibility test for 20.

2. a. Use a factor tree to find the prime factorization of each of these powers of ten: 10^1, 10^2, and 10^3.
   b. Use your results from part (a) to find the prime factorization of 10^8 without sketching a factor tree.

Section 3   Factors and Divisibility   163

Standardized Testing
develops your ability to answer questions in different formats: multiple-choice, open-ended, free response, and performance task.

Journal
Exercise 37 checks that you understand the role of place value in adding or subtracting decimals.

Reflecting ◀▶ on the Se

Write your response to Exercise 37 i
37. Design a number puzzle that inv decimals. Include the solution to

Spiral ◀▶ Review

Write each number in words. (Modul
38. 1.12   39. 0.803   4

42. Find the numbers that fit all thre

Clue I	Clue 2
The number is odd.	The sum its digit

Complete each number fact family. (Toolbox, p. 573)
43. $5 \cdot 8 = 40$ $8 \cdot \underline{?} = 40$ $40 \div \underline{?} = 5$ $\underline{?} \div 5 = 8$
44. $6 \cdot \underline{?} = 42$ $\underline{?} \cdot \underline{?} = 42$ $42 \div \underline{?} = 6$ $\underline{?} \div 6 = 7$
45. $18 \div 9 = \underline{?}$ $\underline{?} \div \underline{?} = 9$ $\underline{?} \cdot 2 = 18$ $\underline{?} \cdot \underline{?} = 18$

Extension ▶ ▶

Extending Decimal Place Value
Use the following list of decimals to answer Exercises 46–49.
0.00009, 0.0008, 1.00002, 0.00001, 0.00015

46. Write each decimal using words. (You may want to first extend your place-value table and fill in the missing place-value names. Then write the decimal in the table.)

47. Write the decimals above in order from least to greatest.

48. Which two decimals above have a sum of one ten-thousandth?

49. Find the difference between 1.00002 and 0.00009.

Extension
problems challenge you to extend what you have learned and to apply it in a new setting.

CALCULATORS & COMPUTERS

There are many opportunities to use calculators, as well as mental-math and paper-and-pencil methods. Online resources and a Technology Book provide opportunities to use computers and calculators to explore concepts and solve problems.

TOOLS FOR LEARNING

Using Calculators

Calculators can be especially useful as a problem solving tool. The questions on this page help make calculator use meaningful.

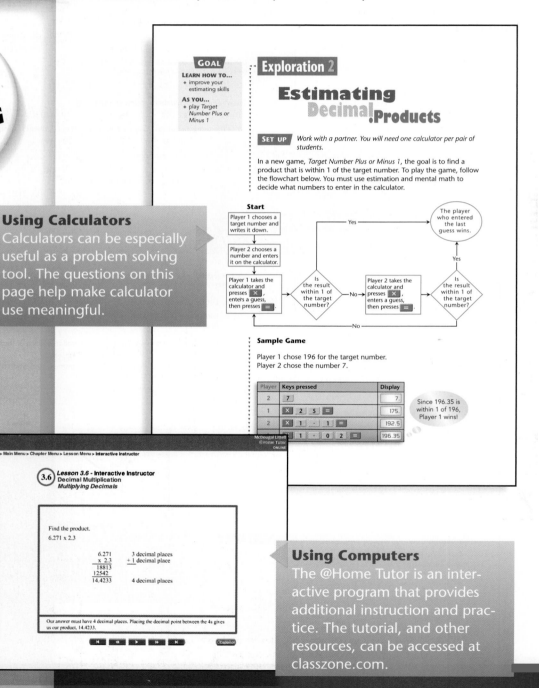

Using Computers

The @Home Tutor is an interactive program that provides additional instruction and practice. The tutorial, and other resources, can be accessed at classzone.com.

ASSESSMENT & PORTFOLIOS

In each module there are a number of questions and projects that help you check your progress and reflect on what you have learned. These pages are listed under *Assessment Options* in the Table of Contents.

E² stands for Extended Exploration—a problem solving project that you'll want to add to your portfolio.

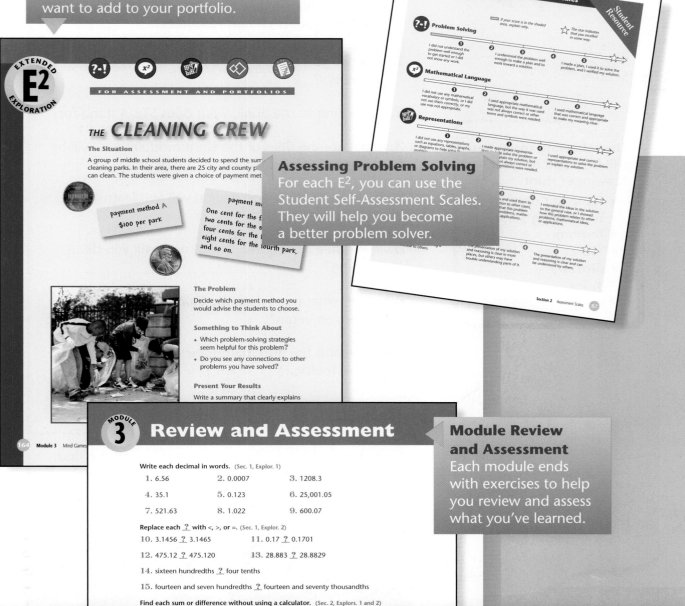

Student Self-Assessment Scales

Student Resource

☐ If your score is in the shaded area, explain why. ☆ The star indicates that you excelled in some way.

?-! Problem Solving

① I did not understand the problem well enough to get started or I did not show any work. ③ I understood the problem well enough to make a plan and to work toward a solution. ⑤ I made a plan, I used it to solve the problem, and I verified my solution.

x² Mathematical Language

① I did not use any mathematical vocabulary or symbols, or I did not use them correctly, or my use was not appropriate. ③ I used appropriate mathematical language, but the way it was used was not always correct or other terms and symbols were needed. ⑤ I used mathematical language that was correct and appropriate to make my meaning clear.

Representations

① I did not use any representations such as equations, tables, graphs, or diagrams to help solve the problem. ③ I made appropriate representations to help solve the problem or explain my solution, but they were not always correct or other representations were needed. ⑤ I used appropriate and correct representations to solve the problem or explain my solution.

③ ...and used them to ...tion to other cases, that this problem problems, mathe applications. ⑤ I extended the ideas in the solution to the general case, or I showed how this problem relates to other problems, mathematical ideas, or applications.

...ar to others. The presentation of my solution and reasoning is clear in most places, but others may have trouble understanding parts of it. The presentation of my solution and reasoning is clear and can be understood by others.

Section 2 Assessment Scales

EXTENDED E² EXPLORATION

?-! x² ◇

FOR ASSESSMENT AND PORTFOLIOS

THE CLEANING CREW

The Situation

A group of middle school students decided to spend the sum cleaning parks. In their area, there are 25 city and county p can clean. The students were given a choice of payment met

payment method A
$100 per park

payment me
One cent for the f
two cents for the s
four cents for the t
eight cents for the fourth park,
and so on.

The Problem

Decide which payment method you would advise the students to choose.

Something to Think About

- Which problem-solving strategies seem helpful for this problem?
- Do you see any connections to other problems you have solved?

Present Your Results

Write a summary that clearly explains

Assessing Problem Solving
For each E², you can use the Student Self-Assessment Scales. They will help you become a better problem solver.

164 Module 3 Mind Games

MODULE 3 Review and Assessment

Module Review and Assessment
Each module ends with exercises to help you review and assess what you've learned.

Write each decimal in words. (Sec. 1, Explor. 1)

1. 6.56   2. 0.0007   3. 1208.3

4. 35.1   5. 0.123   6. 25,001.05

7. 521.63   8. 1.022   9. 600.07

Replace each ? with <, >, or =. (Sec. 1, Explor. 2)

10. 3.1456 ? 3.1465   11. 0.17 ? 0.1701

12. 475.12 ? 475.120   13. 28.883 ? 28.8829

14. sixteen hundredths ? four tenths

15. fourteen and seven hundredths ? fourteen and seventy thousandths

Find each sum or difference without using a calculator. (Sec. 2, Explors. 1 and 2)

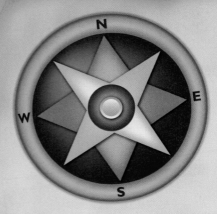

Scavenger Hunt

Your textbook will be an important tool in your study of mathematics this year. Complete the scavenger hunt below to learn more about your textbook and its various resources.

1. Why do you think the title of the book is *Math Thematics*?

2. According to the book, what does STEM stand for?

3. What are the titles of the eight modules you will be studying?

4. In which module and section will you learn about "Building with Nets"?

5. In Module 5 Section 3, what math will you be learning?

6. a. On what page does the Student Resources section begin?

   b. What is the fifth math topic that is reviewed in the Toolbox?

   c. Name one math fact that can be found in the Table of Measures.

   d. In which of the Student Resources can you find the definition of experimental probability?

The following resources will help you on your Scavenger Hunt:
- Table of Contents
- Test-Taking Skills
- Toolbox
- Tables
- Glossary
- Index
- Selected Answers

7. **a.** Use the index to locate pages on which Career Connections appear. Name one of the careers listed and the page number.

   b. Turn to that page and list the person's name and the module theme.

8. What is the title of the Extended Exploration (E^2) in Module 3?

9. On what page is percent first discussed?

10. Give a brief summary of the Module 4 Module Project.

11. What does every Key Concepts page have in common?

12. What is the suggested homework assignment for Exploration 2 of Module 2 Section 4?

13. What is the goal of Module 8 Section 3 Exploration 1?

14. How many exercises are in the Review and Assessment for Module 6?

15. What is the internet address that you can use to find online resources about a module?

16. Use the Table of Measures to find the freezing point of water in degrees Fahrenheit.

17. What is the definition of segment?

18. For more help with Exercise 33 of the Spiral Review on page 136, what page would you review?

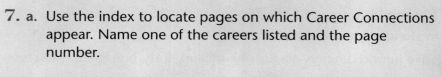

PRE-COURSE TEST

▶▶▶▶▶▶▶▶▶▶▶▶▶▶▶▶▶▶ NUMBERS AND OPERATIONS

Whole Numbers (Toolbox, pp. 565–567)

Write each number in standard form.

1. three thousand, five hundred ninety-six
2. one million, forty-one thousand, seven

Replace each __?__ with >, <, or =.

3. 220,022 __?__ 220,220
4. 7,360,032 __?__ 7,359,661

Round each number or amount to the given place.

5. 18,623 (nearest ten)
6. 1,955,014 (nearest ten thousand)
7. $105.66 (nearest hundred dollars)
8. $25.49 (nearest dollar)

Operations with Whole Numbers (Toolbox, pp. 568–572)

Use mental math to find each sum.

9. 59 + 97
10. 281 + 75
11. $6.09 + $14.32

Add, subtract, multiply, or divide.

12. 4566 + 231
13. 69,304 + 12,999
14. $45.83 + $22.25
15. 5700 − 432
16. 9807 − 1289
17. $60.24 − $49.50
18. 56 × 87
19. 334 × 739
20. 40 × $15.12
21. 6557 ÷ 20
22. 700 ÷ 16
23. 8037 ÷ 99

Number Sense (Toolbox, pp. 573–574)

Find each missing number.

24. 9 × __?__ = 54
25. __?__ + 27 = 35
26. 64 − __?__ = 43

Multiply or divide.

27. 7000 × 300
28. 50,000 ÷ 1000
29. 31,000 × 800

Perimeter and Area (Toolbox, pp. 575–576)

Find the perimeter of each figure.

30.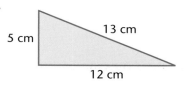

5 cm 13 cm 12 cm

31.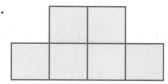

7 in. 4 in. 4 in. 7 in.

Find the area of each figure. Each small square is 1 centimeter by 1 centimeter.

32.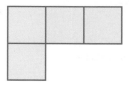

33.

Time Conversions and Elapsed Time (Toolbox, p. 577)

Find how much time has elapsed between the given times.

34. 12:45 P.M. and 7:59 P.M.

35. 10:32 A.M. and 2:10 P.M.

Reading and Making Graphs (Toolbox, pp. 578–579)

Use the bar graph for Exercises 36–38.

36. How many fish were caught in June?

37. In what month were the greatest number of fish caught?

38. About how many more fish were caught in June than in July?

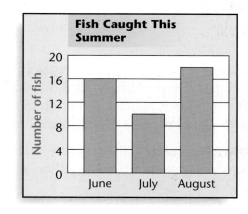

39. Make a pictograph to represent the number of players on each team.

Team	basketball	football	soccer	baseball
Number of players	15	35	25	20

TEST-TAKING SKILLS

Reading a Word Problem

Before you can solve a word problem, you have to understand the information being given and the question being asked.

- Read quickly through the problem once to get a general sense of what the problem is about.

- Read carefully through the problem a second time, focusing on those things that relate to solving the problem.

Solving a Word Problem

- Underline, jot down, and/or make a quick sketch of any information that can be used to solve the problem.

Problem

Clay bought a shirt, a tie, and a pair of pants at a clothing store. <u>The shirt cost $24, the tie cost $17, and the pants cost $28.</u> Clay also used a coupon for <u>$5 off</u> the total price. What was the total amount of money Clay spent at the clothing store?

- Decide which math topic(s) relate to the problem. Think of procedures, formulas, and definitions related to the topics that can be used to solve the problem.

- Solve the problem, making sure that the question answered is the question asked.

- Use estimation to check the reasonableness of your answer.

Prices: $24, $17, $28
Coupon: $5

To find the total amount of money spent, add all of the prices and subtract the value of the coupon.

Total without coupon: 24 + 17 + 28 = $69
Total with coupon: 69 − 5 = $64

Clay spent $64 at the clothing store.

24 + 17 + 28 − 5 ≈ 20 + 20 + 30 − 5 = 65

Keep up with the course.

Ask questions about things you don't understand. Take advantage of extra-help sessions. If you get a problem wrong on a test or on your homework, try to figure out why you got it wrong. If you are absent, find out what material you missed and make up the work.

Become familiar with the test.

Make sure you know the answers to the following questions before you take the test:

- How much time do I have to complete the test?

- How many points are assigned to each type of question?

- About how much time should I spend answering a multiple choice question? a short response question? an extended response question?

- If I can't answer a multiple choice question, is it better to guess, or to leave a blank?

- Am I better off answering the easy, or the more difficult questions first, or should I just answer the questions as they come?

- Is paper provided for scrap work, or should it be done in the white space of the test booklet?

- On which, if any, parts of the test may I use a calculator?

During the Test

- As soon as the test begins, jot down on scrap paper or in the white space of the test booklet any formulas or procedures you're afraid you'll forget.

- Quickly scan the entire test to get an idea of which problems will probably take you the most time to do. Some people prefer to do those problems first. Others do them last.

- Skip over any question you are stuck on. Make a mark next to the question in your test booklet so that you can go back to it later if you have time. Be sure to leave a blank on your answer sheet for the answer to the question.

- Read an entire problem carefully before you start to answer it. Don't assume you know the question that will be asked.

- When answering a multiple choice question, don't assume your answer is correct because it is one of the choices. Always double check your work.

- If you think you can't do a multiple choice question, try substituting each choice back into the problem to see if it is the correct choice.

- If you must guess on a multiple choice question, first try to eliminate any choices that are obviously wrong because they have the wrong units or sign, for example.

- As you write the answer to an extended or short response question, imagine that you are writing an explanation for a fellow student who doesn't know how to solve the problem.

- If you can do part, but not all, of an extended or short response question, write down what you can do. Something written may receive partial credit. Nothing written definitely receives no credit.

Strategies for Answering

Multiple Choice Questions

You can use the 4-step approach to solving problems on page 33 to solve
any problem. If you have difficulty solving a problem involving multiple
choice, you may be able to use one of the strategies below to choose the
correct answer. You may also be able to use these strategies and others to
check whether your answer to a multiple choice question is reasonable.

Strategy: Estimate the Answer

Problem 1

Jared is buying cereal that costs $3.20, milk ●------ Since the question asks for
that costs $1.85, and juice that costs $2.79.   the *total cost*, you need to
What is the total cost?   *add* the costs of the items.

    A. $1.84

    B. $6.84

    C. $7.84 ●------ Estimate: $3.20 + $1.85 + $2.79 ≈ $3 + $2 + $3 = $8,

    D. $17.84   so the correct answer is C.

Strategy: Use Visual Clues

Problem 2

The bar graph shows the tickets sold for the school
play on three different nights. How many more
tickets were sold on Saturday than on Friday?

    F. 95

    G. 115 ●--┐   The horizontal lines are 50 units ----●
             │   apart, so the difference in the
    H. 165   │   heights of the bars is between
             │   100 and 150.
    I. 175   │

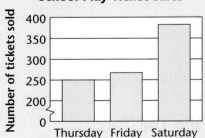

School Play Ticket Sales

          115 is the only one of the given numbers
          that is between 100 and 150, so the correct
          answer is G.

Strategy: Use Number Sense

Problem 3

Evaluate the expression $67 + (112 \times 17) \times 0$. ●------- Notice that 0 is a factor in the product $(112 \times 17) \times 0$. Use the fact that the product of 0 and any number is 0.

A. 0

B. 67 ●----

C. 1971

D. 3043

$67 + 0 = 67$, so the correct answer is B.

Eliminating Unreasonable Choices

The strategies used to find the correct answers for Problems 1–3 can also be used to eliminate answer choices that are unreasonable or obviously incorrect.

Strategy: Eliminate Choices

> Watch out for answer choices based on common errors. For example, the length of the garden is $11 + 10 = 21$ feet, not 10 feet.

Problem 4

A rectangular garden is 11 feet wide. The length of the garden is 10 feet more than the width. What is the perimeter?

F. 42 feet ●---------- *Not the correct answer:* $11 + 21 + 11 + 21 \approx 10 + 20 + 10 + 20 = 60$.

G. 58 feet ●---------- *Not the correct answer:* In the estimate above, the values were rounded down, so the actual perimeter should be greater than 60 feet.

H. 62 square feet ●--- *Not the correct answer:* perimeter is measured in *linear* units.

I. 64 feet ●--------- I is the correct answer: $11 + 21 + 11 + 21 = 64$.

TRY THIS

Explain why the highlighted answer choice is unreasonable.

1. A ribbon that is 64 centimeters long is cut into 4 pieces of equal length. How many centimeters long is each piece?

   A. 14 cm   **B.** 16 cm   **C.** 32 cm   ✗ **D.** 72 cm

2. Which expression has the least value?

   ✗ **F.** $\$10.06 - \$.20$ **G.** $\$5.70 - \$2.90$ **H.** $\$2.01 + \$1.56$ **I.** $\$3.99 + \$4.03$

3. A rug is 10 feet long. The width of the rug is 2 feet less than the length. What is the perimeter?

   A. 18 ft   **B.** 36 ft   ✗ **C.** 18 ft²   **D.** 36 ft²

Test-Taking Skills   xxvii

Multiple Choice

1. A certain airplane can carry 305 passengers. A flight attendant counts 19 empty seats on the plane. How many passengers are on the plane?

   A. 186   B. 286   C. 300   D. 324

2. The heights of wooden pickets in a fence follow the pattern below. What are the heights of the next three pickets?

   4 feet, 4.5 feet, 4 feet, 4.5 feet, . . .

   F. 4 feet, 4.5 feet, 4 feet

   G. 4.5 feet, 4 feet, 4.5 feet

   H. 4 feet, 4 feet, 4.5 feet

   I. 4.5 feet, 4.5 feet, 4 feet

3. Carmen wants to buy a skateboard for $43.50. She has $29.75. How much more money does Carmen need?

   A. $3.75   B. $13.75

   C. $14.00   D. $73.25

4. The bar graph shows how much Sam earned during each month of the summer. How much more did Sam earn in July than in June?

   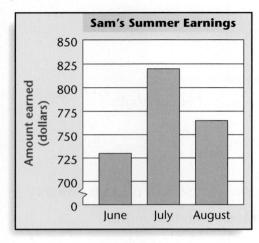

   F. $40   G. $55   H. $75   I. $90

5. What type of polygon is shown?

   A. triangle   B. pentagon

   C. hexagon   D. octagon

6. Raymond bought 5 pounds of apples for $.69 per pound. What is the best estimate for the total cost of the apples?

   F. $.35   G. $3.05

   H. $3.50   I. $35.00

7. Which rule describes the following pattern?

   2, 6, 18, 54, . . .

   A. Add 4 to the previous term.

   B. Multiply the previous term by 4.

   C. Add 3 to the previous term.

   D. Multiply the previous term by 3.

8. Sandra bought the items shown. What is the total cost of the items?

Shampoo	$2.89
Conditioner	$3.73
Hair spray	$1.95

   F. $8.57   G. $9.00

   H. $9.57   I. $857

9. A picture frame has a width of 5 inches. The length is 2 inches more than the width. What is the perimeter of the picture frame?

   A. 10 in.   B. 14 in.

   C. 24 in.   D. 35 in.

Strategies for Answering
Short Response Questions

Scoring Rubric

FULL CREDIT
- answer is correct, *and*
- work or reasoning is included

PARTIAL CREDIT
- answer is correct, but reasoning is incorrect, *or*
- answer is incorrect, but reasoning is correct

NO CREDIT
- no answer is given, *or*
- answer makes no sense

Problem

Sara is organizing a 5 kilometer road race. She wants to have 3 water stations along the race route, with equal distances between the start and the first station, between each station, and between the last station and the finish. How many meters apart should the water stations be placed?

FULL CREDIT SOLUTION

The diagram shows that the 3 water stations divide the race route into 4 equal parts. ●------- The reasoning is the key to solving the problem.

| start | water station | water station | water station | finish |

Divide 5 kilometers by 4 to find the length of each part: ●------------ The steps of the solution are clearly written.
   5 km ÷ 4 = 1.25 km

Convert kilometers to meters:
   1 km = 1000 m, so 1.25 km = 1.25 • 1000 m = 1250 m

The water stations should be 1250 meters apart. ●----------------- The question asked is answered correctly.

PARTIAL CREDIT SOLUTION

First convert 5 kilometers to meters: ●----------------- The reasoning and the conversion are correct.
   1 km = 1000 m, so 5 km = 5 • 1000 m = 5000 m

There are 4 parts, so divide 5000 meters by 4: $4\overline{)5000}$ with 125 above

The water stations should be 125 meters apart. ●------ The answer is not correct because the quotient was not calculated correctly.

PARTIAL CREDIT SOLUTION

$5 \div 4 \times 1000 = 1250$ ●- Without explanation, the reasoning behind this calculation is unclear.

The water stations should be 1250 meters apart. ●- - - - The answer is correct.

NO CREDIT SOLUTION

$5 \div 3 = 1\frac{2}{3}$ ●- The wrong divisor is used and no conversion is done.

The water stations should be $1\frac{2}{3}$ meters apart. ●- - - - - - The answer is not correct.

TRY THIS

Score each solution to the short response question below as *full credit*, *partial credit*, or *no credit*. **Explain your reasoning.**

> Watch Out!
> If a problem involves measurements, don't forget to include units with your solution.

Problem

The mean of the heights of three brothers is 66 inches. If one brother is 68 inches tall, and another brother is 70 inches tall, how tall is the third brother?

1. If the mean of the 3 heights is 66, the sum of the heights must be $66 \times 3 = 198$. Subtract the known heights from 198:

$$198 - 68 - 70 = 60$$

The height of the third brother is 60 inches.

2. Find the mean of the heights:

$$\frac{66 + 68 + 70}{3} = 68$$

The height of the third brother is 68 inches.

3. $68 + 70 = 138$

$198 - 138 = 60$

The height of the third brother is 60 inches.

Short Response

1. Brian made 48 brownies. He gave $\frac{1}{4}$ of the brownies to his grandmother. Then he gave $\frac{1}{2}$ of the remaining brownies to his father. The rest he kept for himself. How many brownies did Brian keep? Explain how you found your answer.

2. The line plot below shows the hours of sleep one person got on each of ten nights. Find the mean, median, and mode of the data. Show your work.

3. Mark is 5 years younger than twice the age of Laura. Write an expression for Mark's age. If Laura is 15 years old, how old is Mark? Show your steps.

4. A carpenter wants to saw a board into 6 pieces of equal length. The board is 1.8 meters long. How many centimeters long will each piece be? Show your work.

5. A class of 30 students is on a field trip. The teacher wants to divide the students into groups with the same number of students in each group. There must be at least 3 students in each group. What are the possible group sizes? Explain how you found your answer.

6. A two-digit number is divisible by 9 and by 5. If the first digit is an even number, what is the two-digit number? Explain how you found your answer.

7. Maria's scores on her science tests are 74, 31, 85, 80, 93, 83, and 93. Find the mean, median, and mode of the test scores. Which average best describes Maria's typical test score? Explain your reasoning.

8. Alvin is buying supplies for a barbecue. He needs 4.75 pounds of hamburger and enough buns for 19 hamburgers. Using the pricing information below, what is the total cost of the supplies that Alvin needs? Show your work.

Hamburger:	$3.40 per pound
Pack of 8 buns:	$2.09

9. A paper bag contains a tile for each of the letters in the word *MISSISSIPPI*. Another paper bag contains a tile for each of the letters in the word *OHIO*. From which bag are you more likely to draw a tile for the letter *I*? Explain how you found your answer.

10. The Venn diagram below shows the number of girls at Highland Middle School on each of three sports teams. What is the total number of girls on each team? Explain how you found your answer.

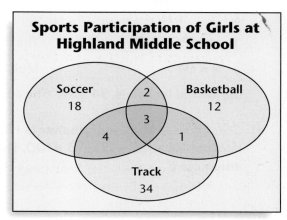

Strategies for Answering

Context-Based Multiple Choice Questions

Some of the information you need to solve a context-based multiple choice question may appear in a table, a diagram, or a graph.

Problem 1

A coach's playbook contains a scale drawing of a basketball court. The actual width of the basketball court is 50 feet. What is the actual length of the basketball court?

A. 4.7 ft   B. 87 ft

C. 94 ft   D. 135 ft

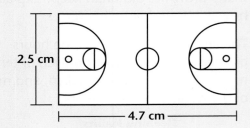

2.5 cm

4.7 cm

Solution

1) From the problem and diagram, you know: ●----------------- Read the problem carefully. Decide what information you are given and how you can use it to solve the problem.

     width on drawing = 2.5 centimeters   actual width = 50 feet

     length on drawing = 4.7 centimeters   actual length = ?

You can use the width on the drawing and the actual width to find the scale of the drawing. Then use the scale to find the actual length.

2) The scale of the drawing is $\frac{2.5\ cm}{50\ ft}$ or $\frac{1\ cm}{20\ ft}$. ●----------------- Find the scale.

3) $\frac{1\ cm}{20\ ft} = \frac{Length\ on\ drawing}{Actual\ length}$ Write a proportion. ●----------- Write and solve a proportion to find the actual length of the car. Use cross products.

     $\frac{1\ cm}{20\ ft} = \frac{4.7\ cm}{x\ ft}$ Substitute values.

     $1 \cdot x = (20)(4.7)$ The cross products are equal.

         $x = 94$ Multiply.

The actual length is 94 feet. The correct answer is C.

4) Check to see that your answer is reasonable. For example, ●---- Use one of the strategies on pages xxvi–xxvii. because 20 x 4.7 ≈ 20 x 5 = 100, the most reasonable answer is C.

Problem 2

A recipe for 8 servings of punch is shown at the right. How many quarts of ginger ale will you need for 4 servings?

F. $\frac{3}{8}$ qt   G. $\frac{3}{4}$ qt

H. 3 qt   I. 6 qt

Punch Recipe

$\frac{1}{2}$ gal sherbet $1\frac{1}{2}$ qt ginger ale

1 pt lemonade

Scoop sherbet into a punch bowl. Pour ginger ale and lemonade over sherbet. Enjoy.

Solution

1) 8 servings ÷ 2 = 4 servings, so you will need half the amount of each ingredient to make 4 servings. • - - - - - - - - Read the problem carefully. Understand what you need to do to solve the problem.

2) $1\frac{1}{2} \div 2 = \frac{3}{2} \times \frac{1}{2} = \frac{3}{4}$ • - Find the amount of ginger ale needed.

You will need $\frac{3}{4}$ quart of ginger ale for 4 servings.

The correct answer is G .

Watch Out!
Be sure that you know what question you are asked to answer. Some choices given may be intended to distract you.

TRY THIS

1. How many gallons of sherbet would be needed to make 2 servings of the punch in Problem 2?

   A. $\frac{1}{8}$ gal   B. $\frac{1}{4}$ gal   C. $\frac{1}{2}$ gal   D. 1 gal

2. The triangles shown are similar. What is the missing side length?

   F. 8 in.   G. 10 in.

   H. 12 in.   I. 15 in.

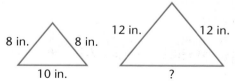

3. The table gives the free throws made and free throws attempted by four players at a basketball practice. Which player made 68% of her free throws?

   A. Gina   B. Terry

   C. Mia   D. Carmen

Player	Free throws made	Free throws attempted
Gina	17	25
Terry	26	40
Mia	9	16
Carmen	20	32

Context-Based Multiple Choice

1. A scale drawing of a yoga mat is shown. If the width of the actual yoga mat is 36 inches, what is the length of the actual yoga mat?

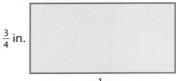

$\frac{3}{4}$ in.

$1\frac{1}{2}$ in.

A. 18 in. B. 27 in.

C. $40\frac{1}{2}$ in. D. 72 in.

2. Which two cans are similar?

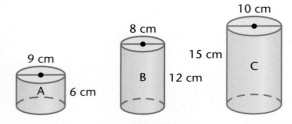

9 cm 8 cm 10 cm
A 6 cm B 15 cm 12 cm C

F. can A and can B   G. can A and can C

H. can B and can C   I. none

In Exercises 3 and 4, use the diagram below.

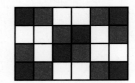

3. What is the ratio of blue squares to red squares?

A. 1   B. $\frac{1}{2}$ C. $\frac{3}{4}$ D. $\frac{4}{3}$

4. What is the ratio of red squares to white squares?

F. $\frac{3}{5}$ G. $\frac{4}{5}$ H. $\frac{5}{4}$ I. $\frac{5}{3}$

In Exercises 5 and 6, use the spinners shown below.

5. The spinner on the left is spun once. What is the probability of spinning a 1?

A. $\frac{1}{3}$ B. $\frac{1}{2}$ C. $\frac{2}{3}$ D. 1

6. The spinner on the right is spun once. What is the probability of spinning a prime number?

F. 0   G. $\frac{1}{3}$ H. $\frac{2}{3}$ I. 1

In Exercises 7 and 8, use the table of data.

Person	Height
Jared	5 ft 9 in.
Paul	6 ft 2 in.
Greg	5 ft 4 in.

7. How much taller is Paul than Greg?

A. 2 in.

B. 10 in.

C. 1 ft 2 in.

D. 1 ft 8 in.

8. What is the mean of the boys' heights?

F. 5 ft 7 in.

G. 5 ft 8 in.

H. 5 ft 9 in.

I. 5 ft 10 in.

BUILDING TEST-TAKING SKILLS (For use after Module 8.)

Strategies for Answering
Extended Response Questions

Scoring Rubric

FULL CREDIT
- answer is correct, *and*
- work or reasoning is included

PARTIAL CREDIT
- answer is correct, but reasoning is incorrect, *or*
- answer is incorrect, but reasoning is correct

NO CREDIT
- no answer is given, *or*
- answer makes no sense

Problem

Peter is starting a lawn mowing business. He buys a lawn mower for $320. Peter has work lined up that will earn him $40 a week. Make a table of values to show the number of weeks in business and the profit for 0, 1, 2, 3, 4, and 5 weeks. Graph the values. Find the number of weeks that Peter has to be in business in order to make back the cost of the lawn mower. Explain how you found your answer.

FULL CREDIT SOLUTION

Let x represent the number of weeks in business. Let y represent profit.

Week, x	0	1	2	3	4	5
Profit, y	−$320	−$280	−$240	−$200	−$160	−$120

●--- The table of values is correct and reflects an understanding of the relationship between the number of weeks and the profit.

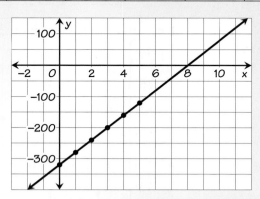

●--- The graph correctly represents the data in the table.

Peter needs to be in business for 8 weeks in order to make back the cost of the lawn mower.   ●------ The answer is correct.

I found my answer by drawing a line through the plotted points. I looked to see where the line crosses the x-axis, since that represents a profit of $0. The line crosses the x-axis at x = 8, so it will take 8 weeks.   ●--- The explanation is clear and reflects correct mathematical thinking.

The table of values is ------● incorrect. The cost of the lawn mower should be represented as a negative amount, not a positive amount.

Week, x	Profit, y
0	$320
1	$360
2	$400
3	$440
4	$480
5	$520

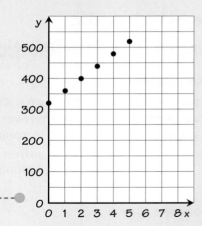

The graph correctly displays the data in the ------------● table, but the data is incorrect.

The answer is correct. ------● Peter will make back the cost of the lawn mower in 8 weeks.

The explanation reflects ---● correct mathematical reasoning.

I found my answer by dividing the cost of the lawn mower by the amount earned per week: $320 ÷ $40 = 8.

TRY THIS

Watch Out!
Scoring is often based on how clearly you explain your reasoning.

1. A student's answer to the problem on page xxxv is given below. Score the solution as *full credit*, *partial credit*, or *no credit*. Explain your choice. If you choose *partial credit* or *no credit*, explain how you would change the answer to earn a score of *full credit*.

Week, x	Profit, y
0	−$320
1	−$280
2	−$240
3	−$200
4	−$160
5	−$120

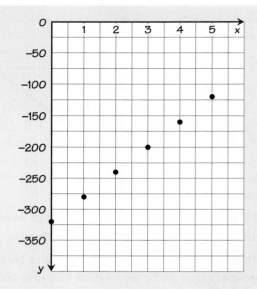

It will take Peter 8 weeks to make back the cost of the lawn mower.

To find my answer, I reasoned that since it took 4 weeks to make back half the cost of the lawn mower, it must take 8 weeks to make back the full cost of the lawn mower.

Extended Response

1. The dimensions of two rectangular prisms are shown. Find the volume of each prism. How could you change one of the dimensions of prism A to make the volume equal to the volume of prism B? Show your work.

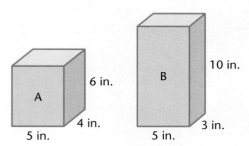

2. The deli at a grocery store sells macaroni salad by weight. Brianna buys 3 pounds of macaroni salad for $8.16. How much would 1 pound 4 ounces of macaroni salad cost? Explain how you found your answer.

3. The highest daily temperatures for one week are listed below. Find the mean, median, mode, and range of the data. Show your work. Which average does not represent the data well? Why?

   –2°F   28°F   6°F   0°F   9°F   10°F   –2°F

4. A carnival game involves throwing a dart on one of the targets shown below. You win by having the dart land within the shaded area of a target. If the dart lands on a chosen random point on a target, on which target is there a better chance of winning? Show your calculations.

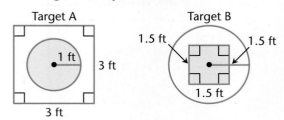

5. The circle graph shows the results of a survey in which 400 middle school students were asked to name their favorite after-school activity. How many more students said that playing sports is their favorite activity than said playing video games? Show your work.

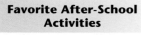

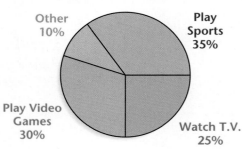

6. The table below shows the number of tickets sold to adults, senior citizens, and children at a movie screening. Make a bar graph of the data that makes it appear like the number of tickets sold to children was double the number sold to senior citizens. Explain how you created this impression.

Ticket type	adult	senior citizen	child
Number of tickets	126	75	98

PATTERNS

and

Problem

Solving

MODULE **1** SECTION OVERVIEW

1 Operations, Estimation, and Mental Math

As you look for patterns in number sentences and everyday situations:
- Learn the order of operations.
- Estimate by rounding.
- Decide when to use estimation, mental math, or a calculator.

2 Patterns and Sequences

As you explore patterns and model sequences:
- Find a rule to extend a pattern.
- Write an equation to find the terms of a sequence.
- Predict terms of a sequence.

3 A Problem Solving Approach

As you play a card swapping game:
- Learn a 4-step approach to solve problems.
- Use several problem-solving strategies.

4 Fractions and Mixed Numbers

As you explore coins and kites:
- Write fractions and mixed numbers.

5 Equivalent Fractions

As you use pattern blocks to make window designs:
- Recognize and find equivalent fractions.
- Write fractions in lowest terms.
- Find a fraction of a whole number.

The Module Project

A Puzzling Problem

You will apply mathematical ideas you have learned as you solve the *30 Pennies in a Row* problem. You will explore different approaches that can also help you with the Extended Exploration (E²) feature in each module and with other problems throughout the year. You will share your solution in a group presentation.

For the Module Project
See pp. 68-69.

IN THIS SECTION

EXPLORATION 1
◆ Order of Operations

EXPLORATION 2
◆ Estimating with Rounding

EXPLORATION 3
◆ Using Mental Math

The Science of Patterns

Setting the Stage

KEY TERM
◆ expression

SET UP *Work in a group of two or three. You will need:* • *Labsheet 1A* • *4 number cubes* • *a pair of scissors* • *a calculator*

Mathematics has been described as the science of patterns. In this module, you will begin studying patterns. Recognizing patterns can help you discover new mathematics, solve problems, and create interesting designs. It might even help you win a game!

Use Labsheet 1A. Follow the directions on the labsheet to play *A Dicey Problem.*

Think About It

▶ The problems you recorded as you played *A Dicey Problem* are examples of mathematical *expressions*. An **expression** can contain numbers, variables, and operations.

FOR ▶ HELP
with *variables*, see
MODULE 1, p. 19

1 When you played the game, what strategies did you use for choosing the numbers and operations?

2 What is the greatest possible value you could get for an expression in one turn of *A Dicey Problem*?

3 **a.** Use a calculator to find the value of your expressions.

   b. Did you get the same answers? If not, why do you think the answers were different?

Exploration 1

1. Order
2. Of
3. Operations

GOAL

LEARN HOW TO...
- follow the order of operations

AS YOU...
- look for patterns in number sentences

KEY TERM
- order of operations

▶ When they played *A Dicey Problem*, Sarah and Josh used the same numbers and operations but got different answers.

Sarah's solution:	Josh's solution:
$4 + 6 \times 5 - 2$ Answer = 32	$4 + 6 \times 5 - 2$ Answer = 48

4 Discussion

a. In what order did Sarah perform the operations in the expression $4 + 6 \times 5 - 2$ to get her answer?

b. In what order did Josh perform the operations?

▶ Mathematics would be very confusing if expressions like $4 + 6 \times 5 - 2$ could have more than one value. To understand each other's work, mathematicians have agreed on an order to follow when performing operations. This order is known as the order of operations.

To answer Questions 5–8, study the number sentences. Each number sentence follows the order of operations.

5 Describe the order in which addition and subtraction are performed to get the answers shown.

  a. $4 + 5 - 3 = 6$ **b.** $30 - 10 - 8 = 12$ **c.** $16 - 8 + 11 = 19$

6 Describe the order in which multiplication and division are performed to get the answers shown.

  a. $10 \cdot 6 \div 3 = 20$ **b.** $24 \div 6 \cdot 2 = 8$ **c.** $60 \div 10 \div 2 = 3$

Another way to show multiplication is to use a dot between the factors. $10 \cdot 6$ means 10×6.

7 Describe the order in which the operations are performed to get the answers shown.

    a. $3 \cdot 6 - 5 = 13$ **b.** $20 - 6 \cdot 2 = 8$

    c. $30 \div 10 + 5 = 8$ **d.** $15 - 4 \cdot 3 + 6 = 9$

8 How do parentheses affect the order in which operations are performed? (*Hint:* Compare these number sentences with the ones in Question 7.)

    a. $3 \cdot (6 - 5) = 3$ **b.** $(20 - 6) \cdot 2 = 28$

    c. $30 \div (10 + 5) = 2$ **d.** $(15 - 4) \cdot 3 + 6 = 39$

9 **Try This as a Class** Use your results from Questions 5–8. Describe the order of operations in a way that is clear and easy to remember.

10 For each problem, write an expression that uses both addition and multiplication and can be used to solve the problem. Then find the value of the expression.

    a. How many feet of fencing are needed to fence the three sides of the garden?

    b. How many beads are needed to make the necklace?

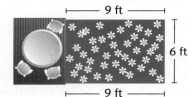

✔ **QUESTION 11**

...checks that you can follow the order of operations.

11 ✔ **CHECKPOINT** Find the value of each expression.

    a. $5 + 3 \cdot 2$ **b.** $12 - 8 + 5$ **c.** $25 \cdot 4 \div 2$

    d. $6 \cdot 5 - 18 \div 3$ **e.** $6 \cdot (5 - 2) \div 9$ **f.** $4 + (14 - 6)$

12 **a.** Use order of operations to find the value of the expressions you wrote when you played *A Dicey Problem*.

    b. Compare your answers in part (a) with the answers you got with your calculator in Question 3. Does your calculator follow the order of operations when it does calculations? Explain.

HOMEWORK EXERCISES ▶ See Exs. 1–13 on pp. 11–12.

31. Compatible numbers can also be used to estimate products.

Example:

26 · 198   **or**   26 · 198

26 · 200 = 5200   25 · 200 = 5000

Without using a calculator, explain how you can tell which estimate in the Example is closer to the exact product.

In Exercises 32–34, explain how to use compatible numbers to estimate each answer.

32. 14 · 2 · 39   **33.** 24 · 389   **34.** 325 + 34 + 40

Reflecting ◀▶ on the Section

Be prepared to report on the following topic in class.

35. a. Choose from the digits 3, 5, 4, 2, and 8. You may not repeat a digit. Copy and fill in the boxes to make the greatest possible product.

$$\begin{array}{c} \boxed{?}\ \boxed{?} \\ \times\ \boxed{?} \end{array}$$

b. Describe how you used estimation, mental math, or a calculator to solve this problem.

Oral Report

Exercise 35 checks that you can choose an appropriate computational method to solve a problem.

Spiral ◀▶ Review

Replace each ? with <, >, or =. (Toolbox, p. 566)

36. 84,987 _?_ 85,132   **37.** 25 thousand _?_ 2500

Find the missing number. (Toolbox, p. 577)

38. 50 min = _?_ sec   **39.** 3 hours = _?_ min

Extension ▶ ▶

Applying Order of Operations

40. Find a sequence of keys that results in each number 1 through 10. You may use only the keys 2 , 5 , × , − , and = . You may use each key as many times as you like or not at all.

Example: The keystrokes below result in 8.

5 × 2 − 2 =

Section 1
Extra Skill Practice

Find the value of each expression.

1. $5 + 7 \cdot 3$

2. $6 \cdot 4 + 7 \cdot 2$

3. $15 - 6 \div 3$

4. $60 \div 15 \cdot 5$

5. $10 + 30 \div 6$

6. $42 - 21 \cdot 2$

7. $(10 + 4) \div 7 + 3$

8. $5 + (12 - 4) \cdot 4$

9. $(19 - 10) \cdot 5 - 8$

10. $16 \div 2 \cdot (5 + 3)$

11. $25 - (14 + 3) + 6$

12. $2 \cdot (5 + 8) - 4 \div 2$

Estimate each answer. If possible, decide whether the estimate is _greater than_ or _less than_ the exact answer.

13. $229 + 68$

14. $323 - 119$

15. $64 + 42$

16. $137 + 22$

17. $31 \cdot 58$

18. $427 - 212$

19. $158 + 43 + 78$

20. $2362 - 1221$

21. $193 \cdot 13$

22. $12 \cdot 62$

23. $98 \cdot 45$

24. $22,352 + 1,649$

Use compatible numbers to find each answer by mental math.

25. $12 + 17 + 8 + 3$

26. $6 + 19 + 14 + 211$

27. $32 + 45 + 5 + 8$

28. $140 + 58 + 60 + 42$

29. $5 \cdot 5 \cdot 12 \cdot 4$

30. $2 \cdot 3 \cdot 3 \cdot 25$

31. $15 \cdot 4 \cdot 6 \cdot 5$

32. $20 \cdot 8 \cdot 5 \cdot 3$

Standardized Testing ◀▶ Multiple Choice

1. Which expression matches this set of directions?

   ◆ First multiply 25 by 9.

   ◆ Next add 16 to the product.

   ◆ Then divide the total by 4.

   Ⓐ $(16 + 25 \cdot 9) \div 4$ Ⓑ $25 \cdot 9 \div 4 + 16$

   Ⓒ $25 \cdot 9 + 16 \div 4$ Ⓓ $16 + (25 \cdot 9) \div 4$

2. Use mental math to decide which expression is equal to $17 + 46 + 13 + 24$.

   Ⓐ $20 + 60$ Ⓑ $46 + 50$ Ⓒ $30 + 70$ Ⓓ $30 + 50 + 25$

Section 2 Patterns and Sequences

sHAPEly Numbers

Setting the Stage ▸▸

SET UP *Work with a partner. You will need pattern blocks.*

KEY TERM
◆ sequence

Do numbers have geometric shapes? The Pythagoreans and other ancient Greeks thought so. They classified numbers based on the patterns that regularly spaced coins or pebbles formed.

For example, they called 6 a triangular number because six pebbles can be arranged to form an equilateral triangle as shown at the right.

> 1 pebble
>
> 2 pebbles
>
> 3 pebbles

The Pythagoreans were a society founded by Pythagoras of Samos (c. 500 B.C.). They studied numbers, music, and geometry.
▼

There are other triangular numbers besides 6. The first four are:

$$1, 3, 6, 10, \ldots$$

> An ordered list of numbers or objects like this is a **sequence**.

Think About It

1 What does each of the following words mean?

   a. pentagonal   **b.** hexagonal   **c.** equilateral

2 Show how the following numbers of pattern blocks can be arranged to form an equilateral triangle.

   a. 3 pattern blocks   **b.** 10 pattern blocks

3 What do you think the fifth triangular number is? Why?

▶ **In this section, you will explore patterns in mathematics. Finding patterns and using them to make predictions is an important problem-solving strategy.**

GOAL

LEARN HOW TO...
- find a rule to extend a pattern
- make a table to organize your work

AS YOU...
- explore patterns using pattern blocks

KEY TERMS
- rule
- term
- term number

Exploration 1

Extending PATTERNS

SET UP *Work with a partner. You will need pattern blocks.*

▶ Pythagoras had a *rule* for finding triangular numbers. He noticed that the third triangular number, 6, was equal to 1 + 2 + 3, and that the fourth triangular number, 10, was equal to 1 + 2 + 3 + 4.

4 **a.** How would Pythagoras have found the fifth triangular number?

b. What is the fifth triangular number? How does this compare with your answer to Question 3?

▶ **Finding a Rule** When you describe how to create or extend a sequence you are giving a **rule** for the sequence.

5 For each of the following sequences:

- ◆ Look for a pattern.
- ◆ Use pattern blocks to build the next two shapes in the sequence.
- ◆ Explain the rule you used.

The three dots tell you the pattern continues in the same way.

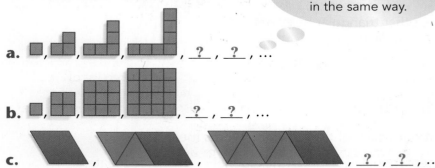

a. ☐ , ☐ , ☐ , ☐ , ? , ? , ...

b. ☐ , ☐ , ☐ , ☐ , ? , ? , ...

c. ▱ , ▱ , ▱ , ? , ? , ...

6 For each of the following sequences:

- ◆ Look for a pattern.
- ◆ Give the next two entries in the sequence.
- ◆ Explain the rule you used.

a. 2, 5, 8, 11, _?_ , _?_ , ...

b. 1, 4, 9, 16, _?_ , _?_ , ...

c. one, ten, hundred, thousand, _?_ , _?_ , ...

7 Discussion

a. What things did you look for when you tried to discover the rules for the patterns in Questions 5 and 6?

b. Are any of the sequences in Question 6 related to sequences in Question 5? If so, which ones? Explain.

c. What do you think the Pythagoreans would have called the numbers in the sequence in Question 6(b)? Why?

▶ Each number or object in a sequence is a **term** and can be labeled with a **term number**. The term number tells you the order or position of the term in the sequence.

> The **2nd term** in the sequence is **3**.

1, **3**, 6, 10, 15, ...

8 Use Pythagoras' rule to find the next term in the sequence above. What is its term number?

▶ **Using a Table** You can use a table to help organize the terms and term numbers of a sequence.

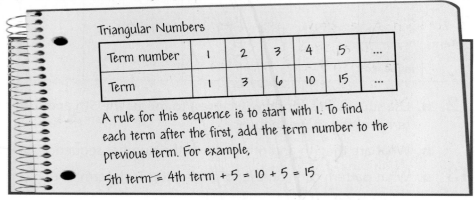

Triangular Numbers

Term number	1	2	3	4	5	...
Term	1	3	6	10	15	...

A rule for this sequence is to start with 1. To find each term after the first, add the term number to the previous term. For example,

5th term = 4th term + 5 = 10 + 5 = 15

9 a. Use the rule to find the next term of the sequence in the table. What is its term number?

b. What would the eighth term be? Explain.

10 ✔ **CHECKPOINT** Make a table showing the term numbers and terms of each sequence. Then find the next two terms of each sequence.

a. 1, 3, 7, 13, 21, _?_ , _?_ , ...

b.  , _?_ , _?_ , ...

HOMEWORK EXERCISES ▶ See Exs. 1–9 on pp. 22–23.

✔ **QUESTION 10**

...checks that you can set up a table to help examine and extend a sequence.

GOAL

LEARN HOW TO...
◆ write an equation
  to find the terms
  of a sequence
◆ make predictions

AS YOU...
◆ model sequences
◆ explore visual
  patterns

KEY TERMS
◆ equation
◆ variable
◆ evaluate an
  expression

Exploration 2

ANALYZING SEQUENCES

SET UP *You will need 20 square tiles or graph paper.*

▶ Like Pythagoras, you can use patterns to predict the terms in sequences. A table can help you see the relationship between the term numbers and the terms of the sequences.

11 How are the sequence of numbers and the sequence of shapes in the table related?

Term number		1	2	3	4	5	6	...
Term	Shape sequence					?	?	...
	Number sequence	2	4	6	8	?	?	...

12 **a.** Use square tiles (or draw pictures) to model the 5th and 6th terms of the shape sequence.

b. What are the 5th and 6th terms of the number sequence?

13 **a.** What pattern can you use to predict the 10th term of the shape sequence?

b. How is each term of the number sequence related to its term number?

c. Predict what the 10th term of the number sequence will be. To check, use your pattern from part (a) to model the 10th shape and count the squares in it.

14 **Try This as a Class**

a. Share your patterns from Question 13(a).

b. Describe the 90th term in the shape sequence.

c. Predict the 90th term of the number sequence.

d. Are the numbers in the number sequence even or odd?

▶ In Question 14, you used a pattern to predict a term of the sequence 2, 4, 6, 8, ... You may have noticed that the number of squares in each term of the shape sequence is equal to 2 times the term number. For example:

number of squares

The 4th term of the shape sequence contains 8 squares.

2 ⟶ $8 = 2 \cdot 4$

4

term number

▶ An **equation** such as $8 = 2 \cdot 4$ is a mathematical sentence stating that two quantities are equal. Sometimes you can use *variables* to write an equation that gives a rule for finding any term of a sequence. A **variable** is a quantity that is unknown or that changes. It can be represented by a letter, a word, or a symbol. To **evaluate an expression** with one or more variables, you substitute a number for each variable. Then you carry out any operations in the expression using the order of operations.

EXAMPLE

Write an equation for the rule for the sequence 2, 4, 6, 8, ... Use the equation to predict the 90th term of the sequence.

SAMPLE RESPONSE

Because the terms and the term numbers change, you can use variables to represent them. Let **t** = the term. Let **n** = the term number.

The term is equal to 2 times the term number.

$$t = 2 \cdot n$$
or $\quad t = 2n$

"2 times n" can be written $2 \cdot n$ or $2n$.

Use this equation to predict the 90th term of the sequence. Evaluate the expression $2 \cdot n$ when $n = 90$.

$$t = 2 \cdot n$$
$$= 2 \cdot 90$$
$$= 180$$

For the **90th term**, the term number **n** is 90.

The 90th term of the sequence 2, 4, 6, 8, ... is 180.

15 Copy the table below and extend it to include the next two terms in the shape and number sequences.

Term number		1	2	3	4	5	6	...
Term	Shape sequence	▪	▪▪	▪▪▪	▪▪▪▪	?	?	...
	Number sequence	1	3	5	7	?	?	...

16 **Try This as a Class**

a. Explain how to sketch the 20th term in the shape sequence.

b. Describe two ways to find the 20th term of the number sequence.

c. Write an equation that can be used to find any term of the number sequence from its term number. Use t for the term and n for the term number.

d. Use your equation to find the 75th term of the number sequence.

e. Are the numbers in the number sequence *even* or *odd*? How can you tell from the shapes in the shape sequence?

f. How can you tell whether a number is *even* or *odd* without sketching a shape?

✔ QUESTION 17

...checks that you can write a rule for finding the terms of a sequence.

17 **✔ CHECKPOINT**

a. How is each term in the number sequence below related to its term number?

Term number	1	2	3	4	...
Term	4	5	6	7	...

b. Write an equation for the rule for the sequence. Be sure to identify what each variable in the equation represents.

c. Use the equation to find the 67th term in the sequence.

HOMEWORK EXERCISES ▶ See Exs. 10–19 on pp. 24–25.

Section 2

Key Concepts

Sequences (pp. 15–17)

A sequence is an ordered list of numbers or objects.

Example

5, 10, **15**, 20, 25, ...

> The 3rd term in the sequence is **15**.

Each number or object of a sequence is a term. The position of each term can be labeled with a term number.

A table can help you see how the term numbers and terms of a sequence are related and write a rule for finding the terms of the sequence.

Example

Term number	1	2	3	4	5
Term	5	10	15	20	25

Rule: Start with 5. Add 5 to each term to get the next term.

or

The term is 5 times the term number.

Equations and Variables (pp. 18–20)

You can use variables to write an equation that shows how a term in a sequence is related to its term number. A variable is a letter, word, or symbol used to represent unknown quantities or quantities that change. To evaluate an expression with one or more variables, substitute a number for each variable. Then carry out any operations in the expression.

Example Write an equation for the rule for the sequence 5, 10, 15, 20, ...

The term t is 5 times the term number n.

$$t = 5 \cdot n \text{ or } t = 5n$$

18 Key Concepts Question Make a table for the sequence 3, 5, 7, 9, 11, ... Extend the table to include the next two terms. Then write a rule for the sequence.

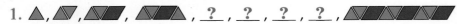

Practice & Application Exercises

In Exercises 1–4, look for a pattern and replace each __?__ with the correct term. Describe the rule you used for each sequence.

1. ▲, ◢◣, ◢◣▰, ◢◣▰◣ , __?__ , __?__ , __?__ , __?__ , ◢◣◢◣◢◣▰

2. 7, 14, 21, 28, __?__ , __?__ , __?__ , __?__ , 63

3. 99, 90, 81, 72, __?__ , __?__ , __?__ , __?__ , 27

4. $\frac{1}{2}, \frac{1}{4}, \frac{1}{6}, \frac{1}{8},$ __?__ , __?__ , __?__ , __?__ , $\frac{1}{18}$

5. At the end of February, Ben began to save for a $240 mountain bike. At the time he had $113 in his savings account. His savings increased to $138 at the end of March and $163 at the end of April. If his savings pattern continues, when will he be able to buy the bike?

6. A middle school class schedule forms a sequence. Each period is the same length. The first three periods begin at 7:40 A.M., 8:30 A.M., and 9:20 A.M.

   a. What rule does the class schedule follow?

   b. Make a table showing the periods of the day and the times they begin. Using your rule from part (a), extend the table to find what time 7th period will begin.

7. **Science** Plants and animals are made up of tiny cells you can only see under a microscope. The pictures show a new starfish starting to grow from a single cell. The cell divides to form two cells. Then each of the new cells divides into two cells, and so on.

  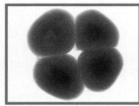 

   a. The numbers of cells in the pictures form a sequence. Make a table and record the sequence.

   b. Describe the pattern that develops as the number of cells increases.

   c. How many cells would be in the 6th term of the sequence?

8. Jimi and Adam both extended the sequence 2, 4, 8, ... Did they both extend the sequence correctly? Explain.

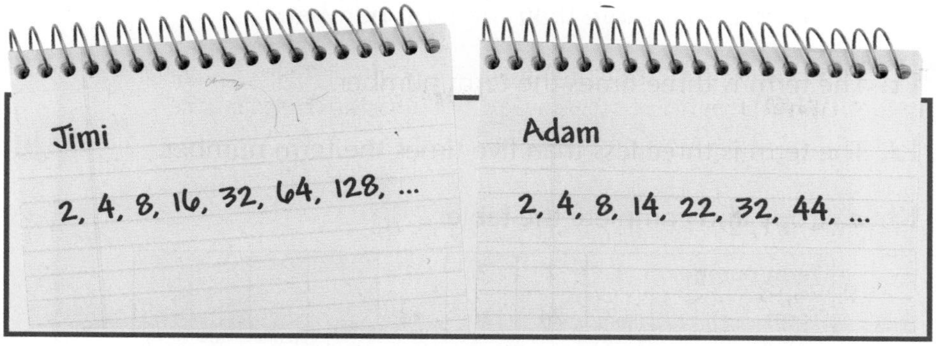

Jimi

2, 4, 8, 16, 32, 64, 128, ...

Adam

2, 4, 8, 14, 22, 32, 44, ...

9. **Challenge**

a. The following table contains the first four pentagonal numbers. What are the 5th and 6th pentagonal numbers?

Term number		1	2	3	4	5	6
Term	Shape sequence			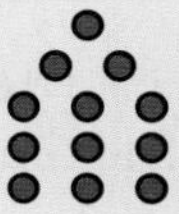	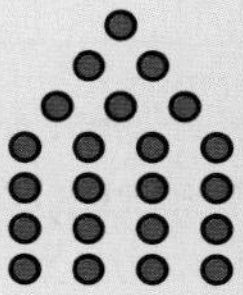	?	?
	Number sequence	1	5	12	22	?	?

b. The following table contains the first four hexagonal numbers. What are the 5th and 6th hexagonal numbers?

Term number		1	2	3	4	5	6
Term	Shape sequence			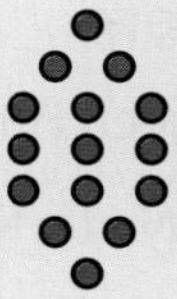	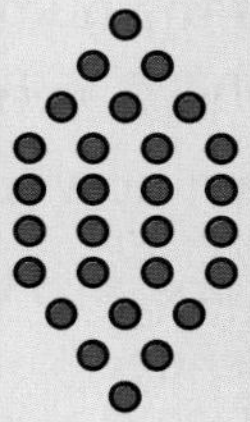	?	?
	Number sequence	1	6	15	28	?	?

c. How is the shape for each hexagonal number related to the shape for the corresponding pentagonal number?

Write an equation for each word sentence. Use _t_ for the term and _n_ for the term number.

10. The term is four more than the term number.

11. The term is three times the term number.

12. The term is three less than five times the term number.

13. **a.** Copy and complete the table.

Term number	1	2	3	4	?	?	?	?
Term	12	24	36	48	?	?	?	?

 b. How are the term numbers and terms related?

 c. Write an equation for the rule for the sequence. Use _t_ for the term and _n_ for the term number.

 d. Use the equation to find the 30th term in the sequence.

14. Repeat parts (a)–(d) of Exercise 13 for the table below.

Term number	1	2	3	4	?	?	?	?
Term	99	98	97	96	?	?	?	?

15. Use the sequence of shapes in the table below.

Term number	1	2	3	4
Term				

 a. Draw a picture of the 5th and 6th terms of the sequence.

 b. Write the number sequence that matches the first six terms of the shape sequence.

 c. Explain how to sketch the 10th term in the shape sequence.

 d. Describe two ways to find the 10th term of the number sequence.

 e. Write an equation that can be used to find any term of the number sequence from its term number. Be sure to identify what each variable in the equation represents.

 f. Use your equation to find the 25th term of the number sequence.

16. Each shape at the right is made with toothpicks. A sequence can be formed by listing the number of toothpicks in each shape.

   a. Make a table and record the first five terms.

   b. Think about the relationship between the terms and the term numbers. Write an equation that can be used to find any term in the sequence.

   c. How many toothpicks would be needed to build the 12th shape?

17. **Challenge** Look back at Exercise 7 on page 22. Explain how you could find the number of cells in the 25th term.

18. **Visual Thinking** Use the shape sequences on pages 18 and 20 to help answer the following questions.

   a. Is the sum of an even number and an odd number *even* or *odd*? How can you tell?

   b. Is the sum of two odd numbers *even* or *odd*? Explain.

R e f l e c t i n g ◀▷on the Section

Be prepared to discuss your response to Exercise 19 in class.

19. *Start with 3 and add 4 to each term to get the next term*
                              and
   the term is 1 less than 4 times the term number

   are both rules for the sequence 3, 7, 11, 15, 19, ….

   For each rule, give an example of a problem that you would use the rule to solve. Explain why you would choose that rule to solve the problem.

Discussion

Exercise 19 checks that you understand how different kinds of rules can be used to create or extend patterns.

S p i r a l ◀▷Review

Write each number in words. (Toolbox, p. 565)

20. 3672   21. 671,598   22. 23,856

Find each sum or difference. (Toolbox, pp. 568, 570)

23. 534 + 682   24. 291 − 156   25. 7256 + 873

26. 5473 − 598   27. 32,567 − 9239   28. 294 + 67 + 141

Draw a picture of each shape.

29. triangle   30. square   31. rectangle

Extra Skill Practice

Look for a pattern and replace each __?__ with the correct term. Describe the rule you used for each sequence.

1. 25, 50, 75, 100, __?__ , __?__ , __?__ , __?__ , __?__ , 250

2. 13, 16, 19, 22, __?__ , __?__ , __?__ , __?__ , __?__ , 40

3. 144, 132, 120, 108, __?__ , __?__ , __?__ , __?__ , __?__ , 36

4. $\frac{1}{3}$, $\frac{1}{6}$, $\frac{1}{9}$, $\frac{1}{12}$, __?__ , __?__ , __?__ , __?__ , __?__ , $\frac{1}{30}$

5. 1, 3, 9, 27, __?__ , __?__ , __?__ , __?__ , __?__ , 19,683

For each sequence,

- copy and complete the table,
- write an equation for the rule for the sequence, and
- use your rule to find the 40th term.

6.

Term number	1	2	3	4	?	?	?	?
Term	499	498	497	496	?	?	?	?

7.

Term number	10	11	12	13	?	?	?	?
Term	100	110	120	130	?	?	?	?

8.

Term number	1	2	3	4	?	?	?	?
Term	14	16	18	20	?	?	?	?

Study Skills ◀▶ Getting to Know Your Textbook

When you begin a new course, it is helpful to get to know your textbook. Then you will be able to find information you need quickly.

1. Look through pages xii–xix. Describe two features of your textbook that are illustrated in these pages.

2. A section of student resources appears at the back of your textbook. Make a list of all these resources.

3. Find the Toolbox. Which page of the Toolbox contains help with rounding whole numbers?

What's the Plan?

Setting the Stage ▸▸▸▸▸▸▸▸▸▸▸▸▸▸▸▸▸▸▸▸▸▸▸▸▸▸▸▸▸▸▸▸

SET UP *Work as a class. You will need 9 index cards numbered 1–9.*

Knowing how to solve problems is important. There is often a pattern to the way good problem solvers approach problems. As you play a game called *Card Swappers*, you will learn a 4-step approach that can help you become a better problem solver.

CARD SWAPPERS

The object of the game is to put nine cards in order from least to greatest in the fewest swaps possible.

A swap is made by exchanging the positions of two cards.

The challenge is that you must predict the number of swaps needed before you see the order of the cards.

▶ **As a class, first practice swapping by putting these cards in order from 1 to 9. Try to use as few swaps as possible. Record your swaps.**

Think About It

1 How many swaps were needed to put the cards in order?

2 Will the number of swaps needed for different arrangements of the cards always be the same? Explain.

Exploration 1

Understand the Problem

SET UP *Work in a group of four. You will need 9 index cards numbered 1–9.*

▶ **You have had some experience swapping cards. Now you will play the game *Card Swappers*.**

You will need two teams. At the start of each game, the cards should be shuffled and placed facing away from both teams.

First

Each team bids the number of swaps they think it may take to put the cards in order.

Next

The cards are turned over so that the numbers can be seen.

Then

The lowest bidding team puts the cards in order from least to greatest.

If the lowest bidding team uses *no more than* the number of swaps they bid, then they win. Otherwise the other team wins.

▶ **One way to understand the game better is to play it several times.**

3 **Try This as a Class** Play *Card Swappers* two times with the whole class divided into two teams.

4 **Discussion** In the *Setting the Stage*, you just needed to put the cards in order from least to greatest in the fewest swaps possible. What new challenges did you face when your class played the game?

▶ **Now work in your group to think more about bidding.**

5 Split up your group and play *Card Swappers* two times.

6 **a.** If you bid 1 swap each time, would you ever win**?** Why**?**

   b. If you bid 9 swaps and get the bid, will you win**?** Why**?**

   c. **Discussion** A bid is called "safe" if you can be sure of always putting the cards in order using at most that many swaps. What could you do to determine the lowest safe bid**?**

7 **Try This as a Class** Describe the problem you need to solve to be successful at the *Card Swappers* game.

▶ To *Understand the Problem* **is the first step in a 4-step approach to solving problems. As you played and thought about** *Card Swappers,* **you developed an understanding of the problem you will solve in Explorations 2 and 3.**

Step 1
Understand the Problem

HOMEWORK EXERCISES ▶ See Exs. 1–5 on pp. 34–35.

Exploration 2 ▸▸▸▸▸▸▸▸▸▸▸▸▸▸▸▸▸▸▸▸▸▸▸▸▸▸▸▸▸▸▸

Make a Plan

GOAL

LEARN HOW TO...
- make a plan to solve a problem
- use several problem solving strategies

AS YOU...
- begin to solve the *Card Swappers* problem

SET UP *Work in a group of four. You will need 9 index cards numbered 1–9.*

▶ **Once you understand the problem you have to solve, the next step is to** *Make a Plan* **for solving it. The plan for solving a problem often involves using problem-solving strategies.**

8 **Discussion** List some strategies you remember using to solve problems in mathematics.

► To find the lowest safe bid in the *Card Swappers* game, you can begin by seeing whether the strategy ***try a simpler problem*** is helpful. You will explore what happens as you play with fewer cards.

Step 2

Make a Plan

| Make an organized list | Try a simpler problem |

9 Imagine playing *Card Swappers* with only one card. How many swaps do you have to make? Explain.

10 Use only the cards numbered 1 and 2.

  a. Play *Card Swappers* several times in your group.

  b. What seems to be the lowest safe bid for two cards? Remember, this is the least number of swaps you can bid and still be certain of putting the cards in order.

11 Use only the cards 1, 2, and 3. Repeat Question 10.

► Your next step is to check your findings. One way to do this is to ***make an organized list***.

12 **a.** List all the possible arrangements for cards 1 and 2.

  b. What is the lowest safe bid for two cards?

13 There are six possible arrangements for cards 1, 2, and 3. What are they?

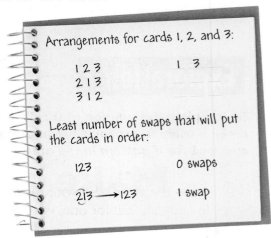

Arrangements for cards 1, 2, and 3:

    1 2 3   1   3
    2 1 3
    3 1 2

Least number of swaps that will put the cards in order:

    123   0 swaps

    2̃1̃3 ⟶ 123   1 swap

14 **a.** For each arrangement found in Question 13, find the least number of swaps that will put the cards in order. Record your swaps.

  b. What is the lowest safe bid for three cards?

15 **Discussion** Think about your answers to Questions 10 and 11. How does using an organized list help you check your answer?

▶ So far you have found the lowest safe bid for three cards. In Exploration 3 you will complete and carry out a plan for bidding successfully in the *Card Swappers* game.

HOMEWORK EXERCISES ▶ See Exs. 6–9 on p. 35.

Exploration 3 ▶▶▶▶▶▶▶▶▶▶▶▶▶▶▶▶▶▶▶▶▶▶▶▶▶▶▶

Carry Out the Plan and Look Back

GOAL

LEARN HOW TO...
◆ carry out the plan
◆ look back

AS YOU...
◆ complete the 4-step approach to solve the *Card Swappers* problem

SET UP *Work in a group of four. You will need 9 index cards numbered 1–9.*

To complete the solution of the *Card Swappers* problem, you could *make a table* to organize the information about the number of swaps and *look for a pattern* in the data.

16 Copy the table. Use your results from Exploration 2 to fill in the lowest safe bid for one, two, and three cards.

Number of cards in the game	1	2	3	4
Least number of swaps to safely bid	?	?	?	?

17 **a.** Use your table to predict the lowest safe bid for four cards. Write your prediction in the table.

b. Play the game with four cards. Does it seem as if your prediction was correct? Explain.

c. Make an organized list to check your prediction. Record your swaps as you did in Question 14(a).

18 Suppose you have more than four cards. Would you want to use an organized list to examine what happens? Explain.

19 **Try This as a Class** Think about your work on the *Card Swappers* problem so far.

    a. Describe the plan you have developed.

    b. Explain what you can do now to find the lowest safe bid for nine cards.

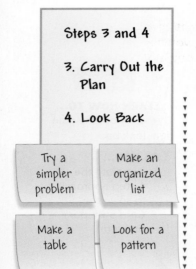

Steps 3 and 4

3. Carry Out the Plan

4. Look Back

| Try a simpler problem | Make an organized list |
| Make a table | Look for a pattern |

Now you are ready for the third and fourth steps of the 4-Step Approach, which are to *Carry Out the Plan* **and** *Look Back.* **You will use these steps to find the lowest safe bid. Then you will use the result to solve the full problem of how to bid successfully in the** *Card Swappers* **game.**

20 Use your strategies from Question 19 to carry out the plan. What is the lowest safe bid for nine cards?

21 **Discussion** Look back at your solution to the problem of finding the lowest safe bid in *Card Swappers*.

    a. Does your solution seem reasonable? Explain.

    b. Do you see any errors in your work? If you do, correct them.

    c. Try to think of another way to find the lowest safe bid for nine cards. If you can, use this method to check your solution to Question 20.

    d. Suppose there are 12 cards in the deck. What is the lowest safe bid?

    e. What is a rule you can use to find the lowest safe bid?

22 When playing *Card Swappers* with 9 cards, what would you bid? Why?

The 4-step problem-solving approach will help you tackle other problems. Some problems have many ways to get to a single correct answer. Other problems may have several correct answers.

4-Step Problem-Solving Approach

1. **Understand the Problem**

2. **Make a Plan**

3. **Carry Out the Plan**

4. **Look Back**

HOMEWORK EXERCISES ▶ See Exs. 10–15 on pp. 35–36.

4-Step Approach to Solving Problems

1. Understand the Problem
- Read the problem carefully, probably several times.
- Restate the problem in your own words.
- Identify the important information in the problem.

2. Make a Plan
- You may try several problem-solving strategies.

If information is missing, you may need to gather it.

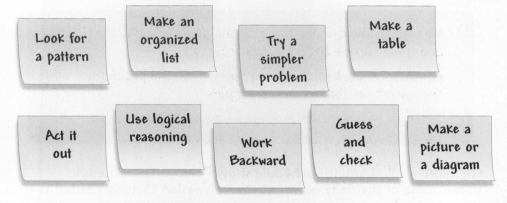

Look for a pattern

Make an organized list

Try a simpler problem

Make a table

Act it out

Use logical reasoning

Work Backward

Guess and check

Make a picture or a diagram

3. Carry Out the Plan
- Solve the problem using the strategies selected.
- You may need to try other strategies.

4. Look Back
- Check that you answered the question being asked.
- Check that your solution seems reasonable.
- Check that your work is accurate.
- Try to find another method. Compare the results.
- Is the problem similar to other problems you have solved?
- Can you generalize your solution or extend it to other situations?

23 **Key Concepts Question** Suppose you play the *Card Swappers* game with 26 cards each showing a letter of the alphabet from A to Z. You must put the cards in alphabetical order. What would be the lowest safe bid?

Section ③

Practice & Application Exercises

YOU WILL NEED

For Ex. 15:
◆ graph paper
(optional)

FOR ▶ HELP

with *computing
with money*, see
**TOOLBOX,
pp. 568, 571**

Canoes carry visitors
among the islands at
the Polynesian Cultural
Center. Polynesians
crossed the Pacific in
giant catamarans to
settle Hawaii and
other islands centuries
before Columbus
ever set sail.
▼

For Exercises 1–4 do parts (a)–(c). Do not solve the problems now.

   a. Describe the problem you need to solve.

   b. State the important information in the problem.

   c. Identify any information missing from the problem.

1. An on-line computer service offers two monthly service contracts. Suppose you spend 8 to 10 hours a month on line. Which contract should you choose?

Standard Contract	**Frequent User Contract**
Monthly fee $4.95	Monthly fee.............$19.95
Hours included.................3	Hours included...............20
Additional hours........$2.50	Additional hours.....:.....$2.00
	* Receive a 10% discount when you use over 50 hours of on-line time.

For Exercises 2–4, use the schedule shown below. This schedule shows some of the daily events at the Polynesian Cultural Center in Hawaii where you can learn about Polynesian culture and traditions. Remember, just do parts (a)–(c) shown at the top of the page.

AFTERNOON EVENTS

Double Hulled Canoe Tour (15 min) 12:30–2:00 and 3:00–7:30
  Tours leave every 15 min with last tour at 7:15.

"Ancient Legends of Polynesia" Canoe Pageant (90 min) 2:30

"The Polynesian Odyssey" (45 min) 3:00 4:00 6:00

"The Living Sea" (45 min) 2:00 5:00 7:00

Ali'i Luaua Buffet Dinner 5:15-7:00

2. Can you attend the activities and shows listed during one visit?

3. How many times a day is the Canoe Tour given if a tour leaves at 2 P.M.?

4. Suppose you plan to arrive at the Polynesian Center at 2:00 P.M. You want at least 45 minutes for the buffet dinner. It takes 15 minutes to get to each event. Can you attend all the events listed on page 34? Explain.

5. Tell whether each problem contains *too much* or *not enough* information. Identify any extra or missing information.

   a. Jon had $25.00. He bought a CD for $12.95 and two pens for $1.75 each. How much money did he spend?

   b. The Coles drove from Ashton to Collins with one stop in Bates. The drive from Ashton to Bates took 2.5 hr, and the entire trip lasted 5 hr. How long did it take the Coles to drive from Bates to Collins?

6. At work Derek must wear a dress shirt, long pants, and a tie. He has three dress shirts (white, blue, and green), two pairs of long pants (tan and black), and two ties (plain and striped). Make an organized list to find how many different outfits he has for work.

7. Solve the problem in Exercise 1.

For Exercises 8 and 9, choose one or more strategies from the list on page 33. Explain how you could use those strategies to solve each problem. You do not need to actually solve it.

8. Marita has to be at school by 8 A.M. It takes her 40 minutes to get up and get dressed in the morning. She needs at least 20 minutes to eat breakfast. Then she has a 15 minute walk to school. What time does Marita need to get up?

9. **Geometry Connection** How many 1-inch equilateral triangles are needed to make a row of triangles that has a perimeter of 20 inches?

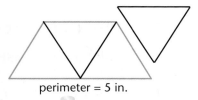

perimeter = 5 in.

10. Use Exercise 9 to answer parts (a)–(c).

    a. Solve the problem.

    b. Describe the plan you used.

    Remember, perimeter is the distance around a figure.

    c. Look back:
    - Did you answer the question asked in the problem?
    - Does your solution seem reasonable? Explain.
    - How can you check your work? Explain.
    - Is the problem similar to other problems you have solved? If so, how is it similar?
    - Can you generalize your solution to a chain of triangles with any perimeter?

▲ The Canoe Pageant uses "dance language" and narration to tell the legends of ancient Polynesia.

Solve each of these problems from pages 34–35.

11. Exercise 3   12. Exercise 4   13. Exercise 8

14. **Challenge** Suppose you have two pots. One pot holds 7 cups and the other holds 4 cups. How can you measure exactly 5 cups of water?

Visu**a**l
T H I N K I N G

Exercise 15 checks that you can use the 4-step approach to solve a problem.

Reflecting on the Section

15. a. Solve the following problem. (*Hint*: graph paper can make it easier to sketch the game board.)

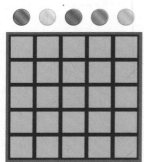

How can five chips be placed on the game board so that each chip does not lie in the same row, column or any diagonal as any other chip?

b. Describe your plan.

c. Find at least one other solution.

Spiral Review

Round each number to the given place. (Toolbox, p. 567)

16. 5632 (nearest hundred)   17. $44.99 (nearest ten dollars)

18. $6.72 (nearest dollar)   19. 34,819 (nearest thousand)

20. 896 (nearest ten)   21. 45,031 (nearest hundred)

Mental Math Multiply. (Toolbox, p. 574)

22. $100 \cdot 100$ 23. $10,000 \cdot 10$ 24. $1000 \cdot 6$

25. $56 \cdot 10$ 26. $300 \cdot 70$ 27. $726 \cdot 100$

28. $80 \cdot 400$ 29. $2000 \cdot 500$ 30. $900 \cdot 70,000$

Mental Math Find the value of each expression. (Module 1, p. 10)

31. $15 - 9 \div 3$ 32. $32(37 + 13)$ 33. $10 \cdot 6 + 5 \cdot 2$

34. Make a table for the sequence 4, 8, 12, 16, …. Extend it to include the next two terms. Then write a rule for the sequence. (Module 1, p. 21)

13. a. Draw the square below on dot paper.

b. Divide the square into two **congruent** parts (parts that have the same shape and size) as shown below.

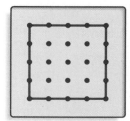 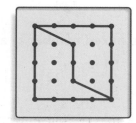

c. What fraction of the square is each congruent part?

d. Find five other ways to divide the square into two congruent parts. Sketch your answers on dot paper.

14. a. Draw this rectangle on dot paper.

b. Divide the rectangle into four congruent parts. Record your answer on dot paper.

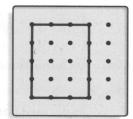

c. What fraction of the rectangle is each part?

d. Find four more ways to divide the rectangle into four congruent parts. Sketch your answers on dot paper.

e. Shade each diagram from parts (b) and (d) to show $\frac{3}{4}$ of the rectangle.

For each pair, explain why the shapes are or are not congruent.

15.   **16.** 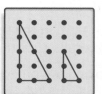   **17.**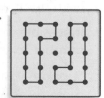

18. Physical Education A running track is $\frac{1}{4}$ of a mile long.

a. How many times must you run around the track in order to run one mile?

b. How many miles will you have run if you run around the track twice? If you run around 6 times?

c. If you run halfway around the track, what fraction of a mile will you have run?

19. **Challenge** Mina ran $\frac{3}{5}$ of a cross-country course. If she ran 6 km, how long is the course?

Rewrite each fraction as a mixed number.

20. $\frac{21}{4}$ 21. $\frac{15}{8}$ 22. $\frac{41}{6}$ 23. $\frac{14}{3}$

Rewrite each mixed number as a fraction.

24. $4\frac{1}{5}$ 25. $1\frac{7}{12}$ 26. $11\frac{1}{2}$ 27. $2\frac{2}{3}$

28. $7\frac{4}{5}$ 29. $3\frac{1}{8}$ 30. $6\frac{5}{7}$ 31. $9\frac{9}{11}$

Visual Thinking Copy the number line. Mark and label a point on the line where you think each fraction or mixed number would be.

32. $\frac{14}{6}$ 33. $\frac{9}{6}$ 34. $2\frac{1}{6}$ 35. $1\frac{2}{3}$

Write each quotient as a mixed number.

36. $26 \div 5$ 37. $52 \div 7$ 38. $98 \div 10$

39. Suppose you roll a 3 on each of your first five turns of *Flex Your Hex*. The sequence below represents the fraction of a hexagon you had after each turn.

$$\frac{3}{6}, \frac{6}{6}, \frac{9}{6}, \frac{12}{6}, \frac{15}{6}, \dots$$

a. Write a rule for finding any term in the sequence from its term number.

b. If possible, write each term in the sequence as a mixed number to show the results after trading.

c. Suppose you keep rolling a 3 on every turn. In how many more turns will you collect 5 hexagons?

40. Naomi's class is playing a trading game similar to *Flex Your Hex* using circles. Naomi just finished a turn and has $3\frac{4}{5}$ circles.

a. How many pieces does it take to make a complete circle in this game?

b. It takes five complete circles to win the game. Can Naomi win on her next turn? Explain.

41. Suppose you are sharing 6 dollars among 4 people. Which form of $6 \div 4$ would you use to describe each share? Explain your choice.

    a. 1 R2   **b.** 1.50   **c.** $1\frac{1}{2}$

Reflecting ◀▶ on the Section

Journal

Exercises 42 and 43 check that you understand mixed numbers.

Be prepared to respond to Exercises 42 and 43 in class.

Here is a shortcut for changing a mixed number to a fraction.

- ◆ **Multiply** the whole number and the denominator.
- ◆ Then **add** the numerator to the product.
- ◆ Write the result over the **original denominator, 3.**

$$2 \times 3 + 1 = 7$$

$$2\frac{1}{3} = \frac{7}{3}$$

42. Look back at the Example on page 45. Use the idea of trading pattern blocks to explain each step in the shortcut.

43. Use the shortcut to write each of the following mixed numbers as fractions.

    a. $1\frac{7}{8}$ **b.** $3\frac{5}{6}$ **c.** $6\frac{3}{4}$

Spiral ◀▶ Review

Describe in words how to find the value of each expression.
(Module 1, p. 10)

44. $4 \cdot (3 + 2)$ **45.** $7 + 10 \div 2$ **46.** $8 - 3 \cdot 2$

Solve each problem. (Module 1, p. 33)

47. Together, a breakfast bar and juice cost $4.00. The breakfast bar costs 90¢ more than the juice. How much does the juice cost?

48. Bruno mailed 30 postcards and letters. It cost $.26 each to mail the postcards and $.41 each for the letters. His total cost was $10.65. How many of each did he mail?

Find each product without using a calculator. (Toolbox, p. 574)

49.   17
    $\times 20$

50.   300
    $\times\ 53$

51. 70000
    $\times\ 627$

Tell whether each statement is true or false. If a statement is false, explain why.

1.

   $\frac{1}{2}$ of the triangle is shaded.

2.

   $\frac{2}{6}$ of the trapezoid is shaded.

3.

   $\frac{3}{4}$ of the rectangle is shaded.

☐ **represents the whole. Write each part to whole relationship as a fraction and as a mixed number.**

4.

5.

6.

Write each fraction as a mixed number.

7. $\frac{10}{3}$ 8. $\frac{14}{9}$ 9. $\frac{17}{4}$ 10. $\frac{5}{3}$ 11. $\frac{21}{2}$

Write each mixed number as a fraction.

12. $1\frac{1}{2}$ 13. $5\frac{4}{9}$ 14. $2\frac{1}{8}$ 15. $3\frac{3}{7}$ 16. $9\frac{4}{5}$

Write each quotient as a mixed number.

17. $11 \div 5$ 18. $35 \div 3$ 19. $18 \div 4$ 20. $19 \div 2$

21. Jake has $\frac{1}{3}$ of the money he needs to buy a kite. If he has \$1.50, how much does the kite cost?

Standardized Testing ◀▶ Free Response

1. Draw each figure. Then shade the part that represents the given fraction.

   A $\frac{4}{6}$ of a rectangle   **B** $\frac{3}{4}$ of a square   **C** $\frac{2}{8}$ of a circle

2. Fill in the missing terms of the sequence. Explain your reasoning.

   $\frac{8}{9}$, __?__ , $1\frac{7}{9}$, $2\frac{2}{9}$, __?__ , __?__ , $3\frac{5}{9}$, 4, __?__

Section 5 Equivalent Fractions

IN THIS SECTION

EXPLORATION 1
◆ Equivalent Fractions

EXPLORATION 2
◆ Finding Equivalents

EXPLORATION 3
◆ Fractions of Whole Numbers

The Same or Different?

Setting the Stage ▶▶▶▶▶▶▶▶▶▶▶▶▶▶▶▶▶▶▶▶▶▶▶▶▶▶▶▶

Although you may not notice them, many everyday objects show a variety of designs and patterns.

Designs for floors range from simple squares and rectangles to many-sided polygons.

Think About It

1 Some of the pattern block shapes can be seen in the sidewalk above. Which can you identify?

2 Use a fraction to describe a part of the sidewalk design.

▶ **Different fractions can name the same part of a whole design. In this section you will find different ways to name parts of floor designs.**

Exploration 1

EQUIVALENT FRACTIONS $\dfrac{2}{4}\ \dfrac{4}{8}\ \dfrac{6}{12}$

SET UP *You will need:* • *Labsheet 5A* • *pattern blocks*

Use the Hexagon Section on Labsheet 5A for Question 3.

3 **a.** Estimate the fraction of the hexagon covered by the star.

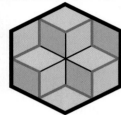

◄ a hexagon-shaped section of a floor design

b. Cover the entire hexagon with **rhombuses** (▰). What fraction of the entire figure does one rhombus represent?

c. Cover just the star portion with **rhombuses** (▰). What fraction of the hexagon do these rhombuses represent?

d. Now cover the entire hexagon with **triangles** (▲). What fraction of the hexagon does one triangle represent?

e. Cover just the star portion with triangles (▲). What fraction of the hexagon do these triangles represent?

f. How are your answers to parts (c) and (e) alike? How are they different?

▶ Fractions that name the same portion of a whole are **equivalent fractions**. Question 3 shows that $\frac{6}{12}$ and $\frac{12}{24}$ are equivalent fractions.

4 **Discussion** Name another fraction that is equivalent to $\frac{6}{12}$ and $\frac{12}{24}$. How do you know it is equivalent?

5 ✔ **CHECKPOINT** Pattern blocks covering part of a hexagon-shaped floor pattern (⬡) are shown below.

✔ **QUESTION 5**

...checks that you can recognize equivalent fractions.

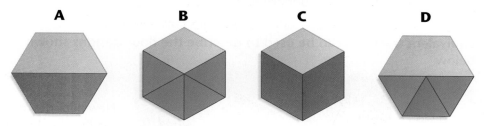

A   **B**   **C**   **D**

a. What fraction of each floor pattern is covered?

b. Which of the fractions in part (a) are equivalent?

6 The floor designs below are formed within the same outlined shape. Each design has a hexagon of clear tile in the center.

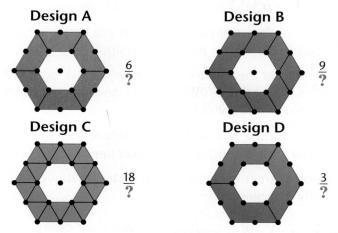

Design A $\frac{6}{?}$

Design B $\frac{9}{?}$

Design C $\frac{18}{?}$

Design D $\frac{3}{?}$

a. Complete the fractions that represent the part of each floor design that has colored tiles.

b. Explain why the fractions in part (a) are equivalent.

7 a. For designs A–C in Question 6, cover each center with the same type of colored tiles used for the outer part of the design. What fraction of each floor design is covered with colored tiles now?

b. What whole number does each fraction in part (a) represent?

HOMEWORK EXERCISES ▶ See Exs. 1–9 on pp. 62–63.

LEARN HOW TO...
- find equivalent fractions
- write a fraction in lowest terms

AS YOU...
- use pattern blocks to make floor designs

KEY TERM
- lowest terms

Exploration 2

FINDING = EQUIVALENTS

SET UP *You will need pattern blocks.*

▶ **Equivalent fractions can be used to describe the floor designs shown below.**

Original floor design made with
6 trapezoids (▰).

New floor design made by replacing
4 trapezoids (▰)
with **triangles (▲).**

8 a. Use **trapezoids (▰)** to create the original floor design.

   b. What fraction of the original floor design will be replaced with **triangles (▲)** to create the new floor design?

   c. Without looking at the picture of the new floor design, how can you determine the number of triangles you will need to replace the 4 trapezoids?

   d. If you were going to replace all of the trapezoids with triangles, how many triangles would you need?

   e. What fraction of the new floor design pictured above is covered with triangles?

9 An equivalent fraction for the part of the new floor design that is covered by triangles can be found as follows.

You replaced 4 of the 6 trapezoids with triangles.

4 trapezoids became 12 triangles.

$$\frac{4}{6} = \frac{4 \cdot ?}{6 \cdot ?} = \frac{12}{18}$$

You would need **18 triangles (▲)** to replace all **6 trapezoids (▰).**

   a. What number must replace each question mark to make the equations true?

   b. How are the products in the middle fraction related to your answers from Questions 8(c) and 8(d)?

10 Copy and complete the equivalent fractions. Be sure to include all the missing steps.

a. $\dfrac{1}{2} = \dfrac{1 \cdot 2}{2 \cdot 2} = \dfrac{2}{?}$

b. $\dfrac{1}{3} = \dfrac{1 \cdot 2}{3 \cdot 2} = \dfrac{2}{?}$

c. $\dfrac{2}{3} = \dfrac{2 \cdot ?}{3 \cdot ?} = \dfrac{?}{12}$

d. $\dfrac{3}{3} = \dfrac{3 \cdot ?}{3 \cdot ?} = \dfrac{?}{12}$

e. $\dfrac{3}{4} = \dfrac{3 \cdot ?}{4 \cdot ?} = \dfrac{?}{12}$

f. $\dfrac{8}{6} = \dfrac{? \cdot ?}{? \cdot ?} = \dfrac{?}{12}$

11 ✔ **CHECKPOINT** Complete each pair of equivalent fractions.

a. $\dfrac{3}{7} = \dfrac{?}{28}$

b. $\dfrac{5}{6} = \dfrac{45}{?}$

c. $\dfrac{2}{5} = \dfrac{?}{30}$

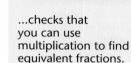

✔ **QUESTION 11**

...checks that you can use multiplication to find equivalent fractions.

▶ **Equivalent fractions can also be used to describe these floor designs.**

Original floor design has $\dfrac{12}{18}$ of the design made from **triangles** (▲).

New floor design made by replacing **triangles** (▲) with **rhombuses** (▰).

12 **Discussion** The following equation can be used to find an equivalent fraction representing the part of the new floor design that is covered by **rhombuses** (▰).

$$\dfrac{12}{18} = \dfrac{12 \div ?}{18 \div ?} = \dfrac{6}{9}$$

a. Use pattern blocks to create the original floor design.

b. How many **triangles** (▲) can be covered with one **rhombus** (▰)? How can you use this information to find how many rhombuses you need to replace all of the triangles?

c. Create the new floor design. Is $\dfrac{6}{9}$ of the new floor design covered with rhombuses? Explain.

d. Why was division used in the equations?

e. What number must replace each question mark?

13 Copy and complete the equivalent fractions.

a. $\dfrac{9}{12} = \dfrac{9 \div 3}{12 \div 3} = \dfrac{3}{?}$ b. $\dfrac{4}{6} = \dfrac{4 \div 2}{6 \div 2} = \dfrac{?}{3}$ c. $\dfrac{8}{16} = \dfrac{? \div ?}{16 \div 8} = \dfrac{?}{?}$

d. $\dfrac{64}{72} = \dfrac{64 \div 8}{? \div ?} = \dfrac{?}{9}$ e. $\dfrac{25}{30} = \dfrac{? \div ?}{? \div ?} = \dfrac{5}{?}$ f. $\dfrac{30}{36} = \dfrac{? \div ?}{? \div ?} = \dfrac{?}{12}$

✔ **QUESTION 14**

...checks that you can use division to find equivalent fractions.

14 ✔ **CHECKPOINT** Complete each pair of equivalent fractions.

a. $\dfrac{40}{64} = \dfrac{?}{8}$ b. $\dfrac{36}{108} = \dfrac{4}{?}$ c. $\dfrac{21}{33} = \dfrac{?}{11}$

▶ **Lowest Terms** Fractions like $\dfrac{2}{3}$ and $\dfrac{3}{4}$ are said to be in **lowest terms** since 1 is the greatest whole number that will divide both the numerator and denominator of the fraction evenly.

15 Tell whether or not each fraction is in lowest terms. Explain how you know.

a. $\dfrac{3}{6}$ b. $\dfrac{21}{29}$ c. $\dfrac{5}{8}$ d. $\dfrac{11}{66}$

▶ **You can write fractions in lowest terms by dividing the numerator and the denominator by the same whole number.**

EXAMPLE

Express $\dfrac{24}{72}$ in lowest terms.

SAMPLE RESPONSE

Step 1   Step 2   Step 3

$$\dfrac{24}{72} = \dfrac{24 \div 2}{72 \div 2} = \dfrac{12 \div 4}{36 \div 4} = \dfrac{3 \div 3}{9 \div 3} = \dfrac{1}{3}$$

16 **Discussion**

a. Why does the number you divide by have to be a common factor of both the numerator and the denominator?

b. Divide by a different common factor in Step 1 of the Example. Show the steps to find the fraction in lowest terms.

c. How can you write $\dfrac{24}{72}$ in lowest terms in fewer than three steps?

17 ✔ **CHECKPOINT** For each fraction, write an equivalent fraction in lowest terms.

a. $\dfrac{7}{14}$ b. $\dfrac{10}{30}$ c. $\dfrac{6}{48}$ d. $\dfrac{25}{125}$

■ **HOMEWORK EXERCISES** ▶ See Exs. 10–29 on pp. 63–64.

QUESTION 17

...checks that you can write fractions in lowest terms.

Exploration 3 ▸▸▸▸▸▸▸▸▸▸▸▸▸▸▸▸▸▸▸▸▸▸▸

Fractions of Whole Numbers

SET UP *Work in a group. You will need:* • *Labsheet 5B*
• *25 pattern blocks*

GOAL

LEARN HOW TO...
◆ find a fraction of a whole number

AS YOU...
◆ make predictions from a sample of pattern blocks

KEY TERMS
◆ sample
◆ population

▶ Fractions can be used to make predictions from a **sample**, which is part of a whole set of objects being studied. Your group has a sample of all the pattern blocks being used by the class. The whole set of pattern blocks is the **population**.

18 What fraction of your group's pattern blocks are triangles?

19 **a. Discussion** Predict what fraction of the pattern blocks in use by the class are triangles. How can you use your answer to Question 18 to help you make your prediction?

  b. In a collection of 250 pattern blocks, how many do you think are triangles? How could you use your answer to part (a) to help you find out?

▶ **Use Labsheet 5B.** For Questions 20 and 21 you will use dot paper to find fractions of whole numbers.

20 Follow the directions for *Dot Grid 1* to find out how many pattern blocks are triangles if $\dfrac{2}{3}$ of the 36 pattern blocks are triangles.

21 Follow the directions for *Dot Grid 2* to find out how many pattern blocks are squares if $\dfrac{3}{4}$ of the 24 pattern blocks are squares.

▶ **You can also use mental math to find a fraction of a whole number.**

22 A class predicts that $\frac{3}{8}$ of their 48 pattern blocks are hexagons.

   a. To find $\frac{3}{8}$ of 48 pattern blocks, you can first think about dividing 48 pattern blocks into how many groups of equal size?

   b. How many pattern blocks will be in each group?

   c. How many groups do you need to make $\frac{3}{8}$?

   d. What is $\frac{3}{8}$ of 48?

   e. How many of the 48 pattern blocks do you predict are hexagons?

✔ QUESTION 23

...checks that you can use mental math to find a fraction of a number.

23 ✔ **CHECKPOINT** Use mental math to find each value.

   a. $\frac{4}{5}$ of 30   **b.** $\frac{5}{6}$ of 18   **c.** $\frac{2}{3}$ of 12

24 **Discussion** Think about the mental math method you used in Questions 22 and 23. Would you use this method to find $\frac{2}{5}$ of 12? Explain why or why not.

25 **a.** Combine your pattern blocks with those of another group. What fraction of the combined pattern blocks are triangles?

   b. Use your answer to part (a) to predict what fraction of the pattern blocks being used by the class are triangles.

   c. In a collection of 250 pattern blocks, how many do you think are triangles?

26 **Try This as a Class** Count how many of the pattern blocks being used by the class are triangles.

   a. What fraction of the class's pattern blocks are triangles?

   b. Was your prediction from Question 19(a) close?

27 **Try This as a Class** Suppose you combined your class's pattern blocks with 250 pattern blocks from another class.

   a. Predict how many of the combined pattern blocks are triangles.

   b. Did you use the fraction from Question 18 or from Question 26(a) to make your prediction? Why?

HOMEWORK EXERCISES ▶ See Exs. 30–49 on pp. 64–66.

Section 5

Key Concepts

Key Terms

Equivalent Fractions (pp. 54–59)

Fractions that name the same portion of a whole are equivalent.

equivalent fractions

Examples

$\frac{1}{2}$, $\frac{2}{4}$, and $\frac{3}{6}$ are equivalent fractions since

$$\frac{1}{2} = \qquad, \qquad \frac{2}{4} = \qquad, \qquad \text{and } \frac{3}{6} = \qquad.$$

Given a fraction, you can find an equivalent fraction by multiplying or dividing the numerator and denominator by the same nonzero whole number.

Examples

$\frac{5}{6} = \frac{5 \cdot 3}{6 \cdot 3} = \frac{15}{18}$, so $\frac{5}{6}$ is equivalent to $\frac{15}{18}$.

$\frac{24}{28} = \frac{24 \div 4}{28 \div 4} = \frac{6}{7}$, so $\frac{24}{28}$ is equivalent to $\frac{6}{7}$.

Lowest Terms (pp. 58–59)

lowest terms

In the example above, $\frac{6}{7}$ is in lowest terms because 1 is the only whole number that will divide both 6 and 7 evenly.

Key Concepts Questions

28 **a.** Divide the numerator and denominator of $\frac{18}{30}$ by 2.

b. Is the result in lowest terms? If not, how can you find an equivalent fraction in lowest terms?

29 Make shaded drawings for the fractions in each pair. Use your drawings to explain whether or not the fractions in each pair are equivalent.

a. $\frac{1}{3}$, $\frac{3}{9}$ **b.** $\frac{3}{8}$, $\frac{1}{4}$ **c.** $\frac{2}{5}$, $\frac{4}{10}$

Section ⑤

Key Concepts

Finding a Fraction of a Whole Number (pp. 59–60)

Example

A sample of 15 fish is taken from a population of fish. $\frac{2}{3}$ of the sample are tuna. Use mental math to find $\frac{2}{3}$ of 15.

Think: Divide 15 into 3 groups of equal size. There are 5 in each group. There are 10 in two groups, so $\frac{2}{3}$ of 15 = 10.

30 Key Concepts Question Which is greater, $\frac{3}{4}$ of 24 or $\frac{3}{10}$ of 70?

Section ⑤

Practice & Application Exercises

YOU WILL NEED

For Ex. 8:
♦ pattern blocks

For Exs. 27–29:
♦ fraction calculator

1. The windows in the photograph below are identical except that the bottom window is partly open.

   a. What fraction of the bottom window is open?

   b. The photograph shows that another fraction is equivalent to the one in part (a). What is the other fraction?

Write two equivalent fractions that tell what part of each figure is shaded.

2.

3.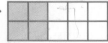

4.

5.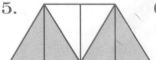

6.

7.

8. Use your pattern blocks to show how $\frac{2}{5}$ is equivalent to $\frac{4}{10}$. Trace around the blocks you used.

9. When special stamps are printed, several related designs may be arranged on a sheet.

   a. Write three equivalent fractions to represent the portion of the stamps that show the purple flower.

   b. What is the value in cents of the two rows of 13¢ stamps?

   c. Write a fraction different from the ones in part (a) that compares the value in cents of the stamps showing the purple flower with the total value in cents of the two rows of stamps.

   d. How is the fraction in part (c) related to the fractions you found in part (a)? Explain.

Complete each pair of equivalent fractions.

10. $\frac{3}{8} = \frac{?}{16}$

11. $\frac{4}{7} = \frac{12}{?}$

12. $\frac{2}{9} = \frac{?}{27}$

13. $\frac{12}{18} = \frac{?}{3}$

14. $\frac{32}{40} = \frac{?}{5}$

15. $\frac{12}{27} = \frac{4}{?}$

Find the next three terms in each sequence.

16. $\frac{1}{2}, \frac{2}{4}, \frac{3}{6}, \frac{4}{8}, \ldots$

17. $\frac{2}{3}, \frac{4}{6}, \frac{6}{9}, \frac{8}{12}, \ldots$

18. $\frac{1}{5}, \frac{3}{15}, \frac{9}{45}, \frac{27}{135}, \ldots$

Choose the fractions in each list that are in lowest terms.

19. $\frac{5}{20}, \frac{4}{20}, \frac{3}{20}$ 20. $\frac{8}{6}, \frac{9}{12}, \frac{5}{8}$ 21. $\frac{4}{8}, \frac{4}{9}, \frac{4}{10}$

Write each fraction in lowest terms.

22. $\frac{12}{20}$ 23. $\frac{24}{36}$ 24. $\frac{13}{52}$ 25. $\frac{5}{60}$

26. **Challenge** Find two pairs of equivalent fractions in the list below. Explain how you know each pair is equivalent.

$$\frac{12}{9} \qquad \frac{5}{4} \qquad 1\frac{3}{4} \qquad 1\frac{2}{6} \qquad \frac{6}{9} \qquad 1\frac{21}{28}$$

Fraction Calculator Use a fraction calculator for Exercises 27–29.

27. Some fraction calculators can be used to find equivalent fractions, in particular equivalent fractions in lowest terms.

   a. Enter the key sequence [1] [8] [/] [2] [4] on your calculator. What number appears on the display?

   b. Now press [SIMP] [=]. What number appears on the display? What did the calculator do to get that number?

   c. Press [SIMP] [=]. What number appears on the display? What did the calculator do?

   d. What happens if you press [SIMP] [=] again? Why do you think this happens?

28. a. Enter the fraction $\frac{16}{28}$ on your calculator.

   b. Press [SIMP] [=] repeatedly to find an equivalent fraction in lowest terms.

29. Use your calculator to tell if each pair of fractions is equivalent.

   a. $\frac{27}{45}, \frac{5}{7}$ b. $\frac{85}{272}, \frac{20}{64}$ c. $\frac{14}{49}, \frac{2}{7}$

Mental Math Use mental math to find each value.

30. $\frac{2}{3}$ of 12   31. $\frac{5}{6}$ of 18   32. $\frac{2}{5}$ of 20   33. $\frac{3}{4}$ of 12

34. $\frac{2}{9}$ of 27   35. $\frac{3}{16}$ of 32   36. $\frac{5}{8}$ of 24   37. $\frac{5}{10}$ of 30

38. If $\frac{2}{3}$ of 6 pattern blocks are rhombuses, how many are rhombuses?

39. If $\frac{4}{5}$ of 10 pattern blocks are triangles, how many are triangles?

40. How many squares are there in a set of 14 pattern blocks that is $\frac{4}{7}$ squares?

41. Ten of Group A's pattern blocks were triangles. When they combined their pattern blocks with those of Group B, they had a total of 32 pattern blocks. When combined, $\frac{3}{4}$ of the pattern blocks were triangles. How many of Group B's pattern blocks were triangles?

Plant Pollen A pollen expert counted the pollen grains in a sample of a pollen deposit to make predictions about the deposit. Use the table of results for Exercises 42 and 43.

Type of pollen	Number of grains in sample
pine	48
grass	36
oak	30
cactus	6
total	**120**

42. What fraction of the sample is each type of pollen? Write each fraction in lowest terms.

   a. pine

   b. grass

   c. oak

   d. cactus

43. Suppose the pollen expert estimates 540 grains are in the deposit. Use your answers to Exercise 42 to estimate the number of grains of each type of pollen in the deposit.

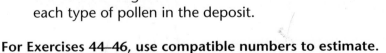

◄ Scientists study plant pollen that has been preserved in the ground to help learn how plants were used by ancient people.

For Exercises 44–46, use compatible numbers to estimate.

Example: $\frac{5}{6}$ of 31 is close to $\frac{5}{6}$ of 30, or about 25.

44. $\frac{2}{3}$ of 34   **45.** $\frac{1}{5}$ of 19   **46.** $\frac{3}{4}$ of 15

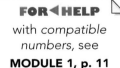

FOR ◄ HELP

with *compatible numbers,* see

MODULE 1, p. 11

47. Challenge A researcher catches 45 fish, tags them, and puts them back in a pond. Later, a sample is taken from the pond and tags are found on $\frac{3}{5}$ of the fish. Estimate how many fish live in the pond. Explain how you made your estimate.

Discussion

Exercises 48 and
49 check that
you understand
equivalent fractions.

Reflecting on the Section

Be prepared to discuss your responses to Exercises 48 and 49 in class.

48. United States coins represent fractions of a dollar. For example, the value of a quarter is 25 cents or $\frac{25}{100}$ of a dollar.

   a. What is $\frac{25}{100}$ in lowest terms?

   b. Why do you think our 25 cent coin is called a quarter?

49. Give two equivalent fractions that tell what part a dime is of a dollar. Are any of your answers in lowest terms? Explain.

Spiral Review

Estimate each answer. If possible, decide whether your estimate is *greater than* or *less than* the exact answer. (Module 1, p. 10)

50. $256 + 88$ 51. $210 \cdot 68$ 52. $78 \cdot 21$

53. $573 - 218$ 54. $81 \div 19$ 55. $8632 - 794$

Use compatible numbers to find each answer by mental math. (Module 1, p. 11)

56. $27 + 18 + 13$ 57. $216 + 139 + 41 + 84$

58. $2 \cdot 35 \cdot 4$ 59. $3 \cdot 8 \cdot 25 \cdot 2$

Use the table to answer Exercises 60 and 61. (Module 1, p. 21)

Term Number	1	2	3	4	5
Term	7	14	21	28	35

60. Describe the relationship between the term and the term number.

61. What is the 60th term of the sequence?

62. Is $\frac{1}{4}$ of the circle shaded? Explain why or why not. (Module 1, p. 46)

Subtract without using a calculator. (Toolbox, p. 570)

63. $\begin{array}{r} 291 \\ -\ 156 \end{array}$ 64. $\begin{array}{r} 9431 \\ -\ 934 \end{array}$ 65. $\begin{array}{r} 3101 \\ -\ 1808 \end{array}$

Section 5

Extra Skill Practice

Write two equivalent fractions that tell what part of each figure is shaded.

1.

2.

3.

For each fraction, write three equivalent fractions.

4. $\frac{2}{5}$ 5. $\frac{4}{9}$ 6. $\frac{4}{16}$ 7. $\frac{3}{8}$ 8. $\frac{8}{24}$

9. $\frac{1}{6}$ 10. $\frac{2}{7}$ 11. $\frac{4}{32}$ 12. $\frac{2}{18}$ 13. $\frac{6}{15}$

Complete each pair of equivalent fractions.

14. $\frac{6}{9} = \frac{?}{54}$ 15. $\frac{3}{7} = \frac{18}{?}$ 16. $\frac{6}{8} = \frac{?}{4}$ 17. $\frac{3}{12} = \frac{?}{48}$

18. $\frac{18}{27} = \frac{2}{?}$ 19. $\frac{17}{51} = \frac{?}{3}$ 20. $\frac{72}{99} = \frac{8}{?}$ 21. $\frac{100}{?} = \frac{5}{6}$

Write each fraction in lowest terms.

22. $\frac{6}{9}$ 23. $\frac{5}{30}$ 24. $\frac{12}{20}$ 25. $\frac{8}{40}$ 26. $\frac{18}{30}$

27. $\frac{21}{48}$ 28. $\frac{12}{24}$ 29. $\frac{4}{15}$ 30. $\frac{30}{100}$ 31. $\frac{9}{24}$

Use mental math to find each value.

32. $\frac{1}{2}$ of 16   33. $\frac{3}{5}$ of 20   34. $\frac{1}{3}$ of 27   35. $\frac{2}{7}$ of 21

36. $\frac{7}{8}$ of 56   37. $\frac{4}{9}$ of 54   38. $\frac{3}{4}$ of 124   39. $\frac{1}{6}$ of 90

Standardized Testing ◀▶ Multiple Choice

1. Which fraction is equivalent to $\frac{28}{36}$?

    A $\frac{12}{18}$ B $\frac{70}{90}$ C $\frac{84}{106}$ D $\frac{128}{136}$

2. Which fraction is in lowest terms?

    A $\frac{7}{84}$ B $\frac{9}{43}$ C $\frac{27}{72}$ D $\frac{18}{100}$

The Module Project

A Puzzling Problem

Throughout this module you have been working with patterns and learning how to solve problems. In this project, you will apply some of the ideas you have learned to solve the *30 Pennies In A Row* problem. You will work as a team to prepare a written report and to share your solution.

Work in a group. You will need:
- *Project Labsheet A*

Understanding the Problem

1 It will help to study the situation before you try to solve the *30 Pennies in a Row* problem.

   a. Read the entire labsheet. Then read *The Situation* again.

   b. Breaking *The Situation* into steps can help you understand it. Suppose that in Step 1 you place 30 pennies in a row. What do you do in Step 2? In Steps 3–5?

2 **Focusing on Patterns** You can use a table to look at the patterns the coins create.

   a. Copy the table. For Steps 2–5, fill in the pattern using *P, N, D, Q,* and *F* to represent the different coins.

Term number	1	2	3	4	5	6	7	8	9	10
Step 1	Term	P	P	P	P	P	P	P	P	P	P
Step 2	Term	?	?	?	?	?	?	?	?	?	?
Step 3	Term	?	?	?	?	?	?	?	?	?	?
Step 4	Term	?	?	?	?	?	?	?	?	?	?
Step 5	Term	?	?	?	?	?	?	?	?	?	?

   b. Describe the sequence of coins in the row for Step 2.

   c. **Discussion** Discuss any relationships you see between each term in the row for Step 3 and its term number.

   d. Describe any patterns you see in the rows for Steps 4–5.

3 Your answer to the problem will be the value of the coins. Is $30 a reasonable estimate of the answer? Is $15 reasonable? Explain.

Making and Carrying Out Your Plan

4 Read *The Problem* again. Choose a strategy or strategies and solve the problem.

Looking Back Now you will look back at your answer to the *30 Pennies in a Row* problem.

 5 a. Check that you solved the problem you were given and that your answer is reasonable.

b. Check your work for computational errors.

c. Can you think of any other way to check your answer? If so, explain your method and use it to check your work.

 6 a. Is this problem like other problems you have solved? Explain.

b. How can you extend the problem to more than 30 coins?

 7 Look at your table from Question 2.

a. Did the coin in position 1 change? in position 2? in position 6?

b. In which positions do the coins seem to change the most? Why?

Presenting the Solution

8 Work as a team to prepare a presentation for the *30 Pennies in a Row* problem.

> **Ideas for Preparing a Team Presentation**
> - Everyone should participate in the presentation.
> - Presentation
>   possible types
>   - lecture/demonstration
>   - panel discussion
>   - news show
>   - skit
>   - musical
>   - magic show
>   use visuals (diagrams, pictures, graphs, tables)
> - Written Report
>   - restate the problem
>   - explain your plan
>   - show your work
>   - include visuals
>   - identify strategies used
>   - verify the solution
>   - extend the solution
>   - look for connections

a. Prepare your written report.

b. Plan how your team will present its solution to the class.

c. Practice your presentation a few times to make sure everyone on your team understands what to do.

 9 As a team, present your solution to the rest of the class.

Find the value of each expression. (Sec. 1 Explor. 1)

1. $54 - 63 \div 7$
2. $12 + 7 \cdot 5$
3. $180 \div (5 \cdot 6)$
4. $7 + 45 - 22 - 9$
5. $24 \div 4 \cdot 2$
6. $(33 + 8) - (5 + 17)$

Estimation For Exercises 7–12, show how to estimate each answer. (Sec. 1 Explor. 2)

7. $42 \cdot 66$
8. $251 - 188$
9. $3122 + 890$
10. $257 + 34 + 85$
11. $186 \cdot 12$
12. $3452 - 2128$

13. **Writing** Marco estimated the difference between $47.98 and $22.31 to be $30. Is his estimate *less than* or *greater than* the actual difference? Explain how you can tell without finding the exact difference. (Sec. 1 Explor. 2)

Mental Math For Exercises 14–17, explain how you can use mental math to find each answer. (Sec. 1 Explor. 3)

14. $67 + 19 + 143 + 31$
15. $7 \cdot 4 \cdot 5 \cdot 25$
16. $5 \cdot 46 \cdot 2$
17. $34 + 158 + 66$

For Exercises 18 and 19, replace each __?__ with the correct term. Describe the rule you used for each sequence. (Sec. 2 Explor. 1)

18. 188, 185, 182, 179, __?__ , __?__ , __?__ , 167

19. 15, 30, 45, 60, __?__ , __?__ , __?__ , 120

For each sequence,
- copy and complete the table,
- write an equation for the rule for the sequence, and
- use your rule to find the 50th term. (Sec. 2 Explor. 2)

20.

Term Number	1	2	3	4	?	?	?
Term	5	6	7	8	?	?	?

21.

Term Number	1	2	3	4	?	?	?
Term	4	8	12	16	?	?	?

22. In Linda Tetley's 6th grade class, Gail, Lita, and Ben have been chosen to fill the positions of class president, vice president, and secretary. Make an organized list to find the number of different ways the three positions can be filled. (Sec. 3 Explor. 2)

23. Tom and Sarah are reading the same book. When Tom asked Sarah what page she was on, she replied that the product of the page number and the next page number was 17,030. What page was she reading? (Sec. 3 Explor. 3)

Tell whether each statement is *true* or *false*. If a statement is false, explain why. (Sec. 4 Explor. 1)

24. $\frac{1}{2}$ of the square is shaded.

25. $\frac{1}{3}$ of the circle is shaded.

26. $\frac{3}{8}$ of the rectangle is shaded.

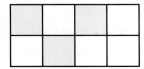

Find the missing number. (Sec. 4 Explor. 2)

27. $6\frac{3}{5} = \frac{?}{5}$ **28.** $\frac{34}{9} = ?\frac{7}{9}$ **29.** $4\frac{2}{7} = \frac{30}{?}$ **30.** $\frac{31}{8} = 3\frac{?}{8}$

31. Write three equivalent fractions for the fraction of the window at the right that is colored red. (Sec. 5 Explor. 1)

32. Which methods below will give a fraction equivalent to $\frac{2}{4}$? Explain. (Sec. 5 Explor. 2)

     a. $\frac{2+2}{4+2}$ **b.** $\frac{2 \cdot 2}{4 \cdot 2}$ **c.** $\frac{2 \div 2}{4 \div 2}$ **d.** $\frac{2-2}{4-2}$

Write each fraction in lowest terms. (Sec. 5 Explor. 2)

33. $\frac{6}{24}$ **34.** $\frac{9}{12}$ **35.** $\frac{25}{30}$ **36.** $\frac{3}{8}$ **37.** $\frac{42}{48}$

Find each value. (Sec. 5 Explor. 3)

38. $\frac{3}{7}$ of 21   **39.** $\frac{5}{6}$ of 24   **40.** $\frac{2}{5}$ of 125   **41.** $\frac{7}{9}$ of 63

Reflecting ▶ on the Module

42. Write a letter to an adult member of your family describing the math you learned in this module and what you liked most and least about the module.

MATH
DETECTIVES

MODULE 2 — SECTION OVERVIEW

1 Probability
As you perform coin tosses and play a game with a number cube:
◆ Find experimental and theoretical probabilities.

2 Assessment Scales
As you explore problems about the World Cup and about string art:
◆ Learn to assess and improve your problem solving skills.

3 Lines, Angles, and Triangles
As you learn to accurately describe and draw geometric figures:
◆ Name basic geometric figures.
◆ Classify angles and triangles.
◆ Decide when a triangle can be formed.

4 Polygons and Angles
As you explore shapes found in puzzles and nature:
◆ Classify polygons.
◆ Sort polygons using a Venn diagram.
◆ Measure and draw angles using a protractor.

The Module Project
Pop-Up Art

Pop-up art is made by cutting and folding paper using geometric shapes and patterns. You will explore some of the techniques and mathematical skills that are used to create pop-ups. Then you will use the mathematics you have learned to design and create a pop-up of your own.

For the Module Project
See pp. 124–125.

Section 1 Probability

IN THIS SECTION

EXPLORATION 1
♦ Experimental Probability

EXPLORATION 2
♦ Theoretical Probability

Detecting Outcomes

Setting the Stage

In this module, you will use clues to solve problems and make decisions just like detectives do when they are solving a mystery. First you will explore *chance* to see how it can help you understand games and make decisions.

Using a coin can solve the mystery of who gets to start a game. In a pick-up basketball game, for example, a coin toss may be used to decide which team gets the ball first.

▲
The Romans used coin flipping to make decisions. The face of the emperor Caesar was on one side of many Roman coins. If Caesar's head came up on a coin toss, it was taken to mean that he approved of the decision.

Think About It

1 Do you think a coin toss is a fair way to decide which team gets the ball first? Why?

2 Suppose your teacher announced that each day from Monday through Friday a coin would be flipped and you would have a quiz if a head appeared. About how many quizzes do you think you would have each week? Explain your answer.

Exploration 1

Experimental Probability

GOAL

LEARN HOW TO...
◆ find experimental probabilities
◆ determine if outcomes are equally likely
◆ use probabilities to make predictions

AS YOU...
◆ perform coin toss experiments

KEY TERMS
◆ experiment
◆ outcome
◆ probability
◆ experimental probability
◆ equally likely

SET UP *Work with a partner. You will need:* • *a coin* • *Labsheet 1A*

Sometimes detectives act out the events of a crime to help solve it. You will flip a coin to find the chance of flipping a head or a tail.

▶ A single flip of a coin is an example of an **experiment**. The result of the flip, a *head* or a *tail*, is an **outcome**.

Use Labsheet 1A for Questions 3–12.

3 With your partner, flip a coin 20 times. Tally the outcomes of your 20 flips in the table.

4 **a.** Which outcome occurred most often in the 20 flips?

  b. What fraction of the flips were heads? What fraction were tails?

▶ A **probability** is a number that tells how likely something is to happen. The fractions you found in Question 4 are probabilities.

5 **Discussion** How can you use the fraction of the flips that were heads from Question 4(b) to describe the chance of getting a head?

▶ A probability found by repeating an experiment a number of times and observing the outcomes is an **experimental probability**.

experimental probability $=$ number of times the outcome occurred
of an outcome $=\dfrac{\text{number of times the outcome occurred}}{\text{number of times the experiment was repeated}}$

FOR◀HELP
with *fractions*, see
MODULE 1, p. 46

EXAMPLE

Suppose **heads** occurred on **23** out of **40** flips of a coin. What is the experimental probability of heads?

SAMPLE RESPONSE

experimental probability of heads $=\dfrac{\text{number of times heads occurred}}{\text{number of times the coin was flipped}} = \dfrac{23}{40}$

---

6 In the table on Labsheet 1A, record the number of heads and tails flipped by four other pairs of students.

7 ✔ **CHECKPOINT** Use your table of data from Question 6.

    a. Find the experimental probability of heads for each pair of students. Are the probabilities the same for each pair?

    b. Suppose you flip the coin again 20 times. What do you expect the experimental probability of heads to be? Why?

8 The table now has data for 100 flips. What is the experimental probability of heads and of tails for the 100 flips?

9 **Try This as a Class**

    a. How can you use the probabilities from Question 8 to predict the number of heads and tails for the whole class?

    b. In the whole class, how many of the flips would you expect to be heads? to be tails?

10 **a.** Collect the coin toss data for the whole class.

    b. How many times was the outcome heads? tails?

    c. How do the number of heads and of tails compare to your predictions in Question 9(b)?

    d. What is the experimental probability of heads for the whole class? the experimental probability of tails?

11 **Discussion** Compare the experimental probability for your 20 flips, for the 100 flips recorded on Labsheet 1A, and for the class's total flips. Which gives you the best idea of the chances of getting heads?

12 ✔ **CHECKPOINT** Suppose you flip a coin 1000 times. About how many times do you expect the result to be heads? tails?

▶ **Outcomes are equally likely if they have the same chance of occurring.**

13 **a.** When you flip a coin, are the chances of getting heads and of getting tails equally likely?

    b. When you spin the spinner at the left, are the chances of the spinner stopping on 1 and stopping on 2 equally likely? Why?

    c. Describe an experiment that has equally likely outcomes.

14 **a.** Based on what you have learned, do you think the toss of a coin is a fair way to decide between two choices? Explain.

    b. Give an example other than a coin flip of a fair way to decide between two choices.

HOMEWORK EXERCISES ▶ See Exs. 1–5 on pp. 81–82.

Section 1
Practice & Application Exercises ▸▸▸▸▸▸▸▸▸

1. What is the experimental probability the spinner stops on B?

Outcome	Total
A	17
B	25
C	18

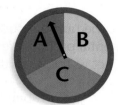

2. An octahedron has eight identical sides numbered 1–8.

   a. What are the possible outcomes when the octahedron is rolled?

   b. Are the outcomes equally likely? Why or why not?

   c. The octahedron was rolled 16 times. The results were:

   6 2 5 1 1 2 7 3
   6 4 3 6 8 5 2 4

   Based on these results, what is the experimental probability of rolling a number less than 6?

3. a. Complete the *Experimental Probability of Heads* column in the table.

John Kerrich's Data for 10,000 Tosses of a Coin		
Number of Tosses	Number of Heads	Experimental Probability of Heads
10	4	?
100	44	?
1,000	502	?
10,000	5,067	?

◀ While a prisoner of war during World War II, mathematician John Kerrich wrote a book about probability and conducted a coin-tossing experiment.

   b. Kerrich got 5,067 heads in 10,000 tosses. How many tails did he get?

   c. What was the experimental probability of getting tails?

4. A bag contains one blue, one green, and one red marble.

   a. What are the possible outcomes when you draw one marble from the bag without looking? Are the outcomes equally likely?

   b. What are the possible outcomes when you draw two marbles at once from the bag without looking? Are the outcomes equally likely?

5. **a.** A number cube was rolled 25 times. On 8 rolls, the outcome was ⚁. What is the experimental probability of rolling ⚁?

   b. On how many rolls was the outcome not ⚁? What is the experimental probability of not rolling ⚁?

   c. What do you notice about your answers in parts (a) and (b)?

   d. Suppose the number cube is thrown 100 times. Based on the experimental probabilities you found, about how many times do you expect to roll a ⚁? to not roll a ⚁?

6. Find the theoretical probability of each event.

   a. The spinner stops on A.

   b. The spinner does not stop on A.

   c. The spinner stops on a vowel.

For Exercises 7 and 8, suppose you pick a card, without looking, from the thirteen heart cards in a standard deck. (An Ace is *not* considered a numbered card.)

Hearts (♥):

7. Are all the outcomes for picking one card equally likely? Explain.

8. **a.** List the possible outcomes for picking a numbered card.

   b. What is the theoretical probability of picking a numbered card?

   c. What is the theoretical probability of picking a non-numbered card? Is there more than one way to find the probability? Explain.

   d. What is the theoretical probability of picking an even-numbered card? an odd-numbered card?

   e. Plot your answers from parts (b)–(d) on a number line.

9. **Basketball** Each season the National Basketball Association (NBA) holds a lottery to decide the order in which its teams will pick new players. Until 1993, each of the 11 teams that did not make the playoffs was assigned from 1 to 11 balls marked with the team's logo. As shown in the table, the number of balls assigned to a team depended on the team's rank for the season. The first ball drawn determined the team that would get first pick.

   a. What was the theoretical probability that the team assigned 11 balls got the first pick? the team assigned 5 balls?

   b. **Writing** Did the team assigned 1 ball have a good chance of getting one of the top new players for the next season? Does this seem reasonable? Explain your thinking.

Rank of Non-Playoff Team	Number of Balls
1st	1
2nd	2
3rd	3
⋮	⋮
11th	11

10. **Open-ended** Give an example of a certain event and of an impossible event in everyday life.

Reflecting ◀▶on the Section

Write your response to Exercise 11 in your journal.

11. a. Develop a strategy for playing the game *Never a Six*. Explain why your strategy helps.

    b. Play the game again to test your strategy.

    c. How does probability relate to your strategy?

Journal

Exercise 11 checks that you can apply probability.

Spiral ◀▶Review

12. In how many different ways can you make 35 cents in change using only nickels, dimes, and quarters? (Module 1, p. 33)

Write the next two terms of each sequence. (Module 1, p. 21)

13. 9, 13, 17, 21, …

14. 2, 5, 9, 14, …

15. Write a rule for finding the terms of each sequence in Exercises 13 and 14.

Extension ▶ ▶

Applying Experimental Probability

16. Have a friend or relative put 10 pennies into a bag—some shiny and the rest dull. Do not look at how many of each are put into the bag!

    a. Take one penny from the bag. Record whether it is shiny or dull in a tally table. Put the coin back in the bag.

    b. Repeat part (a) 29 more times.

    c. Use the data in your table to find the experimental probability of drawing each kind of penny.

    d. Predict how many shiny pennies and how many dull pennies are in the bag. Then check your prediction.

Section 1

Extra Skill Practice

Suppose a number cube was rolled 80 times with the results shown.

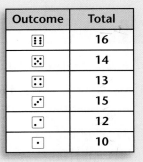

Outcome	Total
⚅	16
⚄	14
⚃	13
⚂	15
⚁	12
⚀	10

1. What is the experimental probability of rolling a 3?

2. What is the experimental probability of rolling an even number?

3. What is the experimental probability of rolling a number less than 5?

4. What is the experimental probability of rolling an odd number?

5. An experiment consists of spinning the spinner once.

   a. What are the outcomes of the experiment?

   b. Are the outcomes equally likely? Why or why not?

Find the theoretical probability of each event.

6. The spinner stops on A.　　　7. The spinner stops on B.

8. The spinner stops on C or F.　　9. The spinner stops on a vowel.

10. If you know that the theoretical probability the spinner stops on G is $\frac{1}{8}$, how can you find the probability that it does not stop on G?

11. Were any of the events in Exercises 6–9 impossible? certain? If so, which ones?

12. Plot each probability you found in Exercises 6–9 on a number line. Label your number line and each point you plot.

Study Skills ◀▶ Managing your Time

The probability of achieving your goals is greater if you learn to manage your time. One way to plan your time is to make a schedule.

1. Beginning with the time you get up in the morning, write a schedule of things you do on a normal school day.

2. a. Suppose that one day you need to spend an hour working on a school project. Neighbors who are away have also asked you to spend 30 minutes cat-sitting and 20 minutes watering their plants. Adjust your schedule to include time for these activities.

   b. Are there any other ways to adjust your schedule to include the activities from part (a)? Explain.

Section ② Assessment Scales

Detecting the Score

Setting the Stage ▸▸▸▸▸▸▸▸▸▸▸▸▸▸▸▸▸▸▸▸▸▸▸▸

People have been reading about the adventures of Sherlock Holmes and Dr. Watson since 1887. Holmes was considered the world's greatest detective because he could solve almost any problem. If detectives were rated on a scale of 1-5, Holmes would easily score a 5.

In the stories, Holmes often describes the methods that made him so successful. Here are a few examples.

"As a rule, when I have heard some slight indication of the course of events, I am able to guide myself by the thousands of other similar cases which occur to my memory." **The Red-headed League**

"...the strangest and most unique things are very often connected not with the larger but with the smaller crimes ..." **The Red-headed League**

"In solving a problem of this sort, the grand thing is to be able to reason backward. That is a very useful accomplishment, and a very easy one, but people do not practice it much." **A Study in Scarlet**

Think About It

1 How would examining similar cases help Holmes solve a problem?

2 Holmes talks about things being connected. What does he mean?

3 Holmes describes reasoning backward as a valuable problem-solving strategy. What other strategies have you used?

LEARN HOW TO...
- use the problem solving scale

AS YOU...
- apply the 4-step approach to solve the *World Cup Problem*
- assess your group's solution

Exploration 1

The Problem Solving SCALE

SET UP *Work in a group.*

▶ To solve problems, Sherlock Holmes used an approach similar to the 4-step approach you used in Module 1 on page 33.

4 Work as a team and use the 4-step problem-solving approach to solve the *World Cup Problem*. Write up an explanation of your team's solution.

> ### World Cup Problem
>
> The World Cup is a world championship soccer tournament that is held every 4 years and is played over several rounds. In the first round of the 2006 finals, 32 teams competed against one another. The teams were divided into eight groups of four teams. Within each group, each team played the other three teams once. How many games were played in the first round of the 2006 World Cup finals?

▲
The World Cup draws a huge audience. In 2006, over 3.3 million fans attended the 64 World Cup matches.

5 **Discussion** For each question, explain what your team did when you solved the *World Cup Problem*.

   a. What did you do to make sure you understood the problem?

   b. What was your plan for solving the problem?

   c. What steps did you use to carry out your plan?

   d. What did you do when you looked back at your solution?

▶ **Assessment Scales** This year you will be using the *Assessment Scales* on page 87 to help improve your problem solving and communication skills.

The first scale is the *Problem Solving Scale*. It is used to assess the application of the 4-step approach to problem solving. You will use the scale to think about your work and how to improve it.

6 How is the problem solving scale related to the 4-step problem-solving approach?

7 If you score a "1" on this scale, you cannot score your work using any of the other assessment scales on page 87. Why?

8 How can you score a "5" on the problem solving scale? a "4"?

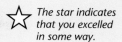

Student Resource

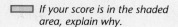 *If your score is in the shaded area, explain why.*

☆ *The star indicates that you excelled in some way.*

 ## Problem Solving

① I did not understand the problem well enough to get started or I did not show any work.

②

③ I understood the problem well enough to make a plan and to work toward a solution.

④

⑤ I made a plan, I used it to solve the problem, and I verified my solution.

 ## Mathematical Language

① I did not use any mathematical vocabulary or symbols, or I did not use them correctly, or my use was not appropriate.

②

③ I used appropriate mathematical language, but the way it was used was not always correct or other terms and symbols were needed.

④

⑤ I used mathematical language that was correct and appropriate to make my meaning clear.

 ## Representations

① I did not use any representations such as equations, tables, graphs, or diagrams to help solve the problem or explain my solution.

②

③ I made appropriate representations to help solve the problem or help me explain my solution, but they were not always correct or other representations were needed.

④

⑤ I used appropriate and correct representations to solve the problem or explain my solution.

 ## Connections

① I attempted or solved the problem and then stopped.

②

③ I found patterns and used them to extend the solution to other cases, or I recognized that this problem relates to other problems, mathematical ideas, or applications.

④

⑤ I extended the ideas in the solution to the general case, or I showed how this problem relates to other problems, mathematical ideas, or applications.

 ## Presentation

① The presentation of my solution and reasoning is unclear to others.

②

③ The presentation of my solution and reasoning is clear in most places, but others may have trouble understanding parts of it.

④

⑤ The presentation of my solution and reasoning is clear and can be understood by others.

▶ **Here is Becky's solution to the *World Cup Problem*.**

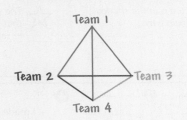

First I used a diagram to find the number of games for one group.
Then I used that to find the number of games for all the groups.

Team 1

Team 2 — Team 3

Team 4

Group A

Team 1 – 3 games
Team 2 – 2 other games
Team 3 – 1 other game
Team 4 – 0 other games
3 + 2 + 1 = 6 games per group
6 × 8 = 14 games in all

14 games were played in the first round of the 2006 World Cup.

9 **Discussion** Discuss each question and explain your answer.

a. Do you think Becky understood the *World Cup Problem*?

b. Do you think Becky had a plan for solving the problem?

c. Do you think she looked back at her solution?

d. Becky gave herself a "5" on the problem solving scale. Do you agree with her scoring? Why or why not?

✔ **QUESTION 10**

… checks that you understand the problem solving scale.

10 ✔ **CHECKPOINT** Use the problem solving scale on page 87.

a. What score would you give your team's solution to the *World Cup Problem*? Why?

b. What could your team do to improve its score?

HOMEWORK EXERCISES ▶ See Exs. 1–4 on p. 93.

GOAL

LEARN HOW TO…
◆ Apply different problem-solving strategies
◆ use the representations scale

AS YOU…
◆ work as a team to solve the *Handshake Problem*

KEY TERM
◆ representations

Exploration 2

The Representations SCALE

SET UP *Work in a group.*

11 **Discussion** Look at Becky's solution to the *World Cup Problem*.

a. Becky started with a diagram. How did the diagram help her solve the problem?

b. Did you make a table, a list, or a diagram to solve the *World Cup Problem*? If not, would using one of these representations have helped you solve the problem? Why or why not?

▶ Diagrams, tables, and graphs are **representations** that can help you solve problems and explain your solutions. You will use the *Representations Scale* to assess and improve your use of representations.

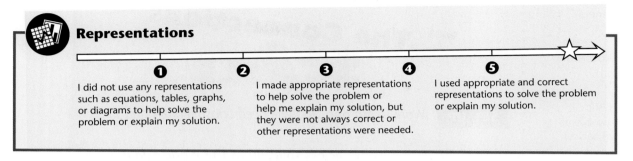

Representations

❶ I did not use any representations such as equations, tables, graphs, or diagrams to help solve the problem or explain my solution.

❷ ❸ I made appropriate representations to help solve the problem or help me explain my solution, but they were not always correct or other representations were needed.

❹ ❺ I used appropriate and correct representations to solve the problem or explain my solution.

12 **Discussion** What score would you give Becky's solution of the *World Cup Problem* on the representations scale? Why?

13 **a.** Work as a team. Use appropriate problem-solving strategies and visual representations to solve the *Handshake Problem*.

> **Handshake Problem**
>
> Five people are hired to work together on a fundraising project. As they are introduced, they shake hands with each other exactly one time. How many handshakes take place?

b. Write an explanation that shows how your team solved the problem.

14 **Discussion**

a. What representations did your team use to solve the problem or to explain your solution?

b. Were your representations appropriate? Explain.

c. Were your representations correct? Explain.

15 ✔ **CHECKPOINT** What score would you give your team on the representations scale? Why?

✔ **QUESTION 15**

...checks that you understand the representations scale.

HOMEWORK EXERCISES ▶ See Exs. 5–8 on pp. 93–94.

GOAL

LEARN HOW TO...
◆ extend solutions to the general case
◆ use the connections scale

AS YOU...
◆ look for connections among problems you have solved

KEY TERMS
◆ connection
◆ general case

Exploration 3

The Connections SCALE

SET UP *Work in a group. You will need Labsheets 2A and 2B.*

▶ **Here is the final part of Becky's solution of the *World Cup Problem*.**

> When I looked at the diagram, I saw that the problem was like the Handshake problem.

16 Try This as a Class Compare Becky's final solution to the *World Cup Problem* with your solution to the Handshake Problem.

   a. How is the *World Cup Problem* like the *Handshake Problem*?

   b. How are the *World Cup* and *Handshake* problems related to the triangular numbers on page 15 in Module 1?

▶ **One type of connection is made when you relate a problem to other problems, mathematical ideas, or applications.**

17 Is there a pattern in the *World Cup Problem* or the *Handshake Problem* that you can extend? Explain.

▶ **You make another type of connection when you identify patterns and extend them to other cases. For example, in Module 1 you predicted the next triangular number and found the lowest safe bid for playing *Card Swappers* with different numbers of cards. The *Connections Scale* is used to assess either type of connection.**

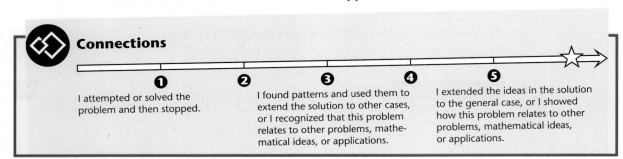

Connections

❶ I attempted or solved the problem and then stopped.

❷

❸ I found patterns and used them to extend the solution to other cases, or I recognized that this problem relates to other problems, mathematical ideas, or applications.

❹

❺ I extended the ideas in the solution to the general case, or I showed how this problem relates to other problems, mathematical ideas, or applications.

18 What score do you think Becky should give her final solution on the connections scale? Why?

▶ **As you work on the string art problem in Questions 19–22, think about the connections scale.**

19 In the design shown, string links each of the six pegs in every way possible. How many linkups are there altogether?

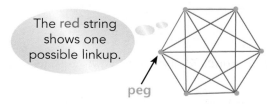

The red string shows one possible linkup.

peg

20 ✔ **CHECKPOINT** Is the string design problem related to any other problems you have solved? Explain.

21 Copy and complete the table to find the number of linkups for different numbers of pegs.

Number of pegs	1	2	3	4	5	6	7
Number of linkups	?	?	?	?	?	?	?

22 **Try This as a Class**

a. How many linkups can be made in a string design with 9 pegs like the one at the right?

b. Explain how you can find the total number of linkups made in a string design with any number of pegs.

c. Compare your method for solving part (b) with those of other class members. If different methods were used, are they all correct?

▶ **One way to score a "5" on the connections scale is by extending a solution to the general case. You did this when you found the number of linkups for any number of pegs. You also did this in Module 1 when you wrote a rule to find any term of a sequence.**

23 **a.** Write a complete explanation that shows how you solved the string art problem. Remember to explain the connections.

b. What score would you give yourself on the connections scale? Why?

HOMEWORK EXERCISES ▶ See Exs. 9–10 on pp. 94–95.

✔ **QUESTION 20**

...checks that you understand connections.

▲
String art designs can be simple or complicated depending on the pattern and the number of pegs used.

Section 2
Key Concepts

Problem Solving Scale (pp. 86–88)

This scale can be used to assess how well you use the 4-step problem-solving approach.

- Did I understand the problem?
- Did I make a plan and get started toward a solution?
- Did I carry out my plan and find a solution?
- Did I look back to make sure my work was correct and my answer was reasonable?
- Did I make sure I answered the right questions?
- Did I try a different method to solve the problem?

Representations Scale (pp. 88–89)

This scale can be used to assess how well you use representations such as equations, tables, graphs, and diagrams.

- Were my representations appropriate?
- Were my representations correct?
- Were there any other representations I should have used?

representations

Connections Scale (pp. 90–91)

This scale can be used to assess your ability to show how a problem relates to other problems, mathematical ideas, or applications or to extend the solution to the general case.

connection

general case

- Did I identify a pattern?
- Did I extend the solution to other cases or to the general case?
- Did I relate the problem to another situation, problem, or mathematical idea?
- Did I clearly show the connections I found?

To extend the solution to the general case, you need to find a rule that will work for any case.

24 **Key Concepts Question Use Labsheets 2A and 2B.** On the labsheets are explanations of how two teams solved the *Handshake Problem*. Score each team on the *problem solving*, *representations*, and *connections scales*.

Section 2
Practice & Application Exercises ▸▸▸▸▸▸▸▸▸▸▸▸

For Exercises 1 and 2, solve each problem and score your solution using the problem solving scale on page 87.

1. A snail starts at the bottom of a well 10 ft deep and crawls up 3 ft each day. Each night the snail slips back 2 ft. How long will it take the snail to reach the top of the well?

2. Use the clues below to find the mystery number.

   ◆ The number is between 0 and 150.

   ◆ If you start with 7 and keep counting by 7s, the number will be on your list.

   ◆ The sum of the digits in the number is 12.

   ◆ The number can be divided evenly by four.

3. a. Find the digit represented by each letter. A letter stands for the same digit throughout the problem. Every letter has a different value.

   b. How can you verify your solution?

```
      C E D
    ×   G K
    ───────
      D D 1
    2 5 7
    ───────
    K K 4 G
```

4. **Challenge** A jeweler had four pieces of gold chain. Each piece has three links. The jeweler wants to join the links to form a closed necklace. Explain how to do this by cutting and rejoining the least number of links.

5. **Geometry Connection** Explain why each drawing is or is not an appropriate and correct solution to the problem: Draw a segment that divides a square into two right triangles.

   a. 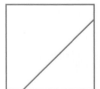   b.    c.

6. a. Half of a boat's crew of 15 men and 15 women could leave to visit a port. The crew lined up. Every ninth person was allowed to leave until half the crew had left. When the last person in line was counted, the counting continued to the front of the line. The crew that remained was all women. In what order did the crew line up? Show how you found your answer.

   b. Use the representations scale on page 87. What score would you give your solution to part (a)? Why?

7. **Create Your Own** Write a word problem that could be solved using one of the visuals shown below.

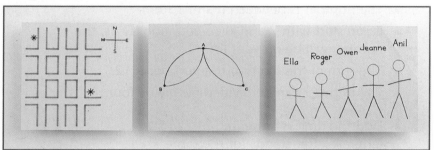

8. Large stained glass windows are made of panels of colored glass held together by an iron frame.

   a. Suppose a glass panel is 4 ft wide and 10 ft long. About how many feet of iron framing are needed to hold two glass panels stacked vertically as shown? to hold three glass panels stacked vertically?

   b. How can you find how many feet of framing are needed to hold any number of glass panels stacked vertically?

   c. Use the representations scale on page 87. What score would you give your solution to part (b)? Why?

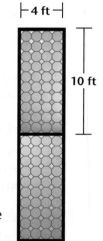

9. Six teams compete in a contest. In the first round every team plays one game against each of the other teams. The top three teams go on to the second round where every team plays against each of the other teams twice. In the third round, the top two teams from the second round play against each other twice.

   a. Find the least and the greatest number of games a team may play. Explain your solution and how it is related to another problem, mathematical idea, or application.

   b. Use the connections scale on page 87. What score would you give your solution to part (a)? Why?

Reflecting on the Section

Write your responses to Exercise 10 in your journal.

Journal

Exercise 10 checks that you can use problem-solving strategies.

10. **Language Arts** The detective Sherlock Holmes uses the clues below in "The Case of the Itinerant Yeggman" by June Thomson.

December 27, 1894 – Letter arrives at mansion. Professor from Germany wants to visit to study design of buildings.

January 25, 1895 – Professor visits mansion.

July 21, 1895 – Mansion robbed. Among items stolen: Priceless prayer book passed down in owner's family.

November 26, 1894 – Letter arrives at old estate. Historian from France wants to visit to study woodwork of rooms.

December 28, 1894 – Historian visits estate.

June 22, 1895 – Estate robbed. Among items stolen: jewelled fan passed down by owner's great grandparents

October 28, 1894 – Letter arrives at country home. Professor from Chicago wants to visit to study design of floor tiling.

November 27, 1894 – Professor visits country home.

May 24, 1895 – Country home robbed. Among items stolen: gold cup passed down by owner's great grandfather.

a. Describe any patterns that you see in the clues.

b. Holmes learns that the owner of a fourth home received a letter on January 25, 1895, and a visit from a professor on February 24, 1895. He suspects that another break-in may occur. Choose the most likely date. Explain your thinking.

   - Apr. 15, 1895
   - July 7, 1895
   - Aug. 20, 1895
   - June 5, 1895

Spiral Review

Find the value of each expression. (Module 1, p. 10)

11. $6 \cdot 5 + 13$ 12. $54 - 81 \div 9$ 13. $144 \div (12 - 8)$

14. Make a table for the sequence 5, 9, 13, 17, … . Extend it to include the next two terms. Then write a rule for the sequence. (Module 1, p. 21)

Section 2

Show how to use the 4-step approach and a diagram, a table, or a graph to solve each problem. Remember to make connections.

1. A school bus travels 3 blocks east, 4 blocks north, 10 blocks west, 2 blocks south, and 1 block east. At this point, the bus is how many blocks north or south of its starting point? How many blocks east or west?

2. An elevator in an office building started at ground level. It rose 5 floors, descended 2 floors, rose 9 floors, descended 3 floors, and rose 7 floors. Which floor is the elevator on?

3. John, Sue, Lisa, and Fernando are student council officers. The council has four officers: president, vice president, secretary, and treasurer. Use the clues below to determine which student is the president.

   ◆ John is neither president nor secretary.
   ◆ A boy holds the office of vice president.
   ◆ Sue is not secretary.
   ◆ The names of the treasurer and the vice president have the same number of letters.

4. The lengths of three sticks are 5 in., 7 in., and 10 in. How can you use these sticks to mark off a length of 8 in.?

5. A restaurant has two types of tables. One type seats two people and the other seats four. If 28 people are in the restaurant, how many full tables of each type can there be?

6. Tickets to the musical cost $8 for students and $12 for all others. If $520 was earned by the sale of 49 tickets, how many student tickets were sold?

Standardized Testing ◀▶ Free Response

Caroline and Juanita are going camping. Their tent weighs 7 pounds. They have two sleeping bags that weigh 3 pounds each, a camp stove that weighs 6 pounds, 14 pounds of food and assorted supplies, 15 pounds of water, 10 pounds of clothing, a 1-pound first-aid kit, and a 3-pound lantern.

Can Caroline and Juanita divide their gear so that each person carries the same amount of weight? Explain.

Section 3 Lines, Angles, and Triangles

Language Clues

IN THIS SECTION

EXPLORATION 1
◆ Geometric Language

EXPLORATION 2
◆ Sides of a Triangle

EXPLORATION 3
◆ Angles of a Triangle

Setting the Stage ▸▸▸▸▸▸▸▸▸▸▸▸▸▸▸▸▸▸▸▸▸▸▸▸▸▸▸▸▸▸▸▸

SET UP *Work with a partner. You will need: • I Describe, You Draw cards from Labsheet 3A • two sheets of unlined paper*

▶ Detectives depend on crime scene investigators to collect evidence to help solve cases. It is very important that the investigators accurately describe the evidence and provide detailed sketches. In this section you will learn to accurately describe and draw geometric figures.

In the game *I Describe, You Draw,* one person describes the design on a card. The other person tries to draw what is described without asking any questions.

I Describe, You Draw

- ◆ Decide who will draw and who will describe.
- ◆ Play the game using the first card.
- ◆ Switch roles and play the game with the second card.

> Be sure your partner does not see your card. Be sure you cannot see the drawing.

Think About It

1 How do the drawings compare with the cards?

2 Did you use mathematical terms to describe the drawing?

3 If you did use mathematical terms, did it help? Explain.

LEARN HOW TO...
- name basic geometric figures

AS YOU...
- describe and draw figures

KEY TERMS
- point
- line
- segment
- ray
- plane
- parallel
- perpendicular

Exploration 1

Geometric Language

To help detectives, the crime scene investigator's written reports must accurately describe the evidence. Using accurate mathematical terms can help you understand and solve problems.

▶ **Terms for Geometric Figures** Special terms and symbols can help you describe geometric figures.

4 Choose the number of the best term for each figure.

a. 		**1.** line
b. 		**2.** segment
c. •————————•		**3.** perpendicular lines
d. •		**4.** ray
e. •————————▶		**5.** parallel lines
f. 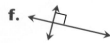		**6.** point

5 **Discussion** Segments and rays are parts of lines.

a. How are lines, rays, and segments alike?

b. How are they different?

▶ **You can use letters and symbols to name geometric figures.**

EXAMPLE

In the diagram:

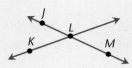

J means **point** J.

$\overline{KL}$ means **segment** KL.

$\overleftrightarrow{KL}$ means **line** KL.

$\overrightarrow{KL}$ means **ray** KL.

The segment includes endpoints K and L and all points between K and L.

The ray starts at endpoint K and passes through L.

6 **Discussion** Use the diagram in the Example to help answer the following questions.

a. Why are two points enough to name a line but one point is not?

b. Are all three letters necessary to name line *JLM*? Explain.

7 **Try This as a Class** In each part below, the name of a figure is printed in red followed by two other names. Are the figures whose names are printed in black the same figures as the one whose name is printed in red? Explain.

a. $\overleftrightarrow{EG}$: $\overleftrightarrow{EF}$, $\overleftrightarrow{GE}$

b. $\overrightarrow{EG}$: $\overrightarrow{EF}$, $\overrightarrow{GE}$

c. $\overline{EG}$: $\overline{EF}$, $\overline{GE}$

8 ✔ **CHECKPOINT** Draw and label the following objects.

a. point *P*

b. ray *SQ*

c. segment *MT*

d. line *UV*

e. $\overrightarrow{YX}$

f. $\overleftrightarrow{ND}$

g. $\overline{RG}$

h. $\overrightarrow{XY}$

✔ **QUESTION 8**

...checks that you can identify and name points, lines, segments, and rays.

▶ **Letters and symbols can also be used to describe relationships between geometric figures.**

EXAMPLE

A **plane** can be thought of as a flat surface that goes on forever in all directions. The floor and walls of your classroom are each part of a plane.

Two lines in a plane are **parallel** if they don't *intersect*, or meet.

$\overleftrightarrow{AB} \parallel \overleftrightarrow{JH}$ means
$\overleftrightarrow{AB}$ and $\overleftrightarrow{JH}$ are parallel.

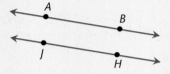

Two lines that intersect at a *right angle* are **perpendicular**. You will learn more about right angles and other types of angles in Exploration 3 on page 103.

$\overleftrightarrow{QV} \perp \overleftrightarrow{UT}$ means
$\overleftrightarrow{QV}$ and $\overleftrightarrow{UT}$ are perpendicular.

The ⌐ tells you the angle is a right angle. The measure of a right angle is 90 degrees.

9 Name two lines in the photo below that have the given characteristic.

   a. They are parallel.   **b.** They are not parallel.

   c. They are perpendicular.   **d.** They are not perpendicular.

10 Look back at the cards you used for *I Describe, You Draw*. If you described the cards again, what geometric terms could you use to help your partner draw the figures correctly?

HOMEWORK EXERCISES ▶ See Exs. 1–7 on p. 108.

Exploration 2

Sides of a Triangle

GOAL

LEARN HOW TO...
- classify triangles by the lengths of their sides
- determine when triangles can be formed

AS YOU...
- construct triangles with sides of different lengths

KEY TERMS
- equilateral triangle
- isosceles triangle
- scalene triangle

SET UP *You will need: • a ruler • Labsheet 3B and scissors, or sticks with different lengths • Labsheet 3C*

Jessie described the design on Card 5 as "a square that is inside a triangle and has one side that lies on the bottom side of the triangle." Jessie's partner made two drawings.

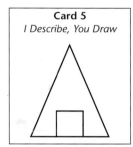

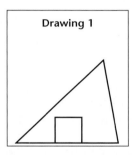

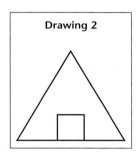

▶ **Types of Triangles** The design on the card would have been easier to describe if Jessie knew how to classify triangles. One way to classify triangles is by the lengths of the sides.

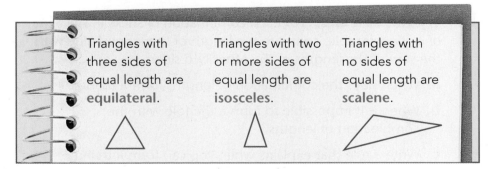

Triangles with three sides of equal length are **equilateral**.

Triangles with two or more sides of equal length are **isosceles**.

Triangles with no sides of equal length are **scalene**.

11 Discussion

    a. What type of triangle is on Card 5? How do you know?

    b. How can you show that the triangle in Drawing 1 is scalene?

    c. Identify the type of triangle in Drawing 2. Why did you classify it that way?

    d. Why can the triangle in Drawing 2 be classified in two different ways?

12 Write a description of the design on Card 5 that does not also describe the other two drawings.

▶ **Constructing Triangles** You can use sticks of different lengths to explore a variety of triangles.

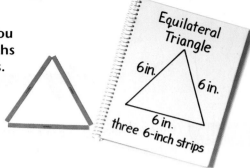

Equilateral Triangle

6 in.   6 in.

6 in.

three 6-inch strips

Use Labsheet 3B for Questions 13 and 14.

✔ **QUESTION 13**

...checks that you can classify triangles based on the lengths of their sides.

13 ✔ **CHECKPOINT** Use the *Sticks of Different Sizes* to construct one example of each type of triangle. List the lengths of the sticks you use for each.

a. an isosceles triangle

b. a scalene triangle

c. an equilateral triangle (different from the one shown above)

Use Labsheet 3C for Questions 14 and 15.

14 Using your sticks, decide whether you can form a triangle for each combination of lengths listed in the *Sides of a Triangle* table. Sketch each triangle you form and record its type and the lengths of its sides in the table.

15 **Try This as a Class** For each combination of sticks in the *Sides of a Triangle* table, compare the length of the longest side with the sum of the lengths of the other two sides.

a. When does the combination of lengths form a triangle?

b. When is it impossible to form a triangle with the combination of lengths?

c. Write a rule that explains when you can form a triangle.

✔ **QUESTION 16**

...checks that you understand when a combination of side lengths will form a triangle.

16 ✔ **CHECKPOINT** Without using sticks, decide which combinations of side lengths can form a triangle. Explain.

a. 5 in., 12 in., and 6 in.   **b.** 9 in., 6 in., and 5 in.

c. 6 in., 8 in., and 10 in.   **d.** 4 in., 1 in., and 3 in.

HOMEWORK EXERCISES ▶ See Exs. 8–15 on p. 108.

Exploration 3

Angles of a Triangle

GOAL

LEARN HOW TO...
- identify types of angles
- classify triangles by their angles
- use the mathematical language scale

AS YOU...
- explore geometric figures around you

KEY TERMS
- angle
- vertex of an angle
- degrees
- right angle
- acute angle
- obtuse angle
- straight angle
- acute triangle
- right triangle
- obtuse triangle

SET UP / *You will need:* • Labsheet 3D

17 Discussion Both red triangles below are isosceles. Besides their side lengths, what makes them look different?

▶ **Naming and Describing Angles** You can use an *angle* measurement to describe how the sides of a roof meet. An **angle** is formed by two rays that have a common endpoint.

EXAMPLE

This angle can be named in any of the following ways:

- angle *B* (written ∠*B*)
- angle *ABC* (written ∠*ABC*)
- angle *CBA* (written ∠*CBA*)

> The endpoint of the rays is the **vertex** of the angle.

18 Try This as a Class

a. Explain how the vertex is used in naming an angle.

b. Write all the possible names that identify the angle marked in red.

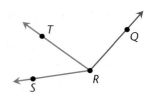

▶ The measure of an angle refers to the size of the opening between the two rays of the angle. Angles are measured in units called **degrees**. The symbol for degrees is °. For example, the measure of an 80 degree angle can be written as 80°.

CLASSIFYING ANGLES

Right Angle
Its measure is 90°.

Acute Angle
Its measure is greater than 0° but less than 90°.

Obtuse Angle
Its measure is greater than 90° but less than 180°.

Straight Angle
Its measure is 180°.

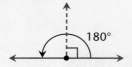

✔ **QUESTION 19**

...checks that you can classify and name angles.

19 ✔ **CHECKPOINT** For each of the following, find an angle of that type in the diagrams below and write all the names that identify the angle.

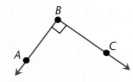

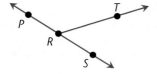

a. right angle

b. acute angle

c. obtuse angle

d. straight angle

▶ **Classifying Triangles by Angles** In Exploration 2, you learned to use the side lengths to classify triangles. You can also classify triangles by the types of angles they have.

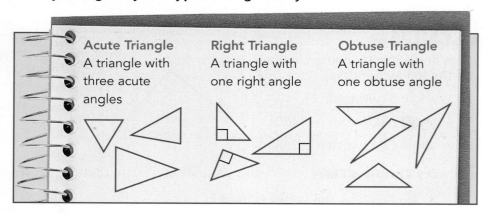

Acute Triangle
A triangle with three acute angles

Right Triangle
A triangle with one right angle

Obtuse Triangle
A triangle with one obtuse angle

Use Labsheet 3D for Questions 20 and 21.

✔ **QUESTION 20**

...checks that you can classify triangles based on their angles.

20 ✔ **CHECKPOINT**

a. For each triangle in the *Angles in a Triangle* table, list the names of its angles in the appropriate columns.

b. Use the definitions above to classify the triangle by the measures of its angles and record the type in the last column.

21 Use Labsheet 3D to help answer each question. It may also help to try drawing triangles on a piece of scrap paper.

    a. Can a triangle have two right angles? Why or why not?

    b. If a triangle has one obtuse angle, what kind of angles will the other two angles be? Why?

22 **Discussion** After examining a triangle, a student decides it is an acute triangle and a right triangle. Is this possible? Explain.

23 Think about how the geometric terms you have learned can help you when playing *I Describe, You Draw.*

    a. Make up an *I Describe, You Draw* card that can be described using the mathematical terms you learned in this section.

    b. Play the game with another student using the cards you created.

    c. How do your drawings compare with the cards?

    d. Which were closer to the drawings on the cards, your drawings in part (b) or your drawings for Cards 1 and 2 from the *Setting the Stage?*

▶ **This year you will use the Mathematical Language Scale to assess and help improve your use of mathematical language.**

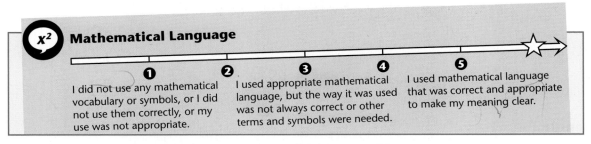

This scale is part of the Assessment Scales on page 87.

24 What score would you give this description on the mathematical language scale? Why?

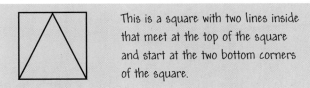

This is a square with two lines inside that meet at the top of the square and start at the two bottom corners of the square.

| HOMEWORK EXERCISES ▶ See Exs. 16–31 on pp. 109–110.

Section ③ Key Concepts

Key Terms

point

line

ray

segment

plane

parallel

perpendicular

equilateral triangle

isosceles triangle

scalene triangle

Basic Geometric Figures (pp. 98–99)

Figure	Words	Symbol
• A	point A	A
←•——•→ A B	line AB or line BA	$\overleftrightarrow{AB}$ or $\overleftrightarrow{BA}$
•——•→ A B	ray AB	$\overrightarrow{AB}$
•——• A B	segment AB or segment BA	$\overline{AB}$ or $\overline{BA}$

Line Relationships (p. 100)

A plane is a flat surface that goes on forever in all directions.
Two distinct lines in a plane either intersect or are parallel.
When lines intersect at a 90° angle, they are perpendicular.

intersecting lines   parallel lines   perpendicular lines

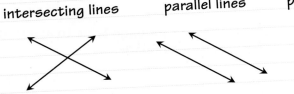

This is a right angle symbol.

Classifying Triangles by Sides (p. 101)

- Equilateral triangles have three sides of equal length.
- Isosceles triangles have two or more sides of equal length.
- Scalene triangles have no sides of equal length.

Triangle Side Lengths (p. 102)

The sum of the lengths of the two shortest sides of a triangle is greater than the length of the longest side.

25 Key Concepts Question A triangle has a 5 in. side and an 11 in. side. The length of the third side is a whole number of inches. What are the possible lengths of the third side?

Section 3
Key Concepts

Naming and Classifying Angles (pp. 103–104)

An angle is formed by two rays that have a common endpoint. The endpoint of the rays is the vertex of the angle. The angle at the right is formed by $\overrightarrow{RQ}$ and $\overrightarrow{RS}$. It can be named $\angle R$, $\angle QRS$, or $\angle SRQ$.

Angles are measured in units called degrees. An angle can be classified by its measure.

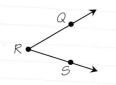

angle

vertex

degrees

Right Angle	**Acute Angle**	**Obtuse Angle**	**Straight Angle**
Its measure is 90°.	Its measure is greater than 0° but less than 90°.	Its measure is greater than 90° but less than 180°.	Its measure is 180°.

right angle

acute angle

obtuse angle

straight angle

Classifying Triangles by Angles (pp. 104–105)

- Acute triangles have three acute angles.
- Right triangles have one right angle.
- Obtuse triangles have one obtuse angle.

acute triangle

right triangle

obtuse triangle

Mathematical Language Scale (p. 105)

To assess your use of mathematical language, ask yourself:
- Was my use of terms and symbols correct?
- Was my use of terms and symbols appropriate?
- Are there other mathematical terms or symbols I should have used to make my meaning clearer?

26 Key Concepts Question Sketch an example of each type of triangle.

a. a triangle that is both right and scalene

b. a triangle that is both acute and isosceles

Section 3

Practice & Application Exercises

Use the points on the line to write each answer using symbols.

X   Y   Z

1. Name three different segments. How are they different?

2. Name three different rays. How are they different?

3. Name the line in six ways.

Write *line, segment, ray, parallel,* or *perpendicular* to best describe each object or pair of objects.

4. flagpole

5. light from car's headlight

6. flagpole and the edge of the road

7. light from headlight and the edge of the road

Use a ruler or a straightedge to draw an example of each type of triangle.

8. equilateral

9. isosceles

10. scalene

A triangle has sides of lengths 20 ft and 15 ft. Tell whether each length *can* or *cannot* be the length of the third side of the triangle.

11. 29 ft   12. 3 ft   13. 5 ft   14. 37 ft

15. Read the story. Then explain Smith's answer to the problem.

Jones said to Smith: "I think I'll sell that piece of land at the bottom of my garden, but I can't make up my mind how much to ask for it. What do you suggest?"

"Well," said Smith, "what are its dimensions?"

Jones drew the diagram below and handed it over.

Smith studied the drawing for a second or two, then passed it back. "If your dimensions are right, you don't get so much as a dime for it," he said laughing.

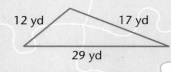

12 yd   17 yd   29 yd

from Puzzles and Brain Twisters, by Fred Walls

Explain what is wrong with each statement.

16. This is ∠JHI.

17. This is $\overrightarrow{CB}$.

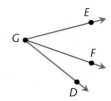

18. This is ∠G.

Classify each angle as *right, acute, straight,* or *obtuse.*

19.

20.

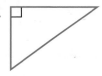

21.

22.

Classify each triangle according to the measures of its angles and according to the lengths of its sides.

23.

24.

25.

26.

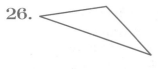

27.

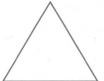

28.

29. a. The shop owner described a missing watch to the detectives. Will the detectives be able to identify the correct watch? If not, how can you improve the description?

The missing watch has a silver band and there are two blue triangles next to the dial.

b. What would you score the shop owner's description on the mathematical language scale? Why?

30. Challenge *Acute-isosceles* is an example of a combination name for a triangle. A name describing the angles (*acute*, *right*, or *obtuse*) is joined with a name describing the number of sides of equal length (*equilateral*, *isosceles*, or *scalene*). List all the combination names that can be written. Then explain which names describe triangles that cannot actually be formed.

RESEARCH

Exercise 31 checks that you understand how important mathematical language is in everyday life.

Reflecting ◀▶ on the Section

31. a. Describe ways in which people may need to use words like line, angle, or triangle in their everyday life or work.

b. What mathematical terms do you use outside of school besides numbers?

Spiral ◀▶ Review

Write each fraction in lowest terms. (Module 1, p. 61)

32. $\frac{6}{18}$ **33.** $\frac{24}{30}$ **34.** $\frac{15}{25}$ **35.** $\frac{18}{27}$

Use mental math to find each value. (Module 1, p. 62)

36. $\frac{1}{4}$ of 28   **37.** $\frac{5}{6}$ of 48   **38.** $\frac{2}{3}$ of 24

Use the following information to answer Exercises 39–41. A bag contains 2 red, 3 blue, and 5 white balls. One ball is drawn from the bag. (Module 2, p. 80)

39. What are the outcomes of the experiment?

40. Find the theoretical probability of the given event.

     a. A red ball is drawn.

     b. A green ball is drawn.

     c. A red or a white ball is drawn.

     d. The ball drawn is not white.

41. Suppose the experiment was repeated 20 times, and the ball that was drawn was put back in the bag after each trial. About how many times would you think a blue ball was drawn? Explain.

Section 3

Extra Skill Practice

Choose the letter of the symbol that matches each term.

1. segment *AB*   A. *A*

2. point *A*   B. $\overrightarrow{AB}$

3. line *AB*   C. $\overline{AB}$

4. ray *AB*   D. $\overleftrightarrow{AB}$

Tell whether each combination of side lengths *can* or *cannot* form a triangle.

5. 20 ft, 12 ft, 10 ft   6. 8 in., 9 in., 18 in.

7. 15 yd, 6 yd, 6 yd   8. 11 ft, 12 ft, 13 ft

Tell whether each statement is *true* or *false*.

9. A right triangle has one right angle.

10. A scalene triangle has two sides of equal length.

11. An obtuse triangle has one obtuse angle.

Classify each angle as *right*, *acute*, *obtuse*, or *straight*.

12.   13.   14.   15.

Standardized Testing ◀▶ Free Response

Find an example of each type of triangle that is formed by putting together two or more of the small triangles. List the numbers of the small triangles you used.

A right   B equilateral

C acute   D isosceles

E scalene   F obtuse

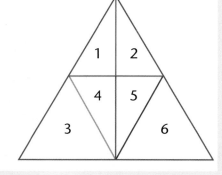

Section 4 Polygons and Angles

Detecting Shapes

IN THIS SECTION

EXPLORATION 1
◆ Naming Polygons

EXPLORATION 2
◆ Measuring Angles

EXPLORATION 3
◆ The Presentation Scale

◂◂ Setting the Stage ▸▸▸▸▸▸▸▸▸▸▸▸▸▸▸▸▸▸▸▸▸▸▸

KEY TERMS
◆ polygon
◆ vertex of a polygon

Sometimes being a detective means examining clues over and over again, hoping to see something you did not see before. For example, examine the drawing at the right. Can you find the five-pointed star**?**

The five-pointed star is an example of a *polygon*. A **polygon** is a closed plane figure made from segments, called sides, that do not cross. Each endpoint of a side is a **vertex**. (The plural of vertex is vertices.) A polygon can be named by listing the vertices in consecutive order.

Think About It

1 List all the polygons in the figure at the left. Record your answers in a table like the one below. (One polygon has been done for you.) Then compute the total score by adding the points described.

◆ 1 point for each triangle
◆ 2 points for each 4-sided polygon
◆ 3 points for each 5-sided polygon
◆ 5 points for each 6-sided polygon

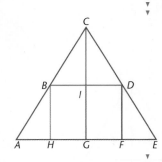

Type	Names	Score
Triangle		
4-sided polygon	*HBIG*	
5-sided polygon		
6-sided polygon		
	TOTAL SCORE	

2 Discussion What is the greatest possible score for the figure**?**

Exploration 1

Naming Polygons

SET UP *Work with a partner. You will need: • index cards or sticky notes • Labsheet 4A • 2 pieces of string, each 3 feet long • scissors*

▶ **Just as examining the clues over and over again can help detectives solve a mystery, sorting polygons in various ways can help you identify their properties.**

3 **Use Labsheet 4A.** Cut out the *Shape Cards*. Then follow the steps below to sort them.

> You may want to tie the ends of the string together.

First

Shapes

Polygons

Place a loop of string on your workspace. Write *Polygons* on an index card and place it in the loop. Write *Shapes* on another card and place it outside the loop.

Then

Shapes

Polygons

Place all the cards with a polygon inside the loop. Place the cards with shapes that are not polygons outside the loop.

▶ **The shapes you placed inside the loop in Question 3 are a set of polygons.**

4 A **regular polygon** is a polygon in which all the sides have the same length and all the angles have the same measure.

   a. Use a loop of string and an index card labeled *Regular Polygons*. Sort the polygon *Shape Cards* so the regular polygons are inside the loop and the non-regular polygons are outside the loop.

   b. What is another name for a regular triangle?

GOAL

LEARN HOW TO...
◆ classify polygons
◆ sort polygons using a Venn diagram

AS YOU...
◆ explore geometric shapes

KEY TERMS
◆ regular polygon
◆ quadrilateral
◆ Venn diagram
◆ trapezoid
◆ parallelogram
◆ rhombus

▶ **Another way to sort polygons is by the number of sides.**

✔ **QUESTION 5**

...checks that you can distinguish polygons based on their number of sides.

5 ✔ **CHECKPOINT** Identify the polygons on the *Shape Cards* that have the given number of sides.

a. eight sides   **b.** four sides

▶ The word **polygon** comes from the Greek **poly-** meaning "many" and **-gon** meaning "angles." Polygons have many angles and sides. Many of the terms used to classify polygons also come from the Greek word parts shown at the right. For example, *pentagon* means "five angles."

Word part	Meaning
tri-	three
quadri-	four
penta-	five
hexa-	six
octa-	eight
deca-	ten
poly-	many
-gon	angle(s)
-lateral	side(s)

6 What is the name of a polygon with eight angles?

7 **Try This as a Class** With the exception of **quadrilateral**, which means "four sides," the names of polygons refer to the number of angles. How are the number of sides and the number of angles of a polygon related?

✔ **QUESTION 8**

...checks that you can name polygons by the number of sides or angles.

8 ✔ **CHECKPOINT** Write a definition of each term and sketch two examples.

a. triangle   **b.** pentagon   **c.** hexagon

▶ **Looking at Two Sets** Objects in one set sometimes share characteristics with objects in another set.

9 Use the quadrilateral *Shape Cards*. Follow the steps below to sort them into two sets.

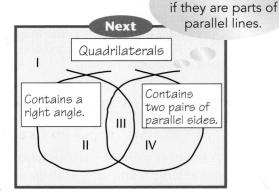

Two sides are parallel if they are parts of parallel lines.

First

Place two overlapping loops on your workspace.

Next

Quadrilaterals

I

Contains a right angle.

Contains two pairs of parallel sides.

II   III   IV

Label three index cards and place them as shown.

Then Place the *Shape Cards* in the correct regions, I, II, III, or IV.

10 **a.** Where did you place the cards that belong to both sets?

b. Why were some cards placed in region I?

▶ Diagrams like the ones you have made with loops are **Venn diagrams**. Venn diagrams use a drawing to show how the objects in sets are related.

11 A quadrilateral that has exactly one pair of parallel sides is a **trapezoid**. In what region(s) did you place the trapezoids? Why?

12 A quadrilateral that has two pairs of parallel sides is a **parallelogram**.

a. In what region(s) did you place the parallelograms? Why?

b. What is another name for parallelograms that contain a right angle?

13 A parallelogram with all sides the same length is a **rhombus**.

a. Where did you place the rhombuses? Explain.

b. What is another name for a rhombus that contains a right angle?

14 ✔ **CHECKPOINT**

a. Sort the parallelogram *Shape Cards* into two sets, a set labeled *Rectangles* and a set labeled *Rhombuses*.

b. Did you have any shapes that belong to both sets? Explain.

15 **a.** What kind of polygon is the five-pointed star in the *Setting the Stage*?

b. Is the five-pointed star a regular polygon? Explain.

c. Sketch a four pointed star.

d. What kind of polygon is a four pointed star?

✔ **QUESTION 14**

...checks that you can sort parallelograms using a Venn diagram.

HOMEWORK EXERCISES ▶ See Exs. 1–4 on p. 120.

LEARN HOW TO...
+ measure an angle
  using a protractor
+ draw an angle
  using a protractor

AS YOU...
+ examine angles in
  geometric figures

KEY TERM
+ protractor

Exploration 2

MEASURING Angles

SET UP *You will need: • a protractor • Labsheet 4B*

Stars like the one you found in the *Setting the Stage* are also found in nature.

Use Labsheet 4B for Questions 16–18.

16 The angles the sea star in the photo makes with its arms, ∠A, ∠B, ∠C, ∠D, and ∠E, determine its shape. Identify each angle as acute, right, or obtuse. Record your answers in the table on Labsheet 4B.

FOR◀HELP

with *ray and vertex,*
see
MODULE 2,
pp. 106–107

▶ **Measuring Angles** The shape of a polygon is also determined by the measures of its angles. To measure an angle, imagine one ray of an angle rotating around the vertex while the other ray is fixed in place. The measure of the angle is the amount of rotation measured in degrees.

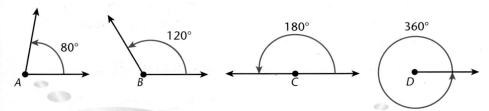

The measure of this angle is 80 degrees. Another way to write this is $m\angle A = 80°$.

There are 360° in a complete rotation, so one degree is $\frac{1}{360}$ of a complete rotation.

17 Try this as a Class

a. What is the measure of half a complete rotation?

b. What does an angle with that measure look like?

c. Estimate the measure of the angles shown in the sea star photo on Labsheet 4B. Record your estimates in the table on the labsheet.

▶ You can use a **protractor** to measure and draw angles.

Student Resource

Using a Protractor

The steps below show how to use a protractor to measure an angle.

First Place the center mark of the protractor on the vertex of the angle.

Next Place the 0° mark on one side of the angle. You may need to extend the sides of the angle.

Then Read the number where the other side of the angle crosses the scale.

 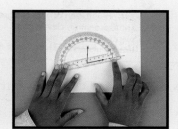 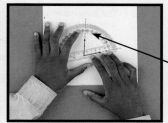

Read the number on the bottom scale since you used its 0° mark.

The measure of ∠ABC is 75°.

18

a. Use a protractor to find the exact measure of each angle in the sea star photo on Labsheet 4B. Record the measures in the table on the labsheet.

b. How close were your estimates in Question 17(c)?

19 Discussion
How can you use what you have learned about measuring angles with a protractor to draw a 62° angle?

20 ✔ CHECKPOINT
Use a protractor to draw an angle with each measure.

a. 90°   **b.** 38°   **c.** 125°

✔ **QUESTION 20**

...checks that you can use a protractor.

HOMEWORK EXERCISES ▶ See Exs. 5–10 on p. 120.

Exploration 3

The **Presentation** Scale

SET UP You will need • your *Handshake Problem* solution • your *String Art Problem* solution

▶ **Presenting Your Solution** So far in Module 2, you have learned about four different scales that help you assess your work. The last scale you will learn about is the presentation scale. This scale helps you assess how well you present your solutions.

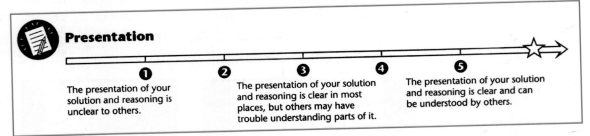

Presentation

❶ The presentation of your solution and reasoning is unclear to others.

❸ The presentation of your solution and reasoning is clear in most places, but others may have trouble understanding parts of it.

❺ The presentation of your solution and reasoning is clear and can be understood by others.

21 **Try This as a Class** Discuss why the presentation of your solution is important.

22 Prepare a team presentation for the *Handshake Problem*.

> Explain your solution so others can understand your reasoning.
>
> Make certain your presentation:
>
> ◆ explains the plan you used,
>
> ◆ uses correct and appropriate mathematical language,
>
> ◆ includes appropriate and correct representations,
>
> ◆ extends the solution to a general case or shows how it is related to other problems, and
>
> ◆ is clear and can be understood by others.

23 Use the presentation scale to score your presentation.

■ **HOMEWORK EXERCISES** ▶ See Exs. 11–12 on pp. 120–121.

Section 4
Key Concepts

▶▶▶▶▶▶▶▶▶▶▶▶▶▶▶▶▶▶▶▶▶▶▶▶

Key Terms

Polygons (pp. 112–114)
A polygon is a closed plane figure made from segments, called sides, that do not cross. A regular polygon is a polygon in which all the sides have equal lengths and all the angles have equal measures.

polygon
regular polygon

Quadrilaterals (pp. 114–115)
Quadrilaterals can be classified by the number of parallel sides. Sides are parallel if they are parts of parallel lines.

quadrilateral

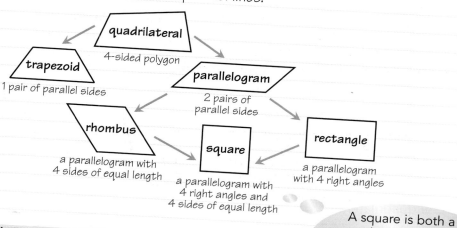

parallelogram
trapezoid

rhombus

A square is both a rectangle and a rhombus. It is also a parallelogram and a quadrilateral.

Venn Diagram (p. 115)
A Venn diagram uses a drawing to show how sets are related.

Venn diagram

Measuring Angles (pp. 116–117)
A complete rotation is 360 degrees, or 360°.

You can use the top scale of the protractor to measure this angle.

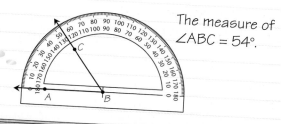

The measure of ∠ABC = 54°.

protractor

24 Key Concepts Question How do you know you should use the top scale to measure ∠ABC?

Section 4

Practice & Application Exercises

1. Which figures are regular polygons? If a polygon is not regular, explain why not.

a.

b.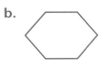

c.

d.

e.

f. (trapezoid)

2. Name each polygon in Exercise 1. Be as specific as possible.

3. **Probability Connection** Suppose you reached into a bag that contained the shapes from Exercise 1 and pulled one out. What is the probability of getting the given shape?

   a. a pentagon

   b. a polygon

   c. a quadrilateral

4. **Challenge** How many triangles are in the figure at the right?

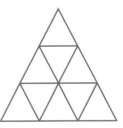

Trace each angle and extend the rays. Then measure each angle.

5.  Z

6.

7.   G

(W)

Use a protractor to draw an angle with each measure.

8. 56°

9. 123°

10. 79°

11. Use your solution to the string art problem to answer parts (a)–(c).

   a. Use the presentation scale to score your solution to the string art problem.

   b. Exchange solutions to the string art problem with a partner. Score your partner's solution using the presentation scale.

   c. Compare your self assessment score with your partner's score. Discuss any differences.

Reflecting ◀▶ on the Section

12. The Venn diagram shows how several shapes can be sorted according to their common properties.

Exercise 12 checks that you can apply ideas about polygons.

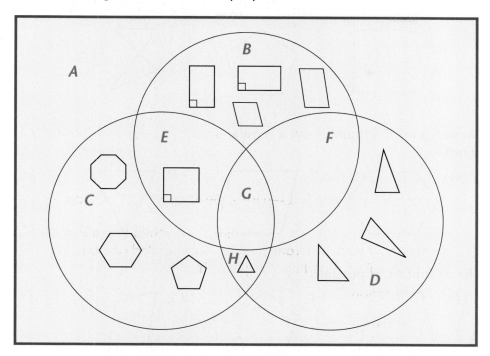

   a. What labels could be used for regions *A*, *B*, *C*, and *D*?

   b. Explain why a square is in region *E*.

Spiral ◀▶ Review

Classify each triangle by its angles. Then classify each triangle by its sides. (Module 2, pp.106–107)

13.

14.

15.

16. A triangle has a perimeter of 12 cm. The length of one side is 5 cm. If the lengths of the sides are whole numbers, what is a possible length for each of the other sides? (Module 2, p. 106)

17. The blue box is to the left of the yellow box. The green box is to the right of the red box. The blue box is to the right of the green box. In what order are the boxes? (Module 1, p. 33)

Section 4

Extra Skill Practice

Is each figure a polygon? If not, explain why not.

1.   2.   3.   4.

Is each figure a regular polygon? If a figure is not a regular polygon, explain why not.

5.   6. 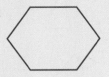 7.   8.

Name each polygon. Be as specific as possible.

9. 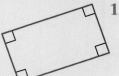 10.   11.   12.

Use a protractor to draw an angle with each measure.

13. 81°   14. 177°   15. 21°

16. 90°   17. 110°   18. 180°

Study Skills ◀▶ Taking Notes

Sometimes it is helpful to include a diagram or another visual representation when you take notes.

1. Look back at the *Key Concepts* on page 119. What does the quadrilateral diagram illustrate?

2. Make a table or a concept map to organize what you know about angles.

EXTENDED **E2** EXPLORATION

Pattern BLOCK Angles

SET UP *You will need pattern blocks or the Extended Exploration Labsheet.*

The Situation
You know that a square has four right (90°) angles and that a straight angle measures 180°.

The Problem
For each polygon in the table, figure out the sum of the measures of the angles without using a measuring tool. How can you find the sum of the measures of the angles of any polygon?

Polygon	Number of sides	Sum of the measures of its angles
triangle	?	?
quadrilateral	?	?
pentagon	?	?
hexagon	?	?
heptagon	7	?
octagon	?	?
nonagon	9	?
decagon	?	?

Something to Think About
Suppose you start by tracing around each pattern block. How can you find and label the angle measures? Use pattern blocks to create the polygons in the table. Trace around each polygon you create.

Present Your Results
Describe how you found the angle measures for each polygon in the table. What relationship did you find between the number of sides of a polygon and the sum of the measures of its angles?

Pop-Up Art

Throughout this module you have been working with various polygons and learning about their characteristics. In this project you will apply some of the ideas you have learned to create pop-up art.

SET UP

Work in a group.
You will need:
- *construction paper*
- *scissors*
- *ruler*
- *glue stick or tape*

Triangles and Angles The photos below show how to make a pop-up cutout.

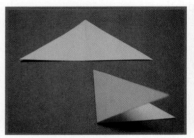

1 **a.** Experiment with isosceles triangles where the sides with the same length form acute, right, or obtuse angles.

   b. What effect do the different angled triangles have on the pop-up? What adjustments did you make in taping down the tabs?

2 Experiment with making a pop-up cutout using equilateral and scalene triangles.

Parallel Segments and Polygons Experiment with the double-slit method shown below to create pop-up polygons.

> This hexagon pop-up is composed of two identical parallelograms.

Step 1	**Step 2**	**Step 3**
Fold a piece of paper in half. Cut two parallel segments across the fold.	Fold the loose section between the cuts backward and forward.	Open the card. Pull the loose section toward you and close the card.

3 **a.** Make two identical trapezoids by using two parallel cuts.

   b. Make two identical trapezoids using two non-parallel cuts.

   c. Explain why you can create trapezoids with either parallel or non-parallel cuts.

Follow the directions below to make a Pop-Up Staircase.

Step 1 Use the double-slit method to construct a pop-up like the one shown.

This cut creates two rectangles.

Step 2 Fold the paper back down along its central fold.

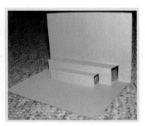

Make a smaller double slit across one of the two new folds.

Fold back the two loose sections between the cuts.

Open the card. Pull the loose sections toward you and re-crease to create a traditional staircase effect.

Step 3 Repeating the double-slit method on some or all of the new folds creates a pop-up staircase.

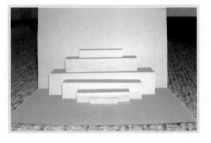

 4 The cuts above created pop-ups that form rectangles. How should the double-slit be cut to form square steps?

Completing the Project To complete the module project, you will create your own pop-up. Your pop-up should include several of the techniques you have learned and can use more than one piece of paper.

 5 Plan the design of your pop-up. Make a drawing or sketch if necessary. Be sure your design includes the following features.

- two different types of quadrilaterals
- perpendicular lines

- two different types of triangles
- parallel lines

 6 Describe how you used each of the mathematical ideas from Question 5 to create your pop-up.

A tetrahedron with sides numbered 1 to 4 was rolled 75 times with the results shown in the table. For Exercises 1-3, find the experimental probability of each event. Write each answer as a fraction. (Sec. 1 Explor. 1)

Outcomes	Total
1	16
2	18
3	22
4	19

1. rolling the number 2

2. rolling an even number

3. rolling a number greater than 4

4. Find the theoretical probability of each event in Exercises 1-3. Write each probability as a fraction. (Sec. 1 Explor. 2)

5. From home, Leon walked 6 blocks east, 5 blocks north, 3 blocks west, and then 7 blocks south on errands. Draw a diagram to show two ways he can get home by walking the fewest blocks. He cannot cut diagonally across any blocks because of buildings. (Sec. 2 Explor. 2)

6. Vina is putting together 1-cm squares as shown. (Sec. 2 Explor. 3)

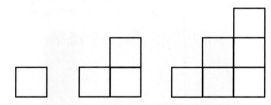

   a. How many squares will she need to build a figure that has a perimeter of 32 cm?

   b. Explain how you can extend your solution in part (a) to the general case.

If possible, sketch each triangle. If it isn't possible, explain why.
(Sec. 3 Explor. 2)

7. a triangle that is obtuse and isosceles

8. a triangle that is both right and equilateral

9. a triangle with side lengths 1 cm, 3 cm, and 7 cm

10. a triangle with side lengths 10 cm, 10 cm, and 10 cm

For Exercises 11-19, use the diagram at the right. Name an example of each figure.
(Sec. 3 Explor. 1 and Explor. 3)

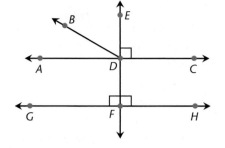

11. an acute angle   12. a segment

13. a ray   14. perpendicular lines

15. a right angle   16. an obtuse angle

17. a line   18. a point

19. parallel lines

20. Complete the Review and Assessment Labsheet for *Identifying Quadrilaterals.* (Sec. 4 Explor. 1)

Use the Venn diagram for Exercises 21-23. (Sec. 4 Explor. 1)

21. Which foods are good sources of vitamin A?

22. How many foods are good sources of vitamins A and D?

23. Why are nuts and citrus fruits outside of the sets?

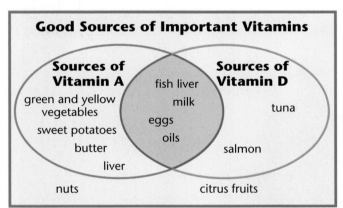

24. Estimate the measure of each angle below. Then trace each angle and use a protractor to measure it. (Sec. 4 Explor. 2)

a.    b.   c.

25. Use a protractor to draw an angle with each measure (Sec. 4 Explor. 2)

a. 85°   b. 33°   c. 170°

R e f l e c t i n g ◀▶ on the Module

26. a. Describe two different mathematical ideas you explored in this module.

   b. What discoveries did you make about these ideas?

1 **Understanding Decimals**
As you play place value games:
- Read and write decimals.
- Compare and order decimals.

2 **Decimal Addition and Subtraction**
As you solve a puzzle:
- Add and subtract decimals.

3 **Factors and Divisibility**
As you develop game strategies:
- Use divisibility tests.
- Find factors and greatest common factors.
- Find prime factorizations.
- Explore powers of a number.

4 **Multiples**
As you explore patterns in a game:
- Find multiples and least common multiples.

5 **Fraction and Mixed Number Multiplication**
As you solve a story puzzle:
- Multiply fractions.
- Use the distributive property.
- Multiply mixed numbers.

6 **Decimal Multiplication**
As you play target number games:
- Multiply decimals.
- Estimate decimal products.

The Module Project
Puzzle Making

Story and logic puzzles can be fun to solve and fun to create. You will explore how to solve several different types of puzzles. Then you will use the mathematics you have learned in this module to create your own puzzle. At the end of the project you will combine your puzzle with those of your classmates in a *Class Puzzle Book*.

For the Module Project
See pp. 194–195.

Section ① Understanding Decimals

Quite a Collection

Setting the Stage

SET UP *Work in a group. You will need:* • base-ten blocks • a number cube

In this module you will discover mathematical ideas as you solve puzzles and develop strategies for playing games. In the *Place Value Game,* you will use base-ten blocks to explore decimal place value.

Follow the steps below to play the *Place Value Game.*

Game Rules Players alternate turns. On each turn follow the steps below. The first person with two flats is the winner.

First	**Next**	**Then**
Roll a number cube. Take the number of **small cubes** shown on the number cube.	Trade in small cubes for a **rod** whenever possible.	Trade in rods for a **flat** whenever possible.

Think About It

1 a. One small cube is what fraction of a rod?

b. One rod is what fraction of a flat?

c. One small cube is what fraction of a flat?

Section 1

Extra Skill Practice

Write the place value of each underlined digit.

1. 0.00<u>5</u>
2. 356<u>4</u>.22
3. 90.<u>2</u>86
4. 116.9<u>8</u>

5. 1<u>2</u>.35
6. 0.0<u>1</u>8
7. 159.<u>5</u>34
8. 5.102<u>6</u>

Write each number as a decimal and as a fraction or mixed number.

9. two tenths
10. five hundred thousandths

11. four thousand and six tenths
12. one and twenty-five hundredths

13. three hundred fifty-six and forty hundredths

Write each decimal in words.

14. 4.2
15. 0.026
16. 531.08
17. 10.205

18. 3.25
19. 1.004
20. 0.01
21. 11.100

Compare each pair of decimals. Use <, >, or =.

22. 6.13 _?_ 6.125
23. 75.001 _?_ 75.0009
24. 3.60 _?_ 3.600

25. 1.999 _?_ 1.9009
26. 0.520 _?_ 0.52
27. 73.04 _?_ 73.401

Order each list of numbers from least to greatest.

28. 6, 6.04, 6.008, 66.002
29. 123.1, 124, 12.3, 1.233, 0.123

30. 1.9, 1.99, 1.099, 1.909
31. 75.24, 7.0652, 7.526, 75.024

Standardized Testing ◀▶ Multiple Choice

Choose the decimal that represents each number.

1. Three thousand fifty-nine and one tenth

   (A) 0.10359
   (B) 359.1
   (C) 3000.69
   (D) 3059.1

2. Four hundred and three thousandths

   (A) 0.4003
   (B) 400.003
   (C) 0.403
   (D) 403,000

Section ② Decimal Addition and Subtraction

A Fitting Puzzle

SET UP *You will need: • Labsheets 2A and 2B • scissors*

Setting the Stage

Adding decimals can be a bit puzzling, especially when the numbers are not aligned in columns for you to add. Solving the *Decimal Puzzle* will help you recognize some key patterns in adding decimals.

Use Labsheets 2A and 2B. Follow the directions on Labsheet 2A to solve the *Decimal Puzzle*.

Think About It

1   **a.** What is the place value of the 9 in the puzzle piece 0.09?

    b. What do you notice about the place value of all the other digits in the same column as the 9?

2   All the cards except two have decimal points in them. What is the place value of the digits without a decimal point?

▶ In this section, you will use base-ten blocks to investigate addition and subtraction of decimals.

Exploration 1

Adding .DECIMALS

SET UP *You will need: • Decimal Puzzle solution • base-ten blocks*

▶ **The example below shows how base-ten blocks can be used to add two of the numbers from the *Decimal Puzzle*.**

EXAMPLE

Find the sum 2.8 + 1.57 using base-ten blocks.

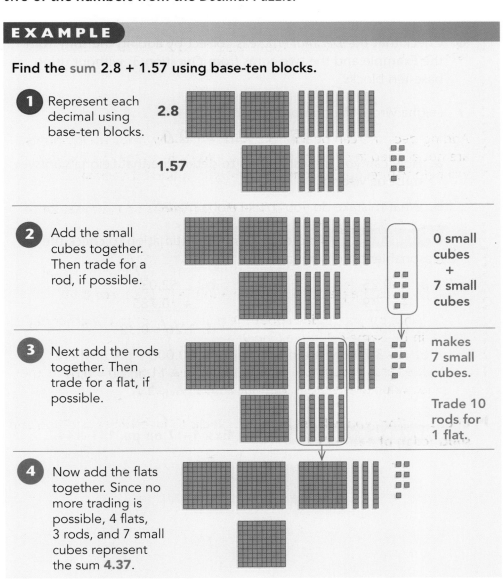

1 Represent each decimal using base-ten blocks.

2.8

1.57

2 Add the small cubes together. Then trade for a rod, if possible.

0 small cubes
+
7 small cubes

3 Next add the rods together. Then trade for a flat, if possible.

makes 7 small cubes.

Trade 10 rods for 1 flat.

4 Now add the flats together. Since no more trading is possible, 4 flats, 3 rods, and 7 small cubes represent the sum **4.37**.

3 The sums below use the remaining numbers from the *Decimal Puzzle*. Use base-ten blocks to find each sum.

a. 4.06 + 0.09   **b.** 3.8 + 3

4 **Discussion** Two students used numbers to record the addition problem modeled in the Example. Did they both represent the problem correctly? Explain.

Rankin wrote:

$$2.8$$
$$+ \ 1.57$$

Jerome wrote:

$$2.80$$
$$+ \ 1.57$$

5 Add the numbers in Question 3(b) using either Rankin's or Jerome's representation.

6 Check that the *Decimal Puzzle* is correct by adding the sum from the Example and the two sums from Question 3, without using base-ten blocks.

7 Leigha wrote the number sentence:

$$1.5 \ + \ 0.11 = \ 2.6$$

a. How can you use estimation to determine that Leigha's answer must be wrong?

b. What mistake do you think Leigha made?

✔ **QUESTION 8**

...checks that you can add decimals.

8 ✔ **CHECKPOINT** Find each sum. Use estimation to check the reasonableness of your answers.

a.   0.25
      + 1.79

b.   52.03
      + 0.785

c. 0.009 + 0.999

d. 1.26 + 0.32

e. n + 3.706 where n = 0.4

f. 10.006 + p + q where p = 11 and q = 0.07

HOMEWORK EXERCISES ▶ See Exs. 1–17 on pp. 143–144.

Subtracting .DECIMALS

SET UP *You will need base-ten blocks.*

▶ **Base-ten blocks can also be used to model decimal subtraction.**

EXAMPLE

Find the difference 1.43 – 0.58 using base-ten blocks.

1 Represent 1.43 using base-ten blocks.

1.43

Trade 1 rod for 10 small cubes.

2 You need to take away 5 rods and 8 small cubes. Since there are only 3 cubes, you must make a trade before you can take 8 cubes away.

Now, take away 8 small cubes.

3 Next you must take away 5 rods. Since there are only 3 rods, you must make another trade before you take 5 rods away.

Now, take away 5 rods.

4 The difference is 8 rods and 5 small cubes, or **0.85**.

9 Use base-ten blocks to find each difference.

   a. 1.62 – 0.8   **b.** 1.62 – 0.80   **c.** 1.62 – 0.08

10 In Question 9, is subtracting 0.8 the same as subtracting 0.80 or subtracting 0.08? Explain.

11 **Discussion** How is subtraction of decimals like subtraction of whole numbers?

12 **Try This as a Class** The subtraction 2.85 – 1.063 is shown below.

a. Explain what is being done in each step.

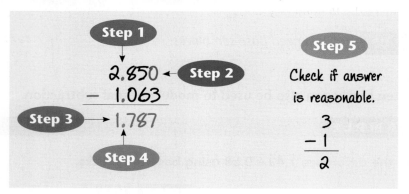

b. Placing zeros so both numbers have an equal number of decimal places is optional when adding decimals. Why is writing a zero in the thousandths place necessary in this subtraction problem?

13 a. To check that the answer was reasonable, 2.850 was rounded to 3. How do you know that 2.850 is closer to 3 than to 2?

b. The subtraction 15 – 8 = 7 can be checked by making sure that 8 + 7 = 15. Show how you could use addition to check the subtraction 2.85 – 1.063 = 1.787.

✔ **QUESTION 14**

...checks that you can subtract decimals and check the results.

14 ✔ **CHECKPOINT** Find each difference. Check your answers using addition.

a. 12001.7 – 120.017   b. 43 – 16.535

c. 17.3 – 17.30   d. 21.5 – 0.009

e. $n – 0.56$ where $n = 2.45$ f. $x – y$ where $x = 0.82$ and $y = 0.015$

15 **Discussion** Explain how you could use estimation to check if each difference in Question 14 is reasonable.

16 Complete this puzzle. Use the digits 0, 1, 2, 3, 4, 5, and 6 to make two decimal numbers that have a difference of 3.866. Each digit can only be used once.

HOMEWORK EXERCISES ▶ See Exs. 18–37 on pp. 145–146.

Section  2

Extra Skill Practice

Find each sum.

1. 12.06
    + 9.4

2. 1.599
    + 70.6

3. 41.75
    + 9.673

4. 6.61
    21.85
    + 4.3

5. 14.9 + 231.07

6. 16.08 + 0.37 + 5.9

7. 27 + 4.6 + 0.017

8. 1.25 + 12.75

9. 0.049 + 0.026

10. 98.2 + 4.7

11. 21.209 + 12.75

12. 33.55 + 0.55

13. 0.007 + 0.763

Find each difference.

14.   4.5
      – 1.7

15.   70.42
     – 35.7

16.   28.4
     – 5.162

17.   86.005
     – 14.32

18. 6.4 – 2.367

19. 147.61 – 5.724

20. 349 – 51.06

21. 12 – 3.5

22. 0.09 – 0.045

23. 132.42 – 61.34

24. 1.089 – 0.6

25. 34.2 – 0.004

26. 13 – 6.347

27. Jana had $30.50. She earns $6.75 baby-sitting one morning, but then spends $4.15 on lunch. Now how much money does Jana have?

Find the next three terms in each sequence.

28. 0.4, 0.54, 0.68, 0.82, ...

29. 5.4, 5.5, 5.7, 6.0, ...

30. 2.5, 2.7, 3.1, 3.7, ...

31. 1.02, 1.12, 1.22, 1.32, ...

Standardized Testing ◀▶ Performance Task

Jim receives $0.10 from his father for mowing the lawn. His father promises that next time Jim mows he will get $0.20, then $0.40 for the third time, and so on.

Jim races to his calculator, does a few calculations, and exclaims, "The tenth time I mow I'll get $51.20!" "No, Jim," says Jim's dad, who takes the calculator and does his own calculation, "the tenth time you mow you'll get $4.60. You are $46.60 too high."

Given the promise, how can both Jim and his dad be right? Show your work.

Paper Clip Products

Setting the Stage

SET UP *Work with a partner. You will need:* • *Labsheet 3A*
• *2 paper clips* • *10 each of two different-colored chips*

Paper Clip Products is a strategy game involving multiplication.

Paper Clip Products

◆ Player 1 starts. Place the paper clips on numbers in the factor list. They may both be on the same factor. Multiply the numbers and place a chip on the product on the game board. (Player 2 will use a different color chip.)

◆ Player 1 and Player 2 alternate turns. On a turn, leave one paper clip where it is, and move the other clip to any factor. Cover the new product with a chip.

◆ A turn ends when a player covers a product or if a product is not on the game board or is already covered.

◆ A player wins by covering three adjacent products horizontally, vertically, or diagonally.

Use Labsheet 3A. Play *Paper Clip Products* twice.

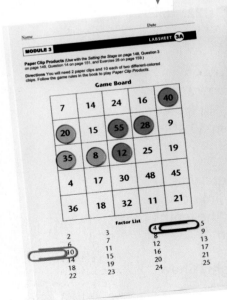

Think About It

1 If you are Player 1, where might you want to place the first two paper clips? Why?

2 What kind of moves did you avoid? Why?

GOAL

LEARN HOW TO...
- use divisibility tests
- find factors
- find the greatest common factor

AS YOU...
- develop a strategy for playing *Paper Clip Products*

KEY TERMS
- divisible
- factor
- greatest common factor (GCF)

Exploration 1

Testing for Divisibility

SET UP   *You will need Labsheets 3A and 3B.*

▶ **To develop a strategy for playing *Paper Clip Products*, you can use a Venn diagram to sort the numbers on the game board.**

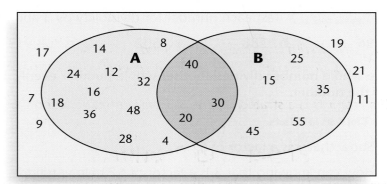

3 **Use Labsheet 3A.**

a. If you put a paper clip on 2, your opponent will be able to cover any number in Set *A*. Explain why.

b. Putting a paper clip on what factor makes it possible for your opponent to cover any number in Set *B*?

c. 20, 30, and 40 are in both Set *A* and Set *B*. Putting your paper clip on what factors would make it possible for your opponent to cover these numbers?

▶ **When a number can be divided evenly by another number, it is divisible by that number.**

4 Look back at your answers to Question 3. Just by looking at a number, how can you tell if it is divisible

   a. by 2?   **b.** by 5?   **c.** by 10?

5 ✔ **CHECKPOINT** Without dividing, tell whether each number is divisible by 2, by 5, or by 10.

   a. 125   **b.** 326   **c.** 270   **d.** 681

✔ **QUESTION 5**

... checks that you can determine whether a number is divisible by 2, by 5, or by 10.

▶ **In Questions 6–8, you will discover divisibility tests for 3 and 9.**

6 The number 351 is divisible by 3. Tell whether each rearrangement of the digits of 351 is still divisible by 3.

    a. 135   **b.** 153   **c.** 315   **d.** 513   **e.** 531

7 **Use Labsheet 3B.** Follow the directions to discover a *Divisibility Test for 3.*

8 **Discussion** The test for divisibility by 9 is similar to the one for 3. Find a divisibility test for 9. Try your divisibility test on the following numbers to be sure it works.

    a. 18   **b.** 54   **c.** 117   **d.** 243   **e.** 5409

✔ **QUESTION 9**

... checks that you can determine whether a number is divisible by 3 or by 9.

9 ✔ **CHECKPOINT** Test each number for divisibility by 3 and by 9.

    a. 96   **b.** 288   **c.** 502   **d.** 68,913

▶ **When one whole number divides another whole number evenly, it is a factor of the number.**

10 **Try This as a Class**

    a. Show that 3 is a factor of 57.

    b. How can knowing that 3 is a factor of 57 help you find another factor of 57?

▶ **Finding Factors To find a complete list of factors, it is helpful to begin with 1 and check in order for pairs of factors.**

EXAMPLE

To find the factors of 12:

$$12 \div 1 = 12$$
$$12 \div 2 = 6$$
$$12 \div 3 = 4$$

1, 2,   3,   4, 6, 12
factors of 12

To find the factors of 4:

$$4 \div 1 = 4$$
$$4 \div 2 = 2$$

1,   2,   4
factors of 4

Since $4 \div 2 = 2$, the factor 2 pairs with itself.

---

11 How do you know when you have found all the factors?

12 ✔ **CHECKPOINT** List all the factors of each number.

    a. 24   **b.** 13   **c.** 32   **d.** 18

✔ **QUESTION 12**

… checks that you can find the factors of a number.

▶ **Common Factors** Developing a strategy for playing *Paper Clip Products* involves finding factors that numbers have in common.

13 Use your lists of factors from Question 12. Find the common factors of each pair of numbers.

    a. 18 and 32   **b.** 18 and 24   **c.** 13 and 18

14 **Use Labsheet 3A.** Suppose the paper clips are on 2 and 3.

    a. Name two different moves you could use to cover 18.

    b. Which move from part (a) should you avoid if you do not want your opponent to cover 32 on the next turn?

15 **Discussion** How is each of the following used in *Paper Clip Products*?

    a. finding the factors of a number

    b. finding common factors of two numbers

▶ The **greatest common factor (GCF)** of two or more numbers is the greatest number that is a factor of each number.

EXAMPLE

Find the greatest common factor of 16 and 20.

SAMPLE RESPONSE

List the factors of each number.

        Factors of 16: ①, ②, ④, 8 , 16

        Factors of 20: ①, ②, ④, 5 , 10 , 20

        Common factors: 1, 2, and 4

The GCF of 16 and 20 is 4.

16 ✔ **CHECKPOINT** Use the common factors you listed in Question 13. Find the greatest common factor of each set of numbers.

    a. 18 and 32   **b.** 18 and 24   **c.** 13 and 18

✔ **QUESTION 16**

… checks that you can find the greatest common factor of a set of numbers.

HOMEWORK EXERCISES ▶ See Exs. 1–30 on pp. 159–160.

GOAL

LEARN HOW TO...
◆ recognize prime and composite numbers
◆ use a factor tree to find prime factors

AS YOU...
◆ develop a strategy for playing *Prime Time*

KEY TERMS
◆ prime
◆ composite
◆ prime factorization
◆ factor tree

Exploration 2

Prime Factors

SET UP   Work with a partner. You will need: • Labsheet 3C
• paper clips • 15 each of two different-colored chips

Prime Time is another strategy game involving factors.

Prime Time

◆ To begin, the first player places two paper clips on factors below the game board. He or she then covers the product of the factors on the game board with a colored chip.

◆ Players alternate turns. On a turn, a player has a choice of three ways to cover a new product.

  Move one paper clip to another factor.
  OR Place another paper clip on any factor.
  OR Take a paper clip off any factor.

◆ A turn ends when a player covers a product. A turn also ends if a product is not on the game board or is already covered.

◆ A player wins by covering three adjacent numbers horizontally, vertically, or diagonally.

17 **Use Labsheet 3C.** With your partner, play three games of *Prime Time*.

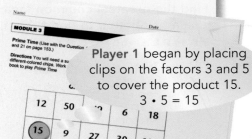

Player 1 began by placing clips on the factors 3 and 5 to cover the product 15.
3 • 5 = 15

Player 2 then placed another clip on 3 to cover 45.
3 • 3 • 5 = 45

▶ All whole numbers greater than 1 are either *prime* or *composite*. A **prime** number has exactly two factors, 1 and the number itself. A **composite** number has more than two factors.

18 Explain why 1 is neither prime nor composite.

19 **Use Labsheet 3C.** Tell whether the numbers in each of the following sets are prime or composite. Explain your answers.

    a. the factors below the game board

    b. the numbers on the game board

20 ✔ **CHECKPOINT** Tell whether each number is prime or composite. Explain your reasoning.

    a. 13   **b.** 305   **c.** 71   **d.** 243

✔ **QUESTION 20**

… checks that you can determine whether a number is prime or composite.

21 **a. Use Labsheet 3C.** Suppose a player covers 20 on the game board. What factors do the paper clips cover?

    b. How many paper clips are on each factor in part (a)?

    c. Besides the factors covered in part (a), are there any other prime numbers that can be used to get a product of 20?

▶ Every composite number can be written as the product of prime factors. This product is the **prime factorization** of the number. A **factor tree** can be used to find the prime factorization.

EXAMPLE

Use a factor tree to find the prime factorization of 12.

SAMPLE RESPONSE

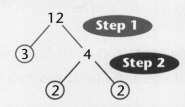

The prime factorization of 12 is 2 · 2 · 3.

22 **Try This as a Class** Use the Example above.

    a. What is done in Step 1? Why is the 3 circled but not the 4?

    b. What is done in Step 2? Why does the factor tree end?

    c. What parts of the tree are used to write the prime factorization?

23 a. Sketch a factor tree for 12 using 2 and 6 for factors in the first step.

b. Why do you think your tree ends with the same circled numbers as the tree in the Example?

c. Why do you not want to use the factors 1 and 12 for factors in the first step of the tree?

24 a. Copy and complete the factor tree for 48 shown below.

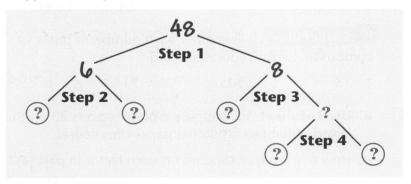

b. Why are more branches necessary to make this tree than to make the factor tree for 12?

c. What is the prime factorization of 48?

25 Discussion

a. What happens when you try to make a factor tree for 47?

b. Does 47 have a prime factorization? Explain.

26 Use a factor tree to find the prime factorization of 36.

27 Try This as a Class Compare your factor tree for 36 with those of your classmates.

a. Did everyone use the same pair of factors in the first branch?

b. Did the same prime factors always show up at the ends of the branches? Why?

28 Discussion Explain how prime factorization is used in the game *Prime Time.*

29 Think about making another *Prime Time* game board using the factors 2, 3, 5, and 7. What are two composite numbers you can put on your game board that cannot be covered?

HOMEWORK EXERCISES ▶ See Exs. 31–44 on pp. 160–161.

Exploration 3

Power^s of Numbers

GOAL

LEARN HOW TO...
- identify powers
- write numbers using exponents

AS YOU...
- investigate a paper folding puzzle

KEY TERMS
- exponent
- base
- power
- standard form

SET UP *You will need:* • *paper for folding* • *a calculator*

▶ **A paper-folding puzzle can help you learn a special notation for writing numbers with repeated factors.**

30 Fold a piece of paper in half and then unfold it. The fold divides the paper into two sections. Predict how many sections the paper would be divided into if you could fold the paper in half 8 times. Explain your reasoning.

▶ **One strategy for solving Question 30 is to look for a pattern.**

31 **a.** Make a table like the one below. Record the number of sections formed by one fold.

Number of folds	Number of sections		
1	2		
2	?		
3	?		

b. Continue folding the paper in half as many times as possible. After each fold, record the number of sections.

c. Look at your table. Each time you make a new fold, how does the number of sections change?

d. Use the pattern to extend the table to 8 folds.

32 How does your prediction in Question 30 compare with the result for 8 folds in Question 31(d)?

33 You can use the pattern you discovered in Question 31(c) to rewrite the number of sections. Label and fill in the third column of your table as shown.

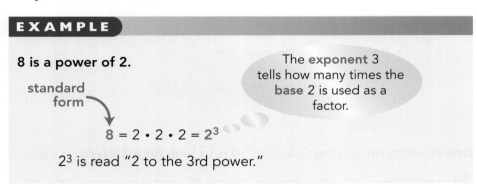

Number of folds	Number of sections	Rewritten form	
1	2	2	
2	4	2 · 2	
3	8	2 · 2 · 2	

▶ **Using Exponents** A short way to write a product like 2 · 2 · 2 is to use an **exponent** to tell how many times the **base** 2 is used as a factor. A number that can be written using an exponent and a base is a **power** of the base.

EXAMPLE

8 is a power of 2.

standard form

$$8 = 2 \cdot 2 \cdot 2 = 2^3$$

The **exponent** 3 tells how many times the **base** 2 is used as a factor.

2^3 is read "2 to the 3rd power."

34 **a.** In your table, label the fourth column *Power of 2*. Fill it in by rewriting each number of sections using an exponent.

b. Discussion How did you write 2 using exponents? Why?

35 How do you read 3^4? What is its value?

✔ **QUESTION 36**

… checks that you can find the value of a number written using an exponent.

36 ✔ **CHECKPOINT** Find the value of each expression.

    a. 3^5 **b.** 5^3 **c.** 10^2 **d.** 7^1

37 Calculator Scientific calculators have a power key y^x. Follow the steps below to find the value of 2^8.

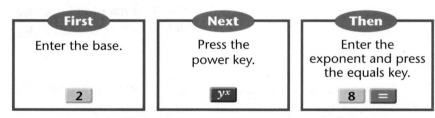

First	**Next**	**Then**
Enter the base.	Press the power key.	Enter the exponent and press the equals key.
2	y^x	8 =

38 **a.** How many sections would be formed if you could fold a piece of paper in half 12 times? Use exponents to write your answer.

b. Use a calculator to find the standard form of your answer in part (a).

▶ **You can use exponents to write prime factorizations. For example, the prime factorization of 75 is 3 · 5 · 5 = 3 · 5² or 3 · 5^2.**

39 Write the prime factorization of each number, using exponents for repeated factors.

a. 40 **b.** 81 **c.** 23

HOMEWORK EXERCISES ▶ See Exs. 45–61 on pp. 161–162.

Section 3
Key Concepts

Key Terms

Divisibility Rules (pp. 149–150)

When a number can be divided evenly by another number, it is divisible by that number.

divisible

You can tell whether a number is divisible by 2, 5, or 10 by looking at the ones digit.

Divisible by	Ones digit
2	0, 2, 4, 6, or 8
5	0 or 5
10	0

A number is divisible by 3 if the sum of its digits is divisible by 3.

A number is divisible by 9 if the sum of its digits is divisible by 9.

Factors and Common Factors (pp. 150–151)

When one whole number divides another whole number evenly, it is a factor of the number.

factor

To find the greatest common factor of a set of numbers, find all the factors the numbers have in common. Then, pick the greatest of these common factors.

greatest common factor (GCF)

Example The common factors of 30 and 45 are 1, 3, 5, and 15. The greatest common factor of 30 and 45 is 15.

Section 3
Key Concepts

Key Terms

prime

composite

prime
factorization

factor tree

exponent

base

power

standard form

Prime and Composite Numbers (pp. 152–154)

All whole numbers greater than 1 are either prime or composite. A prime number has exactly two factors, 1 and the number itself. A composite number has more than two factors.

Every composite number can be written as the product of prime factors. Factor trees can be used to find prime factorizations.

Example Find the prime factorization of 24.

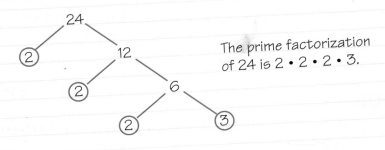

The prime factorization of 24 is 2 • 2 • 2 • 3.

Powers (pp. 155–157)

When a number can be written using an exponent and a base, the number is a power of the base. The example below shows that 64 is the 3rd power of 4.

Example $64 = 4 \cdot 4 \cdot 4 = 4^3$

standard form

*The exponent **3** tells how many times the base **4** is used as a factor.*

You can use exponents to write prime factorizations.

Example The prime factorization of 24, shown above, can be written as $2^3 \cdot 3^1$, or $2^3 \cdot 3$.

Key Concepts Questions

40 How can divisibility rules help you find the prime factorization of 261?

41 Write the prime factorization of 261 using exponents.

Section 3
Practice & Application Exercises

For Ex. 28:
♦ Labsheet 3A

Test each number for divisibility by 2, 3, 5, 9, and 10.

1. 168   2. 53   3. 499   4. 66,780

5. 4326   6. 75   7. 1011   8. 50,436

9. a. If a number is divisible by 9, is it divisible by 3? Explain.

   b. If a number is divisible by 3, is it divisible by 9? Explain.

List all the factors of each number.

10. 28   11. 51   12. 64   13. 72   14. 80

Find the greatest common factor of each set of numbers.

15. 14 and 28   16. 12 and 17   17. 21 and 51

18. 43 and 69   19. 54, 36, and 72   20. 22, 64, and 80

Greatest Common Factors can be used to write fractions in lowest terms.

Example: Write $\frac{12}{30}$ in lowest terms.

$$\frac{12}{30} = \frac{2 \cdot 6}{5 \cdot 6}$$ Use the GCF to write the numerator and denominator as products.

$$= \frac{2 \cdot \overset{1}{\cancel{6}}}{5 \cdot \cancel{6}}$$ Divide the numerator and denominator by the GCF.

$$= \frac{2}{5}$$ lowest terms

FOR ◄ HELP

with *writing fractions in lowest terms,* see
MODULE 1, p. 61

Use the greatest common factor of the numerator and denominator to write each fraction in lowest terms.

21. $\frac{12}{32}$ 22. $\frac{25}{35}$ 23. $\frac{36}{54}$ 24. $\frac{27}{63}$

Mental Math Show how to find each product using mental math. Use what you know about factors and compatible numbers.

Example: 36 • 25 = 9 • 4 • 25 = 9 • 100 = 900

25. 25 • 48   26. 12 • 75   27. 16 • 125

28. **Use Labsheet 3A.**

   a. What numbers on the game board cannot be covered?

   b. Find the factors of each number from part (a).

   c. What do you notice about the factors of the numbers that cannot be covered?

Section 3   Factors and Divisibility   **159**

29. **Displaying Data** You are going to make a pictograph of the data below using the symbol ❋ to represent a number of plant species. You must decide how many plant species each ❋ will represent.

Approximately ▶
60,000 of the
world's 90,000
known plant species
are endangered.
The photo shows a
tumboa plant lying on
a desert in Namibia, a
country of southwest
Africa.

FOR ▶ HELP

with *making a
pictograph*, see
TOOLBOX, p. 579

Endangered Plant Species	
Place	Number of plant species
Namibia	18
Portugal	90
Sicily	48

a. What numbers of plant species can each ❋ stand for so you can make a pictograph using only whole symbols?

b. Use your answer from part (a) to make a pictograph that contains as few symbols as possible. Be sure to tell how many species each ❋ represents.

30. **Challenge** A perfect number equals the sum of all its factors, not including the number itself. The first perfect number is 6 because 6 = 1 + 2 + 3. Find the next perfect number.

Tell whether each number is prime or composite.

31. 25   32. 37   33. 135

34. 51   35. 306   36. 91

Write the prime factorization of each number, using exponents for repeated factors.

37. 42   38. 144   39. 53

40. 280   41. 484   42. 840

43. This diagram organized the prime factors of 20 and 36.

20   36
5 · 2 · 2 · 3 · 3

a. Describe how the prime factorizations of 20 and 36 were used to make the diagram above.

b. How are the numbers in the overlapping region in the diagram above related to the GCF of 20 and 36?

c. Create a similar diagram for the prime factors of 24 and 30 and use it to find the GCF of 24 and 30.

44. **Challenge** The prime factorization of 60 has four prime factors since $60 = 2 \cdot 2 \cdot 3 \cdot 5$. Which two-digit numbers have the most factors in their prime factorizations?

Find the value of each expression.

45. 7^4 46. 5^2 47. 6^3 48. 3^5

49. Write the prime factorization of 1800 using exponents.

Write each of the following as a single number raised to either the 2nd or 3rd power.

50. 36   51. 8   52. 100   53. 125

54. **Computers** The smallest pieces of information stored in computer memory are called bits. One byte of memory is made up of 2^3 bits. One kilobyte of memory is 2^{10} bytes.

 a. In standard form, how many bits are in a byte? How many bytes are in a kilobyte?

 b. A computer with 512 kilobytes can store how many bytes of information? How many bits of information?

 Calculator **In Exercises 55–57, predict which number will be greater or if the two numbers are equal. Then check your prediction with a calculator.**

55. 2^{15} or 3^{15} 56. 10^3 or 3^{10} 57. 4^4 or 16^2

58. a. **Writing** Write each power of ten from 10^1 to 10^9 in exponential and standard form. How does the exponent of each power relate to the number of zeros in the standard form?

 b. A *googol* is 10^{100}. Written in standard form, a *googol* is 1 followed by how many zeros?

59. **Visual Thinking** The number 9 is a square number because you can make a square from 9 square tiles.

 a. Use drawings to find three other square numbers.

 b. Rewrite 9 and each square number from part (a) as a number raised to the 2nd power. Can every square number be written this way? Explain.

The term *googol* was invented by Milton Sirotta, the 9-year old nephew of mathematician Edward Kasner. Kasner asked Milton what he thought such a large number should be called. After thinking briefly, Milton answered that the number could only be called something as silly as... a *googol*!

$2^5 = 32$

$2^4 = 16$

$2^3 = 8$

$2^2 = 4$

$2^1 = 2$

Oral Report

Exercise 61 checks that you can apply your understanding of divisibility and prime factorization.

60. **a.** What mathematical operation is used to go from 32 to 16? from 16 to 8? Does this pattern continue throughout the sequence 32, 16, 8, 4, 2?

    b. Based on the pattern, what is the value of 2^0?

    c. How does this compare with the number of sections after 0 folds in the paper-folding pattern in Exploration 3 on page 155? Explain.

Reflecting ◀▶on the Section

Be prepared to discuss your answer to Exercise 61 in class.

61. **a.** Write the prime factorization of each number in the table.

    b. What do you notice about the prime factors of the numbers that are divisible by 6?

    c. Use your results from part (b) and the divisibility tests you know. Write a divisibility test for 6.

Divisible by 6	Not Divisible by 6
72	44
30	39
114	175
24	63
138	70

Spiral ◀▶Review

62. A bag contains 1 red marble, 2 yellow marbles, and 7 blue marbles. What is the theoretical probability of drawing a red marble from the bag? a green marble? (Module 2, p. 80)

63. If possible, sketch a triangle that is both obtuse and scalene. (Module 2, pp. 106–107)

Decide if the given lengths will form a triangle. (Module 2, p. 106)

64. 3 in., 2 in., 6 in.

65. 4 ft, 22 ft, 25 ft

Write an equation for each word sentence in Exercises 66–69. Use *t* for the term and *n* for the term number. (Module 1, p. 21)

66. The term is three more than the term number.

67. The term is four times the term number.

68. The term is two more than three times the term number.

69. The term is the term number to the third power.

70. Use your equations from Exercises 66–69 to find the first 4 terms of each sequence.

▶ **You will use what you know about multiples to answer Question 8.**

8 Maya met Jim at the mall. They really liked each other but were too shy to say how they felt. Hoping to see Maya, Jim returns to the mall every 5 days. Hoping to see Jim, Maya returns to the mall every 6 days.

   a. List the first seven multiples of 5. What do these multiples represent?

   b. List the first seven multiples of 6. What do these multiples represent?

   c. Look at the two lists of multiples. In how many days will Maya and Jim be at the mall on the same day?

▶ The answer to Question 8(c) is the least common multiple of 5 and 6. The **least common multiple (LCM)** of two or more whole numbers is the least number that is a multiple of all the numbers.

EXAMPLE

Find the least common multiple of 8 and 6.

SAMPLE RESPONSE

List the multiples of each number.
Then circle the common multiples.

Multiples of 8: 8, 16, (24,) 32, 40, (48,) ...

Multiples of 6: 6, 12, 18, (24,) 30, 36, 42, (48,) ...

Common multiples: 24, 48, ...

The LCM of 8 and 6 is 24.

---

9 ✔ **CHECKPOINT** Find the least common multiple of each pair of numbers.

   a. 3 and 9   **b.** 12 and 9   **c.** 25 and 15

10 Use lists of multiples to find all the numbers that "tick-tock" will replace in a game of *Pattern Tick-Tock* if you count to 100. Use *tick* for 8 and *tock* for 12.

✔ **QUESTION 9**

...checks that you can find the LCM of two numbers.

HOMEWORK EXERCISES ▶ See Exs. 1–20 on p. 169.

Section 4

Key Concepts

Multiples (p. 166)
A multiple of a whole number is the product of that number and any nonzero whole number.

Example

18 is a multiple of 6 since 6 • 3 = 18.

Least Common Multiple (LCM) (p. 167)
You can find the least common multiple (LCM) of two or more whole numbers by listing the multiples of each number in order. You can stop when you find a multiple that is common to all the numbers.

Example

multiples of 4: 4, 8, 12, 16, 20, (24), ...

multiples of 6: 6, 12, 18, (24), ...

multiples of 8: 8, 16, (24), ...

The least common multiple of 4, 6, and 8 is 24.

Key Concepts Question

11 Corey painted a row of circles numbered 1 through 100. Every ninth circle was painted yellow and every fifteenth circle was painted with red stripes.

a. Which circles were painted yellow? What do the circles painted yellow represent?

b. Which circles were painted with red stripes? What do these striped circles represent?

c. Which circles were painted yellow with red stripes? What do these circles represent?

Section 4

Practice & Application Exercises

List the first seven multiples of each number.

1. 7
2. 25
3. 99

4. 106
5. 8
6. 32

7. Suppose you can withdraw only multiples of $20 from a bank teller machine. Which amounts can you withdraw?

   a. $40   **b.** $250   **c.** $160   **d.** $220

Find the least common multiple of each set of numbers.

8. 3 and 7
9. 14 and 10
10. 6 and 12

11. 16 and 20
12. 6, 9, and 12
13. 48 and 12

14. 4 and 8
15. 15 and 35
16. 2, 5, and 8

17. The International Fountain in Seattle, Washington, contains special-effect devices called *shooters*. They shoot arcs of water at different time intervals.

   a. Suppose a fountain has one shooter that shoots water every 8 sec and another that goes off every 12 sec. How long after the fountain is turned on will both shooters go off at the same time?

   b. A third shooter shoots water every 6 sec. Suppose all three shooters just went off together. How many seconds will pass before all three go off again at the same time?

Reflecting ◀▶ on the Section

Be prepared to discuss your responses to Exercises 18–20 in class.

18. What is the first multiple of any whole number?

19. The greatest common factor of each of the following pairs of numbers is 1. What is the least common multiple of each pair?

   a. 2 and 3   **b.** 5 and 8   **c.** 4 and 9

20. If the greatest common factor of two whole numbers is 1, what do you think the least common multiple of the numbers will be?

Discussion

Exercises 18–20 check your understanding of multiples and common multiples.

Spiral ◀▶ Review

Find the missing numerator or denominator in each pair of equivalent fractions. (Module 1, p. 61)

21. $\frac{25}{100} = \frac{?}{4}$

22. $\frac{3}{8} = \frac{15}{?}$

23. $\frac{?}{3} = \frac{24}{36}$

Write each fraction as a mixed number. (Module 1, p. 46)

24. $\frac{13}{4}$

25. $\frac{28}{5}$

26. $\frac{29}{8}$

27. The picture at the left shows the stained glass dome of the Great Hall on the third floor of the National Portrait Gallery in Washington D.C.

    a. What fractions do you see in the figure?
       (Module 1, p. 46)

    b. What polygons do you see in the figure?
       (Module 2, p. 119)

Career ▪ Connection

Choreographer and Dancer: Emiko Tokunaga

Choreographers like Emiko Tokunaga create the steps dancers perform. Emiko designs combinations of dance steps to fit a piece of music. A piece of music can be broken into *measures*, which are groups of beats.

28. Emiko would like two dancers to each perform a different combination of steps, repeating the combination as needed so each reaches the final pose at the end of a piece of music.

    a. One dancer is to perform a combination of steps that is 4 measures long while the other is to perform a combination that is 12 measures long. How many measures long must the piece of music be?

    b. Suppose Emiko adds a third dancer. This dancer performs a combination of steps that is 8 measures long. Can the same piece of music be used? Explain.

> Emiko Tokunaga is the artistic director of Tokunaga Dance Ko (TDK). With her sister Yasuko, she started TDK, which has performed around the world. TDK was the first company selected by the Japan-United States Friendship Commission for their cultural exchange program.

Section 4
Extra Skill Practice

List the first seven multiples of each number.

1. 4

2. 12

3. 33

4. 110

Find the least common multiple of each set of numbers.

5. 9 and 27

6. 2, 4, and 9

7. 30 and 50

8. 15 and 45

9. 20, 40, and 60

10. 140 and 210

11. Find all the numbers that "tick-tock" will replace in a game of *Pattern Tick-Tock* if you use *tick* for 6, *tock* for 15, and count to 100.

12. Jackie spent the same amount of money on used CDs as she did on new CDs. If used CDs cost $12 and new CDs cost $16, what is the least amount she could have spent on each?

Standardized Testing ▶ Multiple Choice

For Exercises 1–3, choose the word that makes the statement true.

1. The product of two positive whole numbers is ___?___ a common multiple of the two numbers.

    A sometimes   B always   C never

2. The least common multiple of two whole numbers is ___?___ one of the numbers.

    A sometimes   B always   C never

3. The least common multiple of two whole numbers is ___?___ less than both numbers.

    A sometimes   B always   C never

Section ⑤ Fraction and Mixed Number Multiplication

IN THIS SECTION

EXPLORATION 1
◆ Fraction Multiplication

EXPLORATION 2
◆ Multiplying Mixed Numbers

A Fair Share

⫯⫯⫯**Setting the Stage**

Since ancient times, mathematics problems have been used as puzzles. The story below is an example of such a puzzle.

> Three brave, but not very bright, treasure hunters recovered a small box of priceless Spanish doubloons aboard a sunken ship. They took the coins back to their campsite. Since it was late, they decided to go to sleep and divide the treasure the next day.
>
> One of the treasure hunters, fearing that the others did not understand mathematics well enough to give out fair shares, took $\frac{1}{3}$ of the coins in the middle of the night and fled into the darkness.
>
> Later that night, another treasure hunter awoke and saw that some of the coins were missing. That treasure hunter took $\frac{1}{3}$ of the remaining coins and also fled into the night.
>
> The third treasure hunter awoke and was surprised to see the others gone and many of the coins missing. Trusting that the others left a fair share, the third treasure hunter took the remaining coins and walked away whistling happily.
>
> Which of the treasure hunters ended up with the greatest share of the doubloons?

Think About It

1 Do you think any of the treasure hunters ended up with more than a fair share of doubloons? If so, which one and why?

2 Do you need additional information to solve this puzzle? Explain.

Fraction Multiplication

SET UP   *You will need: • paper for folding • colored pencils*

▶ **Amazingly, you don't need to know how many doubloons were in the box to solve the puzzle—all you need is a piece of paper!**

3 The first treasure hunter took $\frac{1}{3}$ of the treasure. What fraction of the treasure was left for the others?

▶ **Finding a Part of a Part** The second treasure hunter took $\frac{1}{3}$ of the part that was left behind. To find the part of the treasure he took, you must find $\frac{1}{3}$ of $\frac{2}{3}$. When you find a fractional part of a part, you are multiplying fractions.

4 Let a sheet of paper represent the whole treasure. Work through Steps 1–4 to model $\frac{1}{3}$ of $\frac{2}{3}$, or $\frac{1}{3} \cdot \frac{2}{3}$.

$\frac{1}{3}$ of $\frac{2}{3}$

Step 1
Fold the paper into thirds with vertical folds. Shade two of the columns to represent the remaining coins.

Step 2
Refold the paper so only the shaded part is showing.

Step 3
Fold the paper into thirds with horizontal folds. Shade one of the rows using a different color.

Step 4 Unfold your paper and examine your results.

5 Use your unfolded paper to answer parts (a)–(d).

The second hunter took $\frac{1}{3}$ of the $\frac{2}{3}$ left behind by the first hunter.

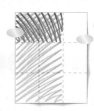

The first hunter took $\frac{1}{3}$ of the whole treasure.

   a. How many small regions is the whole paper divided into?

   b. What fraction of the whole paper is double-shaded?

   c. What fraction of the whole treasure did the second treasure hunter take?

   d. Write the fraction multiplication problem that represents the part the second treasure hunter took.

6 **Try This as a Class**

   a. What fraction of your unfolded paper represents the part of the whole treasure that was left for the third treasure hunter?

   b. Write a fraction multiplication problem that represents the part left for the third treasure hunter.

7 **Discussion**

   a. Which treasure hunter got the greatest share of the treasure?

   b. What fraction of the remaining coins should the second treasure hunter have taken so that everyone got a fair share? Use paper folding to explain.

Remember, this means $\frac{1}{3}$ of $\frac{1}{2}$.

8 Use paper folding to find $\frac{1}{3} \cdot \frac{1}{2}$.

   a. Use vertical folds and shading to model $\frac{1}{2}$ with paper folding.

   b. Use your model from part (a) to find $\frac{1}{3} \cdot \frac{1}{2}$. Remember to use horizontal folds and shade with a different color.

   c. What fraction of the whole paper is double-shaded?

✔ **QUESTION 9**

...checks that you can multiply fractions using a model.

9 ✔ **CHECKPOINT** A student folded paper as shown to find $\frac{2}{3} \cdot \frac{4}{5}$. Use the sketch to find the product.

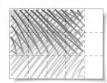

▶ **A Pattern for Multiplication** By looking back at the results of your paper folding, you can discover a method for multiplying fractions without using a model.

10 **Try This as a Class** Make a table of the products you found.

Question Number	Multiplication problem	Product
5(c)–(d)	$\frac{1}{3} \cdot \frac{2}{3}$	$\frac{2}{9}$
6	$\frac{2}{3} \cdot \frac{2}{3}$	?
8	$\frac{1}{3} \cdot \frac{1}{2}$	?
9	$\frac{2}{3} \cdot \frac{4}{5}$	?

   a. How is the numerator of each product related to the numerators in the problem?

   b. How is the denominator of each product related to the denominators in the problem?

   c. Explain how you can multiply two fractions without using paper folding or a sketch.

   d. Use your method from part (c) to find $\frac{3}{4} \cdot \frac{4}{5}$.

11 ✔ **CHECKPOINT** Find each product without using a model. Write each product in lowest terms.

   a. $\frac{3}{7} \cdot \frac{1}{2}$ **b.** $\frac{2}{3} \cdot \frac{3}{5}$ **c.** $\frac{2}{5} \cdot \frac{10}{12}$ **d.** $\frac{3}{4} \cdot \frac{4}{9}$

12 In the story, each treasure hunter took a whole number of coins.

   a. Give two possibilities for the number of coins that could have been in the treasure box.

   b. What do you know about the original number of coins in the treasure box?

FOR ◀HELP

with *writing fractions in lowest terms*, see

MODULE 1, p. 61

QUESTION 11

...checks that you can multiply fractions and write the product in lowest terms.

| **HOMEWORK EXERCISES** ▶ See Exs. 1–15 on pp. 179–180.

GOAL

LEARN HOW TO...
◆ use the distributive property
◆ multiply mixed numbers

AS YOU...
◆ find the weight of the coins in a treasure

KEY TERM
◆ distributive property

1 lb of coins

$\frac{1}{3}$ **lb of coins**

Exploration 2

Multiplying Mixed Numbers

SET UP *Work in a group. You will need pattern blocks.*

▶ Four treasure hunters found a chest containing gold coins. When they divided the treasure, each treasure hunter received $1\frac{1}{3}$ lb of coins. Pattern blocks can be used to find how many pounds of coins were in the chest.

13 If one treasure hunter receives $1\frac{1}{3}$ lb of coins, then the whole treasure contains 4 times that many pounds of coins.

  a. Use pattern blocks to show $4 \cdot 1\frac{1}{3}$.

  b. Group together any rhombuses that can form hexagons, and trade them for hexagons. Record the total number of hexagons and rhombuses you have after the trade.

  c. How many pounds of coins were in the chest?

14 Use pattern blocks to find the number of pounds of coins in the chest if the four treasure hunters each received the given amount.

  a. $1\frac{1}{2}$ lb of coins   **b.** $2\frac{1}{3}$ lb of coins

▶ To multiply an amount by 4, you can add the same amount four times. You can also use the **distributive property** as shown in the Example.

EXAMPLE

Find $4 \cdot \left(1\frac{1}{3}\right)$.

SAMPLE RESPONSE

multiply the 1 by 4

multiply the $\frac{1}{3}$ by 4

$$4 \cdot \left(1 + \frac{1}{3}\right) = (4 \cdot 1) + \left(4 \cdot \frac{1}{3}\right)$$

$$= 4 + \frac{4}{3}$$

$$= 4 + 1\frac{1}{3}$$

$$= 5\frac{1}{3}$$

$1\frac{1}{3} = 1 + \frac{1}{3}$

$4 \cdot \frac{1}{3} = \frac{4}{1} \cdot \frac{1}{3} = \frac{4}{3}$

15 **Discussion** Explain how to find $2\frac{1}{2} \cdot 3$ using the distributive property.

16 ✔ CHECKPOINT Find each product. Show your steps.

a. $6 \cdot 4\frac{1}{2}$ b. $2 \cdot 2\frac{1}{6}$ c. $3\frac{1}{4} \cdot 3$

✔ QUESTION 16

...checks that you can use the distributive property to multiply a whole number and a mixed number.

Karina

Number of pounds of coins if 4 hunters each received $2\frac{1}{3}$ lb of coins:

$4 \cdot 2\frac{1}{3} = \frac{4}{1} \cdot \frac{7}{3}$ Step 1

$= \frac{28}{3}$ Step 2

$= 9\frac{1}{3}$ Step 3

$9\frac{1}{3}$ lb of coins

17 **Try This as a Class** Explain each step of Karina's method for finding $4 \cdot 2\frac{1}{3}$.

18 Use Karina's method to find each product.

a. $3 \cdot \frac{2}{5}$

b. $6 \cdot 1\frac{5}{8}$

c. $4 \cdot 6\frac{1}{2}$

▶ **Multiplying Mixed Numbers** You have learned to multiply fractions and to write a mixed number as a fraction. You can combine these two skills to multiply mixed numbers.

EXAMPLE

Multiply $2\frac{2}{3} \cdot 1\frac{1}{5}$.

SAMPLE RESPONSE

$2 \cdot 3 + 2 = 8$

$1 \cdot 5 + 1 = 6$

$2\frac{2}{3} \cdot 1\frac{1}{5} = \frac{8}{3} \cdot \frac{6}{5}$

$= \frac{8 \cdot 6}{3 \cdot 5}$

$= \frac{48}{15}$ $48 \div 15$

$= 3\frac{3}{15}$

$= 3\frac{1}{5}$

19 Find the product $5\frac{1}{2} \cdot 3\frac{1}{2}$ by first writing the mixed numbers as fractions. Write your answer as a mixed number in lowest terms.

QUESTION 20

...checks that you can multiply mixed numbers.

20 ✔ **CHECKPOINT** Below are three multiplication expressions.

A. $6 \cdot 3\frac{1}{2}$ **B.** $\frac{3}{4} \cdot 1\frac{3}{8}$ **C.** $2\frac{1}{6} \cdot 12\frac{1}{2}$

   a. Find each product in lowest terms.

   b. Did you use the same method to find each product? Explain.

HOMEWORK EXERCISES ▶ See Exs. 16–35 on pp. 180–182.

Section ⑤
Key Concepts

Key Term

Multiplying Fractions (pp. 173–175)

Step 1 Multiply the numerators of the fractions to find the numerator of the product.

Step 2 Multiply the denominators of the fractions to find the denominator of the product.

Example $\frac{3}{4} \cdot \frac{8}{15} = \frac{3 \cdot 8}{4 \cdot 15} = \frac{24}{60} = \frac{2}{5}$

Multiplying Mixed Numbers (pp. 176–178)

One way to multiply a mixed number by a whole number is to use the distributive property.

distributive property

Example $3 \cdot 2\frac{1}{4} = 3 \cdot \left(2 + \frac{1}{4}\right) = (3 \cdot 2) + \left(3 \cdot \frac{1}{4}\right) = 6 + \frac{3}{4} = 6\frac{3}{4}$

You can always write mixed numbers as fractions to multiply.

Example $1\frac{1}{2} \cdot 3\frac{2}{5} = \frac{3}{2} \cdot \frac{17}{5} = \frac{3 \cdot 17}{2 \cdot 5} = \frac{51}{10}$, or $5\frac{1}{10}$

21   **Key Concepts Question** When you multiply two whole numbers other than 0, the product is always greater than or equal to either number. Is this true when you multiply two fractions? Give an example.

Section 5

Practice & Application Exercises

1. **a.** Find $\frac{1}{3}$ of $\frac{5}{8}$.

   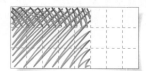

   b. Find $\frac{5}{8}$ of $\frac{1}{3}$.

   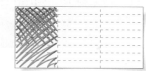

   c. How do the products in parts (a) and (b) compare?

Find each product. Write your answer in lowest terms.

2. $\frac{3}{5} \cdot \frac{1}{2}$ 3. $\frac{4}{9} \cdot \frac{5}{6}$ 4. $\frac{7}{10} \cdot \frac{2}{3}$ 5. $\frac{1}{12} \cdot \frac{1}{12}$

6. $\frac{1}{2} \cdot \frac{4}{5}$ 7. $\frac{9}{16} \cdot \frac{2}{3}$ 8. $\frac{10}{20} \cdot \frac{14}{30}$ 9. $\frac{16}{21} \cdot \frac{3}{4}$

10. **Visual Thinking**

    a. The model at the right was used to multiply two fractions. The double shaded part shows the product. What are the fractions, and what is their product?

    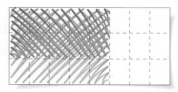

    b. Use your method for multiplying fractions to check your answer to part (a).

    c. Express the product of the fractions in lowest terms.

11. One fifth of a farmer's corn crop is destroyed by hail. Later that summer, $\frac{1}{3}$ of the remaining crop is eaten by insects. To file an insurance claim, the farmer needs to find what part of the total original crop was eaten by insects. The farmer says it is $\frac{1}{15}$. Is this correct? Explain.

12. Three fifths of a group of students surveyed said they would like to visit the National Zoo. If $\frac{5}{6}$ of those $\frac{3}{5}$ also said they would like to visit the Air and Space Museum, what fraction of the students surveyed said they would like to visit both attractions?

13. **Challenge** Read the story puzzle below. How many brownies did the original recipe make?

▲

Don decided to make $\frac{1}{2}$ the number of brownies from a recipe. He changed the recipe by cutting the amount of each ingredient in half.

▲

Later he gave his reduced recipe to his sister Sylvie. She changed it to make only $\frac{1}{4}$ of Don's recipe.

▲

Sylvie gave her recipe to Julio, who made $\frac{2}{3}$ of the amount in Sylvie's recipe. Julio made 30 brownies.

Science Rocks contain small amounts of radioactive elements that decrease over time. Scientists measure the age of rocks using *half lives*, the time it takes for a rock to lose half of its radioactive material.

Example: A rock that has $\frac{1}{4}$ of its radioactive elements is **2 half lives** old since $\frac{1}{4} = \frac{1}{2} \cdot \frac{1}{2}$.

14. How many half lives old is a rock that has $\frac{1}{16}$ of its original radioactive elements?

15. What fraction of its original radioactive elements does a rock have that is 6 half lives old?

Amount of radioactive elements remaining	Number of half lives
1	0
$\frac{1}{2}$	1
$\frac{1}{4}$	2

Mental Math Use the distributive property and mental math to find each product. Write each answer in lowest terms.

16. $3 \cdot 5\frac{1}{4}$

17. $2\frac{1}{3} \cdot 3$

18. $10 \cdot 3\frac{1}{5}$

19. $4 \cdot 2\frac{1}{2}$

20. $5\frac{1}{6} \cdot 5$

21. $6\frac{1}{8} \cdot 8$

Find each product. Write each answer in lowest terms.

22. $2\frac{1}{3} \cdot 3\frac{1}{5}$

23. $6\frac{1}{2} \cdot \frac{2}{3}$

24. $\frac{3}{5} \cdot 2\frac{1}{4}$

25. $1\frac{1}{3} \cdot 2\frac{1}{5}$

26. $7\frac{1}{6} \cdot 1\frac{1}{2}$

27. $1\frac{5}{8} \cdot \frac{3}{13}$

28. Show two methods for finding $3\frac{2}{3} \cdot 5$.

29. **Language Arts** In Mildred Pitts Walter's novel *Justin and the Best Biscuits in the World*, ten-year-old Justin Ward learns about much more than biscuits on a visit to his grandfather's ranch. Justin learns that past generations of Wards were among the many African-American cowhands who helped build the American West.

    As he prepares a lunch of homemade biscuits, stewed raisins, and smoked pork, Justin's grandfather remembers:

    "When I was a boy about your age, I used to go with my father on short runs with cattle. We'd bring them down from the high country onto the plains."

    "Did you stay out all night?" [Justin asks.]

    "Sometimes. That was the time I liked most. The cook often made for supper what I am going to make for lunch."

    a. At home, Justin uses his grandfather's recipe to make biscuits for himself, his mother, and his two sisters. If the recipe serves 12 people, what fraction of the recipe should Justin make?

    b. If the biscuit recipe calls for $1\frac{3}{4}$ cups of all-purpose flour, how much flour should Justin use?

    c. How much flour is needed if the original recipe is increased to serve 30 people?

Predict whether each product will be *greater than* or *less than* $4\frac{4}{5}$.

30. $\frac{2}{3} \cdot 4\frac{4}{5}$

31. $1\frac{1}{12} \cdot 4\frac{4}{5}$

32. $\frac{9}{8} \cdot 4\frac{4}{5}$

33. $4\frac{4}{5} \cdot \frac{2}{5}$

34. Suppose you multiply two fractions that are between 0 and 1. Is the product between 0 and 1 or greater than 1? Give some examples to support your answer.

Discussion

Exercise 35 checks that you can choose a method to multiply mixed numbers.

Reflecting ◀▶ on the Section

Be prepared to discuss your response to Exercise 35 in class.

35. Choose a different method to find each product. Show your work and explain why you chose each method.

    a. $6\frac{1}{8} \cdot 3$ **b.** $10\frac{2}{5} \cdot \frac{1}{3}$

Spiral ◀▶ Review

Write the prime factorization of each number using exponents. (Module 3, p. 158)

36. 44   **37.** 125   **38.** 56   **39.** 117

Estimate each answer. (Module 1, p. 10)

40. \$82 · \$51   **41.** \$178 − \$59   **42.** \$34.69 + \$17.14

Find each sum or difference. (Module 3, p. 143)

43. 5.002 − 1.243   **44.** 12.4 − 9.75   **45.** 1.73 + 15.6 + 0.015

Extension ▶▶

Products in Lowest Terms

46. Find $\frac{3}{20} \cdot \frac{4}{5}$. Write the answer in lowest terms.

Here is another way to find a product like $\frac{3}{20} \cdot \frac{4}{5}$ in lowest terms. Divide a numerator and a denominator by the common factor 4 *before* you multiply.

Divide by 4, the GCF of 4 and 20.

$$\frac{3}{20} \cdot \frac{4}{5} = \frac{3 \cdot \overset{1}{4}}{\underset{5}{20} \cdot 5} = \frac{3 \cdot 1}{5 \cdot 5} = \frac{3}{25}$$

Divide by 4.

47. Find $\frac{5}{12} \cdot \frac{4}{15}$ in lowest terms by dividing by the common factor after you multiply and then before you multiply. Which method is easier for you? Why?

Section 5

Extra Skill Practice

Find each product. Write each answer in lowest terms.

1. $\dfrac{1}{2} \cdot \dfrac{2}{3}$

2. $\dfrac{3}{16} \cdot \dfrac{4}{9}$

3. $\dfrac{5}{12} \cdot \dfrac{6}{25}$

4. $\dfrac{27}{32} \cdot \dfrac{2}{9}$

5. $\dfrac{7}{9} \cdot \dfrac{12}{20}$

6. $\dfrac{10}{39} \cdot \dfrac{13}{20}$

7. $\dfrac{14}{24} \cdot \dfrac{2}{3}$

8. $\dfrac{18}{45} \cdot \dfrac{15}{36}$

9. The string section makes up about $\dfrac{2}{3}$ of a symphony orchestra. Cellos make up about $\dfrac{1}{5}$ of the string section, and about $\dfrac{3}{5}$ of the string section are violins.

   a. About what part of a symphony orchestra are cellos?

   b. About what part of a symphony orchestra are violins?

Find each product. Write each answer in lowest terms.

10. $5 \cdot 4\dfrac{1}{8}$

11. $2 \cdot 6\dfrac{2}{5}$

12. $1\dfrac{1}{8} \cdot 6\dfrac{1}{4}$

13. $2\dfrac{1}{2} \cdot \dfrac{3}{8}$

14. $3\dfrac{1}{5} \cdot 1\dfrac{3}{4}$

15. $2\dfrac{2}{9} \cdot 5\dfrac{1}{3}$

16. Skirts for a school play each require $1\dfrac{2}{3}$ yd of fabric. How much material should be ordered so that 5 skirts can be made?

Standardized Testing ◀▶ Free Response

How many cups of apple juice do you need to make $2\dfrac{1}{2}$ times the recipe?

Beverages

Fruit Smoothie

Blend together:

$\dfrac{1}{3}$ c frozen strawberry puree

$\dfrac{1}{4}$ c frozen banana puree

1 c white grape fruit juice

$3\dfrac{1}{3}$ c apple juice

Section 6 — Decimal Multiplication

IN THIS SECTION

EXPLORATION 1
◆ Multiplying Decimals

EXPLORATION 2
◆ Estimating Decimal Products

Target Games

Setting the Stage

SET UP *Work with a partner. You will need:* • *Labsheet 6A* • *calculator*

Games like darts test your ability to hit a target. The goal of *Target Number* is to find a product close to the target number.

Use mental math and estimation.

Target Number

◆ Player 1 chooses a number to multiply by the constant factor, trying to come as close to the target number as possible. The player then uses a calculator to find the product.

◆ Players take turns challenging each other's product. A player can win a game in two ways–if his or her product is not challenged, or if it is closer to the target number than the challenger's product.

Sample Game 1 Target Number = 226	Constant Factor = 13
Perry multiplies the constant factor by 15.	13 • 15 = 195
Mary challenges by multiplying by 18.	13 • 18 = 234
Perry challenges by multiplying by 16.	13 • 16 = 208 Mary wins!

Mary wins since 234 is closer to the target number than Perry's 208.

Use Labsheet 6A. Play at least three games of *Target Number*.

Think About It

1 In *Sample Game 1*, is there a way that Perry could have successfully challenged Mary? Explain.

Exploration 1

Multiplying Decimals

SET UP *You will need Labsheet 6B.*

Mary and Perry played *Sample Game 2* of *Target Number* as shown.

2 Think about using a decimal to challenge Perry in Game 2. Should the decimal be greater than or less than 58.5? Why?

Sample Game 2 Target Number = 408	Constant Factor = 7
Mary multiplies the constant factor by 59.	7 · 59 = 413
Perry challenges by multiplying by 58.	7 · 58 = 406
Mary decides not to challenge Perry.	Perry wins!

▶ **To successfully challenge another player in *Target Number*, it may be necessary to multiply by a decimal. Decimal products, like fraction products, can be modeled by shading a part of a part.**

EXAMPLE

Model the product 0.2 · 0.6 using a 10 · 10 grid to represent 1 whole.

The 12 double-shaded squares represent the product 0.2 · 0.6.

Step 1
Represent 0.6 by lightly shading six tenths of the grid.

Step 2
Double-shade two tenths or 0.2 of the part shaded in Step 1.

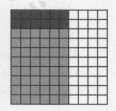

3 Discussion

a. What part of the whole grid is each small square? Write your answer as a fraction and as a decimal.

b. What part of the whole grid is double-shaded? Write your answer as a decimal.

c. What does 0.2 · 0.6 equal?

4 a. Find $\frac{2}{10} \cdot \frac{6}{10}$ in fraction form.

   b. Write your answer from part (a) as a decimal.

   c. Compare your answers from part (b) and Question 3(c). Why is $\frac{2}{10} \cdot \frac{6}{10}$ the same as 0.2 • 0.6?

Use Labsheet 6B for Question 5–7.

5 Use the *Decimal Multiplication Grids* to model the decimal products 0.5 • 0.4 and 0.3 • 0.3.

6 Follow the directions for *Decimal and Fraction Products* to compute decimal products using fraction multiplication.

7 Try This as a Class Look back at your completed *Decimal and Fraction Products* table.

   a. How are the digits in the decimal factors in the first column used to find the digits in the decimal product?

   b. How is the number of decimal places in the decimal product related to the number of decimal places in the factors?

   c. Explain how to multiply 5.2 • 0.04 without finding equivalent fraction products or using a grid. Then find the product.

8 Find 0.5 • 0.4 and 0.3 • 0.3 without using grids or fractions. Then compare the products with those in Question 5.

9 Discussion

   a. How many decimal places will there be in the product 0.3 • 0.2?

   b. Use Labsheet 6B. Why was a zero needed in the tenths place in the decimal product 0.3 • 0.2 in the *Decimal and Fraction Products* table?

   c. To find the product 0.25 • 0.3, you need to write a zero as a placeholder after you multiply the digits. Which is correct, 0.075 or 0.750? Explain.

Find the GCF of each set of numbers. (Sec. 3, Explor. 1)

28. 36 and 48   **29.** 15, 20, and 32   **30.** 26 and 52

Tell whether each number is prime or composite. (Sec. 3, Explor. 2)

31. 22   **32.** 51   **33.** 47   **34.** 111,111

Replace each _?_ with >, <, or =. Explain your choice. (Sec. 3, Explor. 3)

35. 2^5 _?_ 5^2 **36.** 4^3 _?_ 2^6 **37.** 3^3 _?_ $3 \cdot 3 \cdot 3 \cdot 3$

Write the prime factorization of each number, using exponents for repeated factors. (Sec. 3, Explor. 3)

38. 32   **39.** 97   **40.** 300   **41.** 231

42. Mark has swim practice every other day. His brother swims every third day. If they both practice on Monday, what is the next day both Mark and his brother will have practice? (Sec. 4, Explor. 1)

Find each product. Write each answer in lowest terms.
(Sec. 5, Explors. 1 and 2)

43. $\frac{3}{8} \cdot \frac{4}{15}$ **44.** $\frac{5}{7} \cdot \frac{2}{3}$ **45.** $\frac{5}{16} \cdot \frac{8}{9}$ **46.** $\frac{3}{5} \cdot \frac{15}{24}$

47. $6\frac{3}{4} \cdot 1\frac{2}{3}$ **48.** $3\frac{1}{3} \cdot 2\frac{1}{2}$ **49.** $1\frac{5}{8} \cdot \frac{1}{3}$ **50.** $\frac{3}{5} \cdot 4\frac{5}{6}$

Use the distributive property and mental math to find each product. Write each answer in lowest terms. (Sec. 5, Explor. 2)

51. $4 \cdot 1\frac{3}{4}$ **52.** $2\frac{5}{6} \cdot 12$ **53.** $5 \cdot 3\frac{1}{5}$ **54.** $2\frac{3}{5} \cdot 10$

Find each product without using a calculator. Then use estimation to check that your answer is reasonable. (Sec. 6, Explor. 1)

55. $0.4 \cdot 0.32$ **56.** $36.3 \cdot 51$ **57.** $4.7 \cdot 0.006$

Reflecting ◀▶ on the Module

58. Write a letter to an adult member of your family describing the math you learned in this module and what you liked most and least about the module.

MODULE 4 — SECTION OVERVIEW

1 Sets and Metric Measurement

As you study the mammals of Yellowstone Park:

- ◆ Sort data using a sorting grid.
- ◆ Estimate metric length and mass.
- ◆ Convert between metric units.

2 Line Plots and Averages

As you think about the average number of children for families:

- ◆ Create and interpret line plots.
- ◆ Calculate mean, median, and mode.
- ◆ Use a calculator to change a fraction to a decimal.
- ◆ Round decimals.

3 Dividing Decimals and Solving Equations

As you study animals in the wild and in zoos:

- ◆ Divide a decimal by a whole number.
- ◆ Write, model, and solve addition and subtraction equations.

4 Stem-and-Leaf Plots, Decimal Division, and Graphing

As you study dinosaurs:

- ◆ Make and interpret stem-and-leaf plots.
- ◆ Divide by a decimal.
- ◆ Graph ordered pairs on a coordinate grid.

5 Line Graphs and Choosing an Average

As you study population growth:

- ◆ Make and interpret line graphs.
- ◆ Choose an appropriate average.

The Module Project

Be a Reporter

Extra, Extra! Read all about it!

"Study shows that there are over a million pet snakes in the United States."

As a reporter you will collect data about pets or another topic that interests you. The mathematics you learn in this module will help you organize, interpret, and present your results in a newspaper article.

For the Module Project
See pp. 276–277.

INTERNET
Resources and practice at
classzone.com

199

Section ① Sets and Metric Measurement

IN THIS SECTION

EXPLORATION 1
◆ Sorting Data

EXPLORATION 2
◆ Metric Length and Mass

EXPLORATION 3
◆ Converting Metric Units

The Mammals of Yellowstone

Setting the Stage

Yellowstone National Park contains one of the most abundant concentrations of mammals in the lower 48 states. Eighteen kinds of carnivores roam the area. Over 40 other kinds of mammals also live within the park.

An adult bull bison may weigh up to 900 kilograms and stand more than 2 meters high at the shoulder.

An adult red squirrel can have a total length of 38.5 centimeters, including the tail.

An adult grizzly bear may be 2.6 meters long and 1.3 meters tall at the shoulder.

Think About It

1 Would you expect to use the same unit of measure when finding the masses of a bison and a red squirrel? Why?

2 The ear of a red squirrel can be about 31 millimeters long. The claws of an adult grizzly are about 7 centimeters long. What everyday object has a length approximately equal to each of the following measures?

    a. a millimeter   **b.** a centimeter   **c.** a meter

▶ **In this module you will learn about the measurements and habits of different mammals. You will also describe and compare animal data using graphs and averages.**

Exploration 1

S·o·r·t·i·n·g
Data

SET UP *Work in a group. You will need:* • *a set of Yellowstone Mammal Cards from Labsheets 1A and 1B* • *Labsheet 1C*

GOAL

LEARN HOW TO...
- ◆ sort data using a rectangular diagram

AS YOU...
- ◆ explore the characteristics of Yellowstone Park mammals

KEY TERM
- ◆ empty set

3 Follow the steps below to sort the *Mammal Cards* into two sets by the unit of mass.

   a. Divide a piece of notebook paper into two columns and label the columns as shown below.

Mass Measured in Kilograms	Mass Measured in Grams
Set A	Set B

   b. Place the cards for the animals whose mass is measured in grams in the right column, and place the cards for those whose mass is measured in kilograms in the left column. The animal cards in the left column are in Set *A*, and those in the right column are in Set *B*.

4 **Discussion**

   a. What characteristics do the animals on the cards in Set *A* have in common? the animals on the cards in Set *B*?

   b. How would you describe the size of an animal whose mass is measured in kilograms? in grams?

FOR ◄HELP
with *sets*, see
MODULE 2, p. 80

▶ **Looking at Two Sets** The animals on the cards you placed in the left column in Question 3 belong to the set of mammals whose mass is measured in kilograms. Objects in one set sometimes share characteristics with objects in another set.

5 **Use Labsheet 1C.** Sort the *Mammal Cards* into separate piles by placing the cards inside the correct rectangles.

a. Look at the mammals on the cards in Sets *C–F*. Which sets have the large mammals?

b. What is the largest mammal on the cards?

c. Which set has the small animals?

d. What is the smallest animal on the cards?

e. List the mammals in Set *E*.

f. How many mammals are in Set *C*? Set *D*? Set *E*? Set *F*?

g. A set with no objects in it is an **empty set**. Are any of the Sets *C–F* empty sets?

✔ **QUESTION 6**

...checks that you can sort data using a rectangular diagram and list a set of objects.

6 ✔ **CHECKPOINT** Use your *Mammal Cards* and a sorting grid like the one below to sort the mammals by life span and mass. (Draw the diagram large enough to contain the cards.)

	Life span ≤ 10 years ↓	Life span > 10 years ↓
Mass measured in kilograms →	Set *G*	Set *H*
Mass measured in grams →	Set *I*	Set *J*

a. List the mammals in Sets *G–J*.

b. Of the mammals that live less than or equal to 10 years, how many have a mass measured in kilograms? in grams?

c. Of the mammals that live more than 10 years, how many have a mass measured in kilograms? in grams?

d. Do larger mammals or smaller mammals appear to live longer, or does there seem to be little difference?

HOMEWORK EXERCISES ▶ See Exs. 1–7 on pp. 209–210.

Exploration 2

Metric Length and Mass

GOAL

LEARN HOW TO...
- estimate length and mass in metric units

AS YOU...
- build rulers and measure everyday objects

KEY TERMS
- meter (m)
- millimeter (mm)
- centimeter (cm)
- kilometer (km)
- benchmark
- gram (g)
- milligram (mg)
- kilogram (kg)
- metric ton (t)

SET UP *Work in pairs. You will need: • Labsheet 1D • scissors • tape*

7 Think back to the *Mammal Cards.*

   a. Was the length of small mammals measured in meters or centimeters?

   b. Was the mass of large mammals measured in kilograms or grams?

▶ **Metric Length** The metric system is used in most countries today. Metric units of length are based on the **meter (m)**.

The distance between short tick marks is a **millimeter (mm)**.

The distance between long tick marks is a **centimeter (cm)**.

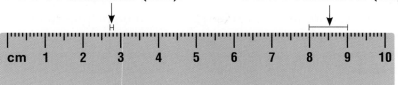

If you continue the ruler up to 100 centimeters, you get a meter. ⟶

A **kilometer (km)** is a metric unit used to measure longer distances such as highway distances. It is also based on the meter.

$$1 \text{ km} = 1000 \text{ m}$$

8 **Use Labsheet 1D.** Cut out the ruler and use it to answer the questions on the labsheet.

▶ **You can use the length of an object you know as a benchmark to estimate lengths. For example, if you know the height of a table in centimeters, you can use it as a benchmark to estimate other heights.**

9 If the table in the picture is about 75 cm high, about how high is the tip of the umbrella?

10 Copy and complete the table. Use your meter tape from Labsheet 1D to find a benchmark for each unit of length.

Length	Benchmark
1 millimeter (mm)	Length of ?
1 centimeter (cm)	Length of ?
1 meter (m)	Length of ?
1 kilometer (km)	Length of ?

11 **Discussion** Share the benchmarks you chose in Question 10 with the class.

12 Use benchmarks to estimate the following:

a. the height of your classroom in meters

b. the length of your shoe in centimeters

c. the width of your thumbnail in millimeters

d. the length of four laps around a running track in kilometers

✔ QUESTION 13

...checks that you can use a ruler to measure length in metric units.

13 ✔ **CHECKPOINT** Check your estimates in parts (a)–(c) of Question 12 by measuring each distance.

▶ **When you measure to find actual lengths, it can be helpful to use decimals to record your measurements.**

EXAMPLE

Find the length of the white-footed mouse's body in centimeters.

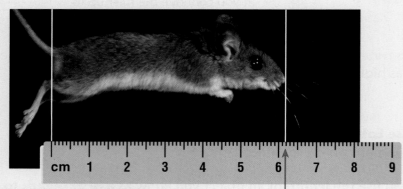

SAMPLE RESPONSE

The body of the white-footed mouse measures 6 cm 2 mm. There are ten divisions in 1 cm, so 2 of these are $\frac{2}{10}$ of a centimeter, or 0.2 cm.

This means that 6 cm 2 mm = 6.2 cm.

14 Discussion

a. Why can 5 m 35 cm be written as 5.35 m?

b. Why can 4.2 cm be written as 4 cm 2 mm?

c. Why can 65 cm be written as 0.65 m?

▶ **Metric Mass** Metric units of mass are based on the **gram**. Sample benchmarks for some common units of mass are shown below.

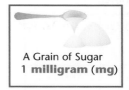

A Grain of Sugar
1 milligram (mg)

Paper Clip
1 gram (g)

1-Liter Bottle of Water
1 kilogram (kg)

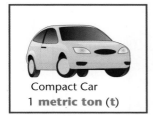

Compact Car
1 metric ton (t)

15

Choose the appropriate metric unit (*metric ton, kilogram, gram,* or *milligram*) for measuring the mass of each animal.

a. a wolf   **b.** a whale   **c.** a flea   **d.** a chipmunk

16 ✔ CHECKPOINT

Estimate the mass of each object using the given unit.

a. a pencil (g)   **b.** a chair (kg)   **c.** your math book (kg)

✔ **QUESTION 16**

...checks that you can estimate mass in metric units.

HOMEWORK EXERCISES ▶ See Exs. 8–27 on pp. 210–211.

Exploration 3

Converting Metric Units

SET UP *You will need Labsheets 1E and 1F.*

GOAL

LEARN HOW TO...
◆ convert between metric units

AS YOU...
◆ relate metric prefixes to place values

Use the Student Resource at the top of page 206 to answer Questions 17–19.

17

a. What does the prefix *kilo-* mean?

b. A kilogram is how many times as large as a gram?

c. Name an animal whose mass would be measured in kilograms.

Metric Prefixes

You can look at the prefixes of metric units of measure to see the relationships between the units. The most commonly used prefixes are in the shaded areas.

The prefixes are like place values, becoming ten times as great each time you move to the left in the table.

Centi- means "hundredth," so 1 **centimeter** is $\frac{1}{100}$ of a **meter**, and 100 centimeters is 1 meter.

Prefix	kilo-	hecto-	deka-	basic unit meter gram	deci-	centi-	milli-
Meaning	1000	100	10	1	0.1 or $\frac{1}{10}$	0.01 or $\frac{1}{100}$	0.001 or $\frac{1}{1000}$

A decimeter is 10 times as long as a centimeter.   A centimeter is 10 times as long as a millimeter.

So a decimeter is 10 · 10, or 100 times as long as a millimeter.

18 a. What does the prefix *milli-* mean?

  b. A millimeter is what fractional part of a meter?

  c. Name an animal whose length would be measured in millimeters.

19 A centimeter is one hundredth of a meter and a millimeter is one thousandth of a meter. How many millimeters are in one centimeter? How do you know?

▶ **Metric Conversions** You may need to convert from one unit to another to compare measurements. Use the photos of the red fox and the badger below for Questions 20 and 21 on the following page.

Red fox

|← 0.8 m →|

Badger

|← 75 cm →|

20 To compare the lengths of the fox and the badger, you can convert 0.8 m to centimeters.

$$1 \text{ m} = 100 \text{ cm}$$
$$0.8 \cdot 1 \text{ m} = 0.8 \cdot 100 \text{ cm}$$
$$0.8 \text{ m} = 80 \text{ cm}$$

Which mammal is longer, the fox or the badger? By how many centimeters?

21 You can also compare the lengths of the fox and the badger in meters.

$$1 \text{ cm} = 0.01 \text{ m}$$
$$75 \text{ cm} = 75 \cdot 0.01 \text{ m}$$

a. Find $75 \cdot 0.01$.

b. The fox is how many meters longer than the badger?

▶ To convert between metric units, it is helpful to know how to multiply by the special multipliers 0.001, 0.01, 0.1, 1, 10, 100, and 1000.

22 **Use Labsheet 1E.** Use your calculator to complete the *Special Multipliers Multiplication Table.*

23 **Use Labsheet 1F.** Use the table of prefix meanings to fill in the missing information for the *Metric Conversions.*

EXAMPLE

Convert 453 mm to meters.

SAMPLE RESPONSE

$$1 \text{ mm} = 0.001 \text{ m}$$
$$453 \text{ mm} = 453 \cdot 0.001 \text{ m} = 0.453 \text{ m}$$

24 **Discussion** How can you check that the answer, 0.453 m, in the Example is reasonable?

25 ✔ **CHECKPOINT** Replace each ? with the number that makes the statement true.

a. 1 g = ? mg   **b.** 1 m = ? km   **c.** 1 metric ton = ? kg
   5 g = ? mg   37 m = ? km   4.2 metric tons = ? kg

✔ **QUESTION 25**

...checks that you can convert between metric units.

HOMEWORK EXERCISES ▶ See Exs. 28–46 on p. 211.

Section 1
Key Concepts

Empty Set (p. 202)
The empty set is a set with no objects in it.

empty set

Metric System (pp. 203–207)
The tables below show the relationships among some commonly used metric units.

benchmark

Units of length are based on the meter. A benchmark for 1 m is the length of an outstretched arm.

kilometer (km)
meter (m)
centimeter (cm)
millimeter (mm)

kilometer (km)	meter (m)	centimeter (cm)	millimeter (mm)
1 km = 1,000,000 mm	1 m = 1000 mm	1 cm = 10 mm	
1 km = 100,000 cm	1 m = 100 cm		1 mm = 0.1 cm
1 km = 1000 m		1 cm = 0.01 m	1 mm = 0.001 m
	1 m = 0.001 km	1 cm = 0.00001 km	1 mm = 0.000001 km

Units of mass are based on the gram. A benchmark for 1 g is the mass of a paper clip.

metric ton (t)
kilogram (kg)
gram (g)
milligram (mg)

metric ton (t)	kilogram (kg)	gram (g)	milligram (mg)
1 t = 1,000,000,000 mg	1 kg = 1,000,000 mg	1 g = 1000 mg	
1 t = 1,000,000 g	1 kg = 1000 g		1 mg = 0.001 g
1 t = 1000 kg		1 g = 0.001 kg	1 mg = 0.000001 kg
	1 kg = 0.001 t	1 g = 0.000001 t	1 mg = 0.000000001 t

26 **Key Concepts Question** The mass of a large horse is about 0.8 metric ton, and the mass of a four-eyed opossum is about 800 g. The mass of the horse is about how many times as great as the mass of the four-eyed opossum?

Practice & Application Exercises

YOU WILL NEED

For Exs. 22–27:
◆ a metric ruler

1. **Connection** Animals can be sorted into sets according to what they eat. *Carnivores* eat meat and *herbivores* eat plants.

Carnivores	Omnivores	Herbivores
Wolf Cougar Brown Bat	Bear	Bison Elk Rabbit

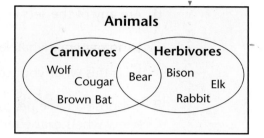

Sorting Grid   **Venn Diagram**

   a. What does the sorting grid tell you about the bear?

   b. What does the Venn diagram tell you about the bear?

   c. What is an omnivore? How can you tell from the diagrams?

Several mammals were sorted by their diets and maximum speeds. The results are shown on the sorting grid below. Use the grid for Exercises 2–7.

	Carnivores ↓	Omnivores ↓	Herbivores ↓
Speed < 60 km/hr →	**Set A** Tiger Domestic Cat	**Set B** Grizzly Bear Patas Monkey Red Fox Raccoon Mouse Squirrel	**Set C** Rabbit Giraffe Donkey Hippopotamus Rhinocerous Elephant Manatee
Speed ≥ 60 km/hr →	**Set D** Cheetah Lion Gray Wolf Coyote Jaguar	**Set E**	**Set F** Horse Pronghorn Antelope

2. List the mammals in Set *A*.

3. List the herbivores that have a maximum speed greater than or equal to 60 km/hr. To which set do they belong?

4. Fill in the blanks to complete the description of Set *B*.

   Set *B* is the set of __?__ that have a maximum speed __?__ 60 km/hr.

5. a. List the animals in Set *D*.

   b. Describe Set *D* in words.

6. Are any of the sets an empty set? What does this mean?

7. a. In general, what seems to be the diet of the fastest mammals?

   b. Is this what you would have expected? Explain.

8. Suppose a table needs to be moved into a classroom. You want to know whether the table will fit through the doorway. Should you measure to the nearest *meter* or *centimeter*? Explain your answer.

9. Suppose you are cutting a board for a shelf in a cabinet. Should you measure to the nearest *centimeter* or *millimeter*? Explain.

Decide which metric unit (*millimeter, centimeter,* or *meter*) to use for the length of each object.

10. an automobile   11. a pencil eraser   12. a dollar bill

Choose the best estimate for each measurement.

13. the width of your classroom   *1 m*   *7 m*   *30 m*

14. the height of a soda can   *1.2 m*   *3.5 cm*   *120 mm*

15. the thickness of a quarter   *8 mm*   *1 cm*   *1 mm*

Decide which metric unit (*milligram, gram, kilogram,* or *metric ton*) to use for the mass of each object.

16. a vitamin pill   17. a baseball bat   18. an airplane

Choose the best estimate for the mass of each object.

19. a bicycle   *15 kg*   *150 g*   *0.5 t*

20. a loaf of bread   *5 g*   *500 g*   *5 kg*

21. a piece of paper   *0.5 kg*   *0.5 g*   *5 kg*

22. Measure the length of this page in centimeters.

23. Measure the thickness of your book in the given metric unit.

   a. millimeters   b. centimeters

Use benchmarks and estimation to draw a segment with each length. Then check your estimates with a metric ruler.

24. 9 cm   25. 25 cm   26. 24 mm   27. 68 mm

Find each product.

28. $2 \cdot 0.01$ 29. $3.4 \cdot 0.001$ 30. $0.4 \cdot 0.01$

31. $0.007 \cdot 10$ 32. $0.35 \cdot 100$ 33. $0.001 \cdot 0.1$

Replace each __?__ with the number that makes the statement true.

34. 5 km = __?__ m   35. 6.5 m = __?__ cm

36. 584 g = __?__ kg   37. 2540 mg = __?__ g

38. 0.6 m = __?__ mm   39. 72 cm = __?__ mm

Use the table to answer Exercises 40 and 41.

40. List the animals in order from least to greatest mass at birth.

41. **Research** A kilogram is a little more than 2 pounds. Which animals in the table have a mass similar to that of a human baby at birth?

Masses of Selected Animals at Birth					
lion	bottlenose dolphin	koala	gorilla	spectacled bear	Thomson's gazelle
1.3 kg	30 kg	0.5 g	2000 g	3200 g	2.7 kg

Replace each __?__ with <, >, or =.

42. 75 mg __?__ 7.5 g   43. 6 t __?__ 600 kg

44. 5.3 km __?__ 5380 m   45. 1500 kg __?__ 0.75 t

Reflecting ▶on the Section

Write your response to Exercise 46 in your journal.

46. Danny had the following six animal cards: octopus, kangaroo, lobster, sea otter, cheetah, and giant clam. He correctly placed his cards in the set *Animals with a Mass Greater than 20 kg* and in the set *Animals that Live in Water*. He found that he had four animals in each set. How can this be, since he had only six cards?

Journal

Exercise 46 checks that you understand set relationships.

Use the Venn diagram below for Exercises 47–50. (Module 2, p. 119)

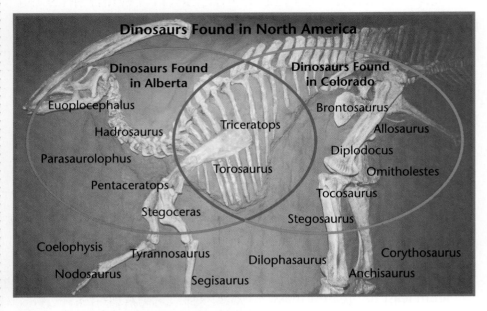

Dinosaurs Found in North America

Dinosaurs Found in Alberta: Euoplocephalus, Hadrosaurus, Parasaurolophus, Pentaceratops, Stegoceras

Dinosaurs Found in Colorado: Brontosaurus, Allosaurus, Diplodocus, Omitholestes, Tocosaurus, Stegosaurus

Triceratops, Torosaurus

Coelophysis, Tyrannosaurus, Dilophasaurus, Corythosaurus, Nodosaurus, Segisaurus, Anchisaurus

47. Find the number of types of dinosaurs that were found in the given area.

   a. Colorado   b. Alberta   c. North America

48. How many types of dinosaurs were found in North America but not in Alberta or Colorado?

49. How many types of dinosaurs found in North America have been found outside of Colorado?

50. What does the Venn diagram tell you about *Triceratops* and *Torosaurus*?

51. Tell where each shape should be placed in the Venn diagram.
(Module 2, p. 119)

Quadrilaterals

Rectangles   Rhombuses

a.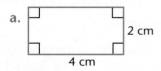
   4 cm, 2 cm

b.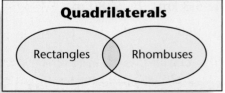
   2 cm, 2 cm, 2 cm, 2 cm

c.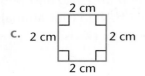
   2 cm, 2 cm, 2 cm, 2 cm

d.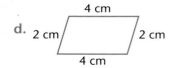
   4 cm, 2 cm, 2 cm, 4 cm

Section 1

Extra Skill Practice

Several mammals were sorted by habitat and whether or not the animals have tails. The results are shown on a sorting grid below.

1. List the mammals that live on land and do not have tails. To which set do they belong?

2. Describe Set *A* in words.

3. How many mammals are in Set *B*?

4. Are any of the sets an empty set? What does this mean?

5. In which set would you place a chimpanzee? Why?

	Live on land	Live in water
Have tails	**Set *A*** Grizzly Bear Armadillo Zebra Tiger Fox Rabbit Bison	**Set *B*** Bottlenose Dolphin Killer Whale Manatee
Do not have tails	**Set *C*** Vampire Bat Pika Koala Gorilla Guinea Pig Orangutan	**Set *D***

Find each product.

6. $3 \cdot 0.01$

7. $2.5 \cdot 0.001$

8. $0.2 \cdot 0.1$

9. $3.48 \cdot 100$

Replace each __?__ with the number that makes the statement true.

10. $350 \text{ cm} = \underline{\ ?\ } \text{ m}$

11. $2930 \text{ mg} = \underline{\ ?\ } \text{ g}$

12. $280 \text{ kg} = \underline{\ ?\ } \text{ g}$

13. $0.4 \text{ t} = \underline{\ ?\ } \text{ kg}$

Study Skills ◀▶ Preparing to do Homework

Looking back at examples and reviewing the key terms can help you prepare to do your homework.

1. Look at an Example in Section 1. What does it show you how to do?

2. a. What are the key terms in Section 1?

   b. Use one of the key terms in a sentence that shows you understand the meaning of the term.

Section ② Line Plots and Averages

IN THIS SECTION

EXPLORATION 1
♦ Line Plots

EXPLORATION 2
♦ Finding Averages

EXPLORATION 3
♦ Appropriate Averages

Animal Averages

Setting the Stage

The Phantom Tollbooth, by Norton Juster, is a story about a boy named Milo who visits a strange land where he has many adventures. One day while resting on the stairs to the land of infinity, Milo is surprised to see what seems to be half of a child.

> "Pardon me for staring," said Milo, after he had been staring for some time, "but I've never seen half a child before."
>
> "It's .58 to be precise," replied the child from the left side of his mouth (which happened to be the only side of his mouth).
>
> "I beg your pardon?" said Milo.
>
> "It's .58," he repeated; "it's a little bit *more* than half."
>
> "Have you always been that way?" asked Milo impatiently, for he felt that that was a needlessly fine distinction.
>
> "My goodness, no," the child assured him. "A few years ago I was just .42 and believe me, that was terribly inconvenient."
>
> "What is the rest of your family like?" said Milo, this time a bit more sympathetically.
>
> "Oh, we're just the average family," he said thoughtfully; "mother, father, and 2.58 children—and, as I explained, I'm the .58."

Think About It

1 **a.** What do you think the word average means?

   b. How do you think the average 2.58 was found?

2 Do you think the average number of children for families in your class is 2.58? Why or why not?

Exploration 1

Line Plots

GOAL

LEARN HOW TO...
- draw and interpret line plots

AS YOU...
- work with data

KEY TERMS
- line plot (dot plot)
- range
- cluster
- gap

▶ To investigate the average number of children in a family, sixth grade students at Anderson School collected data about themselves. The number of children in each student's family is displayed below in a table and in a *line plot*. The line plot, sometimes called a *dot plot*, was created with a data analysis program.

Table

Student	Number of Children in Family	Student	Number of Children in Family
Amanda	4	John	2
Bill	1	Karen	2
Ramon	2	Micki	4
Ladonna	3	Tammy	3
Noreen	5	Massimo	3
Amos	7	Gerald	4
Neil	4	Miya	3
Obed	3		

▲ Anderson school is a rural Montana school located north of Yellowstone Park.

Line Plot

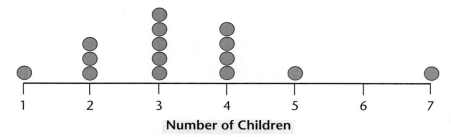

Number of Children in 15 Families

Number of Children

3 Discussion

a. How do you think the data in the table were used to draw the line plot?

b. At what numbers does the scale on the line plot start and end?

4 a. What is the greatest number of children in any of the families? the least number?

b. Did you use the table or the line plot to find the greatest and the least numbers of children? Why?

c. Based on the line plot, what would you report as the average number of students in a family? Why?

5 Discussion Samantha and Ron were absent the day the data were collected.

a. Samantha's family has 6 children. In comparison to the families on the line plot, is the number of children in Samantha's family small, average, or large? Explain.

b. Ron's family has 2 children. Is the number of children in Ron's family small, average, or large in comparison to the other families? Explain.

▶ A **line plot** or **dot plot** displays data using a line marked with a scale. The scale must include the greatest and least values of the data. If you make a line plot before having all your data, you may want to include some extra numbers to the left and right in case the set of data includes surprisingly small or large values.

▶ The **range** of a set of numerical data is the difference between the greatest and least values.

EXAMPLE

Find the range of the numbers 120, 180, 61, 57, and 100.

SAMPLE RESPONSE

Range = greatest value – least value

= 180 – 57

= 123

6 a. What is the range of the numbers of children in the fifteen families?

b. How can the range of the data help you decide what numbers to use on the numerical scale of a line plot?

▶ You have seen how a line plot can be used to display the numbers of children in families. A line plot can also be used to investigate how long animals sleep each day.

7   ✔ CHECKPOINT Use the table below.

   a. Find the range of the data.

   b. Make a line plot for the data. (You may use either **X**'s or **0**'s when constructing your line plot.)

✔ QUESTION 7

...checks that you can draw a line plot.

Sleeping Habits of Selected Animals	
Animal	Hours spent sleeping each day
Asian elephant	4
chimpanzee	10
giraffe	2
gray wolf	13
horse	3
hyena	18
jaguar	11
koala	19
lion	16
mouse	12
okapi	5
rabbit	11
raccoon	13
three-toed sloth	19

8   **Discussion** What do you notice about how the data are distributed in the line plot? Look for *clusters* of data and *gaps* in the data. A **cluster** is a place where the data items are bunched closely together, and a **gap** is a large space where there are no data items.

9   **Try This as a Class** Use the table above and your line plot to help estimate how many hours a day each animal below sleeps. (*Hint:* Look at the clusters of animals in your line plot. Think about what the animals in each cluster have in common.)

   a. donkey   b. cheetah   c. beaver

HOMEWORK EXERCISES ▶ See Exs. 1–9 on p. 226.

GOAL

LEARN HOW TO...
♦ use averages to describe data

AS YOU...
♦ explore data about animals

KEY TERMS
♦ average
♦ mode
♦ median
♦ mean

Exploration 2

FINDING Averages

SET UP *Work in a group. You will need 30 chips.*

Like humans, many animals live together in groups. For example, wolves live in packs. Wolf packs once roamed from the Arctic tundra to Mexico. However, they were considered dangerous predators and were driven out of most areas. By 1926 there were no wolf packs left in Yellowstone Park. In 1995, fourteen wolves were captured in Alberta, Canada, and released in the park. By 2002, at least 148 wolves in 14 packs were living in Yellowstone Park.

2002 Yellowstone National Park Wolf Population													
Pack Name	Agate Creek	Bechler Group	Geode Creek	Buffalo Fork	Tower	Chief Joseph	Leopold	Mollie's	Nez Perce	Rose Creek II	Cougar Creek	Swan Lake	Druid Peak	Yellowstone Delta
Estimated Pack Size	10	4	9	4	2	10	16	12	20	10	10	16	11	14

10 **a.** Make a line plot of the pack sizes.

   b. What is the range of the pack sizes?

11 **Discussion** Why might a wildlife biologist monitoring the Yellowstone wolf population want to know the typical, or most common, number of wolves in a pack?

▶ One way to describe the typical, or **average**, number of wolves in a pack is to find the pack size that occurs most often. The item that occurs most often in a set of data is the **mode**. A set of data may have more than one mode or no mode.

12 **a.** According to the table on page 218, what pack size occurs most often?

b. Using your line plot, how can you determine the pack size that occurs most often?

c. What is the mode of the pack sizes?

d. **Discussion** Suppose two more wolf packs were found, both containing 4 wolves. What would the mode(s) of the 16 packs be?

▶ Another way to describe the average number of wolves in a pack is to find the *middle* pack size.

13 **a.** List the number of wolves in each of the first five packs (starting with the Agate Creek pack) from least to greatest.

b. Using your list from part (a), cross out data items two at a time so that each time you cross out the least and greatest remaining items. The first step is shown below.

$$\cancel{2} \ 4 \ 4 \ 9 \ \cancel{10}$$

c. What is the middle pack size for the five wolf packs?

14 **a.** Now list the number of wolves in the next 6 packs (starting with the Chief Joseph pack) from least to greatest.

b. Using your list from part (a), cross out data items two at a time so that each time you cross out the least and greatest remaining items.

c. **Try This as a Class** Is there a middle pack size for these six wolf packs? If so, what is it? If not, what other number can you think of as being "in the middle"?

▶ The middle item in a set of data listed in numerical order is the **median**. If there is no single middle item, the median is the number halfway between the two data items closest to the middle.

15 What is the median number of wolves in the 14 Yellowstone Park wolf packs?

▶ Suppose the 14 Yellowstone Park wolf packs all had the same number of wolves in them. Then the average pack size would be the number of wolves in any pack. Since the packs don't all have the same number of wolves, we must level off or balance the number of wolves in the packs to find the common size.

FOR▶HELP

with *pictographs,*
see
TOOLBOX, p. 579

16 a. Follow the steps below to balance the pack size in the first five wolf packs in the table on page 218.

Step 1: Use chips on a piece of paper to make a pictograph of the number of wolves in each of the first five wolf packs. Let each chip represent one wolf.

Step 2: Move the chips so that each of the packs has as close to the same number of wolves as possible.

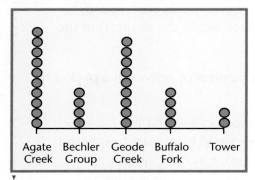

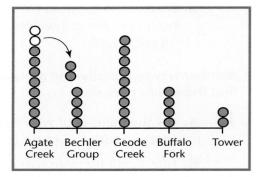

b. How many wolves are in each pack after the moves?

▶ **The common or average pack size you found in Question 16(b) is an approximation of the mean. In this case, the mean tells you how many wolves would be in each pack if all five packs had the same number of wolves.**

17 Try This as a Class

a. How can you find the mean of the number of wolves in the 14 Yellowstone Park packs without using chips?

b. What is the mean of the number of wolves in the 14 wolf packs?

✔ **QUESTION 18**

...checks that you can find the mean, the median, and the mode of a set of data.

18 ✔ CHECKPOINT Most elephants live in herds that consist of many adults and their young. The number of young elephants in eight different herds is listed below. Find the mean, the median, and the mode.

27, 16, 31, 27, 11, 51, 40, 93

▲
A herd of African elephants can have anywhere from 10 to 200 members.

19 Discussion

a. If the average number of children in a family is 2.58, could this average be the mean? the median? the mode? Explain.

b. Repeat part (a) if the average number of children is 2.5.

HOMEWORK EXERCISES ▶ See Exs. 10–17 on p. 227.

Exploration 3

Appropriate
Averages

GOAL

LEARN HOW TO...
- write a fraction as a decimal using a calculator
- choose appropriate averages
- round decimal quotients

AS YOU...
- find the average number of children for different families

SET UP *Work in a group. You will need:* • *11 chips* • *calculator*

▶ **Average family size has fallen in most areas of the world over the past 30 years. In the United States, the mean number of children per family decreased to 2.1 in 2002. Since families have whole numbers of children, it may seem strange for the mean number of children to be a decimal. To see how this can happen, you will explore the mean number of children for four families.**

Family A	Family B	Family C	Family D
2 children	0 children	1 child	0 children

20 **a.** Find the median and the mode for the data in the table.

b. What operations would you have to perform to find the mean?

21 **a.** Use chips to make a pictograph showing the number of children for each family. Let each chip stand for 1 child.

b. Can you move the chips so that each family has the same number of chips? Explain.

22 **a.** Suppose you can divide each of the three chips into four equal-sized parts. If you move the parts so that each family has the same number of parts, how many parts does each family get?

b. What fraction of a whole chip does each family get?

23 **Discussion** Look at your answers to Question 20(b) and Question 22(b).

    a. What fraction does 3 ÷ 4 equal?

    b. What decimal does 3 ÷ 4 equal?

    c. What is the mean number of children in the four families?

    d. Do you think the mean, the median, or the mode best describes the number of children for the four families? Explain.

▶ A fraction represents a division. In Question 22 you found that 3 chips divided by 4 equals $\frac{3}{4}$ of a chip. You can use division to write any fraction as a decimal.

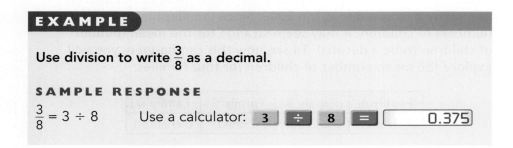

EXAMPLE

Use division to write $\frac{3}{8}$ as a decimal.

SAMPLE RESPONSE

$\frac{3}{8} = 3 \div 8$ Use a calculator: 3   ÷   8   =   0.375

24 **a.** Add a Family E with 8 children to the pictograph you made in Question 21.

    b. If you move the chips so that each family has as close to the same number of chips as possible, how many chips are left over?

    c. Calculator What fraction of a chip should each family get? Use division to write this as a decimal.

    d. Find the mean, the median, and the mode for the five families.

    e. Compare the averages you found in part (d) with the averages you found in Question 20(a) and Question 23(c). Which average changed the least?

    f. Which average changed the most?

    g. Which average do you think best describes the number of children in the five families? Why?

25 Calculator Use division to write $\frac{4}{7}$ as a decimal.

▶ **Rounding** Some quotients, like the one you found in Question 25, have many decimal places. You can round a decimal to a specific place value to make it easier to work with.

26 a. 🖩 Calculator Use a calculator to find the mean of the number of offspring for the three baboon troops in the table.

Baboon troop	Number of adults	Number of offspring
A	30	34
B	14	16
C	35	39

Baboons live in groups called troops.

b. Is the mean closer to 29.6 or 29.7? Explain.

c. In part (b), to what place value was your chosen answer rounded?

EXAMPLE

To the nearest hundredth, find the mean number of adults in the three troops of baboons from Question 26.

SAMPLE RESPONSE

Find the mean of 30, 14, and 35.

$(30 + 14 + 35) \div 3 = 79 \div 3$

[7] [9] [÷] [3] [=]

26.333333

hundredths place

You can round decimals in the same way you round whole numbers.

Look at the digit to the right of the hundredths place.

The 3 in the thousandths place is less than 5, so 26.333333 is closer to 26.33 than to 26.34.

27 Discussion Use the Example above.

a. Why is the 3 in the thousandths place compared with 5?

b. Explain how to round 26.333333 to the nearest thousandth.

28 ✔ **CHECKPOINT** Calculator Write each fraction as a decimal. Round your answers to the nearest hundredth.

a. $\frac{2}{3}$ **b.** $\frac{5}{9}$ **c.** $\frac{1}{7}$ **d.** $\frac{8}{5}$

✔ **QUESTION 28**

...checks that you can write fractions as decimals and round decimals.

29 a. 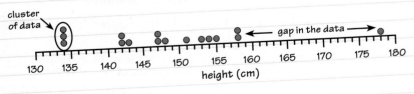 Calculator For each table below, find the mean, the median, and the mode of the data. If necessary, round to the nearest hundredth.

TV Family 1900's	Number of Children
Brady Bunch	6
Dr. Quinn, Medicine Woman	4
Partridge Family	5
Full House	3
Family Matters	2
Cosby Show	5

TV Family 2000's	Number of Children
The George Lopez Show	2
Malcolm in the Middle	4
Reba	3
According to Jim	3
Family Affair	3
My Wife and Kids	3
Like Family	3

b. Which average or averages (mean, median, or mode) do you think best describe the number of children in the TV families of the 1900s? the TV families of the 2000s? Explain.

30 In the *Phantom Tollbooth*, Milo is told that the average number of children in a family is 2.58. How does this compare to the average number of children in the TV families in Question 29?

HOMEWORK EXERCISES ▶ See Exs. 18–37 on pp. 227–229.

Section ② Key Concepts

Key Terms

line plot

range

cluster

gap

Line Plot (Dot Plot) (pp. 215–217)

A line plot (also called a dot plot) displays data using a line marked with a scale. The scale must include the greatest and least values of the data. The range is the difference between the greatest and least values.

Heights of 16 Anderson School Sixth Graders

cluster of data

gap in the data

130 135 140 145 150 155 160 165 170 175 180

height (cm)

Section 2
Key Concepts

Averages (pp. 218–220)

An average is a number used to describe a typical item in a set of data. The mean, the median, and the mode are types of averages.

Example Data: 6, 3, 2, 4, 6, 3

Sum of data = 24
Number of items = 6
mean = 24 ÷ 6 = 4

Ordered data: 2, 3, 3, 4, 6, 6
modes: 3 and 6
2, 3, 3, 4, 6, 6
median = (3 + 4) ÷ 2 = 3.5

For some situations, and depending on the data, some averages may be more appropriate to use than others.

Writing a Fraction as a Decimal (pp. 221–224)

You can use division to write any fraction as a decimal.

Example $\frac{3}{7} = 3 \div 7 \approx 0.4285714286$

Rounding Decimals (pp. 223–224)

It is often helpful to round a decimal to a particular place.

Example Round 0.4285714286 to the nearest thousandth.

5 ≥ 5

0.429 ←— Round the 8 up to 9.

Key Concepts Questions

Use the line plot on page 224 for Questions 31–33.

31 What are the range, the mean, the median, and the mode of the heights of the 16 Anderson School sixth graders? If necessary, round to the nearest hundredth.

32 Which average, the mean, the median, or the mode, do you think best describes the typical height of the 16 Anderson School sixth graders?

33 Ramon, a 136 cm tall sixth grader, was absent the day the heights were measured. In comparison to the 16 students on the line plot, is he short, tall, or of average height? Explain.

Use the line plot for Exercises 1–4.

National Basketball Association All Star Basketball Players, 2006

Height (inches)

▲
Tim Duncan, one
of the 2006 NBA All
Stars.

1. What is the range of the heights of the players?

2. How many players are over 82 inches?

3. What ~~are the two~~ middle heights?

4. What heights occur most often?

5. A pet store owner kept track of how long it took to sell a shipment
   of tropical fish. She recorded how many weeks each fish was kept
   before it was sold. The results are shown in the list below.

   1, 2, 3, 1, 5, 1, 1, 2, 1, 1, 2, 6

   a. Find the range of the data.

   b. Make a line plot for the data.

Use the table below for Exercises 6–9.

Average Life Spans of Some Yellowstone Park Mammals									
Animal	pika	porcupine	dwarf shrew	gray wolf	grizzly bear	bison	bobcat	little brown bat	striped skunk
Life span (years)	6	6	2	16	25	20	12	30	3

6. Make a line plot for the data using X's for the symbols.

7. Is there a life span on your line plot that occurs more frequently
   than the others? If yes, what is it?

8. Is there a life span on your line plot that has the same number of
   X's to the right of it as there are to the left of it? Explain.

9. What can you conclude about the life spans of the animals?

Find the mean, the median, and the mode(s) of each data set.

10. masses of 8 butterflies (mg): 12, 18, 15, 8, 11, 17, 18, 13

11. weights of 7 kittens (ounces): 5, 8, 12, 4, 12, 3, 5

12. litter sizes of 10 coyotes: 4, 6, 4, 8, 7, 6, 7, 9, 5, 4

13. lengths of 5 babies (in.): 19, 22, 21, 20, 18

14. the heights of the NBA All Star players in the line plot on page 226.

15. **Writing** The average depth of a local lake is reported to be 2 ft. Do you think you can wade across the lake? What information might be hidden when reporting this average?

16. **Open-ended** Find a set of six whole numbers that have a mean, a median, and a mode of 50. The numbers cannot all be the same.

17. **Challenge** The mean of nine test scores is 61.

    a. What is the sum of the scores?

    b. If a score of 100 is added to the group of scores, what is the new mean?

18. The masses (in kilograms) of six animals in a zoo are listed as 5, 8, 24, 30, 32, and 1020. The zookeeper reported the average mass to be 186.5 kg. Which average did the zookeeper use? Is this average appropriate? Explain.

19. The grade book below shows Thom's scores on his quizzes. He told his mom he had an average of 92 for his quiz scores.

    a. Which average is he using?

    b. Is this an appropriate average in this case? Why?

Subject . . . STEM 6	Assignment	Quiz 1	Quiz 2		Quiz 3	Quiz 4		Quiz 5	Quiz 6		Quiz 7	Quiz 8	
Section . . . 3													
		1st week				2nd week			3rd week Oct 3			4th week	
Month / Date . . .	Sept.	14 15 16 17 18			21 22 23 24 25			28 29 30 1 2			5 6 7 8 9		
Students . . .		M T W T F			M T W T F			M T W T F			M T W T F		
Thom Wilson		92 85			78 92			71 77			80		
Kamala Pramar		98 79			84 90			90 89			75		
Sarah Adams		82 84			91 92			80 80			83		

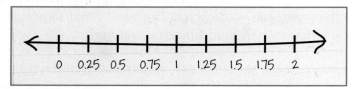

Calculator Write each fraction in Exercises 20–27 as a decimal rounded to the nearest hundredth.

20. $\frac{5}{8}$ 21. $\frac{8}{11}$ 22. $\frac{1}{8}$ 23. $\frac{5}{6}$

24. $\frac{4}{3}$ 25. $\frac{9}{8}$ 26. $\frac{2}{5}$ 27. $\frac{7}{4}$

28. Look at Exercises 20–27. How can you tell whether a fraction is greater than 1 or less than 1 without doing any calculations?

29. Copy the number line and mark a point for each fraction from Exercises 20–27.

```
<----+---+---+---+---+---+---+---+---->
     0  0.25 0.5 0.75  1  1.25 1.5 1.75  2
```

Round each decimal to the given place.

30. 0.3962 (tenths)   31. 0.3962 (thousandths)

32. 13.695 (hundredths)   33. 4.346 (tenths)

34. 56.6 (ones)   35. 102.342 (hundredths)

36. **Gymnastics** Six judges each score a gymnast from 1 through 10 points. The highest and lowest scores are not used. The mean of the remaining four scores is the final score. The table shows the top women's scores for the balance beam in the 2004 Olympic Games in Athens, Greece.

GYMNAST	JUDGES' SCORES					
Carly Patterson, USA	9.80	9.75	9.80	9.75	9.75	9.80
Alexandra Eremia, ROM	9.70	9.70	9.70	9.65	9.70	9.70
Catalina Ponor, ROM	9.80	9.80	9.80	9.75	9.75	9.80

a. Why do you think the highest and lowest scores are not used in finding the mean?

b. **Calculator** Use a calculator to find the posted score for each gymnast. Round to the nearest thousandth.

c. Who won the gold medal in the balance beam?

Reflecting on the Section

Be prepared to discuss your response to Exercise 37 in class.

37. Look back at the table and line plot of the *Number of Children in 15 Families* on page 215.

   a. What are the mean, median, and mode of the data set? If necessary, round to the nearest hundredth.

   b. Which average, the mean, median, or mode, do you think best decribes the average number of children in the families? Explain.

   c. What type of information shows up clearly in the table? What type of information is difficult to see?

   d. What type of information shows up clearly in the line plot?

   e. What do you see as the advantages of the table? of the line plot?

Discussion

Exercise 37 checks that you understand the meaning of mean, median, and mode and can choose an appropriate average.

Spiral Review

For Exercises 38–40, use the bar graph below. (Toolbox, p. 578)

38. Which bird has the widest wingspan? the narrowest?

39. Estimate the greatest difference between the wingspans of the seabirds.

40. Estimate the difference between the wingspans of the gulls.

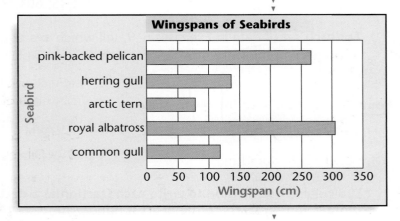

Write each decimal as a fraction in lowest terms. (Module 3, p. 134)

41. 0.5   42. 1.9   43. 0.75   44. 0.04

Find the value of each expression. (Module 1, p. 10)

45. $2 + \dfrac{6}{2}$ 46. $5 \cdot 12 - 7$ 47. $77 - 10 \cdot 2$

Section 2

Extra Skill Practice

Use the table for Exercises 1–5.

Average Life Spans									
Animal	cat	dog	goat	guinea pig	horse	pig	rabbit	sheep	white mouse
Life span (years)	12	12	8	4	20	10	5	12	3

1. Make a line plot of the data.   2. What is the range of the data?

3. How many of the animals have a life span greater than 8 years?

4. What are the mean, the median, and the mode of the life spans of the animals? If necessary, round to the nearest hundredth.

5. Which average, the mean, the median, or the mode, do you think best describes the life span of the animals? Explain.

For Exercises 6–9, find the mean, the median, and the mode(s) for each set of data.

6. 10, 12, 9, 8, 15, 12   7. 4, 4, 2, 3, 4, 6, 5

8. 16, 9, 13, 9, 12, 16, 9   9. 245, 601, 322, 212

10. For each set of data in Exercises 6–9, tell which average or averages you think are most appropriate to use. Explain your choices.

Round each decimal to the given place.

11. 12.457 (hundredths)   12. 5.02841 (tenths)

13. 367.125 (hundredths)   14. 0.9912 (thousandths)

Calculator Use division to write each fraction as a decimal. Round your answers to the nearest hundredth.

15. $\frac{9}{48}$ 16. $\frac{8}{15}$ 17. $\frac{4}{3}$ 18. $\frac{14}{9}$ 19. $\frac{17}{21}$

Standardized Testing ◄►Free Response

Find five whole numbers that have a mean of 4, a median of 3, and a mode of 2.

Section 3 Dividing Decimals and Solving Equations

LITTLE CRITTERS

Setting the Stage ▸▸▸▸▸▸▸▸▸▸▸▸▸▸▸▸▸▸▸▸▸▸▸▸▸▸

Numerous small mammals, including martens, squirrels, and pikas, live in Yellowstone National Park. A pika is a stocky tailless animal about the size of a hamster. Pikas live between the tree line and the mountain peaks. Scientists believe pikas would be one of the first mammals to fall victim to global warming, so they are very carefully monitored.

Pika
body length: 185 mm
mass: 145 g
▼

◀ Marten
body length: 400 mm
mass 1.1 kg

▲
Squirrel
body length: 20 cm
mass: 220 g

Think About It

1 **a.** Which animal is shorter, the pika or the squirrel? by how many centimeters?

b. Estimation The mass of the squirrel is about how many times the mass of the pika?

2 **a.** The marten is how many times as long as the squirrel?

b. The mass of the squirrel is what fraction of the mass of the marten?

▸ The body length and mass given for each animal are averages. In Exploration 1, you will look more closely at how averages may have been calculated.

Exploration 1

Dividing).Decimals

> **SET UP** *You will need Labsheets 3A and 3B.*

3 The masses of four pikas are 0.14 kg, 0.15 kg, 0.18 kg and 0.13 kg.

    a. Find the sum of the masses.

    b. What do you need to do next to find the mean of the masses of the pikas?

▶ **Using a Grid to Divide To find the mean of the masses of the pikas you need to divide a decimal by a whole number. You can model the division on a 10 x 10 grid.**

4 **Use Labsheet 3A.** Follow the directions on the labsheet to find the *Mean Mass of Four Pikas* using a 10 x 10 grid.

5 **Use Labsheet 3A.** The total body length of 6 martens is 2.40 m. Follow the directions and use the grids on the labsheet to find the *Mean Body Length of Six Martens*.

6 ✔ **CHECKPOINT** Use Labsheet 3B. Use the *Decimal Division Grids* to find the quotients 0.06 ÷ 3, 0.36 ÷ 9, and 2)‾1.30‾.

✔ **QUESTION 6**

...checks that you can use grids to divide a decimal by a whole number.

▶ **Estimating a Quotient You can use compatible numbers to quickly check that a quotient seems reasonable.**

EXAMPLE

The total mass of five raccoons is 27.5 kg. Could the mean of the masses of the raccoons be 0.45 kg? Why or why not?

SAMPLE RESPONSE

Estimate 27.5 ÷ 5 to check whether 0.45 is a reasonable answer.

    27.5 ÷ 5 is slightly greater than 25 ÷ 5.

25 ÷ 5 = 5, so the answer of 0.45 is *not* reasonable.

7 Try This as a Class Copy each division at the right.

a. Use estimation to place the decimal point in each quotient. Explain your reasoning.

b. How do you think the numbers in each quotient in part (a) were determined?

c. Look at the position of the decimal points in each quotient and dividend you wrote in part (a). How can you place the decimal point without estimating?

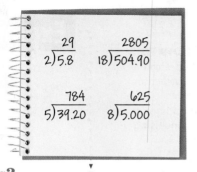

$$\begin{array}{r} 29 \\ 2\overline{)5.8} \end{array} \qquad \begin{array}{r} 2805 \\ 18\overline{)504.90} \end{array}$$

$$\begin{array}{r} 784 \\ 5\overline{)39.20} \end{array} \qquad \begin{array}{r} 625 \\ 8\overline{)5.000} \end{array}$$

8 ✓ CHECKPOINT Find each quotient. Estimate to check that each answer seems reasonable.

a. $3\overline{)106.23}$ b. $3.78 \div 14$ c. $5\overline{)258.65}$

✓ QUESTION 8

...checks that you can divide a decimal by a whole number.

▶ **Remainders** Sometimes a division has a remainder. For these divisions, you have to write zeros to the right of the dividend to continue to divide.

EXAMPLE

$$\begin{array}{r} 2.5 \\ 8\overline{)20.2} \\ \underline{-16} \\ 4\,2 \\ \underline{-4\,0} \\ 2 \end{array}$$
remainder

$$\begin{array}{r} 2.52 \\ 8\overline{)20.20} \\ \underline{-16} \\ 4\,2 \\ \underline{-4\,0} \\ 20 \\ \underline{-16} \\ 4 \end{array}$$
Write a zero.

$$\begin{array}{r} 2.525 \\ 8\overline{)20.200} \\ \underline{-16} \\ 4\,2 \\ \underline{-4\,0} \\ 20 \\ \underline{-16} \\ 40 \\ \underline{-40} \\ 0 \end{array}$$
Write another zero.

9 Try This as a Class

a. Divide 15 by 4.

b. How is 15 related to 15.0 and 15.00?

c. In part (a), how did you know when to write another zero and when to stop?

10 Find each quotient. Use estimation to check that each quotient seems reasonable.

a. $29.2 \div 8$ b. $6\overline{)7.05}$ c. $4\overline{)21.25}$ d. $\dfrac{12}{5}$

HOMEWORK EXERCISES ▶ See Exs. 1–16 on p. 241.

GOAL

LEARN HOW TO...
◆ write addition and subtraction equations
◆ solve addition equations using models

AS YOU...
◆ examine the diets of animals in a zoo

KEY TERMS
◆ solution of an equation
◆ solving an equation

Exploration 2

Writing and Modeling Equations

SET UP You will need algebra tiles.

▶ **Modeling Equations** Animals living in captivity may not have access to the foods they would eat when living in the wild. To keep the animals healthy, zoo nutritionists prepare special diets for each animal based on its natural diet and nutritional needs. For example, each prairie dog is fed 125 g of food per day. The daily feeding consists of fruits and vegetables plus 50 g of grains, seeds, and nuts. Here are three ways to model the amount of food each prairie dog is fed, where x represents the mass of the fruits and vegetables.

Verbal statement:	Mass of fruits and vegetables	plus	Mass of grains, seeds, and nuts	equals	Total mass of food
Equation:	x g	+	50 g	=	125 g

Balance model:

x g (fruits, vegetables)
+
50 g (grains, seeds, nuts) = 125 g (total)

11 **Try This as a Class** Examine the diagram above.

a. Why does the balance scale work as a model for an equation?

b. What is the value of x, the mass of the fruits and vegetables?

c. Explain how you found the value of x in part (b).

▶ **Balance models can help you visualize an equation and remember that both sides represent the same amount. Equations can be used to describe a variety of situations.**

EXAMPLE

Suppose 19 prairie dogs, including 11 juveniles, live in the "prairie dog town" at a zoo. Write an equation to model the total number of prairie dogs in the "town."

SAMPLE RESPONSE

Let a = the number of adult prairie dogs.

Number of adult prairie dogs	plus	number of juvenile prairie dogs	equals	total number of prairie dogs
a	$+$	11	$=$	19

12 **a.** Why is 10 not a reasonable value for a in the Example?

b. How many adult prairie dogs live in the "town" in the Example?

13 One day at a zoo, a 170 kg male spectacled bear was fed 11.3 kg of food. Its meal included 3.3 kg of a nutritionally complete meatloaf, 4.0 kg of fruits and vegetables, plus other foods. Choose a variable to represent the number of kilograms of other foods. Then write an equation to model the amount the bear was fed.

▶ **Sometimes equations that model situations involve subtraction.**

EXAMPLE

After spending $7.00 for a poster of a prairie dog, Maria had $16.00. How much money did she have before purchasing the poster?

SAMPLE RESPONSE

Amount before purchase	minus	cost of poster	equals	amount remaining
x	$-$	$7.00	$=$	$16.00

14 How much money did Maria have before buying the poster?

▲
Spectacled bears are the only bears native to South America. They are small bears whose mass is usually less than 200 kg.

QUESTION 15

...checks that you
can use equations to
model situations.

15 ✔ **CHECKPOINT** Describe a situation that can be represented using a subtraction equation. Write an equation to represent the situation. Use one variable and be sure to tell what it represents.

16 Give a situation that each equation could model.

    a. $j + 3 = 8$ **b.** $15 - c = 4$

▶ **Algebra Tiles** You can use algebra tiles to model equations. The ☐+☐ tile represents the variable. The + tile represents 1.

EXAMPLE

You can model the equation $x + 5 = 8$ with algebra tiles as follows:

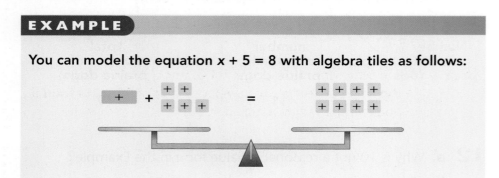

17 a. Use algebra tiles to model the Example above.

    b. Remove two + tiles from the side of the equation with the ☐+☐ . What must you do to the other side to keep the equation balanced?

    c. How many + tiles must ☐+☐ represent in the Example for the equation to be balanced? How did you get your answer?

    d. Use your answer from part (c) to complete the equation $x = \underline{\ ?\ }$.

▶ The value of a variable that makes an equation true is a **solution of the equation**. The process of finding solutions is **solving an equation**.

18 a. Write an equation represented by the algebra tile model.

        + + + + = ☐+☐ + + +

    b. Use algebra tiles to model the equation in part (a).

    c. How can you get the ☐+☐ tile alone on one side of the equation while keeping the two sides balanced?

    d. Solve the equation you wrote in part (a).

19 ✔ **CHECKPOINT** Repeat Question 18 for this algebra tile model.

+ ‖ + ‖ + ‖ + ‖ + = ‖ + ‖ + ‖ + ‖ + ‖ +

✔ **QUESTION 19**

...checks that you can use a model to solve an addition equation.

20 During the spring and summer, nine prairie dogs living in the wild consume about 8 kg of food per week. Their weekly diet consists of 6 kg of grass plus other vegetation.

a. Choose a variable to represent the number of kilograms of other vegetation. Then write an equation to model the amount the nine prairie dogs eat in a week.

b. Use algebra tiles to model and to solve your equation from part (a).

21 **Challenge** How does the number of grams of food a prairie dog in the wild eats each day compare with the 125 g of food a prairie dog living in a zoo is fed each day?

▌ **HOMEWORK EXERCISES** ▶ See Exs. 17–32 on pp. 241–243.

Exploration 3 ▸▸▸▸▸▸▸▸▸▸▸▸▸▸▸▸▸▸▸▸▸▸▸▸

Using Inverse Operations

GOAL

LEARN HOW TO...
◆ use inverse operations to solve addition and subtraction equations

AS YOU...
◆ examine the diets of zoo animals

KEY TERM
◆ inverse operations

22 Each day, a 1200 kg female giraffe living in a zoo is fed 8.6 kg of hay in addition to other foods. Altogether, she eats 12.7 kg of food. Let x = the number of kilograms of other foods.

a. Write an addition equation that describes the amount of food the giraffe eats each day.

b. What can you do to both sides of the equation to get x alone?

c. Why is it difficult to represent this situation with algebra tiles?

▶ Addition and subtraction are **inverse operations**. They "undo" each other. Inverse operations are helpful in solving equations.

Here are keys to solving an equation:

 ◆ Use inverse operations to get the variable alone on one side.
 ◆ Keep the equation in balance by keeping both sides equal.

▶ When you use symbols and variables to solve an equation, you are solving the equation *algebraically.*

EXAMPLE

Here are two methods for solving the equation $x + 4 = 5$.

Solve using tiles.   Solve algebraically.

$$x + 4 = 5$$

Subtract 4 from both sides.

$$
\begin{aligned}
x + 4 &= 5 \\
-4 &\quad -4 \\
\hline
x + 0 &= 1
\end{aligned}
$$

$$x = 1$$

Check to see that the solution is correct.

$$x + 4 = 5$$

Substitute 1 for x.

$$1 + 4 \stackrel{?}{=} 5$$

$$5 = 5 ✔$$

Both sides are equal, so the solution is correct.

---

23 Try This as a Class

 a. In the Example, what was done to the equation to get *x* alone?

 b. Describe the steps in checking the solution. Why is the question mark included in the check process?

 c. Why is it important to check the solution?

24 Tim solved the equation $x + 47 = 65$ as shown at the right. Check to see whether Tim's solution is correct.

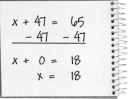

$$x + 47 = 65$$
$$\underline{-47 \quad -47}$$
$$x + 0 = 18$$
$$x = 18$$

25 ✔ **CHECKPOINT** Solve each equation. Check each solution.

  a. $n + 18 = 102$ **b.** $12 = a + 5$ **c.** $n + 5.6 = 14.3$

✔ **QUESTION 25**

...checks that you understand how inverse operations can help you solve equations.

▶ Inverse operations can also be used to solve equations where a number is subtracted from a variable.

EXAMPLE

Solve the equation $x - 4.8 = 13.5$.

SAMPLE RESPONSE

$$x - 4.8 = 13.5$$
$$\underline{+4.8 \quad +4.8}$$
$$x + 0 = 18.3$$
$$x = 18.3$$

Add 4.8 to both sides.

---

26 a. What was done to the equation in the Example to get x alone?

  b. Why was this operation chosen?

  c. Check the solution by substituting 18.3 for x. Is the solution correct?

27 Solve your equation from Question 22(a) to find the number of kilograms of other foods the giraffe was fed.

28 Solve each equation. Check each solution.

  a. $n - 3.7 = 6$ **b.** $16 = k - 7$ **c.** $27 = 12 + p$ **d.** $z - 5.8 = 14.7$

29 ✔ **CHECKPOINT** A student's solution of the equation $n - 1.3 = 1.5$ is $n = 2$. A check of this solution is shown.

  a. What does the check tell you?

  b. What is the solution of the equation?

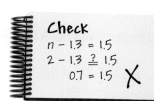

Check
$$n - 1.3 = 1.5$$
$$2 - 1.3 \stackrel{?}{=} 1.5$$
$$0.7 = 1.5 \quad \text{✗}$$

✔ **QUESTION 29**

...checks that you understand how to verify a solution.

HOMEWORK EXERCISES ▶ See Exs. 33–57 on pp. 243–244.

Section 3 Key Concepts

Dividing a Decimal by a Whole Number (pp. 232–233)

Divide as though both numbers were whole numbers.

Write the decimal point in the quotient directly above the decimal point in the dividend.

$$\begin{array}{r} 0.15 \\ 4\overline{)0.60} \\ \underline{4} \\ 20 \\ \underline{20} \\ 0 \end{array}$$

← Write a zero to the right of the dividend when the division does not come out evenly.

Modeling Equations (pp. 234–237)

Balance models can help you visualize an equation and remember that the expressions on either side of an equation must be equal. Algebra tile models can help you solve (find a solution of) an equation.

Using Inverse Operations (pp. 237–239)

The goal when you solve an equation is to get the variable alone on one side of the equation. One method that can help you reach the goal is to use inverse operations. Inverse operations "undo" one another. Addition and subtraction are inverse operations. Remember that any operation done on one side of the equation must also be done on the other side to keep the equation balanced.

Example Addition "undoes" the subtraction when you solve an equation.

Solve $n - 6.3 = 4.5$.

$$\begin{array}{rcl} n - 6.3 & = & 4.5 \\ + 6.3 & & + 6.3 \\ \hline n + 0 & = & 10.8 \\ n & = & 10.8 \end{array}$$

Add 6.3 to both sides.

Check that $n = 10.8$.

$$n - 6.3 = 4.5$$
$$10.8 - 6.3 \overset{?}{=} 4.5$$
$$4.5 = 4.5 \checkmark$$

Substitute your solution in the equation.

10.8 is the solution of the equation $n - 6.3 = 4.5$.

Key Concepts Questions

30 Find the quotient $1.6 \div 5$. Use estimation to check that the quotient seems reasonable.

31 Explain how the steps in the Example above keep the equation "balanced" and help to solve the equation.

Section 3

Practice & Application Exercises

YOU WILL NEED

For Exs. 21–23, 46:
◆ algebra tiles

Estimation Use compatible numbers to check the position of the decimal point on each quotient. If a quotient is incorrect, give the correct quotient.

1. $4\overline{)783.2}$ quotient 19.58

2. $20\overline{)41}$ quotient 2.05

3. $7\overline{)21.14}$ quotient 30.2

4. At the beginning of a trip, the trip odometer in Brianna's car read 0 miles. After 4 days of travel, the odometer read 994.8 miles. What is the mean of the distances she drove each day?

Find each quotient. Use estimation to check that each quotient seems reasonable.

5. $6\overline{)0.48}$

6. $8\overline{)4.976}$

7. $13.08 \div 12$

8. $124.5 \div 6$

9. $37.3 \div 4$

10. $11\overline{)215.6}$

11. **Geometry Connection** The perimeter of a square is 5.23 cm. Find the length of one side.

12. The Pentagon Building is one of the largest office buildings in the world. Its outermost wall is in the shape of a regular pentagon with a perimeter of about 1.6 km. How many *meters* long is one side of the Pentagon?

◀ The Pentagon Building, in Arlington, Virginia, is the headquarters for the Department of Defense of the United States government.

Choosing a Method Use pencil and paper or mental math to write each fraction as a decimal.

13. $\dfrac{7}{8}$

14. $\dfrac{12}{200}$

15. $\dfrac{9}{5}$

16. $\dfrac{756}{1000}$

Write an equation that each model represents.

17.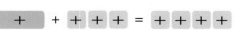

18.

19. **Open-ended** Describe a situation that can be modeled by the equation $n + 4 = 6$. Be sure to tell what the variable represents.

20. **Open-ended** Describe a situation that can be represented using a subtraction equation. Write an equation to model the situation. Use one variable and tell what it represents.

Make an algebra tile model that represents each equation. Then use the model to find the solution.

21. $6 = x + 4$ 22. $x + 3 = 11$ 23. $7 + x = 13$

Social Studies In 1933, the 20th Amendment to the Constitution set January 20 as the inauguration date for the President and January 3 as the inauguration date for members of Congress. Write an addition equation to model each situation. Let y = the number of years served.

24. Dwight D. Eisenhower, the first President limited to two terms by a later amendment to the Constitution, served from 1953 to 1961.

25. Barbara Jordan, the first African-American woman from a Southern state elected to the House of Representatives, served from 1973 to 1979.

26. Dalip Singh Saund, the first Asian-American elected to the House of Representatives, served from 1957 to 1963.

Write an addition equation to model each situation. Use one variable and tell what it represents.

27. The track team gets 2 new members, raising the membership to 20.

28. Of the 12 people in the 200 m dash, 5 of them set a new "personal best."

29. Alice won 3 medals. She now has 17 medals.

Write a subtraction equation to model each situation. Use one variable and tell what it represents.

30. Anna sold 70 prints. She has 8 left over.

31. After paying $5.75 for lunch, John received $4.25 in change.

32. The number of customers on a paper route drops to 28 after 4 people cancel their subscriptions to the newspaper.

Solve each equation. Check each solution.

33. $a + 19 = 47$ **34.** $8 + w = 110$ **35.** $q - 26 = 37$

36. $53 = v - 19$ **37.** $b - 27 = 16$ **38.** $10 = 8 + n$

39. $0.66 + x = 2.4$ **40.** $p - 5.6 = 2.74$ **41.** $1.5 = n - 3$

42. $y - 1.8 = 2.7$ **43.** $n + 0.06 = 4$ **44.** $1.69 = x - 17.4$

45. Is 6 a solution of the equation $0.2 + n = 8$? Explain.

46. Challenge Write an equation that the model below represents. Then use algebra tiles to solve the equation.

+		+ +		+ + + + +
+	+	+	=	+ + + +

Banking For Exercises 47–49, write an equation to model each banking situation. Identify the variable you use. Solve each equation and check your solution.

Midstate Bank

SAVINGS
WITHDRAWAL
$165.00

CURRENT
BALANCE
$357.49

47. Shellie withdrew money from her bank account to buy a used mountain bike. What was the balance in her account before the withdrawal?

48. Darius is saving money for a trip with the Spanish club. What was the increase in his savings this month?

Midstate Bank   SAVINGS ACCOUNT

BEGINNING BALANCE	ENDING BALANCE
$1271.63	$1453.95

49. Darius expected his ending balance to be $1450.24. What was the amount of interest he forgot to include?

50. Writing Describe how you would solve the equation $n - 49.75 = 682.94$ using a calculator.

Choosing a Method Tell whether you would use mental math or paper and pencil to solve each equation. Then solve.

51. $17.3 + a = 62.1$ **52.** $b - 11 = 4$ **53.** $y - 237 = 54$

54. $t - 8 = 20.5$ **55.** $11 = 6 + s$ **56.** $c + 35 = 88$

Reflecting ◀▶ on the Section

57. Research the terms of three former members of Congress from your state who were elected after 1933 and who served full terms. Let y = the number of years served. Write and solve both an addition equation and a subtraction equation to model each situation. Check each solution.

Spiral ◀▶ Review

Round each decimal to the given place. (Module 4, p. 225)

58. 64.37 (ones)   **59.** 13.403 (hundredths)

60. 2.97 (tenths)   **61.** 0.3611 (thousandths)

Tell whether each combination of side lengths can form a triangle. Explain your reasoning. (Module 2, p. 106)

62. 2 in., 6 in., 7 in.   **63.** 5 cm, 8 cm, 3 cm

64. 2 ft, 35 ft, 13 ft   **65.** 1 m, 0.7 m, 0.4 m

Find each value. (Module 1, p. 62)

66. $\frac{3}{5}$ of 35   **67.** $\frac{9}{10}$ of 80   **68.** $\frac{7}{8}$ of 24

Find each product. (Module 3, p. 178)

69. $\frac{3}{5} \cdot \frac{7}{9}$ **70.** $\frac{9}{10} \cdot 1\frac{2}{3}$ **71.** $2\frac{3}{4} \cdot 1\frac{1}{8}$

Tell whether each number is divisible by 2, 3, 5, 9, and 10. (Module 3, p. 157)

72. 75   **73.** 630   **74.** 253

Stem-and-Leaf Plots

SET UP *You will need Labsheet 4A.*

GOAL

LEARN HOW TO...
♦ make and interpret a stem-and-leaf plot

AS YOU...
♦ compare dinosaur data

KEY TERM
♦ stem-and-leaf plot

▶ A *Euoplocephalus* seems large compared with animals alive today, but how did it compare with other plant-eating dinosaurs? Because the sizes of dinosaurs varied so much, an average size may not tell you much. Instead, it may be more useful to make a **stem-and-leaf plot**.

Some Plant-Eating Dinosaurs	
Dinosaur	**Length (feet)**
Anatosaurus	40
Ankylosaurus	25
Centrosaurus	20
Chasmosaurus	16
Corythosaurus	33
Edmontonia	23
Edmontosaurus	43
Euoplocephalus	18
Hadrosaurus	33
Pachyrhinosaurus	20
Panoplosaurus	23
Parasaurolophus	33
Parksosaurus	7
Sauropelta	25
Styracosaurus	18
Tenontosaurus	24
Torosaurus	20
Triceratops	30

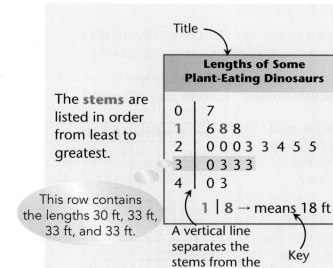

The **stems** are listed in order from least to greatest.

Lengths of Some Plant-Eating Dinosaurs

Title

```
0 | 7
1 | 6 8 8
2 | 0 0 0 3 3 4 5 5
3 | 0 3 3 3
4 | 0 3
```

1 | 8 → means 18 ft

The **leaf** of each data value is written to the right of its stem.

This row contains the lengths 30 ft, 33 ft, 33 ft, and 33 ft.

A vertical line separates the stems from the leaves.

Key

3 Discussion Use the stem-and-leaf plot above.

a. Explain what "4 | 0 3" means.

b. How many of the plant-eating dinosaurs were 18 ft long?

c. Why do you think the numbers 0 through 4 were used as the stems in the stem-and-leaf plot?

d. Was the *Euoplocephalus* long or short compared with the other plant-eating dinosaurs in the table? Explain.

4 **a.** Are the answers to parts (b) and (d) of Question 3 easier to determine from the table or from the stem-and-leaf plot? Explain.

   b. What information from the table do you lose by showing the data in a stem-and-leaf plot?

   c. Why does a stem-and-leaf plot require a key?

Use Labsheet 4A for Questions 5 and 6.

5 **Try This as a Class** Follow the directions on the labsheet to complete the stem-and-leaf plot for the *Weights of Plant-Eating Dinosaurs*.

6 Look at your stem-and-leaf plot from Question 5.

   a. Why is there no leaf for the stem 1?

   b. What are the modes of the plant-eating dinosaur weights?

   c. What is the median of the weights?

   d. How did the weight of a *Euoplocephalus* compare with the weights of the other plant-eating dinosaurs in the table?

   e. How are the stem-and-leaf plots for the weights and lengths of the plant-eating dinosaurs similar? How are they different?

▶ Stem-and-leaf plots can also be used to compare the lengths of predatory dinosaurs with the lengths of the plant-eating dinosaurs they ate.

✔ QUESTION 7

...checks that you can make and interpret a stem-and-leaf plot.

7 ✔ **CHECKPOINT** Make a stem-and-leaf plot for the lengths of the predatory dinosaurs in the table.

   a. How did an 18-foot-long *Euoplocephalus* compare in length with the predatory dinosaurs?

   b. Use your stem-and-leaf plot and the one on page 249. How did the lengths of the plant-eating dinosaurs compare with the lengths of the predatory dinosaurs?

Some Predatory Dinosaurs	
Dinosaur	**Length (feet)**
Albertosaurus	26
Allosaurus	35
Chirostenotes	7
Daspletosaurus	30
Deinonychus	13
Dromaeosaurus	6
Dromiceiomimus	11
Microvenator	4
Nanotyrannous	17
Ornithomimus	13
Struthiomimus	13
Troodon	8
Tyrannosaurus rex	40
Velociraptor	7

HOMEWORK EXERCISES ▶ See Exs. 1–14 on pp. 257–258.

GOAL

LEARN HOW TO...
- divide by a decimal

AS YOU...
- explore the feeding habits of predatory dinosaurs

Dividing. by a)Decimal

SET UP *You will need Labsheet 4B.*

Some scientists believe that dinosaurs ate, slept, and moved more like birds than like lizards. Assuming that is true, scientists can calculate how much and how often dinosaurs ate.

▶ **A 6-kilogram *Microvenator* needed to eat about 0.4 kg of meat a day. Suppose the animals it hunted had a mass of about 0.05 kg each.**

8 What would you do to find out how many animals a *Microvenator* needed to catch each day?

Use Labsheet 4B for Questions 9 and 10.

9 One way to find how many animals a *Microvenator* needed to catch each day is to divide 0.4 by 0.05. Follow the directions on the labsheet to model the division 0.4 ÷ 0.05 on the *Animal Division Grid.*

10 ✔ **CHECKPOINT** Use the *Division Grids* to find 0.60 ÷ 0.15, 0.28 ÷ 0.04, and 0.45$\overline{)0.9}$.

✔ **QUESTION 10**

...checks that you can use a grid to divide by a decimal.

11 **Discussion** Look for patterns in the divisions.

	dividend		
6$\overline{)12}$	18$\overline{)36}$	60$\overline{)120}$	600$\overline{)1200}$

divisor

a. How is the divisor of 6 in the first division related to each of the other divisors?

b. How is the dividend of 12 related to each of the other dividends?

c. Write another division problem that has the same divisor and dividend relationship with the first division.

d. Find all five quotients. What do you notice about them?

e. What happens to a quotient when you multiply the dividend and the divisor by the same number?

▶ In Section 3, you divided a decimal by a whole number. You can use this skill and the pattern you found in Question 11 to divide a decimal or a whole number by a decimal.

FOR◄HELP
with *multiplying by powers of ten*, see
MODULE 4, p. 208

12 **Try This as a Class** A 68-kilogram *Deinonychus* needed to eat a mean of about 2.6 kg of meat per day. Suppose a *Deinonychus* ate 12.48 kg of a *Hadrosaurus* all at once. To find out in how many days it needed to eat again, you can do this division:

$$2.6\overline{)12.48}$$

a. What is the least power of ten that 2.6 can be multiplied by to make it a whole number?

b. If you multiply the divisor by the number you found in part (a), what must you do to the dividend to keep the quotient from changing?

c. Rewrite the division by performing the operations described in parts (a) and (b). Then find the quotient. In how many days did the *Deinonychus* need to eat again?

13 **Discussion** To find the quotient $0.25\overline{)28}$, Roland rewrote the division as $25\overline{)280}$. Is this correct? Explain.

✔ **QUESTION 14**

...checks that you can divide by a decimal.

14 ✔ **CHECKPOINT** Find each quotient.

a. $0.9\overline{)0.072}$ b. $0.426 \div 0.12$ c. $2.4\overline{)9}$

15 A *Velociraptor* had a mass of about 70 kg and ate about one fourth of its own body weight in meat at one sitting.

a. How much would a *Velociraptor* eat at one sitting?

b. Suppose a pack of *Velociraptors* ate a 448-kilogram *Tenontosaur*. For about how many *Velociraptors* did the *Tenontosaur* provide a full meal?

HOMEWORK EXERCISES ▶ See Exs. 15–30 on pp. 258–259.

Exploration 3

SET UP *You will need Labsheets 4C and 4D.*

GOAL

LEARN HOW TO...
- graph pairs of values on a coordinate grid

AS YOU...
- play the game *Guess My Rule*

KEY TERMS
- ordered pair
- coordinate grid
- axes
- origin

▶ **In Exploration 2, you learned that a *Microvenator* needed to eat about 0.4 kg of meat a day.**

16 a. Copy and complete the following table.

Number of days	1	2	6	14
Kilograms of meat needed	0.4	0.8	?	?

b. How would you find the kilograms of meat needed for *d* days?

▶ **In Module 1, you learned that relationships like the one between the number of days and the kilograms of meat a *Microvenator* needed to eat can be written as equations.**

First Choose a variable to represent each of the quantities that are unknown or may change.

Let *d* = the number of days.   Let *m* = the kilograms of meat.

Next Represent the word relationship with symbols and variables.

The kilograms of meat are equal to 0.4 times the number of days.

$$m \qquad = \qquad 0.4 \cdot \qquad d$$

17 Discussion

a. What operation is used in the expression 0.4*d*?

b. Why do you think the symbol for the operation was omitted?

c. Give an example of an expression in which the multiplication symbol could not be omitted.

▶ As you play *Guess My Rule,* you will practice writing equations to represent word relationships.

Guess My Rule

Players alternate turns. On your turn:

◆ Your partner takes a rule card without showing it to you.

◆ You try to guess the hidden rule by giving input values (numbers) one at a time. Your partner will apply the rule on the card to the input and tell you the result, or the output.

◆ You can give at most ten input values, and you can try guessing the rule after any of them. Your turn ends when you correctly guess the rule, or when you have made three incorrect guesses.

The player who correctly guesses the most rules wins.

Sample Turn

Input I	Output O	Guess	Response
2	4	$O = I + 2$	Incorrect
0	0	(no guess made)	
3	6	$O = 2 \cdot I$	Correct

18 **Use Labsheet 4C.** Play *Guess My Rule* using the eight rule cards. Give the rules as equations in which the variable I represents the input and O represents the output.

19 Did you use a special strategy for choosing the input values when you were guessing a rule? If so, describe your strategy.

▶ Each input and output value in *Guess My Rule* can be written as an **ordered pair.** An example is shown in the table below.

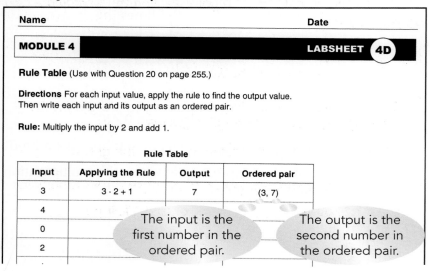

Name _____ Date _____

MODULE 4 **LABSHEET** **4D**

Rule Table (Use with Question 20 on page 255.)

Directions For each input value, apply the rule to find the output value. Then write each input and its output as an ordered pair.

Rule: Multiply the input by 2 and add 1.

Rule Table

Input	Applying the Rule	Output	Ordered pair
3	$3 \cdot 2 + 1$	7	(3, 7)
4			
0			
2			

The input is the first number in the ordered pair.

The output is the second number in the ordered pair.

20 **Use Labsheet 4D.** For each input value, apply the rule to find the output value. Then write each input and its output as an ordered pair. Record your results in the *Rule Table*.

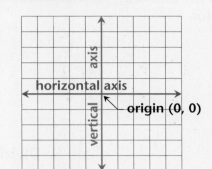

Graphing on a Coordinate Grid

Student Resource

Ordered pairs can be graphed as points on a **coordinate grid**. The grid is formed using two number lines as *axes*. The **axes** intersect at the point (0, 0), called the **origin**.

horizontal axis *vertical axis* *origin (0, 0)*

To graph the ordered pair **(2, 3)** on a coordinate grid, follow these steps.

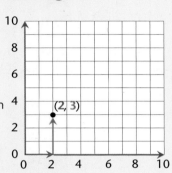

Step 1 Number a scale on each axis.

Step 2 Start at the origin. The first coordinate, **2**, tells you how far to move horizontally.

Step 3 The second coordinate, **3**, tells you how far to move vertically.

Step 4 Plot the point. This is the graph of (2, 3).

---

21 Read the *Student Resource* above. Describe the steps you need to take to graph each ordered pair.

   a. (1, 4)
   b. $\left(2\frac{1}{2}, 3\right)$

Use Labsheet 4D for Questions 22–25.

22 Write the ordered pair for each point *A–D* on the *Coordinate Grid* on your labsheet.

23 ✔ **CHECKPOINT** On the *Empty Coordinate Grid*, graph the ordered pairs you listed in the *Rule Table*.

24 **a.** Draw segments connecting the points you plotted on the *Empty Coordinate Grid* in order from left to right.

   b. What do you notice about the points on the graph?

25 Use your graph from Question 24 to produce the missing value.

   a. input 3.5, output = _?_
   b. output 11, input = _?_

✔ **QUESTION 23**

...checks that you can graph ordered pairs.

HOMEWORK EXERCISES ▶ See Exs. 31–51 on pp. 259–261.

Section ④

Key Concepts

Stem-and-Leaf Plots (pp. 249–250)

One way to compare data is to make a stem-and-leaf plot.

**Total Points Scored in a Girls'
Basketball Championship Game**

stems

0	1 1 3 5 5 5 8
1	0 3 4 7
2	0 2 9

title

leaves

key → 1|4 → means 14 points scored by a player

Dividing by a Decimal (pp. 251–252)

Write a 0 in the tenths place.

Example Find 0.8)0.052.

$$0.8\overline{)0.052}$$
×10 ×10

$$\begin{array}{r} 65 \\ 8\overline{)0.520} \\ \underline{48} \\ 40 \\ \underline{40} \\ 0 \end{array}$$

Write a 0.

$$\begin{array}{r} 0.065 \\ 8\overline{)0.520} \end{array}$$

Multiply both numbers by a number that makes the divisor a whole number.

Divide as you would whole numbers. Add zeros if necessary.

Place the decimal point in the quotient directly above the decimal point in the dividend.

Coordinate Grid (pp. 254–255)

The numbers in an ordered pair give the location of a point on a coordinate grid.

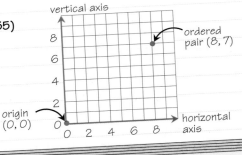

vertical axis

ordered pair (8, 7)

origin (0, 0)

horizontal axis

Key Concepts Questions

26 Use the stem-and-leaf plot above showing the points scored in a basketball game. Find the range, median, and mode of the data.

27 **a.** When dividing by a decimal, how do you know when to add a zero in the dividend? in the quotient?

b. How do you know when the division is complete?

Section 4

Practice & Application Exercises

YOU WILL NEED

For Exs. 35–43, 45–46, and 49:
♦ graph paper

For Exercises 1–3, use the stem-and-leaf plot showing the scores on a math test.

1. What was the low score in the class? the high score?

2. How many students scored in the 70s?

3. Find the mean, the median, and the mode of the scores.

Math Test Scores

```
 6 | 2
 7 | 2  3  5  8
 8 | 2  6  6  6  8
 9 | 5  5  8
10 | 0
```

8 | 2 represents a score of 82

Use the table and the partially completed stem-and-leaf plot to answer Exercises 4-8.

Small and Medium-Sized Predatory Dinosaurs		
Dinosaur	Mass (kg)	Meat Consumption (kg per day)
Chirostenotes	50	2.1
Deinonychus	68	2.6
Dromaeosaurus	45	1.9
Dromiceiomimus	144	4.6
Microvenator	6	0.4
Ornithomimus	153	4.8
Struthiomimus	150	4.7
Troodon	50	2.1
Velociraptor	73	2.7

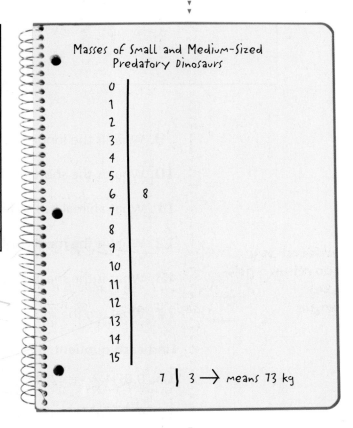

Masses of Small and Medium-Sized Predatory Dinosaurs

```
 0 |
 1 |
 2 |
 3 |
 4 |
 5 |
 6 | 8
 7 |
 8 |
 9 |
10 |
11 |
12 |
13 |
14 |
15 |
```

7 | 3 → means 73 kg

4. Which dinosaur's mass is shown in the stem-and-leaf plot?

5. Why were the numbers 0 through 15 used for the stems?

6. Copy and complete the stem-and-leaf plot.

7. Make a stem-and-leaf plot for the meat consumption of the dinosaurs.

8. **Writing** Compare your stem-and-leaf plots from Exercises 6 and 7. Do they have the same gaps or clusters of data? Explain why you think the plots are alike or different.

Choosing a Data Display Use the bar graph or the stem-and-leaf plot to answer Exercises 9–14. For each question, tell which display you used and why.

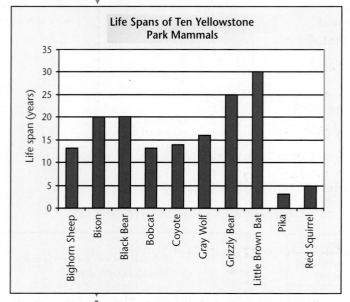

Life Spans of Ten Yellowstone
Park Mammals

```
0 | 3  5
1 | 3  3  4  6
2 | 0  0  5
3 | 0
```

1 | 4 means 14 years

9. What is the longest life span?

10. What is the shortest life span?

11. What animal has a life span of 16 years?

12. What is the median of the life spans?

13. What is the mean of the life spans?

14. What are the modes of the life spans?

Find each quotient. Show your work.

15. $0.07\overline{)4.2}$

16. $3\overline{)0.06}$

17. $0.3\overline{)0.84}$

18. $0.5\overline{)0.365}$

19. $2.4\overline{)45}$

20. $0.8\overline{)4.9}$

21. $0.002\overline{)0.571}$

22. $7.5\overline{)16.2}$

23. $6.25\overline{)5.6375}$

24. Which of the following division problems have the same quotient?

$1.8 \div 0.9$ $0.09\overline{)18}$ $0.09\overline{)0.18}$ $9\overline{)0.18}$

Section 4

Extra Skill Practice

Use the stem-and-leaf plot for Exercises 1–4.

1. What is Mark's lowest score?

2. What is his highest score?

3. On how many tests did Mark score an 80?

Mark's Science Test Scores
7 | 7 9 9
8 | 0 0 3 3 3 7 7 8 9
9 | 2 4 4 6
10 | 0
9 | 2   means a score of 92

4. Find the mean, the median, and the mode of Mark's scores.

Find each quotient.

5. $0.08\overline{)5.6}$

6. $0.5\overline{)1.28}$

7. $1.8\overline{)6.12}$

8. $0.009\overline{)0.108}$

9. $0.04\overline{)1.174}$

10. $7.5\overline{)70.125}$

11. $6.12\overline{)34.884}$

12. $0.021\overline{)0.1953}$

Name the point that is the graph of each ordered pair.

13. $(7, 3)$

14. $\left(4, 3\frac{1}{2}\right)$

15. $(0, 5)$

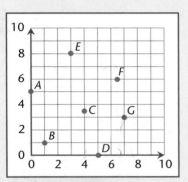

Write the coordinates of each point.

16. B

17. D

18. F

19. The table shows how many hours a machine runs (input) and how many T-shirts it produces (output).

Hours	1	2	3	4	5	20
T-shirts	18	36	54	?	90	?

a. Write a rule for the output based on the input.

b. Use your rule to find the missing values in the table.

Standardized Testing ◀▶ **Performance Task**

Explain why the quotient is always greater than the dividend when the divisor is between 0 and 1. Include at least one example in your explanation.

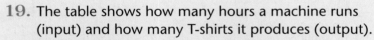

$$\text{Divisor is between 0 and 1.} \overline{)\begin{array}{c}\text{Quotient is greater}\\ \text{than dividend.}\\ \hline \text{Dividend is positive.}\end{array}}$$

Population Growth

Setting the Stage

The graph below shows how the world population has increased from the year 1000 to 2003.

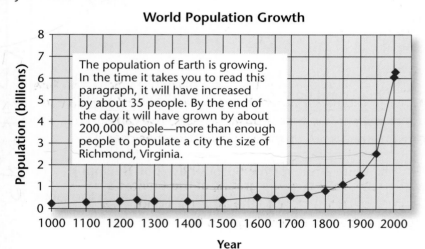

World Population Growth

The population of Earth is growing. In the time it takes you to read this paragraph, it will have increased by about 35 people. By the end of the day it will have grown by about 200,000 people—more than enough people to populate a city the size of Richmond, Virginia.

Population (billions) — vertical axis: 0 to 8

Year — horizontal axis: 1000 1100 1200 1300 1400 1500 1600 1700 1800 1900 2000

Think About It

1 About what year did the world's population reach 1 billion?

2 Was the population increasing faster during the period from 1500 to 1600 or during the period from 1800 to 1900? How can you tell just by looking at the graph?

3 **a.** What was the approximate population of the world in 1950? in 2000?

b. What was the average population increase per year from 1950 to 2000?

4 Suppose the world's population is increasing at the rate you found in Question 3(b).

   a. How much will the population grow today?

   b. How much will it increase in the time it takes you to read the paragraph on the graph?

   c. How do your answers compare to the claims made in the paragraph on the graph?

Exploration 1

Representing Population Data

SET UP *You will need Labsheets 5A and 5B.*

GOAL

LEARN HOW TO...
- make a line graph

AS YOU...
- investigate changes in animal populations

KEY TERM
- line graph

▶ A **line graph** shows changes that take place over time. The line graph in the *Setting the Stage* shows how the world population has changed over the past thousand years. You can also use a line graph to see how an animal population has changed.

5 **Use Labsheet 5A.** Follow the directions on the labsheet to make two line graphs of the *California Condor Population* close to the time the condor was placed on the endangered species list.

6 Look at your line graphs from Question 5.

   a. In what year was the condor population the least?

   b. Which graph did you use to answer part (a)? Why did you use that graph?

   c. How are the scales for the two graphs different?

   d. If you were writing an article claiming that the condor population did not change much from 1953 to 1984, which graph would you choose? Why?

   e. What does the other graph seem to show?

▲
The California condor is the largest bird in North America. It has been on the endangered species list since 1967. An "endangered species" is one that is in danger of becoming extinct throughout all or a significant portion of its range.

▶ In Question 6, you saw how the scale on a line graph affected how the California condor population appeared to change from 1953 to 1984. Now let's look at the condor population from 1997 to 2003.

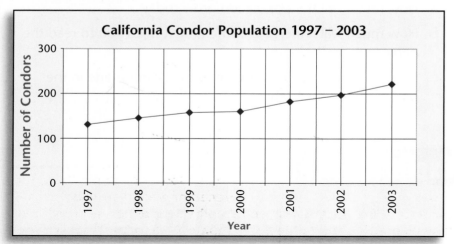

California Condor Population 1997 – 2003

7 **Discussion**

a. Describe the changes in condor population from 1997–2003.

b. How could you alter the scale on the vertical axis to make it look like the condor population increased rapidly from 1997 to 2003?

c. How could you alter the scale on the horizontal axis to make it look like the condor population increased rapidly from 1997 to 2003?

✔ **QUESTION 8**

...checks that you can make a line graph.

8 ✔ **CHECKPOINT**

a. Choose a different scale for at least one of the axes in the *California Condor Population* graph above.

b. **Use Labsheet 5B**. Follow the directions on the labsheet to create your own line graph of the *California Condor Population* from 1997 to 2003.

c. Write a brief paragraph about the change in the condor population shown by your graph. Include predictions for years beyond 2003.

HOMEWORK EXERCISES ▶ See Exs. 1–9 on pp. 271–272.

Choosing an
AVERAGE

SET UP *You will need: • Labsheet 5C • calculator*

▶ **When the population of a species reaches low enough numbers, the species may be placed on the threatened or endangered list. Each year since 1980, the U.S. Fish and Wildlife Service has recorded how many mammal, bird, reptile, fish, amphibian, and insect species are listed as endangered or threatened.**

The timber wolf has been listed ▶ as a "threatened species" in all or part of 30 states. A threatened species is one that is likely to become endangered in the foreseeable future.

9 **Try This as a Class** Suppose after examining the U.S. Fish and Wildlife data a reporter began an article as follows:

> ### Number of Endangered and
> ### Threatened Mammals Off
> ### the Charts in 2002!
>
> Prior to 2002, an average of 57 mammal species appeared on the threatened and endangered lists. Yet in 2002, the U.S. Fish and Wildlife Service reported a whopping 74 mammal species as threatened or endangered. In 2002 close to twenty more species, nearly 35% more, are in danger of disappearing. Why has the number of mammal species listed risen by more than a third in 2002? Scientists say it is a result of the change in...

a. Do you think the average of 57 mammals is the *mean*, the *median*, or the *mode*? Why?

b. Does the average of 57 mammal species mean that in 2001, fifty-seven mammals were listed as endangered or threatened?

FOR ◀ HELP
with *mean, median,* and *mode* see
MODULE 4, p. 225

10 Use Labsheet 5C.

    a. Find the mean, the median, and the mode of the data in the *Endangered or Threatened Mammal Species Graphs.*

    b. Did the reporter use the mean, the median, or the mode in Question 9?

    c. Why do you think the average in part (b) was used?

    d. Why is it not appropriate for the reporter to compare the number of species listed as endangered or threatened in 2002 to the average for 1980–2001 used in the article?

    e. What information can you get from the line graph that is not represented by the mean, median, or mode?

✔ QUESTION 11

...checks that you can choose an appropriate average and make an appropriate graph for a set of data.

11 ✔ CHECKPOINT Data for the number of species of insects listed as endangered or threatened are shown below.

Year	Number	Year	Number	Year	Number
1980	14	1988	18	1996	29
1981	13	1989	19	1997	37
1982	13	1990	21	1998	37
1983	13	1991	23	1999	37
1984	13	1992	25	2000	42
1985	13	1993	26	2001	44
1986	15	1994	28	2002	44
1987	15	1995	29		

    a. Find the mean, the median, and the mode of the data.

    b. What average from part (a) would you report as the typical yearly number of insect species listed as endangered or threatened?

    c. Make a graph to display the numbers of endangered or threatened insect species. Explain why you think the graph you chose is an appropriate way to display the data.

▶ **When an animal population no longer exists, it is said to be "extinct." The table on the following page contains information about ten dinosaurs that lived in North America from 65 million to 80 million years ago.**

Name	Length (m)	Mass (metric tons)	Usually walked on	Diet
Albertosaurus	11	2.7	2 legs	carnivore
Centrosaurus	6	13.6	4 legs	herbivore
Chasmosaurus	5.2	1.4	4 legs	herbivore
Edmontosaurus	13.1	3.4	2 legs	herbivore
Euoplocephalus	6.1	2.5	4 legs	herbivore
Pachycephalosaurus	5.5	1.8	2 legs	herbivore
Parasaurolophus	10.1	3.5	2 legs	herbivore
Tanius	10.7	2.7	2 legs	herbivore
Triceratops	7.99	6.4	4 legs	herbivore
Tyrannosaurus	15.2	7.3	2 legs	carnivore

12 **Discussion**

   a. How would you describe the average diet of the dinosaurs?

   b. Which average, the mean, the median, or the mode, did you use to answer part (a)? Explain.

   c. What is the average number of legs walked on by the dinosaurs in the table? Explain which average you chose to use.

   d. When is the mode the most appropriate average to use?

13 **a.** Find the mean, the median, and the mode of the masses of the dinosaurs.

   b. The mass of the *Centrosaurus* is quite a bit greater than the masses of the other nine dinosaurs. Find the mean, median, and mode of the masses of the other nine dinosaurs.

   c. Compare your answers to parts (a) and (b). Which average, the mean, the median, or the mode, was most affected by the large mass?

   d. **Discussion** Which average in part (a) best describes the average mass of the ten dinosaurs in the table?

14 **Try This as a Class** Without actually finding the mean, median, and mode, decide which average will best describe the average length of the ten dinosaurs. Explain your choice.

HOMEWORK EXERCISES ▶ See Exs. 10–18 on pp. 273–274.

Key Term

line graph

Key Concepts

Line Graphs (pp. 264–266)

A line graph is often used to show change over time. This line graph shows the population density (number of people per square mile) of the United States during the period 1790–1890.

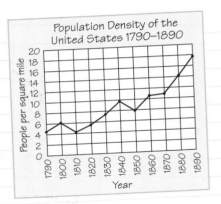

Misleading Graphs (pp. 265–266)

Changing the scales on a line graph can give a different impression of the data.

Choosing an Average (pp. 267–269)

The mean is the most commonly used average. The mean is affected by extreme data.

The median is rarely affected by extreme data values, but if the data are clustered around two different numbers with a large gap in between, the median may give you a false impression of the typical data value.

The mode is best used with categorical data. Movie titles and favorite colors are examples of categorical data.

Key Concepts Questions

15 Use the line graph above. During which 10-year intervals did the number of people per square mile in the United States decrease?

16 **a.** How could you change the numerical scale on the bar graph to make it look like a lot more money was made on the weekend than on weekdays?

b. Do you think the mode would be an appropriate average to use to describe the fundraiser data? Explain.

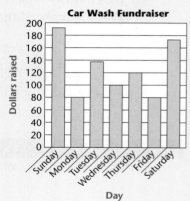

Section 5

1. As part of the wolf recovery program in Yellowstone National Park, wildlife biologists track the number of pups that are born and survive until the end of each year.

Year	Number of wolf pups born
1995	9
1996	11
1997	49
1998	37
1999	38
2000	73

   a. Use the data in the table to create a line graph.

   b. Using your graph, write a brief summary about the number of wolf pups born from 1995 to 2000.

2. The *2000 Living Planet Report* shows the following graphs for two animal populations. Study the graphs.

   Lesser White-Fronted Goose

   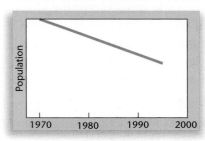

   Silvery Gibbon Monkey

   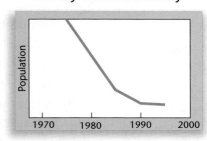

   a. What information do the graphs give about the population of the Lesser White-Fronted Goose? the Silvery Gibbon?

   b. What do you notice about these graphs that may make the information misleading?

Use Labsheet 5D for Exercises 3–5.

3. Look at Graph 1 on Labsheet 5D.

   a. Which state has the greatest percent of people that drive to work alone?

   b. For each state, estimate the difference between the percent of people who carpool or use public transit and the percent of people who drive alone. Which state has the greatest difference?

4. Complete Part II of Labsheet 5D to create a new double bar graph of the ways people get to work.

5. a. In Vermont, the percent of commuters who carpool or use public transit to get to work is about one half the percent of commuters who drive alone. Do Graph 1 and Graph 2 both show this relationship? Explain.

   b. Which graph seems to show that very few people carpool or use public transit? How does it show this?

   c. Which graph would you use if you wanted to show that a large percent of workers in these five states carpool or use public transit? Why?

   d. How are the scales different for each graph?

6. In 1972, Yellowstone Park began a *Do Not Feed The Bears* campaign to minimize contact between bears and humans. Bear-proof trash cans and dumpsters were installed at campgrounds and picnic areas. The effect of the campaign can be seen in the graph.

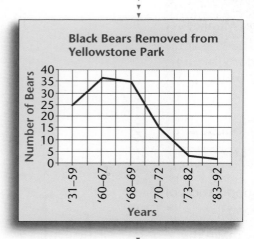

Black Bears Removed from Yellowstone Park

   a. Explain how you could alter either the horizontal or the vertical scale of the graph to make it appear that the number of black bears that had to be removed from the park for unfavorable contact with humans has decreased even more rapidly since the 1972 *Do Not Feed the Bears* campaign.

   b. Explain how you could alter either the horizontal or the vertical scale to make the 1972 *Do Not Feed the Bears* campaign appear less effective.

   c. What do you notice about the scale for the years?

   d. Do you think this is an appropriate way to display the data? Explain.

Tell whether you would use a *line graph*, a *bar graph*, or a *stem-and-leaf plot* for each situation.

7. After a bench press contest, the local gym wants to display the heaviest weights that different contestants were able to press.

8. Your principal wants to see how the number of students has changed over the past six years.

9. The Humane Society wants to compare the number of female and male dogs, female and male cats, and female and male birds it has placed in homes this year.

10. **Science** The chart lists the number of moons for each planet in our solar system.

    a. Find the mean, the median, and the mode of the data.

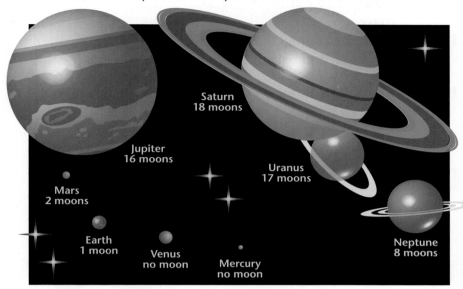

Saturn
18 moons

Jupiter
16 moons

Uranus
17 moons

Mars
2 moons

Earth
1 moon

Venus
no moon

Mercury
no moon

Neptune
8 moons

    b. Which, if any, of the averages would you use to describe the typical number of moons for a planet in our solar system? Why?

Tell whether the *mean*, the *median*, or the *mode* best describes each set of data. Explain your choice.

11. Number of bees in eight hives

| 293 | 355 | 25 | 92 | 470 | 600 | 71 | 50 |

12. Number of ants in five colonies

| 8200 | 7004 | 5216 | 60,000 | 8991 |

13. Number of students in nine college classes

| 18 | 14 | 52 | 15 | 20 | 61 | 21 | 22 | 22 |

14. **Open-ended**

    a. List the ages of five people in your family. Explain which type of average you think is most appropriate to use to describe the data.

    b. List the ages of five of your friends. Which average best describes these ages?

    c. Combine your lists from parts (a) and (b). Which average would you use to describe these ages?

Challenge Tell which type of average you think was used to make each statement. Explain your reasoning.

15. More students at Glenmore Middle School chose swimming as their favorite sport than chose any other sport.

16. The Swansons just had their first child. The average height of the mother, father, and baby is 5 ft 6 in.

17. A group of students took a survey and found that the average person uses a toothbrush 2.8 times a day.

RESEARCH

Exercise 18 checks that you understand how graphs and averages can be misleading.

Reflecting ◀▶ on the Section

18. a. Find a line graph or bar graph in a magazine or newpaper.

    b. What is the graph trying to show about the data?

    c. How could you change the scale on the graph so that it gives a different message?

    d. Was an average used with the graph? If so, does the average give the same message as the graph?

Spiral ◀▶ Review

Give two ways to name each figure. If two ways are not possible, explain why. (Module 2, pp. 106–107)

19.
W • —————— • T

20.
C ∕ A →

21.
A ——— Y →
P ↘

22. You place 2 blue, 1 red, and 3 green marbles in a bag. You choose a marble without looking. What is the probability of choosing the marble described? (Module 2, p. 80)

    a. blue marble

    b. yellow marble

    c. green or red marble

    d. marble that is not red

23. Find the prime factorization of 84. (Module 3, p. 158)

In Exercises 1–6, use the graph below showing the number of grizzly bears removed from Yellowstone Park before and after the 1972 *Do Not Feed the Bears* campaign was put into effect.

1. What impression does the line graph give you about the number of grizzlies removed before and after the 1972 campaign?

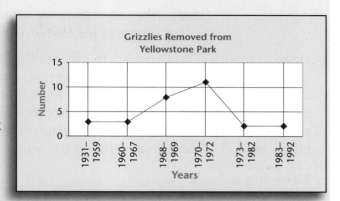

2. Describe a way you could change the vertical scale to create a different impression of the data.

3. Use the method you described in Exercise 2 to draw another line graph for the data.

4. Would a bar graph be an appropriate way to display the data? a circle graph? a line plot? a stem-and-leaf plot? Explain why or why not.

5. What would you report as the average number of grizzlies removed for the 4 time intervals before the campaign in 1972? for the 2 time intervals after the campaign? Tell which type of average you would report and why.

6. How do your averages compare to the numbers of black bears removed during the same time? See Exercise 6, p. 272.

Standardized Testing ◀▶ Open-ended

1. Explain which type of average, mean, median, or mode, best represents the Asian elephant population in the countries listed.

Estimated Populations of Asian Elephants in 2000				
Country	Bangladesh	Cambodia	China	Laos	Vietnam
Number	195	200	250	950	109

2. Which of the averages could be misleading?

The Module Project

Be a Reporter

Extra! Extra! Read all about it!

> *"Study shows that there are over a million pet snakes in the United States."*

How do reporters find answers to questions like "How many pet snakes are in the United States?" Using mathematics, of course! Your project is to collect data about a topic that interests you and to write a newpaper article about the topic. The mathematics you have learned in this module will help you organize, interpret, and present your results in the article.

SET UP

You will need:
* *Project Labsheet A*

Choosing a Topic

1 With your group, decide on a topic to investigate and what you want to find out about that topic. You may choose one of the topics below or come up with your own idea.

* Junk food   * Computers   * TV viewing
* Shopping   * Phone use   * Reading
* Sports   * Music   * Pets

Designing a Survey Over the next few days, you will design a *survey* to collect information about your topic. A survey is a set of questions that you ask a group of people.

2 Decide what population, or group of people, you are interested in (for example, just sixth graders or just teachers).

3 **Use Project Labsheet A.** Follow the steps on the *Survey Worksheet* to write the questions for your survey.

Survey on Pets
1. How many pets do you own?

2. Name each kind of pet you own and how many of each kind you own.

3. What is your favorite pet?

Collecting Your Data Over the next week, you will probably only be able to survey a sample of your population. Usually, the larger the sample, the more accurate your results will be.

4 What do you think your sample size should be in order for your results to be accurate?

5 Now collect your data.

Displaying Your Data After you collect your data, you need to show how people answered your survey questions. Visual displays can quickly help readers understand your results.

6 For each of your survey questions, decide whether a bar graph, a double bar graph, a line plot, a stem-and-leaf plot, or a line graph will best represent the data you are collecting. Consider whether one type of display provides information that another does not.

7 Create your displays. Make sure that anyone looking at them can understand the results of your survey.

Choosing an Average Sometimes a single number can give readers a good idea of what a set of data is like. Now you will look closely at the information you have collected and choose one or more averages to summarize and describe your data.

8 If possible, find the mean, the median, and the mode for the results of each of your survey questions.

9 Think about which average best represents your data for each of your survey questions. Write a paragraph describing your survey results. Be sure you include each of the averages you chose.

Summarizing Your Results Besides gathering data, a newspaper reporter must also present data to readers. Newspaper articles often have visual displays as well as a written summary of the results of a survey.

10 Write your own newspaper article summarizing your group's survey results. Include information on whom you surveyed and why you picked your topic.

11 Include one or more visual displays of your data in your article. These should be described either in the text of the article or in a caption below the display.

12 Write a headline for your article. It should catch your readers' interest and describe what the article is about.

13 Read your entire newspaper article. Make sure it is clear and accurately represents the data you collected.

You will need: • *graph paper* (Ex. 30)

Replace each ? with the value that makes the statement true. (Sec. 1, Explor. 3)

1. 8 km = ? m
2. 2.3 cm = ? mm
3. 1300 mg = ? g
4. 2.3 kg = ? g
5. 5 m = ? cm
6. 4 metric tons = ? kg

Use the table to answer Exercises 7–13. (Sec. 2, Explors. 1–3)

7. What is the range of the speeds?

8. Make a line plot of the data.

9. How many animals have a maximum speed less than 20 mi/hr?

10. Are there any clusters or gaps in the data? Explain.

11. Use the table and your line plot to help estimate the maximum speed of each animal below.

    a. Bison
    b. Pika

12. Find the mean, the median, and the mode(s) of the data. If necessary, round your answers to the nearest tenth.

13. Which average, the mean, the median, or the mode, do you think best describes the maximum speed of the animals? Explain.

Maximum Speed of Some Yellowstone Park Mammals	
Animal	Speed (mi/hr)
Beaver	6
Coyote	43
Elk	45
Gray Wolf	42
Grizzly Bear	30
Ground Squirrel	8
Mule Deer	35
Rabbit	35
Raccoon	15
Red Fox	48
Red Squirrel	12
White-tailed Deer	30

Find each quotient. (Sec. 3, Explor. 1)

14. $6\overline{)21.03}$
15. $18\overline{)354.69}$
16. $\dfrac{7}{10}$

17. Jon bought 45 baseball cards. He now has 315. Write an equation to model the situation. Identify the variable you use. (Sec. 3, Explor. 2)

Solve each equation. Check each solution. (Sec. 3, Explors. 2 and 3)

18. $d - 33 = 18$
19. $25 + f = 47$
20. $2.6 + k = 7.3$
21. $s - 1.75 = 3.8$
22. $0.1 + x = 8$
23. $15 = w - 6$

Find each quotient. (Sec. 4, Explor. 2)

24. $1.4\overline{)1653.54}$
25. $50\overline{)48.944}$
26. $2.5\overline{)3.06}$

Use the stem-and-leaf plot below to answer Exercises 27–29. (Sec. 4, Explor. 1)

Copperhead Snake Lengths

6	1 5 5
7	2 7 7 7 9
8	0 1 6 6 6
9	0 0 1

7 | 2 means 72 cm

27. What is the length of the longest snake in the stem-and-leaf plot?

28. What is the range of the snake lengths?

29. Find the median and the mode(s) of the snake lengths.

30. a. Graph the ordered pairs in the table on a coordinate grid. (Sec. 4, Explor. 3)

Input	3	7	4	8
Output	7	15	9	17

b. Draw segments to connect the points in order from left to right.

c. Use your graph to predict the missing values.

input $5\frac{1}{2}$, output = ?   output 10, input = ?

Use the graphs to answer Exercises 31–33. (Sec. 5, Explor. 1)

Graph 1

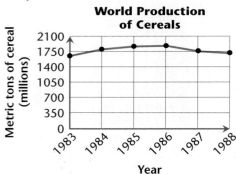

Graph 2

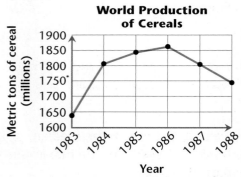

31. The median annual cereal production in the world was 1.8 billion metric tons in the years 1983 through 1988. Which graph do you think shows this fact the best? Why?

32. Which graph would you use to try to show that cereal production in the world did not change much in the years 1983 through 1988? Why?

33. What changes were made to the graph on the left to create the different view of the data shown by the graph on the right?

Reflecting ◀▶ on the Module

34. **Writing** Mathematics can be a powerful tool. Explain how you think people use mathematics to discover and to show how the population and the environment change.

CREATING THINGS

The Module Project

Creating Cubes

Origami is an ancient Japanese art of paper-folding. It can be used to create animals and other shapes. No scissors or glue are needed. With your knowledge of fractions and measurement learned in this module, you will follow steps to create a cube by paper folding.

More on the Module Project
See pp. 357–359.

INTERNET
Resources and practice at
classzone.com

281

Section ① Comparing Fractions

IN THIS SECTION

EXPLORATION 1
◆ Fraction Number Sense

EXPLORATION 2
◆ Common Denominators

Paper Folding

Setting the Stage

SET UP *You will need: • Labsheet 1A • scissors • tape*

SADAKO AND THE THOUSAND PAPER CRANES

by Eleanor Coerr with paintings by Ronald Himler

This story takes place in Japan. In the excerpt below, Chizuko visits her friend, Sadako, who is very ill and in the hospital.

> Chizuko was pleased with herself. "I've figured out a way for you to get well," she said proudly. "Watch!" She cut a piece of gold paper into a large square. In a short time she had folded it over and over into a beautiful crane.
>
> Sadako was puzzled. "But how can that paper bird make me well?"
>
> "Don't you remember that old story about the crane?" Chizuko asked. "It's supposed to live for a thousand years. If a sick person folds one thousand paper cranes, the gods will grant her wish and make her healthy again." She handed the crane to Sadako. "Here's your first one."

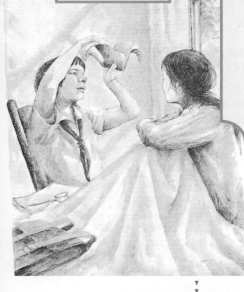

Think About It

1 As the story continues, Sadako folds 644 paper cranes and her classmates fold the rest. Together they fold 1000 cranes.

   a. What fraction of the cranes does Sadako fold?

   b. Write the fraction from part (a) as a decimal.

   c. Write the fraction of the cranes Sadako's classmates fold as a decimal.

2 Use Labsheet 1A. Paper folding can be fun, but cranes are challenging to make. Instead follow the directions in parts (a)–(d) to fold a strip of paper into a trihexaflexagon.

  a. Complete Steps 1 and 2 on the labsheet.

  b. What fraction of the strip is marked with a 1? Be sure to count both the front and the back of the strip.

  c. Complete Steps 3–6 on the labsheet.

  d. Complete Steps 1–4 below.

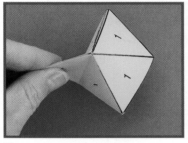

1 Pinch two adjacent triangles together with your thumb and index finger.

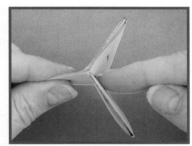

2 Push on the line segment directly across from the two pinched triangles.

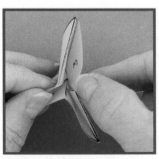

3 Using both thumbs pull open the flexagon from the top center point.

4 A different number will appear on all the triangles.

Note: If your flexagon did not open, pinch two different adjacent triangles and try again.

▶ **When you think of using mathematics to create things, you may imagine spaceships, skyscrapers, robots, and other examples of modern technology. But even the designs of simple things involve mathematics. In this module you will see how mathematics is used to create things.**

GOAL

LEARN HOW TO...
◆ use number sense to compare fractions

AS YOU...
◆ fold fractions strips

KEY TERM
◆ inequality

Exploration 1

Fraction Number Sense

SET UP   *You will need:* • Labsheet 1B • scissors

▶ The Japanese art of creating things by folding paper is called *origami*. In this exploration, you will fold paper to make fraction strips. An example of a completed strip is shown below.

The dashed segments show where the paper is folded to form three equal-sized pieces.

Each piece is labeled as $\frac{1}{3}$ of a strip.

| $\frac{1}{3}$ | $\frac{1}{3}$ | $\frac{1}{3}$ |

Use Labsheet 1B for Questions 3 and 4.

3 Cut out the *Fraction Strips* for thirds, sixths, and twelfths. Fold each strip along the dashed segments, and label each part with the fraction name. (The strip for thirds is already labeled.)

4 Cut out the blank strips and fold them so that one strip is folded into halves, one is folded into fourths, and one is folded into eighths. Label each part with the fraction name.

5 Explain how you folded a strip into eighths.

▶ You can use your strips to compare fractions and to develop your number sense about fractions.

Use fraction strips to compare $\frac{2}{3}$ and $\frac{10}{12}$.

SAMPLE RESPONSE

The original strips are the same length, so you are comparing parts of the same whole.

| $\frac{1}{12}$ | $\frac{1}{12}$ | $\frac{1}{12}$ | $\frac{1}{12}$ | $\frac{1}{12}$ | $\frac{1}{12}$ | $\frac{1}{12}$ | $\frac{1}{12}$ | $\frac{1}{12}$ | $\frac{1}{12}$ | $\frac{1}{12}$ | $\frac{1}{12}$ |

| $\frac{1}{3}$ | $\frac{1}{3}$ | $\frac{1}{3}$ |

First Fold the strip for thirds to show $\frac{2}{3}$.

Then Fold the strip for twelfths to show $\frac{10}{12}$ and place it directly above the $\frac{2}{3}$ strip.

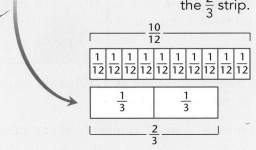

You can see that $\frac{10}{12}$ of a strip is longer than $\frac{2}{3}$ of a strip, so $\frac{10}{12} > \frac{2}{3}$.

▶ A statement such as $\frac{10}{12} > \frac{2}{3}$ that uses the symbol > or < to compare two numbers is an **inequality**.

6 Use your fraction strips to compare each fraction with $\frac{1}{2}$. Replace each _?_ with >, <, or =.

a. $\frac{4}{8}$ _?_ $\frac{1}{2}$
b. $\frac{4}{12}$ _?_ $\frac{1}{2}$
c. $\frac{7}{8}$ _?_ $\frac{1}{2}$

d. $\frac{2}{3}$ _?_ $\frac{1}{2}$
e. $\frac{1}{4}$ _?_ $\frac{1}{2}$
f. $\frac{2}{6}$ _?_ $\frac{1}{2}$

7 **Discussion** Look at your results in Question 6. Just by looking at its numerator and denominator, how can you tell whether a fraction is equal to $\frac{1}{2}$? greater than $\frac{1}{2}$? less than $\frac{1}{2}$?

8 a. Explain how you can use your answers to Question 6, parts (c) and (f), to compare $\frac{7}{8}$ and $\frac{2}{6}$.

b. Write an inequality that compares $\frac{7}{8}$ and $\frac{2}{6}$.

QUESTION 9

...checks that you can compare fractions with $\frac{1}{2}$.

9 ✔ **CHECKPOINT** Use mental math to compare each fraction with $\frac{1}{2}$. Then replace each __?__ with >, <, or =.

  a. $\frac{2}{9}$ _?_ $\frac{13}{15}$ **b.** $\frac{5}{10}$ _?_ $\frac{1}{12}$ **c.** $\frac{5}{12}$ _?_ $\frac{8}{14}$

▶ **Other Patterns** There are other relationships between numerators and denominators that will help you compare fractions.

10 **a.** On each of your fraction strips, fold one part over so the rest of the parts are face down. Arrange the parts facing up in order from shortest to longest and record the fractions in that order.

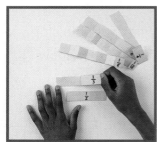

   b. The numerators of the fractions showing on your fraction strips are all 1. What do you notice about the order of the denominators?

   c. Which fraction is greater, $\frac{1}{9}$ or $\frac{1}{4}$? Explain how you decided.

   d. Explain how to order $\frac{2}{6}$, $\frac{2}{4}$, $\frac{2}{3}$, $\frac{2}{2}$, and $\frac{2}{8}$ from least to greatest.

11 **a.** Turn each fraction strip over so the one section you folded is underneath. For each strip, write the fraction that names the part of the strip you can see.

   b. What relationship do you notice between the numerator and the denominator of each fraction?

   c. Arrange the folded strips so the parts you see are in order from shortest to longest and record the fractions in that order.

   d. Which fraction is greater, $\frac{6}{7}$ or $\frac{10}{11}$? Explain how you decided.

   e. Order $\frac{100}{101}$, $\frac{150}{151}$, $\frac{1000}{1001}$, and $\frac{50}{51}$ from least to greatest.

QUESTION 12

...checks that you can use number sense to compare fractions.

12 ✔ **CHECKPOINT** Replace each __?__ with >, <, or =.

  a. $\frac{3}{15}$ _?_ $\frac{3}{10}$ **b.** $\frac{1}{9}$ _?_ $\frac{1}{11}$ **c.** $\frac{8}{9}$ _?_ $\frac{10}{11}$

HOMEWORK EXERCISES ▶ See Exs. 1–15 on p. 291.

Common Denominators

GOAL

LEARN HOW TO...
- use common denominators to write equivalent fractions
- use decimals to compare fractions

AS YOU...
- choose a method to compare fractions

KEY TERMS
- common denominator
- least common denominator

SET UP *You will need a calculator.*

▸ Thelma wants to fold a one-inch strip into thirds. Her ruler does not show thirds of an inch. She thinks $\frac{1}{3}$ is a little less than $\frac{3}{8}$.

13 **Discussion** Use one of the number sense methods you learned in Exploration 1 to compare $\frac{1}{3}$ and $\frac{3}{8}$.

▸ **Using Equivalent Fractions to Compare** One way to compare fractions with different denominators is to find equivalent fractions that are easy to compare.

14 **a.** Copy and complete each list of equivalent fractions.

$$\frac{1}{3} = \frac{?}{6} = \frac{?}{9} = \frac{?}{12} = \frac{?}{15} = \frac{?}{18} = \frac{?}{21} = \frac{?}{24} = \frac{?}{27}$$

$$\frac{3}{8} = \frac{?}{16} = \frac{?}{24} = \frac{?}{32} = \frac{?}{40}$$

b. Use the fractions with 24 as the denominator to compare $\frac{1}{3}$ and $\frac{3}{8}$. Was Thelma correct?

c. Suppose you continue to list equivalent fractions for $\frac{1}{3}$ and $\frac{3}{8}$. What is the next denominator common to both lists?

▸ A **common denominator** of two or more fractions is a common multiple of their denominators. The **least common denominator** of two or more fractions is the least common multiple (LCM) of their denominators. The least common denominator of $\frac{1}{3}$ and $\frac{3}{8}$ is 24, which is the LCM of 3 and 8.

> **FOR ◂ HELP**
> with *least common multiples,* see
> **MODULE 3, p. 168**

15 **Try This as a Class** Complete the following to compare $\frac{5}{8}$ and $\frac{7}{10}$.

   a. Find the least common denominator of $\frac{5}{8}$ and $\frac{7}{10}$.

   b. What else must you do to compare the two fractions in part (a)?

   c. Is $\frac{5}{8}$ *greater than*, *less than*, or *equal to* $\frac{7}{10}$?

EXAMPLE

Use a common denominator to compare $\frac{5}{6}$ and $\frac{7}{9}$.

SAMPLE RESPONSE

First Find a common multiple of the denominators.

multiples of 6: 6, 12, **18**, ...

multiples of 9: 9, **18**, ...

18 is the least common multiple of 6 and 9, so **18** is also a common denominator of $\frac{5}{6}$ and $\frac{7}{9}$.

Then Write equivalent fractions using a common denominator.

$$\frac{5}{6} = \frac{15}{18} \qquad\qquad \frac{7}{9} = \frac{14}{18}$$

$$\frac{15}{18} > \frac{14}{18}, \text{ so } \frac{5}{6} > \frac{7}{9}.$$

---

16 **Discussion** Suppose you use 54 as the common denominator to write equivalent fractions in the Example.

   a. What will the new numerators be?

   b. Will the final answer be the same? Explain.

✔ QUESTION 17

...checks that you can compare fractions using a common denominator.

17 ✔ **CHECKPOINT** Replace each __?__ with >, <, or =.

   a. $\frac{5}{7}$ __?__ $\frac{3}{4}$
   b. $\frac{13}{15}$ __?__ $\frac{4}{5}$
   c. $\frac{17}{20}$ __?__ $\frac{21}{25}$

▶ **Using Decimals to Compare** When the common denominator is difficult to find, you may choose to compare fractions by changing the fractions to decimals.

18 Write $\frac{22}{100}$ and $\frac{3}{8}$ as decimals. Use the decimals to compare the fractions.

19 🖩 Calculator Complete the following to compare $\frac{9}{44}$ and $\frac{8}{31}$.

   a. Enter 9 ÷ 4 4 = to change $\frac{9}{44}$ to a decimal.
   Explain why these are the correct keys to press.

   b. Use your calculator to change $\frac{8}{31}$ to a decimal.

   c. Use the decimals from parts (a) and (b) to compare $\frac{9}{44}$ and $\frac{8}{31}$.

20 Write each fraction as a decimal rounded to the nearest
   hundredth. Then replace each __?__ with >, <, or =.

   a. $\frac{5}{13}$ __?__ $\frac{4}{11}$

   b. $\frac{17}{26}$ __?__ $\frac{55}{100}$

   c. $\frac{22}{250}$ __?__ $\frac{16}{189}$

21 Would you use *number sense, mental math, paper and pencil*, or a
   calculator to compare $\frac{10}{11}$ and $\frac{120}{121}$? Explain.

22 Thelma wants to fold a one-inch strip into fifths. She thinks $\frac{1}{5}$ is
   less than the $\frac{1}{4}$ mark on her ruler. Is she correct? Explain.

23 In the *Setting the Stage*, $\frac{4}{9}$ of one side of the strip used to make
   the trihexaflexagon was labeled with a 1, and $\frac{1}{3}$ of the same side
   was labeled with a 3.

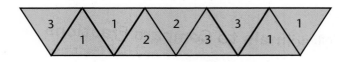

   a. What fraction of this side of the strip was labeled with a 2?

   b. Use the side of the strip in part (a). Compare the fraction of
   the strip labeled with a 2 to the fraction of the strip labeled
   with a 3.

HOMEWORK EXERCISES ▶ See Exs. 16–32 on pp. 291–293.

Key Concepts

inequality

Inequality (pp. 284–285)

A statement that uses the symbol > or < to compare two numbers is an inequality.

Using Number Sense to Compare Fractions (pp. 285–286)

- See if the numerators or the denominators are the same.

Examples $\frac{1}{2} > \frac{1}{3}$, since the numerators are equal and 2 < 3.

$\frac{2}{5} < \frac{3}{5}$, since the denominators are equal and 2 < 3.

- See if one fraction is greater than $\frac{1}{2}$ and the other is less than $\frac{1}{2}$.

Example $\frac{3}{4} > \frac{1}{2}$ and $\frac{2}{9} < \frac{1}{2}$, so $\frac{3}{4} > \frac{2}{9}$.

- See if both fractions are one part less than a whole.

Example $\frac{7}{8} > \frac{6}{7}$, since $\frac{7}{8}$ is closer to a whole.

common denominator

least common denominator

Using a Common Denominator to Compare Fractions (pp. 287–288)

You can write equivalent fractions to compare any two fractions.

Example $\frac{2}{3} > \frac{5}{8}$, since $\frac{16}{24} > \frac{15}{24}$.

24 is the least common denominator.

Using Decimals to Compare Fractions (pp. 288–289)

You can use decimals to compare any two fractions.

Example $\frac{3}{10} = 0.3$ and 4 ÷ 11 results in ⎡0.3636364⎤ ,

so $\frac{3}{10} < \frac{4}{11}$.

24 **Key Concepts Question** What method would you use to compare each pair of fractions? Explain.

a. $\frac{7}{15}$ and $\frac{3}{5}$ b. $\frac{6}{9}$ and $\frac{8}{9}$ c. $\frac{5}{13}$ and $\frac{12}{19}$

Section 1

1. **Visual Thinking** Is the fraction strip folded into fifths? Explain.

Write an inequality or equation that compares each fraction with $\frac{1}{2}$.

2. $\frac{5}{8}$ 3. $\frac{2}{4}$ 4. $\frac{2}{3}$ 5. $\frac{5}{12}$

Write the fractions in order from least to greatest.

6. $\frac{5}{7}, \frac{5}{10}, \frac{5}{6}, \frac{5}{100}, \frac{5}{3}$ 7. $\frac{9}{10}, \frac{99}{100}, \frac{2}{3}, \frac{49}{50}$

Mental Math Use number sense to compare the fractions.
Replace each ? with >, <, or =.

8. $\frac{7}{15}$? $\frac{7}{12}$ 9. $\frac{59}{60}$? $\frac{58}{59}$

10. $\frac{47}{100}$? $\frac{24}{36}$ 11. $\frac{19}{20}$? $\frac{5}{6}$

12. $\frac{15}{22}$? $\frac{15}{23}$ 13. $\frac{11}{18}$? $\frac{9}{20}$

14. **Algebra Connection** The inequality $x < \frac{3}{4}$ means that x represents any number less than $\frac{3}{4}$. Give two values for x that are fractions and that make the inequality a true statement.

15. **Writing** Kyra and Chloe each bought a pizza and ate half of it. Explain how it is possible that Kyra ate more pizza than Chloe did.

Use a common denominator to compare the fractions. Replace each ? with >, < or =.

16. $\frac{7}{12}$? $\frac{3}{4}$ 17. $\frac{3}{5}$? $\frac{5}{8}$

18. $\frac{7}{20}$? $\frac{3}{8}$ 19. $\frac{5}{6}$? $\frac{4}{7}$

20. $\frac{17}{30}$? $\frac{8}{15}$ 21. $\frac{6}{12}$? $\frac{15}{30}$

Use decimals to compare. Replace each ? with >, <, or =.

22. $\dfrac{93}{126}$ __?__ $\dfrac{321}{400}$

23. $\dfrac{65}{121}$ __?__ $\dfrac{15}{29}$

24. $\dfrac{225}{276}$ __?__ $\dfrac{24}{25}$

Choosing a Method Use mental math, paper and pencil, or a calculator to compare the fractions. Replace each __?__ with >, <, or =.

25. $\dfrac{11}{17}$ __?__ $\dfrac{51}{82}$

26. $\dfrac{45}{160}$ __?__ $\dfrac{101}{200}$

27. $\dfrac{22}{25}$ __?__ $\dfrac{4}{5}$

28. If you could use the calculator for only one comparison in Exercises 25–27, which one would it be? Why?

29. **Probability Connection** Trinja bought 50 of the 540 raffle tickets sold by a sports booster club. Nathan bought 42 of the 490 raffle tickets sold by another booster club. Who is more likely to win a prize?

30. **Industrial Technology** A mechanic needs a socket wrench to remove a bolt. A $\frac{1}{4}$-inch socket is too small. A $\frac{3}{8}$-inch socket is too large. Choose the letter of the size the mechanic should try next. Explain your choice.

    A. $\dfrac{7}{32}$ in.   B. $\dfrac{13}{32}$ in.   C. $\dfrac{5}{16}$ in.   D. $\dfrac{3}{16}$ in.

31. **Challenge** The seven colored shapes shown are used in the Chinese tangram puzzle. Copies of the red triangle can be put together to form each of the other pieces.

    a. Write a fraction that describes what part of the whole square each group of pieces represents.

    Group A   Group B

    Group C

    b. Which group represents the greatest fraction?

    c. Which group represents the least fraction?

Reflecting ◀▶on the Section

Write your response to Exercise 32 in your journal.

32. What types of fractions would you compare using each method? Give an example for each method.

   ◆ number sense

   ◆ a calculator

   ◆ a common denominator

Journal

Exercise 32 checks that you can choose an appropriate method to compare fractions.

Spiral ◀▶Review

Write each fraction as a mixed number (Module 1, p. 47)

33. $\dfrac{11}{2}$ 34. $\dfrac{27}{12}$ 35. $\dfrac{31}{7}$ 36. $\dfrac{13}{3}$

37. Make a stem-and-leaf plot of these daily high temperatures in degrees Fahrenheit for a city in the Midwest during July. (Module 4, p. 256)

July Temperatures:

78, 82, 64, 61, 69, 56, 59, 77, 72, 78, 89, 87,
85, 91, 90, 84, 82, 68, 72, 78, 77, 98, 85, 87,
101, 80, 78, 82, 69, 71, 91

Extension ▶ ▶

Combining Inequalities

Two inequalities can be combined in one math statement. For example, $\dfrac{1}{25} < \dfrac{1}{20}$ and $\dfrac{1}{20} < \dfrac{1}{10}$ can be written as $\dfrac{1}{25} < \dfrac{1}{20} < \dfrac{1}{10}$. Find a fraction that can be used to replace each __?__ .

Read as
"$\dfrac{1}{25}$ is less than $\dfrac{1}{20}$ and $\dfrac{1}{20}$ is less than $\dfrac{1}{10}$."

38. $\dfrac{1}{4} < \underline{\ ?\ } < \dfrac{1}{2}$ 39. $\dfrac{3}{8} < \underline{\ ?\ } < \dfrac{5}{8}$

40. $\dfrac{4}{7} < \underline{\ ?\ } < \dfrac{3}{4}$ 41. $\dfrac{3}{7} < \underline{\ ?\ } < \dfrac{5}{6}$

Compare the fractions. Replace each ? with >, <, or =.

1. $\dfrac{5}{6}$? $\dfrac{5}{8}$

2. $\dfrac{15}{16}$? $\dfrac{30}{32}$

3. $\dfrac{7}{12}$? $\dfrac{1}{4}$

4. $\dfrac{3}{8}$? $\dfrac{3}{14}$

Use a common denominator to compare the fractions. Replace each ? with >, <, or =.

5. $\dfrac{5}{8}$? $\dfrac{3}{10}$

6. $\dfrac{11}{8}$? $\dfrac{4}{9}$

7. $\dfrac{3}{5}$? $\dfrac{1}{3}$

8. $\dfrac{6}{7}$? $\dfrac{10}{11}$

Use decimals to compare the fractions. Replace each ? with >, <, or =.

9. $\dfrac{13}{51}$? $\dfrac{19}{40}$

10. $\dfrac{67}{92}$? $\dfrac{17}{23}$

11. $\dfrac{32}{73}$? $\dfrac{27}{65}$

12. $\dfrac{89}{117}$? $\dfrac{107}{205}$

13. $\dfrac{12}{133}$? $\dfrac{23}{197}$

14. $\dfrac{6}{35}$? $\dfrac{9}{75}$

Use mental math, paper and pencil, or a calculator to compare the fractions. Replace each ? with >, <, or =.

15. $\dfrac{5}{12}$? $\dfrac{1}{6}$

16. $\dfrac{19}{101}$? $\dfrac{71}{111}$

17. $\dfrac{19}{30}$? $\dfrac{3}{4}$

18. $\dfrac{1}{12}$? $\dfrac{1}{14}$

19. $\dfrac{25}{26}$? $\dfrac{33}{34}$

20. $\dfrac{2}{111}$? $\dfrac{4}{222}$

21. $\dfrac{1}{8}$? $\dfrac{2}{9}$

22. $\dfrac{3}{14}$? $\dfrac{1}{16}$

Study Skills ◀▶ Reviewing for Assessment

One way to review for assessment is to read or make a summary of what you have learned. The important ideas are summarized on the *Key Concepts* page at the end of the section.

1. Find the *Key Concepts* page for this section. If you want to know more about using a common denominator to compare fractions, what other pages can you turn to?

Another way to review is to pair-share by sharing ideas with a partner before and after exploring a new topic.

2. Before you begin the next section, read the *Exploration* titles. Pair up and share with your partner everything you already know about the listed topics. Plan to get together with your partner to share what you have learned after you have completed the section.

▶ Converting *Li* to our customary miles made it easier to understand the length of the Great Wall.

Sometimes customary units of measurement can be easier to understand if they are converted to a familiar unit of measurement.

Use Labsheet 2A with Questions 12–14.

12 a. Complete Part I of the labsheet.

b. Why is 1 in. written as a fraction of a foot and a fraction of a yard?

13 a. The Great Wall of China is about 8 yd thick at the bottom. Which fact from the labsheet should you use to see how the thickness of the Great Wall of China compares to your height in feet?

b. Complete Part II of the labsheet to convert 8 yd to feet.

c. The thickness of the Great Wall of China is about how many times your height?

14 Ur was an ancient walled city in Southwest Asia. Its walls were over 1044 in. thick.

a. 1044 in. may be hard to imagine. Which conversion fact could you use to convert inches to feet?

b. Complete Part III of the labsheet to convert 1044 in. to feet.

c. Suppose you and your classmates stand shoulder to shoulder across the top of one of the walls at Ur. About how many students are needed to reach from one side of the wall to the other?

◀ The walls of Ur were destroyed by attackers in 2006 B.C. Shown here is a stairway on a stone tower, part of an ancient wall still standing in the city of Ninevah.

d. How many yards thick were the city walls at Ur? How does this compare to the length of your classroom?

15 ✔ **CHECKPOINT** Replace each ? with the number that makes the statement true.

a. 3 yd = _?_ in.   **b.** 90 in. = _?_ yd   **c.** 3 mi = _?_ ft

d. $\frac{1}{2}$ mi = _?_ yd   **e.** 16 ft = _?_ yd   **f.** 2 ft = _?_ in.

✔ **QUESTION 15**

...checks that you can convert between customary units of measure.

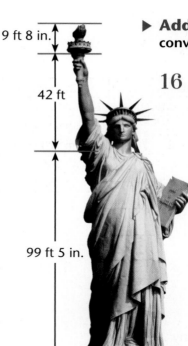

9 ft 8 in.

42 ft

99 ft 5 in.

▶ **Adding and Subtracting Measurements** You may need to convert between units when you add or subtract measurements.

16 **Discussion** To find the height of the Statue of Liberty from the base to the tip of the torch, a student added the measurements of its parts.

a. Is the height of the Statue of Liberty closer to 150 ft or 151 ft? Explain.

b. To simplify the measurement, the student wrote 150 ft 13 in. as 151 ft 1 in. What do you think *simplify* means in this case?

c. In other calculations the student wrote 10 yd 7 ft as 11 yd 4 ft. Why is this not simplified?

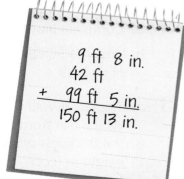

9 ft 8 in.
42 ft
+ 99 ft 5 in.
150 ft 13 in.

▶ **When you subtract measurements, you may need to regroup first.**

EXAMPLE

In order to subtract 9 in. from 5 in., you must regroup.

There are 12 in. in a foot.
5 in. + 12 in. = 17 in.

3 ft 5 in.
− 2 ft 9 in.

Do not forget to decrease the number of feet!

2   17
3 ft 5 in.
− 2 ft 9 in.
        8 in.

17 In a subtraction problem, a student correctly converted 4 yd 1 ft to 3 yd 4 ft. Why are these measurements equal?

✔ **QUESTION 18**

...checks that you know how to add and subtract customary measurements.

18 ✔ **CHECKPOINT** Add or subtract. Simplify answers when possible.

a.   8 in.
     + 10 in.

b.   7 ft 8 in.
      − 5 ft 9 in.

c.   6 mi 1280 yd
      + 2 mi   927 yd

d.   4 yd 2 ft
      + 2 yd 1 ft

e.   6 yd
      − 2 yd 2 ft

f.   5 mi   963 yd
      − 2 mi 1258 yd

19 Suppose a wall similar to the Great Wall of China is to be built along highways from California to New York through the cities listed in the table.

   a. Find the total distance. Simplify if possible.

   b. How does this distance compare with the number of miles in 10,000 *Li*?

From	To	Distance
San Francisco, CA	Salt Lake City, UT	735 mi 1672 yd
Salt Lake City, UT	Lincoln, NE	881 mi 475 yd
Lincoln, NE	Chicago, IL	524 mi 528 yd
Chicago, IL	Cleveland, OH	343 mi 546 yd
Cleveland, OH	New York City, NY	461 mi 282 yd

HOMEWORK EXERCISES ▶ See Exs. 14–33 on pp. 303–304.

Section 2

Key Concepts

Key Terms

Measuring Length in Customary Units (pp. 296–298)

Length can be measured in inches, feet, yards, or miles. You can use benchmarks to estimate lengths. To find more accurate measurements, you can use a ruler.

inches (in.)

feet (ft)

Example Measure the length of a paper clip.

yards (yd)

miles (mi)

To the nearest inch:

2 in.

To the nearest $\frac{1}{2}$ in.

$\frac{4}{2}$ in. or 2 in.

To the nearest $\frac{1}{4}$ in.

$1\frac{3}{4}$ in.

You can use combinations of units to write a measurement. For example, NBA All-Star basketball player Shaquille O'Neal is 7 ft 1 in. tall.

20 Key Concepts Question An object is $5\frac{3}{8}$ in. long. What is its length to the nearest inch? $\frac{1}{2}$ in.? $\frac{1}{4}$ in.?

Key Concepts

Converting Customary Units of Length (pp. 298–299)

To convert between customary units of length you first need to choose an appropriate relationship.

$$1 \text{ ft} = 12 \text{ in.} = \frac{1}{3} \text{ yd} = \frac{1}{5280} \text{ mi} \qquad 1 \text{ in.} = \frac{1}{12} \text{ ft} = \frac{1}{36} \text{ yd}$$

$$1 \text{ yd} = 3 \text{ ft} = 36 \text{ in.} = \frac{1}{1760} \text{ mi} \qquad 1 \text{ mi} = 1760 \text{ yd} = 5280 \text{ ft}$$

Then you can multiply by the conversion fact to convert one customary unit to another.

Adding and Subtracting Lengths in Customary Units (pp. 300–301)

You may need to convert between units when adding or subtracting measurements. You may need to regroup first when subtracting measurements.

Example

$$\begin{array}{r} 2 \text{ ft } 10 \text{ in.} \\ - \ 1 \text{ ft } 11 \text{ in.} \\ \hline \end{array} \qquad \begin{array}{r} \overset{1}{\cancel{2}} \text{ ft } \overset{22}{\cancel{10}} \text{ in.} \\ - \ 1 \text{ ft } 11 \text{ in.} \\ \hline 11 \text{ in.} \end{array}$$

21 Key Concepts Question Your windows are 72 in. long. To make curtains, you need fabric the length of the window plus 9 in. How many yards of fabric do you need?

Section ②

Practice & Application Exercises

YOU WILL NEED

For Exs. 4, 33:
◆ customary ruler or tape measure

In Exercises 1–3 use a benchmark to estimate the measurement.

1. length of your pencil, to the nearest inch

2. height of the room you sleep in, to the nearest yard

3. distance from your shoulder to the tip of your middle finger with your arm outstretched, to the nearest foot

4. Use a ruler or a tape measure to find the actual measurement in Exercises 1–3. Were your estimates close to the actual measurements?

Name an object that has a length close to each measurement.

5. 8 in.   **6.** 4 ft   **7.** 15 ft   **8.** 25 yd

For each situation in Exercises 9–11, name an appropriate customary unit for measuring.

9. checking that the height of a basketball hoop meets NBA regulations

10. finding the length of a route when planning a car trip

11. deciding on the right size paper for a loose leaf binder

12. Social Studies The cubit was a unit of length used in ancient Egypt.

  a. Use inches to measure your cubit.

  b. The standard Egyptian cubit was about 18 in. long. Is this *longer* or *shorter* than your cubit?

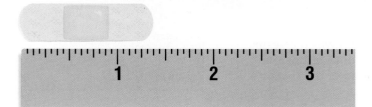

1 cubit

13. What is the length of the bandage to the nearest measure?

  a. $\frac{1}{2}$ in.   b. $\frac{1}{4}$ in.   c. $\frac{1}{8}$ in.

Replace each _?_ with the number that makes the statement true.

14. 6 yd = _?_ ft   **15.** $5\frac{1}{2}$ yd = _?_ in.   **16.** 12,320 yd = _?_ mi

17. 54 in. = _?_ ft   **18.** 11 ft = _?_ yd   **19.** $8\frac{1}{4}$ ft = _?_ in.

Write each measurement as a fraction of a yard.

20. 15 in.   **21.** 2 ft   **22.** 5 ft   **23.** 1 ft 6 in.

17 in. concrete

8 in. cement

12 ft soil with lime

6 ft packed soil

(not drawn to scale)

24. **Writing** Four students' measurements of a table's length are 66 in., $5\frac{1}{2}$ ft, 5 ft 6 in., and 1 yd 2 ft 6 in. Explain how they can all be correct.

25. **Airport Runways** The diagram at the left shows the runway layers at the Denver International Airport. Find the total thickness of the runway in a combination of yards, feet, and inches.

Find each sum or difference. Simplify answers when possible.

26.   3 yd 2 ft
     + 7 yd 1 ft

27.   1382 yd
     + 1576 yd

28.   3 yd 1 ft
     − 2 yd 2 ft

29.   8 ft 9 in.
     − 3 ft 11 in.

30.   6 ft 9 in.
     + 3 ft 5 in.

31.   9 yd
     − 1 yd 2 ft

32. **Challenge** For the ship shown to pass through the locks safely, the gate between Locks 1 and 2 must be opened so water flows from Lock 1 to Lock 2. When the water levels in the two locks are equal, how much has the water level in Lock 1 dropped?

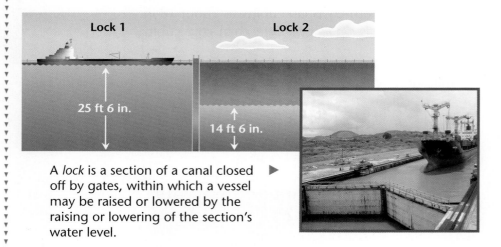

Lock 1

Lock 2

25 ft 6 in.

14 ft 6 in.

A *lock* is a section of a canal closed off by gates, within which a vessel may be raised or lowered by the raising or lowering of the section's water level.

RESEARCH

Exercise 33 checks that you understand how to use benchmarks.

Reflecting ◀▶ on the Section

33. a. Measure the length of your stride in inches. Measure from the heel of one foot to the heel of the other foot.

    b. Use your stride length from part (a) as a benchmark. Estimate the number of steps it would take you to walk 3,784,000 yd (one estimate of the length of the Great Wall of China).

Spiral ◀▶Review

Replace each ? with >, <, or =. (Module 5, p. 290)

34. $\dfrac{2}{5}$? $\dfrac{7}{15}$ **35.** $\dfrac{1}{6}$? $\dfrac{3}{8}$ **36.** $\dfrac{5}{7}$? $\dfrac{9}{13}$

37. In how many different ways can you make change for a half-dollar coin using only nickels, dimes, and quarters? (Module 1, p. 33)

Extension ▶ ▶

Writing Measurements in Mixed Units

Sometimes when measuring it is helpful to have a measurement such as $1\dfrac{3}{4}$ yd in a combination of yards, feet, and inches.

Example:

Convert $1\dfrac{3}{4}$ yd to yards, feet, and inches.

First, convert $\dfrac{3}{4}$ yd to feet: 1 yd = 3 ft

$$\dfrac{3}{4} \cdot 1 \text{ yd} = \dfrac{3}{4} \cdot 3 \text{ ft}$$

$$\dfrac{3}{4} \text{ yd} = \dfrac{9}{4} \text{ or } 2\dfrac{1}{4} \text{ ft}$$

Next, convert any fraction of a foot to inches:

$$1 \text{ ft} = 12 \text{ in.}$$

$$\dfrac{1}{4} \cdot 1 \text{ ft} = \dfrac{1}{4} \cdot 12 \text{ in.}$$

$$\dfrac{1}{4} \text{ ft} = 3 \text{ in.}$$

So, $1\dfrac{3}{4}$ **yd = 1 yd 2 ft 3 in.**

38. Convert each of the following lengths into the mixed units given.

   a. $2\dfrac{1}{3}$ yd = ? yd ? ft

   b. $1\dfrac{2}{3}$ ft = ? ft ? in.

   c. 14 ft = ? yd ? ft

Section 2

You will need: • *customary ruler* (Exs. 1–4)

Measure the length of the needle as directed.

1. to the nearest inch

2. to the nearest $\frac{1}{2}$ in.

3. to the nearest $\frac{1}{4}$ in.

4. to the nearest $\frac{1}{8}$ in.

Replace each _?_ with the number that makes the statement true.

5. $2\frac{1}{4}$ ft = _?_ in.

6. $3\frac{1}{10}$ mi = _?_ yd

7. $12\frac{1}{2}$ ft = _?_ yd

8. 3900 ft = _?_ mi

9. 18 in. = _?_ yd

10. 42 in. = _?_ ft

11. $3\frac{3}{4}$ yd = _?_ ft

12. 3080 yd = _?_ mi

13. 5 yd = _?_ in.

14. 4 mi = _?_ ft

15. 8 in. = _?_ ft

16. 46 in. = _?_ yd

Find each sum or difference. Simplify answers when possible.

17.
    6 ft 3 in.
+ 10 ft 4 in.

18.
    3 yd 4 ft
+   12 ft

19.
    8 yd 1 ft
– 7 yd 2 ft

20.
    9 ft 8 in.
+ 2 ft 4 in.

21.
  13 yd 2 ft
–   6 ft

22.
  11 yd
– 1 yd 2 ft

23.
    1122 yd
+ 709 yd

24.
    6 ft 1 in.
– 5 ft 9 in.

25.
    4 ft 9 in.
+   16 in.

Standardized Testing ◀▶ Performance Task

You are given three strips of paper. One is 2 ft 9 in. long, the second is 3 ft 4 in. long, and the third is 3 ft 2 in. long. Without cutting the strips, describe how to attach the three strips of paper together to create a single strip exactly 3 yd long.

2 ft 9 in.

3 ft 2 in.   3 ft 4 in.

——— 3 yd ———

Section ③ Addition and Subtraction of Fractions

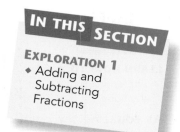

Flex This!

Setting the Stage ▸▹▸▹▸▹▸▹▸▹▸▹▸▹▸▹▸▹▸▹▸▹▸▹

SET UP *You will need: • Labsheet 3A • scissors • tape*

Have you ever played around with a scrap of paper or a gum wrapper, folding it into different shapes before throwing it away? Well that's exactly what Arthur H. Stone did in 1939 with the strips he cut from American-size paper that was too big for his British-size folder. But not all of Arthur's folded strips ended up in the trash. The ones he kept became known as *flexagons*. In fact, the hexagon you folded in Section 1 was Arthur's first flexagon.

After showing his creations to some friends, Arthur soon had others making and discovering new flexagons. The pictures below show how to work a flexagon called a *tetra-tetraflexagon*.

> A *flexagon* is a polygon made from paper, which when folded can reveal hidden surfaces.

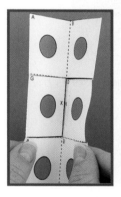   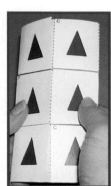

Follow the directions on Labsheet 3A to make a tetra-tetraflexagon.

Think About It

1 The tetra-tetraflexagon you made has 24 shapes on it. When the flexagon is open flat, what fraction of the shapes appear

   a. facing you?   **b.** on the back side?   **c.** hidden inside?

GOAL

LEARN HOW TO...
♦ add and subtract fractions

AS YOU...
♦ explore the measurements of several flexagons

Exploration 1

Adding and Subtracting Fractions

SET UP *You will need your fraction strips from Section 1.*

▶ Arthur Stone's first flexagon designs were made from tiny strips of paper. Variations of the flexagon you made in the *Setting the Stage* are shown here. You can find the widths of these flexagons by adding the widths of the columns.

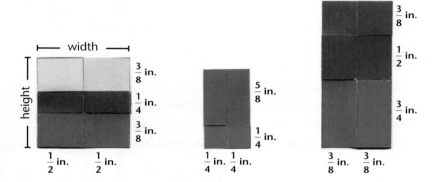

2 Use your fraction strips to find the sum. Each sum represents the width of one of the flexagons above.

    a. $\frac{1}{2} + \frac{1}{2}$ **b.** $\frac{1}{4} + \frac{1}{4}$ **c.** $\frac{3}{8} + \frac{3}{8}$

3 **Discussion**

    a. How can you add fractions with the same denominator without using fraction strips?

    b. Show that you get the same answer for $\frac{5}{12} + \frac{2}{12}$ using your method from part (a) or using strips.

Section 3
Practice & Application Exercises

Find each sum. Write each answer in lowest terms.

1. $\frac{1}{3} + \frac{4}{9}$

2. $\frac{3}{10} + \frac{3}{5}$

3. $\frac{1}{4} + \frac{4}{5}$

4. $\frac{5}{6} + \frac{3}{10}$

5. $\frac{4}{9} + \frac{2}{9} + \frac{1}{9}$

6. $\frac{1}{2} + \frac{1}{4} + \frac{3}{8}$

Find each difference. Write each answer in lowest terms.

7. $\frac{6}{7} - \frac{2}{7}$

8. $\frac{5}{6} - \frac{1}{6}$

9. $\frac{3}{4} - \frac{5}{8}$

10. $\frac{2}{3} - \frac{1}{6}$

11. $\frac{5}{9} - \frac{2}{5}$

12. $\frac{7}{12} - \frac{1}{10}$

13. **Algebra Connection** Evaluate each expression when $n = \frac{5}{8}$. Write each answer in lowest terms.

    a. $n + \frac{7}{8}$

    b. $\frac{15}{16} - n$

    c. $\frac{1}{2} + n - \frac{2}{3}$

Displaying Data The circle graph shows the approximate results of a survey about the ages of Internet users.

14. a. About what fraction of Internet users were over 17 years old?

    b. A circle graph shows the division of a whole into parts. Write a fraction for the part that is labeled 3–17.

    c. What does the fraction you wrote in part (b) tell you about the Internet users surveyed?

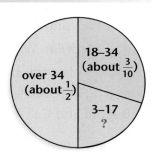

Ages of Internet Users (October 2003)

18–34 (about $\frac{3}{10}$)

over 34 (about $\frac{1}{2}$)

3–17 ?

15. **Solving Equations** In Module 4 you learned to solve one-step equations with whole numbers and decimals. These same steps can be used in solving one-step equations with fractions.

    a. Explain the steps you should use to solve the equation $n + \frac{1}{3} = \frac{5}{7}$.

    b. Solve the equation in part (a).

16. **Music** In written music, the shape of a note shows how long the note should be held. A dot to the right of a note tells you to add on half the value of the note to make it last longer. Use the chart to help you find the value of each note or combination of notes.

quarter note = $\frac{1}{4}$

whole note = 1

A whole note is held four times as long as a quarter note.

half note = $\frac{1}{2}$ eighth note = $\frac{1}{8}$

a.   b. 🎵   c.

d.    e. 🎵   f.

17. **Challenge** On the map, $\frac{1}{4}$ in. represents about 100 mi. A student measures $\frac{3}{8}$ in. between Medellín and Bogotá, $\frac{1}{2}$ in. between Bogotá and Cali, and $\frac{1}{2}$ in. between Cali and Medellín. What is the total mileage of a trip beginning and ending in Medellín with stops in Bogotá and Cali as shown?

Medellín

Bogotá

Cali   COLOMBIA

18. **Writing** Ito and Uri were doing their homework together. Ito said that $\frac{1}{3} + \frac{5}{12} = \frac{6}{15}$. Uri disagreed with Ito, but neither could get the other to change his mind. Convince one of the boys that he is wrong. Be specific in your explanation. Use a model if necessary.

Oral Report

Exercise 19 checks that you understand addition and subtraction of fractions.

Reflecting ◀▶ on the Section

Be prepared to report on the following topic in class.

19. Find a situation where addition or subtraction of fractions is used to create something. Give an example of how mathematics is used in the situation.

Spiral ◀▶ Review

Replace each ? with the number that makes the statement true.
(Module 5, p. 302)

20. 21 in. = ? ft   21. 2 mi = ? yd   22. 16 ft = ? yd

Add or subtract. Simplify answers when possible. (Module 5, p. 302)

23.   4 ft 8 in.
     + 2 ft 10 in.

24.   6 mi
     − 2 mi 1318 ft

25.   5 yd 18 in.
     − 2 yd 23 in.

Use the Venn diagram. (Module 2, p. 119)

26. Find the number of cities listed in the given section of the diagram.

     a. capitals

     b. seaports

     c. capitals and seaports

     d. capitals or seaports

     e. neither a capital nor a seaport

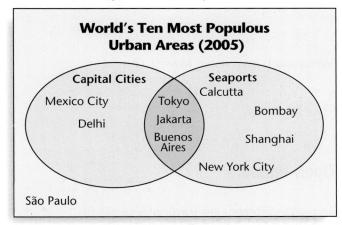

Use compatible numbers to find each sum by mental math.
(Module 1, p. 11)

27. 12 + 15 + 8   28. 45 + 7 + 33

29. 16 + 10 + 14 + 9   30. 43 + 7 + 33

Find each missing number. (Toolbox, p. 573)

31. 45 ÷ ? = 5   32. ? · 8 = 96

33. ? − 12 = 25   34. ? ÷ 9 = 17

35. 12 · ? = 180   36. 7 + ? = 30

Find each sum. Write each answer in lowest terms.

1. $\frac{1}{6} + \frac{3}{10}$

2. $\frac{1}{8} + \frac{3}{8}$

3. $\frac{2}{3} + \frac{5}{18}$

4. $\frac{7}{12} + \frac{5}{18}$

5. $\frac{8}{11} + \frac{1}{3}$

6. $\frac{7}{15} + \frac{7}{15}$

Find each difference. Write each answer in lowest terms.

7. $\frac{12}{13} - \frac{1}{13}$

8. $\frac{7}{8} - \frac{11}{20}$

9. $\frac{9}{10} - \frac{1}{2}$

10. $\frac{7}{8} - \frac{2}{16}$

11. $\frac{3}{4} - \frac{3}{7}$

12. $\frac{11}{12} - \frac{1}{10}$

Find each sum or difference. Write each answer in lowest terms.

13. $\frac{1}{3} + \frac{9}{10}$

14. $\frac{4}{7} + \frac{3}{14}$

15. $\frac{3}{4} + \frac{1}{6}$

16. $\frac{2}{3} - \frac{9}{16}$

17. $\frac{7}{24} + \frac{7}{8}$

18. $\frac{4}{5} - \frac{1}{2}$

Find the value of each expression. Write each answer in lowest terms.

19. $\frac{7}{10} - \frac{3}{20} + \frac{4}{5}$

20. $\frac{5}{8} + \frac{5}{36} - \frac{1}{4}$

21. $\frac{8}{9} - \frac{2}{7} + \frac{1}{2}$

22. $\frac{5}{7} - \frac{1}{28} + \frac{3}{4}$

23. $\frac{2}{9} + \frac{1}{5} + \frac{7}{30}$

24. $\frac{5}{6} + \frac{1}{8} - \frac{1}{12}$

Evaluate each expression when $n = \frac{3}{4}$. Write each answer in lowest terms.

25. $n + \frac{7}{8}$

26. $\frac{5}{6} - n$

27. $\frac{1}{2} + n - \frac{2}{3}$

Standardized Testing ◀▶ Open-ended

1. For each problem, find two fractions with different denominators that have the number shown below as their common denominator. Then write an example showing how to add or subtract the two fractions you chose.

   a. common denominator: 16

   b. common denominator: 24

   c. common denominator: 10

   d. common denominator: 15

2. Pick one of your examples from Question 1. Write a word problem that can be solved using the addition or subtraction you showed.

FOR ASSESSMENT AND PORTFOLIOS

ADD a Square

SET UP *You will need: • the Extended Exploration Labsheet • scissors*

The Situation

Changing the area of a figure may have a surprising effect on its perimeter. In this activity you will explore how the perimeter changes when you add squares to a polygon made up of five squares. Begin by forming a polygon with five 1 in. by 1 in. squares from the labsheet. Add squares to the original polygon until the perimeter reaches 18 in. (*Note:* Added squares must share at least one complete side with another square and they should not overlap.)

The Problem

What is the least number of squares you can add to get a perimeter of 18 in.? What is the greatest number of squares you can add to get a perimeter of 18 in.? Sketch the shapes that give the least and greatest areas for a polygon with a perimeter of 18 in.

Something to Think About

◆ Try several different polygons made with five 1 in. by 1 in. squares. You might want to try these shapes.

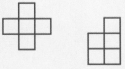

◆ Can you predict how the perimeter will change when you add a square in a certain position?

◆ It may be helpful to organize your work in a table which includes sketches and area and perimeter measurements.

Present Your Results

Explain what approaches you tried. Then describe your solutions. Include any tables and sketches you made. Will you get the same results if you start with any polygon made up of five 1 in. by 1 in. squares? Explain.

Masks

Setting the Stage

SET UP *You will need Labsheet 4A.*

Throughout history, masks have been used in many different cultural celebrations. On November 1st and 2nd, many Mexican-Americans celebrate *Día de Muertos*, the Day of the Dead. This holiday honors relatives and friends who have died during the year. It is traditional to make and display papier-mâché masks like the one shown.

◀ Special masks, called *calaveras*, are made by the entire family.

Think About It

1 About how long and wide would a mask have to be to cover your face?

2 **Use Labsheet 4A.** List the measurements on the mask that have the given characteristic.

　a. less than 1 in.　　　　**b.** greater than 1 in.

Adding **Mixed** Numbers

SET UP *Work with a partner. You will need:* • *Labsheet 4A*
• *customary ruler*

A relief mask has a design that is raised from a flat background. You can glue string, yarn, cotton balls, or even seashells on a cardboard mask to create a raised design.

▸ **To estimate how much material is needed for a mask, you may need to estimate a sum of mixed numbers.**

3 **Use Labsheet 4A.** The length of string, in inches, needed to outline the jaw on the mask is $1\frac{5}{8} + 1\frac{3}{4} + 1\frac{5}{8}$.

   a. Round each measurement to the nearest whole number and find the sum to estimate the length of string.

   b. Is your estimate *less than*, *equal to*, or *greater than* the sum? Explain.

▸ **Using a Ruler** **To find the actual amount of string needed to outline the jaw, you can use a ruler to add the measurements.**

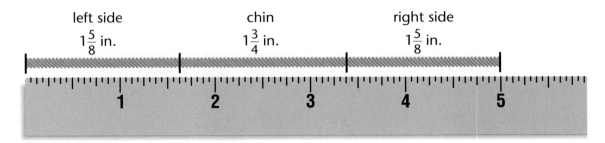

left side	chin	right side
$1\frac{5}{8}$ in.	$1\frac{3}{4}$ in.	$1\frac{5}{8}$ in.

4 **a.** Use the ruler to find $1\frac{5}{8} + 1\frac{3}{4} + 1\frac{5}{8}$. Compare your answer with your estimate in Question 3.

   b. Another way to find the sum is to measure off 3 in. and then measure off lengths for $\frac{5}{8}$ in., $\frac{3}{4}$ in., and $\frac{5}{8}$ in. Why does this method work?

5 a. Estimate $2\frac{2}{3} + 3\frac{3}{4}$ by rounding each number to the nearest whole number.

b. Why is it difficult to find the actual sum $2\frac{2}{3} + 3\frac{3}{4}$ using a ruler?

▶ **Using Paper and Pencil** You can find the sum of mixed numbers by adding the whole numbers and the fractions separately.

EXAMPLE

Find $2\frac{2}{3} + 3\frac{3}{4}$.

SAMPLE RESPONSE

Add the **whole** numbers.

Add the **fractions**.

$$
\begin{array}{rl}
2\frac{2}{3} &= 2\frac{8}{12} \\
+\, 3\frac{3}{4} &= +\, 3\frac{9}{12} \\
\hline
& 5\frac{17}{12} = 6\frac{5}{12}
\end{array}
$$

6 Try This As a Class

a. In the Example, why were $\frac{2}{3}$ and $\frac{3}{4}$ written as $\frac{8}{12}$ and $\frac{9}{12}$?

b. Why was $5\frac{17}{12}$ written as $6\frac{5}{12}$?

7 Find $4\frac{3}{4} + 1\frac{5}{8}$ without a ruler. Then check your answer using a ruler.

8 Discussion Explain the steps Paulo used to find $2\frac{2}{3} + 3\frac{3}{4}$.

9 a. Use Paulo's method to find $1\frac{4}{5} + 6\frac{2}{3}$.

b. Do you prefer Paulo's method or the one in the Example? Why?

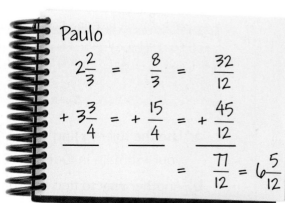

Paulo

$$
\begin{array}{rl}
2\frac{2}{3} &= \frac{8}{3} = \frac{32}{12} \\
+\, 3\frac{3}{4} &= +\,\frac{15}{4} = +\,\frac{45}{12} \\
\hline
&= \frac{77}{12} = 6\frac{5}{12}
\end{array}
$$

10 ✔ **CHECKPOINT** Find each sum. Then write each sum in lowest terms.

   a. $10\frac{1}{4} + 2\frac{5}{6}$ **b.** $\frac{3}{5} + 4\frac{3}{8}$ **c.** $6\frac{1}{4} + 5\frac{3}{8} + 3\frac{3}{4}$

✔ **QUESTION 10**

...checks that you can add mixed numbers.

11 **a. Use Labsheet 4A.** Is 20 in. of string enough to outline the jaw, the mouth, and each pair of rectangles that make the eyes on the *Mask*?

   b. Did you use *paper and pencil* or *estimation* to find your answer? Explain.

HOMEWORK EXERCISES ▶ See Exs. 1–14 on p. 325.

Exploration 2 ▶▶▶▶▶▶▶▶▶▶▶▶▶▶▶▶▶▶▶▶▶▶▶

Subtracting **Mixed Numbers**

GOAL

LEARN HOW TO...
 ◆ subtract mixed numbers

AS YOU...
 ◆ design a pin

SET UP *Work with a partner. You will need a customary ruler.*

Artists are often inspired by patterns found in nature or in the arts and crafts of other cultures. Suppose you use the pattern on this Native American blanket to make a raised design for a pin.

12 Describe how to use mental math to determine that 5 in. of string is needed to outline this rectangular pin.

$1\frac{1}{8}$ in.

$1\frac{3}{8}$ in.

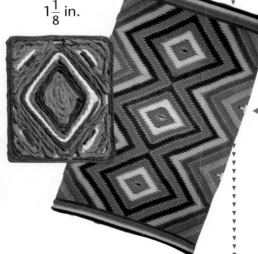

◀ Traditional blanket design made by Navajo weavers of the Southwest.

▶ **Using a Ruler** Suppose you have $6\frac{3}{4}$ in. of string. You can use a ruler to see how much string is left after the pin is outlined.

1 Start with $6\frac{3}{4}$ in. of string.

2 Take away 5 in. of string.   **3** This much is left.

13 **a.** Write a subtraction problem to represent the subtraction shown in the ruler diagram.

b. Find the answer. How can you do this without the ruler?

14 Use a ruler to find $4\frac{1}{2} - 3\frac{1}{4}$.

▶ **Using Pencil and Paper** To subtract mixed numbers without a ruler, you can find a common denominator as you did to add mixed numbers.

15 **a.** Copy the subtraction problem in Question 14.

b. Rewrite the problem using equivalent fractions with a common denominator.

c. Find the difference. Explain how you subtracted.

d. Compare your answer with the answer from Question 14.

16 Gwen has $14\frac{3}{4}$ in. of string and uses $5\frac{3}{8}$ in. to outline a feature on a mask. How much string does she have left?

17 **Try this as a Class** Use the problem shown.

a. Why was $1\frac{1}{2}$ rewritten as $1\frac{4}{8}$?

b. Can you subtract $\frac{4}{8}$ from $\frac{3}{8}$? Explain.

$$\begin{array}{rcrcr} 3\frac{3}{8} & = & 3\frac{3}{8} & = & 2\frac{11}{8} \\ -1\frac{1}{2} & = & -1\frac{4}{8} & = & -1\frac{4}{8} \\ \hline \end{array}$$

c. Show that $3\frac{3}{8} = 2\frac{11}{8}$.

d. Find the difference of $2\frac{11}{8}$ and $1\frac{4}{8}$.

18 Find $6\frac{1}{2} - 3\frac{2}{3}$. Check your answer using addition.

19 Paulo used the same method to subtract mixed numbers as he did to add them. Explain the steps Paulo used to find $2\frac{1}{5} - 1\frac{7}{10}$.

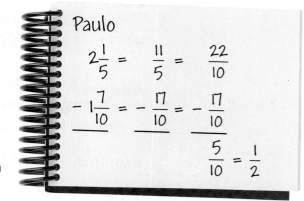

Paulo
$$2\frac{1}{5} = \frac{11}{5} = \frac{22}{10}$$
$$-1\frac{7}{10} = -\frac{17}{10} = -\frac{17}{10}$$
$$\frac{5}{10} = \frac{1}{2}$$

20 Use Paulo's method to find $4\frac{1}{3} - 2\frac{2}{9}$.

21 **Try This as a Class** Consider the problem $6 - 2\frac{1}{4}$.

    a. Explain why you can write 6 as $5\frac{4}{4}$.

    b. Why would you want to write 6 as $5\frac{4}{4}$ to find the difference?

    c. Find the difference.

22 If you have 9 yards of yarn and use $3\frac{3}{4}$ yards in a craft project, how much is left for your next craft project?

▶ **Using Mental Math** Addition and mental math can be used to solve subtraction problems when one number is a mixed number and the other is a whole number.

23 **Discussion** Explain how you can find the difference $4 - 2\frac{1}{3}$ by finding the number to add to $2\frac{1}{3}$ to get 4: $2\frac{1}{3} + \underline{\ ?\ } = 4$.

24 Use mental math to find each difference.

    a. $10 - 7\frac{3}{8}$ **b.** $8\frac{3}{4} - 5$ **c.** $11 - 6\frac{2}{3}$

25 ✔ **CHECKPOINT** Find each difference. Write each answer in lowest terms. Check your answers using addition.

    a. $5\frac{3}{7} - 2\frac{1}{2}$ **b.** $4\frac{3}{8} - 2$ **c.** $10\frac{2}{3} - 3\frac{2}{5}$

    d. $6 - 3\frac{1}{9}$ **e.** $3\frac{5}{8} - 1\frac{3}{4}$ **f.** $5\frac{1}{4} - 4\frac{5}{6}$

✔ **QUESTION 25**

...checks that you can subtract mixed numbers.

26 **a.** Sketch your own design for a pin the size of a rectangle that is $1\frac{7}{16}$ in. by $\frac{7}{8}$ in.

    b. Suppose you have 6 in. of red yarn. Calculate how much will be left after you use it to outline your pin.

HOMEWORK EXERCISES ▶ See Exs. 15–31 on pp. 326–327.

Section 4
Key Concepts

Adding Mixed Numbers (pp. 319–321)

- **Estimating** One way to estimate a sum or difference of mixed numbers is to round to the nearest whole number.

Example $2\frac{1}{2} + 3\frac{2}{3} \approx 3 + 4 = 7$

- **Using paper and pencil** Add the whole numbers and the fractions separately.

*Write fractions with a **common** denominator.*

Example
$$2\frac{1}{2} = 2\frac{3}{6}$$
$$+ 3\frac{2}{3} = + 3\frac{4}{6}$$
$$5\frac{7}{6} = 6\frac{1}{6}$$

Simplify so that the fraction is less than 1 and in lowest terms.

Subtracting Mixed Numbers (pp. 321–323)

- **Using paper and pencil** First subtract the fractions. Then subtract the whole numbers. You may need to regroup a whole.

Regroup 4 as $3\frac{6}{6}$.

Example
$$4\frac{1}{3} = 4\frac{2}{6} = 3\frac{8}{6}$$
$$- 1\frac{5}{6} = - 1\frac{5}{6} = - 1\frac{5}{6}$$
$$2\frac{3}{6} = 2\frac{1}{2}$$

Write in lowest terms.

- **Using mental math** Think of a related addition sentence when subtracting from a whole number.

Example To find $8 - 3\frac{5}{6}$, think $3\frac{5}{6} + \underline{?} = 8$.

If you add $\frac{1}{6}$, you get 4. So you need to add $4\frac{1}{6}$ to get 8.

27 Key Concepts Question Find each sum or difference. Use estimation to check that each answer is reasonable.

a. $7\frac{5}{6} + 2\frac{3}{4}$ b. $7 - 1\frac{4}{5}$ c. $10\frac{1}{4} - 6\frac{5}{8}$

Section 4

Practice & Application Exercises

YOU WILL NEED

For Ex. 26:
◆ fraction calculator

Estimate each sum by first rounding each mixed number to the nearest whole number and then adding.

1. $5\frac{3}{5} + 4\frac{1}{8}$ 2. $7\frac{2}{7} + 2\frac{6}{7}$ 3. $2\frac{1}{3} + 3\frac{1}{8}$

Find each sum. Write each answer in lowest terms.

4. $2\frac{1}{8} + 1\frac{3}{4}$ 5. $4\frac{2}{3} + 5\frac{1}{2}$ 6. $1\frac{2}{3} + 4\frac{4}{5}$

7. $2\frac{1}{3} + 6\frac{5}{8}$ 8. $\frac{5}{7} + 1\frac{5}{14}$ 9. $1\frac{8}{9} + 3\frac{5}{6}$

Mental Math Show how to use compatible numbers to find each sum. (*Hint:* To add three or more mixed numbers, see if any have fractional parts with a sum of 1.)

10. $4\frac{1}{3} + 18\frac{1}{2} + 5\frac{2}{3}$ 11. $8\frac{4}{5} + 6\frac{1}{3} + 4\frac{3}{8} + 1\frac{1}{5} + 2\frac{5}{8}$

FOR ◄ HELP

with *compatible numbers*, see
MODULE 1, p. 11

12. Sonya is making costumes for a play. She needs $1\frac{1}{2}$ yd of ribbon for one costume, $3\frac{2}{3}$ yd of ribbon for another costume, and $2\frac{1}{4}$ yd of ribbon for a third costume. What is the total amount of ribbon she needs?

13. **Estimation** Another way to estimate is to first round to the nearest half.

  a. Explain why $3\frac{3}{8}$ was rounded to $3\frac{1}{2}$ instead of 3.

  b. Do you think $8\frac{1}{2}$ is a low or a high estimate? Explain.

  c. Find the exact sum and compare it with the estimate.

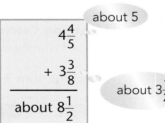

about 5

$4\frac{4}{5}$

$+ 3\frac{3}{8}$

about $3\frac{1}{2}$

about $8\frac{1}{2}$

14. Estimate $11\frac{2}{7} + 4\frac{3}{5}$ by first rounding to the nearest half.

Find each difference. Write each answer in lowest terms. Use addition to check your answers.

15. $3\frac{2}{5} - 2\frac{1}{4}$

16. $4\frac{2}{3} - 2\frac{8}{9}$

17. $2\frac{1}{8} - 1\frac{3}{4}$

18. $23\frac{1}{2} - 5\frac{6}{7}$

19. $17 - 9\frac{5}{11}$

20. $4\frac{5}{12} - 3\frac{13}{36}$

Use mental math to find each difference. Explain your steps.

21. $7 - 3\frac{1}{3}$

22. $5\frac{3}{5} - 2$

23. $3 - 1\frac{1}{4}$

24. **Photography** The image on an instant photograph is $3\frac{5}{8}$ in. long and $2\frac{7}{8}$ in. wide. What are the dimensions of a piece of cardboard you would need to make a mat with a $\frac{3}{4}$ in. border around the top and sides and 1 in. along the bottom?

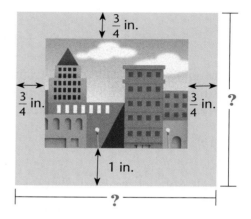

25. Kele is $2\frac{7}{8}$ in. taller than Sharon. Rosa is $2\frac{1}{2}$ in. shorter than Kele but $\frac{5}{8}$ in. taller than Gary.

   a. Who is taller, Sharon or Gary? by how much?

   b. Find the difference between Kele's height and Gary's height.

26. **Fraction Calculator** Another way to add and subtract mixed numbers is by using a calculator.

   a. To find the sum $3\frac{7}{8} + 1\frac{3}{4}$, enter these keystrokes:

   b. Press [Ab/c]. What did this do?

   c. Estimate $3\frac{7}{8} + 1\frac{3}{4}$ to check that the answer displayed is reasonable.

   d. Use a calculator to find $6\frac{1}{2} - 1\frac{4}{5}$. Estimate to check that the answer displayed is reasonable.

27. A plumber needs to replace the middle pipe in the diagram. Find the length of the middle pipe.

$\vdash 2\frac{3}{4}$ ft $\dashv$? $\dashv$ $3\frac{1}{2}$ ft $\dashv$

$\vdash$ $8\frac{1}{2}$ ft $\dashv$

28. Woodworking Nails are sometimes referred to in units called "pennies." A 2-penny nail is 1 in. long. Each increase of a penny means an increase of $\frac{1}{4}$ in. in length up to 3 in.

a. What is the length of a 4-penny nail?

b. A carpenter hammers a 4-penny nail through a board that is $\frac{3}{4}$ in. thick. If the nail is hammered in straight, how far will the nail stick out of the board?

Interpreting Data Use the table to answer Exercises 29 and 30.

Gold Medal Results for Olympic High Jump 1996–2004			
Winner	Country	Height	Year
Charles Austin	United States	7 ft 10 in.	1996
Sergey Klyugin	Russia	7 ft $8\frac{1}{2}$ in.	2000
Stefan Holm	Sweden	7 ft $8\frac{3}{4}$ in.	2004

◄ Stefan Holm was the 2004 Olympic gold medalist in the high jump.

29. How much higher did Austin jump than Stefan Holm?

30. How much higher did Holm jump than Sergey Klyugin?

Reflecting ◄► on the Section

Write your response to Exercise 31 in your journal.

31. Mary and Russ each tried to find $4\frac{3}{15} - 1\frac{10}{15}$. Explain what is wrong with each student's work.

Mary

$4\frac{3}{15}$
$-1\frac{10}{15}$
$3\frac{7}{15}$ ✗

Russ

$3\;4\frac{3}{15}$
$-1\frac{10}{15}$
$2\frac{3}{15}$ ✗

Journal

Exercise 31 checks that you understand mixed number subtraction.

Find each sum or difference in lowest terms. (Module 5, p. 312)

32. $\frac{1}{5} + \frac{4}{25}$ **33.** $\frac{5}{6} - \frac{3}{4}$ **34.** $\frac{7}{10} + \frac{2}{3}$

Write each fraction as a decimal rounded to the nearest hundredth. (Module 4, p. 225)

35. $\frac{13}{25}$ **36.** $\frac{4}{7}$ **37.** $\frac{5}{8}$

Find the prime factorization of each number. (Module 3, p. 158)

38. 126   **39.** 98   **40.** 153

Tell whether each event is *certain*, *impossible*, or *neither* when you roll a single number cube. (Module 2, p. 80)

41. odd number   **42.** multiple of 8   **43.** number less than 7

Use mental math to find each value. (Module 1, p. 62)

44. $\frac{1}{3}$ of 27   **45.** $\frac{2}{5}$ of 15   **46.** $\frac{5}{6}$ of 48

Extension ▶ ▶

Making Connections about Regrouping

47. a. A flight leaves at 1:37 P.M. and arrives at 4:16 P.M. Show how to use subtraction with regrouping to find the elapsed time.

b. How is the regrouping you use when you add and subtract time measurements like the regrouping you use when you add and subtract mixed numbers? How is it different?

48. Make a list of different types of numbers or measurements that you know how to add and subtract. Describe similarities and differences in how regrouping is used for the items on your list.

49. Make up a money or measurement system of your own. It can be totally imaginary (for example, using zings and zangs) or it can use real objects as units. Explain how the units in your system are related. Then show how to use regrouping to add and subtract with your system.

> **FOR ▶ HELP**
> with *elapsed time*, see
> **TOOLBOX, p. 577**

Section 4

Extra Skill Practice

Find each sum. Write each answer in lowest terms.

1. $1\frac{1}{2} + 6\frac{3}{4}$

2. $5\frac{5}{16} + 3\frac{7}{8}$

3. $2\frac{3}{5} + 7\frac{1}{2}$

4. $4\frac{3}{4} + 3\frac{1}{6}$

5. $2\frac{7}{12} + 1\frac{8}{15}$

6. $6\frac{2}{3} + 5\frac{4}{7}$

Find each difference. Write each answer in lowest terms. Use addition to check your answers.

7. $4\frac{5}{9} - 2\frac{1}{2}$

8. $36\frac{2}{3} - 4\frac{1}{6}$

9. $18\frac{3}{4} - 14\frac{1}{7}$

10. $12\frac{7}{8} - 10\frac{3}{4}$

11. $16\frac{4}{9} - 7\frac{5}{6}$

12. $7\frac{2}{7} - 3\frac{5}{14}$

Use mental math to find each difference.

13. $8\frac{3}{4} - 5\frac{1}{2}$

14. $6\frac{5}{8} - 2$

15. $12 - 9\frac{11}{16}$

16. $21 - 6\frac{7}{10}$

17. $32\frac{1}{2} - 14$

18. $7\frac{1}{3} - 4\frac{2}{3}$

Find each sum or difference. Write each answer in lowest terms.

19. $33\frac{1}{3} - 16\frac{1}{2}$

20. $2\frac{1}{3} + 3\frac{8}{9}$

21. $7\frac{3}{5} - 6\frac{3}{4}$

22. $1\frac{7}{32} + 2\frac{3}{8}$

23. $4\frac{5}{9} - 1\frac{3}{5}$

24. $11\frac{3}{4} + 16\frac{5}{6}$

Standardized Testing ◀▶ Multiple Choice

1. Mrs. Quant bought a beef roast that weighed $5\frac{1}{4}$ lb and a ham that weighed $8\frac{1}{2}$ lb. How many pounds of meat did she buy?

   A $3\frac{1}{4}$ lb   **B** $13\frac{1}{3}$ lb   **C** $13\frac{3}{8}$ lb   **D** $13\frac{3}{4}$ lb   **E** none of these

2. After being cooked, the $8\frac{1}{2}$-lb ham loses $\frac{5}{8}$ of a pound. Mrs. Quant slices $4\frac{1}{3}$ lb for sandwiches and serves the rest for dinner. How much ham is served for dinner?

   A $3\frac{1}{2}$ lb   **B** $3\frac{7}{12}$ lb   **C** $3\frac{11}{24}$ lb   **D** $12\frac{5}{24}$ lb   **E** none of these

Section 4   Addition and Subtraction of Mixed Numbers   **329**

Section 5 Area

The Taj Mahal

Setting the Stage

The Taj Mahal, a gigantic domed structure, is the most visited attraction in India. It was created in the 17th century by Emperor Shah Jahan to honor the memory of his beloved wife Mumtaz Mahal. The design of the Taj Mahal is based on the number four and its multiples.

Think About It

1 The garden at the Taj Mahal was laid out in four squares of the same size. Each square was divided into four flower beds, with 400 flowers in each bed. How many flowers were in the garden?

2 The central chamber of the Taj Mahal was built in the shape of an octagon. How is an octagon related to the number 4?

Customary
U·N·I·T·S for AREA

GOAL

LEARN HOW TO...
- measure area using customary units
- convert between customary units of area

AS YOU...
- explore the size of the Taj Mahal

KEY TERMS
- area
- square inch (in.^{2})
- square foot (ft^2)
- square yard (yd^2)

SET UP *Work with a partner. You will need:* • *customary ruler* • *yardstick or measuring tape* • *newspaper or other large paper* • *scissors*

When describing a building, architects often refer to the area of its surfaces. The **area** of a surface is the number of square units that cover it. The area of the floor of the main building of the Taj Mahal is 34,596 ft^2. To find out whether the size of this floor makes the Taj Mahal "gigantic," you will explore area.

3 Draw two squares, one with sides 1 in. long and the other with sides 1 ft long. Cut out your squares.

▸ **The area of the small square is 1 square inch (1 in.^{2}). The large square is 1 ft x 1 ft and has an area of 1 square foot (1 ft^2).**

1 in.

1 in.

The area of the square is 1 in. x 1 in. = 1 in.^{2}

4 a. Use your model of a square foot to estimate the area of the top of your desk.

b. Do you think that using your squares is a good way to find area? Explain.

5 Discussion The area of a rectangle can be found by multiplying its length by its width.

a. How can you use this relationship to estimate area?

b. How can you use this relationship to find the actual area?

6 a. Copy the table.

b. For each item, choose an appropriate unit of measure for its area.

c. Estimate each area in the units you chose.

d. Measure the length and width of each item in the units you chose. Then calculate the actual area.

Item	Unit (in.^{2} or ft^2)	Estimated area	Actual area
this page	?	?	?
top of your desk	?	?	?
chalkboard	?	?	?

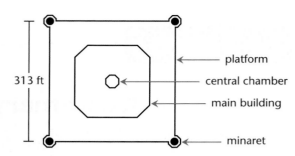

platform
central chamber
main building
minaret

313 ft

7 a. The Taj Mahal stands on a square platform that is 313 ft on each side. What is the area of this square in square feet?

b. The floor area of the main building is 34,596 ft². What is the area of the part of the platform that is not covered by the main building?

8 a. Estimation Estimate the area of your classroom in square feet. Explain your method.

b. Check your estimate by measuring the length and the width and finding the area.

c. About how many of your classroom areas does it take to cover the area of the main building of the Taj Mahal?

d. Would you describe the Taj Mahal as "gigantic"? Explain.

▶ **Converting Units of Area** To express the area covered by a large building like the Taj Mahal, you may want to convert square feet to a larger unit.

9 Try This As a Class Use your model of a square foot.

a. There are 3 ft in 1 yd. How many square feet form **1 square yard (1 yd²)?** Make a sketch showing how to arrange square feet to form a square yard.

b. How can you convert an area measurement given in square feet to square yards?

10 Use your models of a square inch and a square foot.

a. How many square inches form one square foot?

b. How can you convert an area measurement given in square inches to square feet?

✔ **QUESTION 11**

...checks that you can convert between customary units of area.

11 ✔ **CHECKPOINT** The floor of the main building of the Taj Mahal has an area of 34,596 ft². What is its area in square yards?

HOMEWORK EXERCISES ▶ See Exs. 1–6 on p. 340.

Area of a Parallelogram

GOAL

LEARN HOW TO...
◆ find the area of a parallelogram

AS YOU...
◆ investigate geometric shapes in the tile work of the Taj Mahal

KEY TERMS
◆ square centimeter (cm²)
◆ square meter (m²)
◆ intersect
◆ height (of a parallelogram)
◆ base (of a parallelogram)

SET UP *You will need: • Labsheet 5A • scissors • metric ruler • centimeter graph paper*

Thirty-seven specialists including artists, stone cutters, engineers, architects, calligraphers, and inlayers designed the Taj Mahal and supervised the 20,000 workers who built it.

This section of flooring from a terrace at the Taj Mahal is inlaid with white marble and red sandstone tiles.

12 What geometric shapes do you see in the pattern in the floor?

▶ **The design and construction of the terrace must have involved measuring lengths and finding areas. You can use centimeter graph paper to investigate the dimensions and areas of geometric shapes.**

Square units are also used to measure area in the metric system. Since each small square is 1 cm by 1 cm, it has an area of **1 square centimeter (1 cm²)**.

1 linear unit (1 cm)

1 square unit (1 cm × 1 cm = 1 cm²)

13 **Try This as a Class**

   a. How are linear units and square units different?

   b. How many centimeters are in 1 m?

   c. How many square centimeters are there in **1 square meter (1 m²)**? Explain.

14 **Discussion** Chen drew this parallelogram on graph paper. He says that it has an area of 3 cm². Is he correct? Explain.

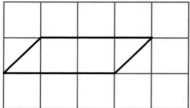

15 On graph paper, draw a different parallelogram that is not a rectangle. Estimate the area of the parallelogram.

16 **a.** Lines or segments that meet at a point **intersect**. Recall that if they meet at a right angle they are also perpendicular. Inside the parallelogram you drew in Question 15, draw a segment that extends from one side to the opposite side and is perpendicular to those sides.

b. The length of the segment you drew in part (a) is the **height** of the parallelogram. The sides that are perpendicular to the height are the **bases** of the parallelogram. Find the height and the length of a base of your parallelogram.

c. Cut out your parallelogram. Then cut it into two pieces along the segment you drew.

d. Form a rectangle using the two pieces of your parallelogram. Record the length, width, and area of this rectangle.

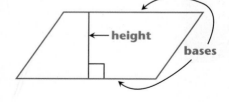

e. How do the length and the width of your rectangle compare with the length of the base and the height of your original parallelogram?

f. What is the area of your parallelogram? Explain.

17 **Try This as a Class** Use your results from Question 16.

a. How do the areas of the parallelograms and the rectangles constructed in Question 16 compare?

b. Use the length of the base and the height to write a formula for finding the area of a parallelogram.

c. What are the two different formulas that can be used to find the area of a rectangle?

18 Draw two parallelograms that are not rectangles on graph paper, one with an area of 12 cm² and the other with an area of 18 cm². What are the length of the base and the height of each parallelogram you drew?

19 ✔ **CHECKPOINT** **Use Labsheet 5A.** Follow the directions on the labsheet to find the areas of *Parallelograms A-D*.

20 Suppose each parallelogram-shaped marble tile in the photo on page 333 has a base length of 8 in. and a height of 4 in. What is the area of each parallelogram-shaped tile?

| **HOMEWORK EXERCISES** ▶ See Exs. 7–15 on pp. 340–341.

✔ **QUESTION 19**

...checks that you can find the area of a parallelogram.

Exploration 3 ▶▶▶▶▶▶▶▶▶▶▶▶▶▶▶▶▶▶▶▶▶▶▶▶▶▶▶

Area of a TRIANGLE

SET UP *Work with a partner. You will need:* • *Labsheet 5B* • *scissors* • *colored pencil* • *metric ruler*

▶ Some of the designs created on this wall of the Taj Mahal can be made using rectangles and triangles. You can use what you know about the area of parallelograms to find the area of triangles.

Any side of a triangle can be the **base**. The diagrams below show the length of the base *(b)* and the **height** *(h)* of several triangles.

GOAL

LEARN HOW TO...
◆ find the area of a triangle
◆ find a missing dimension

AS YOU...
◆ explore geometric designs found in wall panels at the Taj Mahal

KEY TERMS
◆ base (of a triangle)
◆ height (of a triangle)

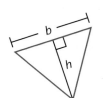 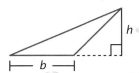

h represents the height.

b represents the length of the base.

21 **Discussion** How is the segment that shows the height of a triangle related to the base?

22 Follow these steps to create two triangles.

   a. Draw a triangle.

   b. Start at any vertex and draw a segment perpendicular to the opposite side or the opposite side extended.

   c. Color the base.

   d. Measure the length of the base and the height to the nearest tenth of a centimeter. Record your measurements inside the triangle.

   e. Cut out your triangle.

   f. Trace around the triangle to make another one that is identical to it. Cut out the second triangle.

23 **a.** Arrange the triangles from Question 22 to form a parallelogram that has the colored side of the first triangle as a base.

   b. Find the length of a base and the height of this parallelogram to the nearest centimeter.

   c. Calculate the area of your parallelogram.

   d. How is the area of one of the triangles related to the area of the parallelogram?

   e. What is the area of one triangle?

   f. How are the length of the base and the height of the parallelogram you formed related to the length of the base and the height of your original triangle?

24 **Try This as a Class** Use your results from Question 23 to write a formula for finding the area (*A*) of a triangle.

25 Use your formula to find the area of your original triangle using each of the other two sides as the bases.

✔ **QUESTION 26**

...checks that you can find the area of a triangle.

26 ✔ **CHECKPOINT** **Use Labsheet 5B** Follow the directions on the labsheet to find the areas of *Triangles A–D*.

27 **Discussion** Suppose you know that the area of a parallelogram is 28 cm² and the height is 4 cm. Explain how you can find the length of the base.

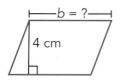

► **Find Unknown Values** When you want to find a missing
dimension, you can use an equation to organize your thinking and
find the unknown value by solving the equation. In Module 4, you
solved addition and subtraction equations. Now you will learn to
solve multiplication and division equations.

EXAMPLE

Find the length of the base of the triangle.

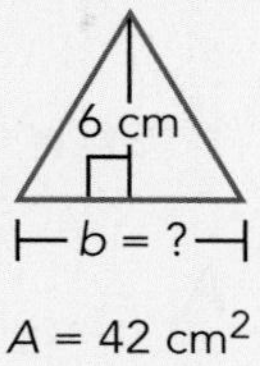

$A = 42 \text{ cm}^2$

SAMPLE RESPONSE

$A = \frac{1}{2} \cdot b \cdot h$	Use the formula for area.
$42 = \frac{1}{2} \cdot b \cdot 6$	Substitute the values you know.
$42 = 3 \cdot b$	$\frac{1}{2} \cdot 6$ equals 3.
$42 \div 3 = b$	To find the missing factor, you can divide.
$14 = b$	

The length of the base is 14 cm.

28 **Discussion**

    a. In the Example, why can you solve for *b* by dividing by 3?

    b. Explain how inverse operations can be used to solve each
    equation.

        ◆ $r + 5 = 11.2$

        ◆ $7y = 154$

        ◆ $\frac{w}{4} = 17$

29 A parallelogram has an area of 5.4 cm².

    a. The base is 0.9 cm long. Use the formula for the
    area of a parallelogram to write an equation. Let *h*
    represent the height.

    b. How can you use division to solve your equation for *h*?

30 Try This as a Class Braedy started to find the height of a triangle with a base $\frac{5}{8}$ in. long and an area of 10 in.^{2}, but he stopped before he finished the problem. His work is shown below.

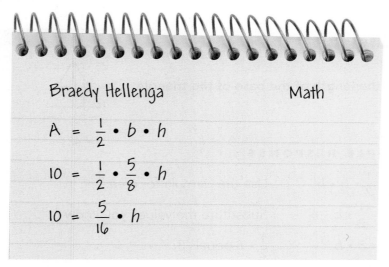

Braedy Hellenga   Math

$$A = \frac{1}{2} \cdot b \cdot h$$

$$10 = \frac{1}{2} \cdot \frac{5}{8} \cdot h$$

$$10 = \frac{5}{16} \cdot h$$

a. What is the next step in solving the equation?

b. Finish Braedy's work to find the height of the triangle in inches.

c. When Braedy asked his older sister for help, she told him to multiply both sides of the equation by $\frac{16}{5}$. How is $\frac{16}{5}$ related to the $\frac{5}{16}$ in the last step on his paper?

d. Finish the problem using his sister's suggestion. Compare the answer with your answer in part (b).

e. Describe how you could use the method suggested by Braedy's sister to solve the equation $\frac{3}{4} \cdot x = 12$.

✔ **QUESTION 31**

...checks that you can use an equation to find a missing dimension.

31 ✔ **CHECKPOINT** For each of the following, write and solve an equation to find the missing length.

a. A parallelogram has a base 4 cm long and an area of 20.4 cm^2. Find the height of the parallelogram.

b. A triangle has a height of 10 in. and an area of $8\frac{3}{4}$ in.^{2} Find the length of its base.

HOMEWORK EXERCISES ▶ See Exs. 16–29 on pp. 341–342.

Section 5
Key Concepts

Key Terms

Units of Area (pp. 331–332)

Area (A) is measured in square units.

You can use the relationships between units in the customary system to convert between square inches, square feet, and square yards.

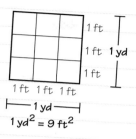

$1 yd^2 = 9 ft^2$

Relationships between units in the metric system can be used to convert between square centimeters and square meters.

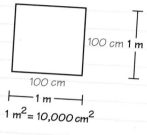

$1 m^2 = 10,000 cm^2$

area

square inch (in.²)

square foot (ft²)

square yard (yd²)

square centimeter (cm²)

square meter (m²)

Formulas for Area
Parallelograms (pp. 333–335)

Example

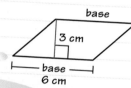

The **height** is the perpendicular distance between the bases.

Area = length of base • height

$A = b \cdot h = 6 \text{ cm} \cdot 3 \text{ cm}$

The area is 18 cm².

Triangles (pp. 335–336)

Example

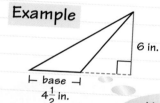

You may have to extend the base.

$\text{Area} = \frac{1}{2} \cdot \text{length of base} \cdot \text{height}$

$A = \frac{1}{2} \cdot b \cdot h = \frac{1}{2} \cdot 4\frac{1}{2} \text{ in.} \cdot 6 \text{ in.}$

The area is $13\frac{1}{2}$ in.²

intersect

base

height

32 Key Concepts Question Figure *GCEF* is a parallelogram, and figure *CDE* is a triangle. Find the area of the entire figure in square yards.

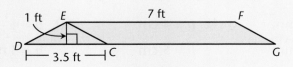

Section 5

Key Concepts

Finding Unknown Values (pp. 337–338)

You can write and solve an equation to find a missing dimension or other unknown value.

Example Fran bought 3.5 lb of coffee beans for $23.80. What is the cost of one pound?

Let c = cost per pound.

$$3.5c = 23.80$$
$$3.5c \div 3.5 = 23.80 \div 3.5$$
$$1c = 23.80 \div 3.5$$
$$c = \$6.80$$

33 Key Concepts Question Find the unknown value in the equation $6x = 39$.

Section 5

Practice & Application Exercises

YOU WILL NEED

For Ex. 13:
- metric ruler
- Labsheet 5A

For Ex. 15:
- graph paper
- a ruler

For Ex. 16:
- metric ruler
- Labsheet 5B

For Ex. 28:
- graph paper

For Ex. 37:
- centimeter graph paper
- tracing paper

Estimation Estimate the area of each object in customary units and explain your method. Then measure the length and width and use an area formula to check your estimates. How did you do?

1. seat of a chair

2. a window

Replace each $\underline{?}$ with the missing measurement.

3. $81 \text{ ft}^2 = \underline{?} \text{ yd}^2$

4. $36 \text{ in.}^2 = \underline{?} \text{ ft}^2$

5. $266 \text{ yd}^2 = \underline{?} \text{ ft}^2$

6. $18 \text{ ft}^2 = \underline{?} \text{ in.}^2$

7. How many square meters are in a square kilometer? Explain.

Find the area of a parallelogram with the given dimensions.

8. $b = 3.5 \text{ mm}$
   $h = 2.7 \text{ mm}$

9. $b = 4 \text{ cm}$
   $h = 5 \text{ cm}$

10. $b = 4\frac{1}{2} \text{ ft}$
    $h = 3 \text{ ft}$

11. The groundskeeper at a high school is in charge of mowing the soccer and football fields. How many more square yards of grass does the groundskeeper have to mow on the soccer field than on the football field?

12. Shane wants to carpet his bedroom. The dimensions of his rectangular room are 12 ft x 15 ft. The carpet he has chosen costs $11.95 a square yard. How much will the carpet for Shane's room cost?

13. **Use Labsheet 5A.** Find the areas of *Parallelograms E–H.*

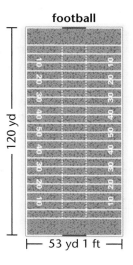

football

120 yd

⊢ 53 yd 1 ft ⊣

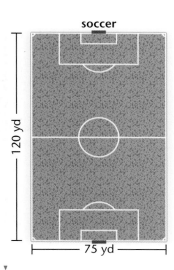

soccer

120 yd

⊢ 75 yd ⊣

14. **Open-ended** Sketch two different parallelograms that each have an area of 24 cm² and are not rectangles. Be sure to label the length of the base and the height.

15. a. Draw a parallelogram on graph paper.

    b. Find the height by measuring the distance between a pair of parallel sides. Use this measurement and the length of the corresponding base to find the area of the parallelogram.

    c. Repeat part (b) using the other pair of parallel sides.

    d. Are the areas in parts (b) and (c) the same? Why or why not?

16. **Use Labsheet 5B.** Find the areas of *Triangles E–H.*

Find the area of each figure.

17.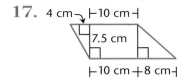
4 cm ⊢10 cm⊣
7.5 cm
⊢10 cm ⊣8 cm⊣

18.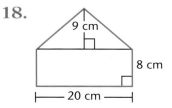
9 cm
8 cm
⊢ 20 cm ⊣

Write and solve an equation to find the missing dimension for each figure.

19.
h = ?
⊢8 ft⊣
Area = 24 ft²

20.
15 in.
⊢ b = ? ⊣
Area = 390 in.²

21.
3 in.   3 in.
2 in.   2 in.
x = ?
Perimeter = 14 in.

22. The multipurpose room of a school building has a rectangular floor with an area of 5828 ft². The length of the floor is 94 ft. What is the width of the floor?

Find the unknown value in each equation.

23. $2 \cdot 9x = 72$

24. $5y = 125$

25. $\frac{3}{8}m = 12$

26. $\frac{x}{12} = 7$

27. Create Your Own The area of a polygon can be found by dividing it into polygons whose areas you know how to find.

    a. Using one triangle, one rectangle, and one parallelogram that is not a rectangle, draw a polygon that has an area of 50 cm².

    b. Label the base length and height of each polygon used.

28. Challenge Copy the polygon onto graph paper. Then find its area in square units.

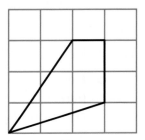

Reflecting ◀▶on the Section

Be prepared to discuss your response to Exercise 29 in class.

29. a. What happens if you use a segment that is not perpendicular to a base as the height of a parallelogram or a triangle? Explain.

    b. For what type of parallelogram does the height equal the length of a side? Explain.

    c. For what type of triangle does the height equal the length of a side? Explain.

Spiral ◀▶Review

Use inverse operations to solve each equation. (Module 4, p. 240)

30. $16.3 + w = 34$

31. $\frac{2}{3} + r = \frac{7}{8}$

32. $p - 0.7 = 3.5$

33. **a.** For each input value, apply the rule to find the output value. Record the results in a table like the one below. (Module 4, p. 256)

Rule: Output = 2 • input – 3

Input	2	5	6	10
Output	?	?	?	?

b. Write each input and its output from part (a) as an ordered pair.

c. On a coordinate grid, graph the ordered pairs you listed in part (b). Draw segments connecting the points in order from left to right.

d. Use your graph to predict the input for an output of 2.

Draw an example of each polygon. (Module 2, p. 119)

34. hexagon   **35.** pentagon   **36.** trapezoid

Extension ▶ ▶

Area of an Irregularly Shaped Figure

You can estimate areas using grid squares.

First Trace the outline of the figure.

Next Place the tracing on a piece of centimeter graph paper.

Then Count the complete grid squares. Add on the area from the partially filled grid squares. You can use a fraction to estimate a part of a grid square or combine parts to form whole squares.

37. **a.** On the map, the area of Madagascar is about how many square centimeters? Explain how you made your estimate.

b. An area on the map that is 1 cm by 1 cm represents how many square kilometers?

c. Estimate the actual area of Madagascar.

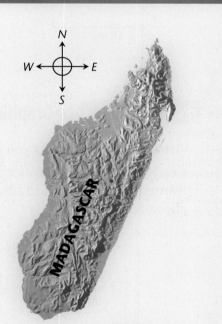

N
W ←⊕→ E
S

1 cm is about 200 km.

Section 5

Extra Skill Practice

Replace each ? with the number that makes the statement true.

1. $168 \text{ ft}^2 = \underline{?} \text{ in.}^2$ 2. $5 \text{ ft}^2 = \underline{?} \text{ in.}^2$ 3. $96 \text{ in.}^2 = \underline{?} \text{ ft}^2$

4. $117 \text{ ft}^2 = \underline{?} \text{ yd}^2$ 5. $4\frac{1}{2} \text{ yd}^2 = \underline{?} \text{ ft}^2$ 6. $1 \text{ yd}^2 = \underline{?} \text{ in.}^2$

Find the area of each parallelogram.

7. $b = 38.2$ mm

    $h = 24$ mm

8.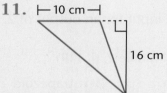

9. $b = 3\frac{1}{4}$ cm

    $h = 7$ cm

Find the area of each figure.

10.

11.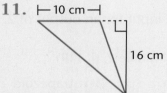

12.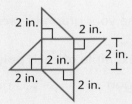

Write and solve an equation to find the missing dimension.

13.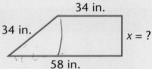

Perimeter = 148 in.

14.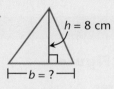

Area = 36 cm²

15.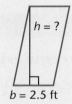

$b = 2.5$ ft

Area = 12.5 ft²

Study Skills ▶ Graphic Organizers

Visual displays can help you relate ideas and organize information.

Copy and extend the concept map to connect ideas you have learned about area. Add on units of measure, formulas, and notes about relationships.

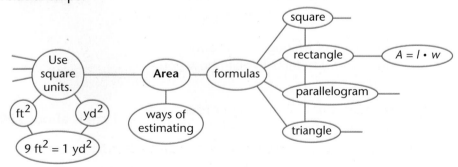

Section 6 Division with Fractions

Designing a Border

Setting the Stage

Glazed ornamental tiles were used to create inlaid borders in the Taj Mahal. In this section you will design a tile and use it to create a border similar to the ones found in the Taj Mahal.

An Islamic ▶ ornamental tile

Think About It

▶ Tiles are often used to create borders around doors and windows. The tile above is $2\frac{1}{2}$ in. long along the bottom edge. Three tiles laid end-to-end will create a $7\frac{1}{2}$ in. border.

1 What length border would 5 tiles laid end-to-end cover? Explain.

2 How many tiles are needed for a 10 in. long border?

3 There are times you may need only part of a tile to finish a border. If only $\frac{2}{5}$ of a tile is needed to complete a border, how much of the $2\frac{1}{2}$ in. tile would you need? Explain.

GOAL

LEARN HOW TO...
- divide whole numbers and mixed numbers by fractions

AS YOU...
- design a border for the cover of your math book

KEY TERM
- reciprocals

Exploration 1

Dividing $\frac{\text{by}}{\text{a}}$ Fraction

SET UP *You will need: • customary ruler • Labsheet 6A*

▶ **The numbers you multiplied in Question 3 had a product of 1. Now you will explore other pairs of numbers whose products are 1. Such pairs of numbers are reciprocals.**

4 Find each product. Write each answer in lowest terms.

   a. $\frac{11}{8} \cdot \frac{8}{11}$ **b.** $2 \cdot \frac{1}{2}$ **c.** $\frac{4}{9} \cdot 2\frac{1}{4}$

5 Write 2 and $2\frac{1}{4}$ as fractions greater than one. How are the numerators and denominators of the two numbers in each part of Question 4 related?

6 **a.** By what number can you multiply $\frac{4}{7}$ to get a product of 1?
   b. What is the reciprocal of $\frac{4}{7}$?

7 **Discussion** Are $2\frac{3}{4}$ and $2\frac{4}{3}$ reciprocals? Explain.

✔ QUESTION 8

...checks that you can find the reciprocal of a number.

8 **✔ CHECKPOINT** Write the reciprocal of each number.

   a. $\frac{8}{9}$ **b.** 3   **c.** $\frac{1}{5}$ **d.** $1\frac{4}{5}$

▶ **Suppose you use $\frac{1}{2}$ in. x $\frac{1}{2}$ in. square tiles to create a border for the cover of your math book as shown at the top of the next page.**

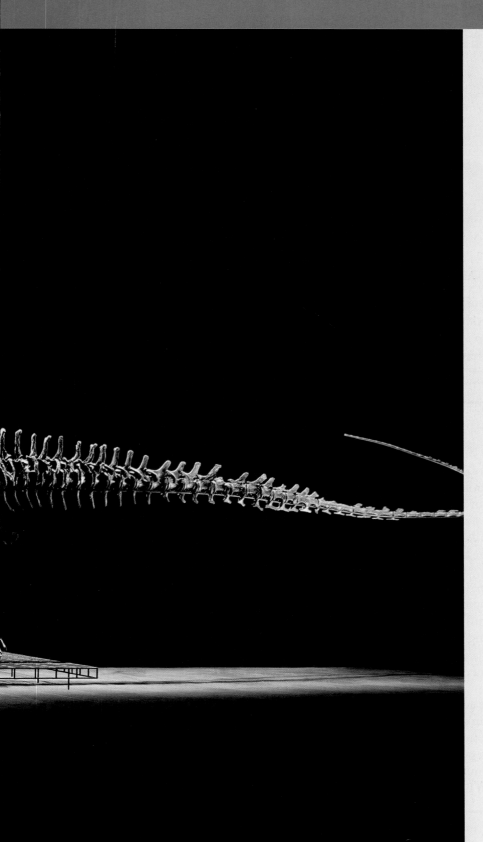

MODULE 6 — SECTION OVERVIEW

1 Exploring Ratios

As you explore the use of props in a movie:

- ◆ Make comparisons using ratios
- ◆ Write equivalent ratios

2 Rates

As you simulate a sandbag brigade:

- ◆ Use rates to make predictions
- ◆ Find unit rates

3 Using Ratios

As you find body ratios:

- ◆ Write a ratio as a decimal
- ◆ Use ratios and scatter plots to make predictions

4 Proportions

As you compare the jumping abilities of humans and animals:

- ◆ Use cross products to find equivalent ratios
- ◆ Write and use a proportion to solve a problem

5 Geometry and Proportions

As you look at how artists use models and scale drawings:

- ◆ Identify similar and congruent figures
- ◆ Use proportions to find missing side lengths

6 Percents and Circle Graphs

As you examine Olympic softball data:

- ◆ Relate fractions, decimals, and percents
- ◆ Find a percent of a number
- ◆ Display data in a circle graph

INTERNET
Resources and practice at
classzone.com

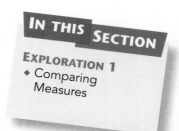
Take a Closer Look

Setting the Stage

Comparing things and making predictions based on those comparisons is an important use of mathematics. In the poem *One Inch Tall*, Shel Silverstein makes comparisons to describe what the world would be like if you were only one inch tall.

From

Where the Sidewalk Ends

by Shel Silverstein

ONE INCH TALL

If you were only one inch tall, you'd ride a worm to school.
The teardrop of a crying ant would be your swimming pool.
A crumb of cake would be a feast
And last you seven days at least,
A flea would be a frightening beast
If you were one inch tall.

If you were only one inch tall, you'd walk beneath the door,
And it would take about a month to get down to the store.
A bit of fluff would be your bed,
You'd swing upon a spider's thread,
And wear a thimble on your head
If you were one inch tall.

You'd surf across the kitchen sink upon a stick of gum.
You couldn't hug your mama, you'd just have to hug her thumb.
You'd run from people's feet in fright,
To move a pen would take all night,
(This poem took fourteen years to write—
'Cause I'm just one inch tall).

1 If the author spent the same amount of time writing each verse of the poem, about how many years did he take to write one verse?

2 If you were only one inch tall, do you think a thimble would fit on your head? Why or why not?

Exploration 1 ▸▸

COMPARING MEASURES

SET UP *Work with a partner. You will need:* • *Labsheet 1A* • *pennies*

GOAL

LEARN HOW TO...
◆ make comparisons using ratios
◆ recognize and write equivalent ratios

AS YOU...
◆ explore how characters in movies can appear to be shorter or taller than their actual heights

KEY TERMS
◆ ratio
◆ equivalent ratios

▶ **Shel Silverstein used comparisons with everyday objects so readers could imagine the world from the perspective of a one-inch tall person. Several movies, such as** *Honey I Shrunk the Kids* **and** *The Lord of the Rings***, also used everyday objects to create an illusion of different sizes.**

Set designers for *The Lord of the Rings* had to make the Hobbits appear smaller than other characters in the film. To do this they created almost every prop in at least two different sizes. In one scene, two different size mugs and two different size tables were used to make Frodo appear to be smaller than Gandalf. In this exploration, you will compare the sizes of the props.

▲
Many areas in New Zealand have served as locations for scenes in *The Lord of the Rings*.

3 **Use Labsheet 1A.** Measure the mug shown on the labsheet.

4 **Discussion** A larger mug looks exactly like the one on Labsheet 1A, but it is 6 pennies tall.

   a. How can you compare the heights of the two mugs in pennies?

   b. *Without measuring*, predict the large mug's height in squares.

   c. Describe a way you can use pennies and squares to check your prediction in part (b).

   d. What is the large mug's height in squares? How does this compare with your prediction?

   e. How does the small mug's height in squares compare with the large mug's height in squares?

▶ To find the height of the large mug in squares, it can be helpful to use a special type of comparison called a *ratio*. The comparison below is an example of a ratio.

The ratio of the height of the small mug in pennies to the height of the large mug in pennies is 4 to 6.

▶ The **ratio** of two numbers or measures can be written several ways:

using the word "to"	with a colon	as a fraction
4 to 6	4 : 6	$\frac{4}{6}$

✔ **QUESTION 5**

...checks that you can write a ratio to compare two quantities.

5 ✔ **CHECKPOINT** Write the ratio of the small mug's height in squares to the large mug's height in squares in three ways.

6 **Discussion** If you compare the large mug's height in squares to the small mug's height in squares, do you get the same ratio as in Question 5? Explain.

▶ **Equivalent Ratios** The heights of the two mugs do not change; therefore, the two ratios used to compare their heights, 4 : 6 and 6 : 9, must be equivalent. Two ratios are **equivalent ratios** if they can be written as equivalent fractions.

7 **Try This As A Class**

  a. Write the ratios 4 : 6 and 6 : 9 as fractions.

  b. How you can show that the ratios in part (a) are equivalent?

  c. Name two more ratios that are equivalent to the ratio 6 : 9.

To make sure the size differences appeared correctly during the scene, it was important that the ratios of the heights of the items on Gandalf's table to the heights of the matching items on Frodo's table be equivalent.

8 **a.** Suppose the heights of the tables where Frodo and Gandalf sat have a ratio in inches of 18 : 27. Is this equivalent to the ratio of the heights of the mugs? Explain.

  b. Gandalf is 6 ft tall. If the ratio of Frodo's height to Gandalf's height is equivalent to the ratio of the small mug's height to the large mug's height, how tall would Frodo be?

9 **Try This As A Class**

  a. In Shel Silverstein's poem, a person 1 in. tall surfs on a stick of gum. If a stick of gum is 3 in. long, write a ratio of *the person's height to the length of a stick of gum* in fraction form.

  b. Write an equivalent ratio with a numerator of 6 ft. What did you do to find the denominator?

  c. What do the numerators represent in the fractions in parts (a) and (b)? What do the denominators represent?

  d. Equivalent ratios can help filmmakers decide what size to make props. Suppose you are making a movie of the poem *One Inch Tall*. If a 6-ft person plays the person in the poem, how long would you need to make the stick of gum?

  e. How does the length in part (d) compare to a typical surfboard? What other items might Mr. Silverstein have used as a realistic size surfboard for a one-inch tall person?

10 ✔ **CHECKPOINT** Which ratios are equivalent to the ratio 6 : 14?

  3 to 7 $\frac{21}{9}$ 12 : 28   9 : 17

✔ **QUESTION 10**

...checks that you can recognize equivalent ratios.

█ **HOMEWORK EXERCISES** ▶ See Exs. 1–17 on pp. 369–371.

Key Terms

ratio

equivalent ratios

Ratios (p. 366)

A ratio is a special type of comparison of two numbers or measures. Ratios can be written in different ways. The order of the numbers in a ratio is important.

Example You can write the ratio of the number of cashews to the number of pretzels in three different ways.

The snack mix has 10 cashews for every 4 pretzels.

10 to 4   10 : 4 $\frac{10}{4}$

Equivalent Ratios (p. 367)

Sometimes a ratio can be shown another way by separating each measure into the same number of groups.

You can compare half the number of cashews with half the number of pretzels.

Example

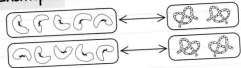

5 cashews   to   **2** pretzels

Equivalent ratios can be written as equivalent fractions.

10 : 4 is equivalent to 5 : 2 because $\frac{10}{4}$ and $\frac{5}{2}$ are equivalent fractions.

11 **Key Concepts Question** Suppose that in a can of mixed nuts there are 12 peanuts for every 9 cashews.

    a. Write the ratio of *the number of cashews to the number of peanuts* in each of the three forms.

    b. Find a ratio that is equivalent to the one in part (a).

    c. Is the ratio of *the number of peanuts to the number of cashews* equivalent to the ratio in part (a)? Explain.

Section ①
Practice & Application Exercises

▶▶▶▶▶▶▶▶▶▶▶

Tell whether the ratios are equivalent.

1. $\frac{3}{5}$ and $\frac{9}{15}$

2. $\frac{5}{12}$ and $\frac{10}{8}$

3. $\frac{4}{3}$ and $\frac{16}{9}$

4. 1 : 6 and 5 : 30

5. 9 : 2 and 32 : 8

6. 12 : 6 and 8 : 4

7. **Volleyball** Before serving in the game of volleyball, players often announce the ratio of their score to the opposing team's score. Suppose Team A has 4 points and Team B has 6 points. The score ratio 6 to 4 is announced. Which team is serving the ball?

8. Write the ratio of the number of dogs to the number of paws in each picture.

   a.   b.

   c. Are the ratios you found in parts (a) and (b) equivalent? If so, explain why.

9. For each of the following, find the number *n* that makes the ratios equivalent.

   a. $\frac{6}{5} = \frac{n}{20}$

   b. 18 : 24 and *n* : 8

10. **Open-ended** Suppose you were one inch tall. How high would a water fountain you could drink from be? Explain how you determined your answer.

11. On the back lot of MGM Studios in Florida sits the *Honey I Shrunk the Kids* playground, where you can crawl through 30-foot blades of grass or view a dog's nose taller than a grown man.

a. Write a ratio that compares the height of a 3-foot child to the height of the grass.

b. Suppose the height of the dog's nose is $\frac{2}{3}$ the height of a blade of grass. Write a ratio that represents the height of the dog's nose to the height of a person who is 6 feet tall.

12. **Gliders** The flight performance of a glider, which is an aircraft with no engine, can be measured using a glide ratio. A glide ratio compares the gliding distance with the change in height.

change in height 500 m

gliding distance 9000 m

Otto Lilienthal built the first controllable glider in the late 1800s.

a. Write the glide ratio for the glider in three ways.

b. Suppose the glider's height changes half as much and it travels half as far. Write this ratio in three ways.

c. Are the ratios you found in parts (a) and (b) equivalent? If so, explain why.

d. Find another ratio equivalent to the ones you wrote in parts (a) and (b). Explain how you found the ratio.

13. a. For every three steps Sam takes, Gandalf takes one step. Write this comparison as a ratio in three ways.

b. Suppose Gandalf takes nine steps. How many steps will Sam take?

c. Suppose Sam takes twelve steps. How many steps will Gandalf take?

14. **Movie Sets** Miniatures of the Argonaths in the movie *The Lord of the Rings* were created in a ratio of 1 ft to 60 ft. That means that every 1 ft on the miniature represented 60 ft in real life.

   a. How much would 2 ft on the miniature represent in real life?

   b. Write a ratio for 2 ft on the miniature to the real life length in fraction form. What happens if you simplify the fraction?

   c. The miniature is 8 ft tall. Find *n* in the ratio 8 : *n* to make it equivalent to the ratio 1 : 60. How tall is the Argonath in real life?

15. **Language Arts** Think of some things you would or would not be able to do if you were one inch tall. Then write another verse for the poem *One Inch Tall*.

16. **Challenge** The poem *One Inch Tall* says, "If you were only one inch tall, you'd walk beneath the door, and it would take about a month to get down to the store." Imagine that you are one inch tall. Estimate the distance to the store in the poem. Explain how you found your answer.

Reflecting ◀▶on the Section

17. Pick an object such as a pencil or a book to use as a measuring tool. Use the object as a unit of length to measure several other objects. Make sketches that compare the objects you measured and write the ratios that can be formed from the sketches.

RESEARCH

Exercise 17 checks that you can use ratios to compare.

Spiral ◀▶Review

Find each quotient. (Module 5, p. 352)

18. $8 \div \frac{5}{6}$

19. $\frac{7}{9} \div \frac{2}{3}$

20. $14 \div \frac{5}{8}$

Choosing a Method Use mental math or paper and pencil to find each answer. (Module 3, p. 190; Module 4, p. 256)

21. $0.48 \div 0.6$

22. $5.24 \cdot 0.01$

23. $43.6 \div 0.5$

24. $27 \cdot 0.001$

25. $3.6 \div 0.4$

26. $0.76 \cdot 0.8$

Complete each pair of equivalent fractions. (Module 1, p. 61)

27. $\frac{9}{12} = \frac{?}{4}$

28. $\frac{20}{4} = \frac{?}{1}$

29. $\frac{8}{10} = \frac{?}{25}$

Section 1

Extra Skill Practice

Use the chart at the right. Write each ratio in three ways.

1. the number of pencils to the number of pens

2. the number of folders to the number of notebooks

3. the number of folders to the number of book covers

School Store Inventory Supply	
pencils	256
pens	120
erasers	60
notebooks	32
folders	37
book covers	183

Draw a picture of the objects to show each ratio.

4. The ratio of the number of stars to the number of squares is five to three.

5. The ratio of the number of forks to the number of spoons is 4 : 8.

6. The ratio of the number of cars to the number of tires is $\frac{1}{4}$.

Tell whether the ratios are equivalent.

7. 6 : 5 and 24 : 20

8. 13 to 5 and 10 to 26

9. 21 : 8 and 8 : 21

10. $\frac{8}{24}$ and $\frac{2}{3}$

11. 7 : 12 and 21 : 32

12. $\frac{6}{8}$ and $\frac{9}{12}$

Study Skills ◀▶ Using Mathematical Language

To read and to talk about mathematics, you need to understand the language. When you need help, use your book as a resource.

1. Find the Glossary in the book. What does the Glossary tell you that the word *ratio* means?

2. Find the Table of Symbols in this book. What does the table tell you about how to read 8 : 12?

3. Find the Table of Measures in this book. What information does the table give you about the length of 1 meter?

4. Find the Index in this book. Look up *measurement*. What ideas about measurement does this book include?

Section 2 Rates

The SANDBAG BRIGADE

Setting the Stage ▸▸▸▸▸▸▸▸▸▸▸▸▸▸▸▸▸▸▸▸▸▸▸▸▸▸▸▸▸▸▸▸

SET UP *Work as a class. You will need: • object to represent a sandbag • watch or clock to time seconds • tape measure*

In the summer of 1993, one of the most costly floods in U.S. history left a wake of destruction across a nine-state region in the Midwest. Many young volunteers helped fight the floodwaters.

> Muddy water lapped at his shoulders, and the sky threatened rain. But Jesse Blaise, 12, stood his soggy ground. He was working hard to protect the North Lee County Historic Center in Fort Madison, Iowa, from the great Mississippi River flood of 1993. Shawn Pulis, 14, worked nearby. "Volunteers brought us boatloads of sandbags," he says. "We stacked them around the building."
>
> The volunteers worked around the clock for 13 days. It paid off. The water receded to the riverbed. The building stood. "I was so tired," says Shawn, "but I felt really good."
>
> ["The Great Flood of 1993," Barbara Brownell]

Follow the steps to simulate a sandbag brigade.

Step 1 Line up ten students side by side.

Step 2 Hand an object representing a sandbag from one end of the line to the other.

Step 3 Record how far the object is passed and how long it takes.

Think About It

1 Suppose your class's brigade is 100 ft long. About how long will it take to pass a sandbag from one end to the other?

2 Suppose it takes one minute to pass a sandbag from one end of a brigade to the other. About how long do you expect the brigade to be?

GOAL

LEARN HOW TO...
- use rates to make predictions
- find unit rates

AS YOU...
- analyze data from your class's sandbag brigade

KEY TERMS
- rate
- unit rate

Exploration 1

Using RATES and UNIT RATES

▶ You can use ratios and the data from your class's sandbag brigade to make predictions.

3 a. What unit was used to measure the distance the sandbag was passed in your class?

b. What unit was used to measure the time it took?

c. Write a ratio that compares the distance the sandbag was passed with the time it took. Label the units of measure.

▶ Ratios like the one you wrote in Question 3(c) that compare two quantities measured in different units are **rates**. Rates can be used to describe how one measure depends on another measure.

EXAMPLE

30 miles per gallon (mi/gal) is a rate that describes how far a car can travel on one gallon of gas.

30.48 cm for every 12 in. is a rate used to convert measurements from inches to centimeters and vice versa.

4 **Try This as a Class** Explain how you can use the rates in the Example on page 374 to answer each question.

    a. How many gallons of gas does the car need to travel 60 mi?

    b. How many gallons are needed to travel 80 mi?

    c. How many centimeters are in 30 in.?

    d. How many centimeters are in 36 in.?

5 **Try This as a Class** Discuss which of the four answers in Question 4 were easy to find and why.

▶ **Using a Table** One way to answer questions involving rates is to make a table.

6 Suppose a brigade of students passes a sandbag 15 ft in 5 sec.

    a. Make a table that predicts how far a sandbag can be passed in 5, 10, 15, 20, 25, and 30 seconds.

Distance passed (feet)	15	?	?	?	?	?
Time (seconds)	5	10	15	20	25	30

    b. Explain how you predicted the distance a sandbag can be passed in 30 sec.

    c. Explain two ways to predict how far a sandbag can be passed in 60 sec.

7 ✔ **CHECKPOINT** Use the rate in Question 6. Predict how long it will take to pass a sandbag 150 ft.

✔ **QUESTION 7**

...checks that you can use a rate to make a prediction.

> The data in the table you created in Question 6(a) represent equivalent rates.
>
> $$\frac{15 \text{ feet}}{5 \text{ seconds}} \text{ is equivalent to } \frac{30 \text{ feet}}{10 \text{ seconds}}.$$

8 Show that $\frac{15}{5}$ and $\frac{30}{10}$ are equivalent.

9 **Discussion** Suppose a sandbag can be passed 15 feet in 5 sec. How can you use equivalent rates to predict how far the sandbag can be passed in 8 sec?

▶ To answer Question 9, it is helpful to find a *unit rate*. A **unit rate** gives an amount per one unit. For example, 30 mi/gal is a unit rate because it gives the distance a car can travel on one gallon of gas.

EXAMPLE

To find a unit rate for the sandbag brigade in Question 6, you need to find an equivalent rate with a denominator of one second.

First Write the given rate as a fraction.

Then Set up a rate for the number of feet per one second.

$$\frac{15 \text{ feet}}{5 \text{ seconds}} = \frac{x \text{ feet}}{1 \text{ second}}$$

10 **a.** What value of x will make the rates in the Example equivalent?

b. Explain how you found the value of x.

c. Use the value of x to complete the following statement:
A sandbag can be passed _?_ feet per second.

d. Show how the unit rate can be used to find the distance a sandbag can be passed in 12 sec.

11 **Try This as a Class** You can also find a unit rate that shows how long it will take to pass a sandbag one foot.

> Notice that the order in the rates has been changed to seconds : feet.

a. Find a value for y so that the rates below are equivalent.

$$\frac{5 \text{ seconds}}{15 \text{ feet}} = \frac{y \text{ seconds}}{1 \text{ foot}}$$

b. Explain how you found the value for y.

c. Use the value of y to complete the following statement:
It takes _?_ seconds to pass a sandbag one foot.

d. Show how the unit rate can be used to find how long it will take the brigade to pass a sandbag 175 ft.

✔ **QUESTION 12**

...checks that you can find a unit rate.

12 ✔ **CHECKPOINT** Find the unit rate for each rate.

a. 250 mi in 5 hr

b. 56 marbles in 4 bags

c. $4.00 for 5 pens

d. 800 turns per 60 sec

HOMEWORK EXERCISES ▶ See Exs. 1–21 on pp. 377–379.

Section 2

Key Concepts

Key Terms

Rates (pp. 374–375)

A rate is a ratio that compares two quantities measured in different units.

rate

Example $2 for 5 limes is a rate.

Rates may be equivalent.

Example

Price (dollars)	2	4	6	8
Number of limes	5	10	15	20

The pairs of numbers in the table are equivalent rates.
$$\frac{\$2}{5 \text{ limes}} = \frac{\$4}{10 \text{ limes}}$$

Unit Rates (p. 376)

A unit rate gives an amount per one unit.

unit rate

Example Find a unit rate equivalent to the rate "$2 for 5 limes."

$$\frac{\$2}{5 \text{ limes}} = \frac{x}{1 \text{ lime}}$$

$$\$2 \div 5 = \$.40$$

$$\frac{\$2}{5 \text{ limes}} = \frac{\$.40}{1 \text{ lime}}, \text{ or } \$.40 \text{ per lime}$$

13 Key Concepts Question Use the rate from the Examples. What is the cost of 25 limes? 12 limes? Explain your method.

Section 2

Practice & Application Exercises

YOU WILL NEED

For Ex. 18:
♦ Labsheet 2A
♦ your class's brigade data

For Exs. 22–25:
♦ calculator

For Ex. 28:
♦ graph paper

Tell whether the rates are equivalent.

1. $\dfrac{4.2 \text{ m}}{2 \text{ jumps}}, \dfrac{10.5 \text{ m}}{5 \text{ jumps}}$

2. $\dfrac{48 \text{ breaths}}{3 \text{ min}}, \dfrac{95 \text{ breaths}}{5 \text{ min}}$

3. $15 for 6 lb, $20 for 8 lb

4. $2 for 5 pens, $8 for 20 pens

5. 12 laps in 3 hr, 3 laps in 1 hr

6. 35 mi in 2 hr, 145 mi in 4 hr

7. $\dfrac{65 \text{ words}}{1 \text{ min}}, \dfrac{195 \text{ words}}{3 \text{ min}}$

8. $\dfrac{3 \text{ measures}}{12 \text{ beats}}, \dfrac{7 \text{ measures}}{21 \text{ beats}}$

Find a unit rate for each rate.

9. $54 for 18 hr

10. 700 mi on 20 gal

11. 150 ft in 100 steps

12. 500 turns in 8 min

13. 17 pages in 5 min

14. $3 for 5 oranges

15. Suppose pens are packaged in two ways: $2.64 for 6 pens or $3.80 for 10 pens. Which package is the better buy? Explain.

16. **Research** Go to the grocery store. Find and record the prices for different quantities of the same item. Compare unit rates to determine which quantity is the better buy.

17. **Science** Mars travels around the sun at a rate of about 15 mi in one second. How far does Mars travel in one minute? in one hour?

Sun

Mars
15 mi per second

FOR ◀HELP

with *graphing on a coordinate grid*, see

MODULE 4, p. 256

18. **Use Labsheet 2A.** You will need your class's brigade data.

   a. Complete the table of *Sandbag Brigade Data.*

   b. Graph the data in the table. Draw segments to connect the points you graphed in order from left to right.

   c. Use your graph to predict how far a sandbag can be passed in 18 sec.

   d. Use a ruler to extend the line of your graph to predict how long it will take to pass a sandbag 140 ft.

   e. Use unit rates to make the predictions in parts (c) and (d). Then compare the predictions you made using unit rates with those you made using the graph.

19. While visiting Italy, some American students found a CD that cost 15 euros. At that time, four United States dollars were worth 3 euros. How much did the CD cost in United States dollars?

20. Writing Gloria Jones drives 15 mi to work in about half an hour.

    a. Write her rate of travel in miles per hour.

    b. Why do you think this rate is called her "average" speed?

Reflecting ◀▶ on the Section

Write your response to Exercise 21 in your journal.

21. At top speed, a zebra can run 176 ft in 3 sec. A roadrunner can run 220 ft in 10 sec. A gray wolf can run 66 ft in one second. Which animal is the fastest? Which is the slowest? Explain.

Journal

Exercise 21 checks that you understand how to use rates to make comparisons.

Spiral ◀▶ Review

Calculator Write each fraction as a decimal rounded to the nearest hundredth. (Module 4, p. 225)

22. $\frac{5}{6}$ **23.** $\frac{12}{23}$ **24.** $\frac{45}{62}$ **25.** $\frac{84}{116}$

Find the mean, median, and mode(s) for each set of data.
(Module 4, p. 225)

26. 75, 86, 73, 80, 86, 80   **27.** 48, 52, 75, 47, 83, 48

Extension ▶ ▶

A Doubling Rate

28. Suppose you put $100 in a bank account where your money doubles every ten years. The table shows how it will grow.

Number of years	0	10	20	30	40
Money in account	$100	$200	$400	$800	$1600

    a. Copy the coordinate grid and plot the data shown in the table. Connect the points in order from left to right.

    b. How is the rate of growth for money in the account different from other rates in this section? (*Hint:* Are the ratios of years to money in the account equivalent?)

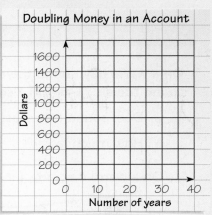

Section ② Extra Skill Practice

Tell whether the rates are equivalent.

1. $\dfrac{150 \text{ words}}{3 \text{ min}}$, $\dfrac{450 \text{ words}}{9 \text{ min}}$

2. $7 for 5 lb, $16.20 for 9 lb

3. 204 mi on 6 gal, 68 mi on 2 gal

4. $\dfrac{212 \text{ heartbeats}}{4 \text{ min}}$, $\dfrac{343 \text{ heartbeats}}{7 \text{ min}}$

Find a unit rate for each rate.

5. 24 km in 3 hr

6. 1500 m in 5 min

7. $45 for 6 books

8. 7 pages in 4 min

9. 84 mi on 3 gal

10. 250 ft in 200 steps

Tell which is the better buy or if neither is the better buy.

11. $4.20 for 8 oranges or $5.76 for 12 oranges

12. $2.24 for 16 oz of apple juice or $3.36 for 24 oz of apple juice

13. Saturn travels around the sun at a rate of about 6 mi in one second.

   a. How far does Saturn travel in one minute?

   b. How far does Saturn travel in one hour?

14. Copy and complete the table of equivalent rates.

Number of pages read	5	10	15	20	?
Time (minutes)	8	?	?	?	40

Standardized Testing ◀▶ Performance Task

On a warm day, sound travels 13,224 ft in 12 sec. On a cool day, sound travels 7140 ft in 7 sec.

1. a. Does sound travel faster through warm air or through cool air?

   b. How much faster?

2. On a warm day, how far does sound travel in 15 sec?

Section ③ Using Ratios

IN THIS SECTION

EXPLORATION 1
◆ Comparing Ratios

EXPLORATION 2
◆ Estimating Ratios

EXPLORATION 3
◆ Predicting with a Graph

BODY RATIOS

Setting the Stage ▸▸▸▸▸▸▸▸▸▸▸▸▸▸▸▸▸▸▸▸▸▸▸▸▸▸▸▸▸▸▸▸▸

In the Jonathan Swift classic *Gulliver's Travels*, Lemuel Gulliver is shipwrecked and swims to the island of Lilliput, where the people have an average height of slightly less than six inches. Since Gulliver's only clothes were those he was wearing, the Lilliputians had to make new clothing for him.

> ## GULLIVER'S TRAVELS *by Jonathan Swift*
>
> The seamstresses took my measure as I lay on the ground, one standing at my neck, and another at my mid-leg, with a strong cord extended, that each held by the end, while the third measured the length of the cord with a rule of an inch long. Then they measured my right thumb, and desired no more; for by a mathematical computation, that twice round the thumb is once round the wrist, and so on to the neck and the waist; and by the help of my old shirt, which I displayed on the ground before them for a pattern, they fitted me exactly.

Think About It

1　The height of a Lilliputian is about what fraction of your height?

2　What two measurements did the Lilliputians take in order to make a shirt for Gulliver?

3　**a.** What do you think Gulliver meant by "twice round the thumb is once round the wrist"?

　b. What do you think he meant by "and so on to the neck and the waist"?

　c. Do you think these comparisons would be true for all the students in your class?

<table>
<tr><td>**GOAL**</td></tr>
</table>

LEARN HOW TO...
◆ use measurements to decide whether a ratio is reasonable
◆ write a ratio as a decimal

AS YOU...
◆ compare your own body ratios with those in *Gulliver's Travels*

Exploration 1

Comparing RATiOS

SET UP *Work in a group. You will need:* • *scissors* • *string* • *metric ruler*

▶ **In this exploration, you will test whether the ratios used by the Lilliputians can be used to accurately predict your body measurements.**

4 Have someone in your group help you measure as shown.

First

Cut a piece of string equal to the distance around your wrist.

Then

Wrap this string around the base of your thumb.

5 **a.** About how many times did the string go around your thumb?

b. Did others in your group get about the same results?

c. How does the relationship you observed compare with Gulliver's claim that "twice around the thumb is once around the wrist"?

6 a. Suppose the distance around a classmate's thumb is 5 cm. What do you expect the distance around the wrist to be?

b. Write the measurements from part (a) as a ratio in two ways:

(**distance around thumb : distance around wrist**)

$$\underline{?} : \underline{?} = \frac{?}{?}$$

▶ **To compare the ratio of your body measurements to Gulliver's ratio, it may be helpful to write the ratio as a single decimal number. For example, the ratio *3 to 4* is *0.75 to 1*, or more simply, *0.75*.**

FOR◄HELP

with *writing a fraction as a decimal*, see
MODULE 4, p. 225

7 Copy and complete the table as you answer parts (a) and (b).

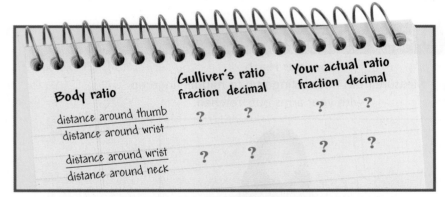

a. Use the relationship described by Gulliver on page 381 to write each body ratio as a fraction and as a decimal.

b. Wrap string to find the ratios for your body. Measure the length of the string in millimeters. Write each ratio as a fraction and as a decimal rounded to the nearest hundredth.

8 ✔ **CHECKPOINT** Look at your table from Question 7.

a. How do Gulliver's ratios compare with your ratios? Which form of the ratios did you use to compare? Explain your choice.

b. Do you think Gulliver's ratios are reasonable estimates? Explain.

✔ **QUESTION 8**

...checks that you can decide whether a ratio is reasonable.

9 Discussion Suppose the distance around a person's thumb is 9 cm. Explain how you can use ratios to predict the distance around the person's neck and waist.

HOMEWORK EXERCISES ▶ See Exs. 1–6 on p. 390.

GOAL

LEARN HOW TO...
- find a ratio to describe data
- use a ratio to make predictions

AS YOU...
- look for other body ratios

KEY TERM
- "nice" fraction

Exploration 2

Estimating RATiOS

SET UP *Work in a group of four. Your group will need: • Labsheet 3A • scissors • string • metric ruler*

▶ **Now you will explore whether other body ratios are about the same for most people. Use the Student Resource below to help you measure.**

10 Estimation Do you think your reach is *more* or *less* than 1 m?

How To Measure

For your reach
Measure from middle fingertip to middle fingertip with your arms outstretched.

For the radius
Rest your elbow on a desk with your hand in the air. Measure from the tip of the elbow to the wrist.

For your height
Measure from the top of your head to the bottom of your feet with your shoes off.

For the tibia
Measure from the ankle bone along the outer side of the leg to just below the knee.

Use Labsheet 3A for Questions 11 and 12.

11 **a.** In the *Body Measurements Table*, record each of the given measurements for each person in your group. Round each measurement to the nearest 0.5 cm.

 b. Include the data from two other groups in your table. (You will use these in Exploration 3.)

12 **a.** For each person in your group, find the decimal form of each ratio in the *Body Ratios Table*. Round to the nearest hundredth. Record your results in the table.

 b. Which columns of your table have ratios that are about the same for everyone?

 c. Find and record the mean of the ratios in each column.

▶ Ratios are often expressed as fractions. **"Nice"** fractions, such as $\frac{1}{3}$, $\frac{1}{4}$, and $\frac{2}{5}$, are common fractions that are easy to visualize and easy to compute with mentally.

EXAMPLE

Find a "nice" fraction for $\frac{5}{11}$.

SAMPLE RESPONSE

Using mental math:

 5 is about half of 11,

 so $\frac{1}{2}$ is a "nice" fraction for $\frac{5}{11}$.

$\frac{1}{2}$ is a **"nice"** fraction because it is easy to compute with. For example, it is easier to find $\frac{1}{2}$ of 16 than $\frac{5}{11}$ of 16.

Using decimals:

 $\frac{5}{11} \approx 0.45$

 This is close to 0.5, or the "nice" fraction $\frac{1}{2}$.

---

13 **Try This as a Class**

 a. Which of the following "nice" fractions is closest to $\frac{7}{24}$: $\frac{1}{2}$, $\frac{1}{3}$, $\frac{1}{5}$, or $\frac{1}{6}$?

 b. How did you decide which fraction was best in part (a)?

 c. Name two fractions that the "nice" fraction $\frac{3}{4}$ could replace.

As you answer Questions 14–16, record the "nice" fractions you find to describe your data in your *Body Ratios Table*.

14 Use Labsheet 3A.

    a. Discussion Which ratio below is closest to the mean of your group's tibia to height ratios? Explain how you know.

$$\frac{1}{1} \quad \frac{1}{2} \quad \frac{1}{3} \quad \frac{1}{4} \quad \frac{1}{5} \quad \frac{1}{6}$$

    b. Use your ratio from part (a) to predict the tibia length of a person who is 150 cm tall.

✔ **QUESTION 15**

...checks that you can find and use a fraction to make a prediction.

15 ✔ **CHECKPOINT**

    a. What "nice" fraction is close to the mean of the radius to height ratios?

    b. Suppose a person's radius is 18 cm long. About how tall do you expect the person to be?

16 a. Write a "nice" fraction that is close to the mean of the reach to height ratios.

    b. Suppose a person is 180 cm tall. About how long do you think the person's reach is?

17 Use your results from Questions 14–16. Draw and label a sketch of a 6-inch tall Lilliputian that shows the measure of the reach, the tibia, and the radius.

HOMEWORK EXERCISES ▶ See Exs. 7–15 on pp. 390–391.

Predicting with a GRAPH

SET UP *Work in a group. You will need: • completed Labsheet 3A • Labsheet 3B • uncooked spaghetti • graph paper*

▶ **In Explorations 1 and 2 you used ratios to make predictions. You can also use a graph to make predictions from data.**

Use Labsheet 3B for Questions 18–20 and 22.

18 **Try This as a Class** Follow the steps below to make predictions about height and reach using a graph.

Step 1

Place a piece of uncooked spaghetti on the *Reach Compared to Height Graph* so it lies close to most of the points. Try to have about the same number of points on one side of the spaghetti as on the other side.

Step 2

Draw a line segment on the *Reach Compared to Height Graph* along the edge of your spaghetti. The segment you drew on the graph is a **fitted line**. It can be used to predict unknown measurements using known ones.

19 **a.** How can the fitted line help you predict a person's height if you know the person's reach is 135 cm?

b. What do you expect the reach of a person 152 cm tall to be?

20 Discussion Look at the scales used on the *Reach Compared to Height Graph*. Why do you think the labeling on the scales starts at a height of 120 cm and at a reach of 110 cm?

Use your data from Labsheet 3A for Questions 21 and 22.

FOR ◄HELP

with *plotting points*, see

MODULE 4, p. 256

21 Use the data on the heights and the lengths of the tibias from all three groups in your *Body Measurements Table*. You will make a graph similar to the *Reach Compared to Height Graph*.

a. Look at the height data. What are the shortest and the tallest heights?

b. Look at the tibia data. What are the shortest and the longest lengths of the tibias?

c. Use your answers from parts (a) and (b) to draw and label the scales for your graph. You do not have to start your labeling at (0, 0).

d. Plot a point representing the height and the length of the tibia for each person.

e. The type of graph you made is a **scatter plot**. What do you notice about the points in your scatter plot?

f. Follow the steps in Question 18 to draw a fitted line for your scatter plot.

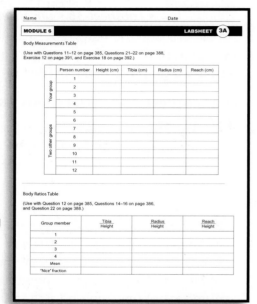

✔ QUESTION 22

...checks that you can use a scatter plot and a fitted line to make a prediction.

22 ✔ CHECKPOINT Use your graph from Question 21.

a. Suppose a person's tibia is 42 cm long. About how tall do you expect the person to be?

b. Use the fitted line on your scatter plot to complete the *Points on the Line Table* on Labsheet 3B.

c. How do the tibia to height ratios in the *Points on the Line Table* compare with the "nice" fraction you recorded in the *Body Ratios Table* on Labsheet 3A?

HOMEWORK EXERCISES ▶ See Exs. 16–20 on pp. 392–393.

Section 3
Key Concepts

Using Ratios (pp. 382–386)
Different forms of ratios are useful in different situations.

- Using the decimal form can help you to compare ratios. To find the decimal, first write the ratio as a fraction. Then divide the numerator by the denominator.

Example length of one step = 64 cm
height = 151 cm

$$\frac{\text{step length}}{\text{height}} = \frac{64}{151}$$

$$151\overline{)64.000} \quad 0.423$$

The ratio is about 0.42 or 0.42 to 1.

- "Nice" fractions, like $\frac{1}{2}$, $\frac{2}{3}$, or $\frac{3}{4}$, are often used to describe ratios in a simple way, making computation easier. Look to see if the decimal form is close to a "nice" fraction.

Example The ratio 0.42 is close to 0.4, which equals the "nice" fraction $\frac{4}{10}$, or $\frac{2}{5}$. This ratio can be used to estimate the height of a person whose step length is 60 cm.

$$\frac{\text{step length}}{\text{height}} = \frac{2}{5} = \frac{60}{?} \qquad \frac{2 \times 30}{5 \times 30} = \frac{60}{150}$$

The height of the person is probably about 150 cm.

Using Scatter Plots (pp. 387–388)
A scatter plot is a graph that shows the relationship between two sets of data.

When the points lie close to a line, you can use a fitted line to make predictions from the data.

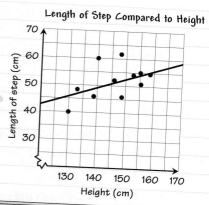

Length of Step Compared to Height

Length of step (cm) / Height (cm)

23 Key Concepts Question

a. Use the "nice" fraction in the second Example above to estimate the step length of a person 145 cm tall.

b. Use the scatter plot above and the fitted line to predict the step length of a person who is 145 cm tall.

YOU WILL NEED

For Exs. 12 and 18:
♦ completed Labsheet 3A

For Exs. 17 and 18:
♦ graph paper
♦ piece of uncooked spaghetti or a clear plastic ruler

1. Use the ratio 1 : 2 as an estimate for the body ratios *thumb to wrist, wrist to neck,* and *neck to waist.*

   a. Suppose the distance around Gulliver's wrist is 20 cm. Estimate his thumb, neck, and waist measurements.

   b. **Create Your Own** Make and label a sketch of Gulliver's shirt. Select reasonable measurements for the cuffs and neckline.

2. Each oval has a vertical height of 12 mm.

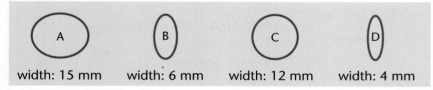

width: 15 mm   width: 6 mm   width: 12 mm   width: 4 mm

   a. For each oval, write the ratio of the width to the height as a decimal.

   b. What does the ratio of the width to the height tell you about the general shape of the ovals?

Write each ratio as a decimal rounded to the nearest hundredth.

3. 7 : 9   4. 6 : 11   5. 2 : 7   6. 8 : 19

7. Solve the following problems to see how an archaeologist might be able to use body ratios.

   a. A human radius 27 cm long was found. Estimate the person's height. (Use 1 : 6 as the ratio for *length of radius to height.*)

   b. A human tibia 46 cm long was discovered at the same site as the radius in part (a). Estimate the person's height. (Use 1 : 4 as the ratio for *length of tibia to height.*)

   c. Do you think both bones are from the same person? Explain.

Write a "nice" fraction for each ratio.

8. 5 : 26   9. 0.31   10. $\frac{12}{38}$ 11. 0.6 to 1

12. **Use the data from Labsheet 3A.** Write a "nice" fraction that compares the length of the tibia with the length of the radius.

13. Some students dropped a ball from different heights. They recorded how high it bounced from each drop height.

    a. The ratio of *bounce height to drop height* was about 0.81. Write a "nice" fraction close to 0.81.

    b. Predict how high the ball will bounce when they drop it from a height of 5 ft.

    c. On one drop the ball bounced to a height of 28 in. Estimate the drop height the students used.

14. **Home Involvement** Find at least two other people whose ages are different from yours. Record the body measurements shown on page 384 for them. Compare the ratios of these measurements with the "nice" fractions you found for your group. Prepare a presentation of your findings.

15. **Volleyball** Volleyball net heights are different for women and men. The women's net is set at 7 ft $4\frac{1}{8}$ in. The men's net is set at 7 ft $11\frac{5}{8}$ in.

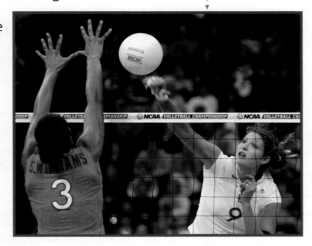

    a. Round each net height to the nearest inch. Write a ratio of *women's net height to men's net height* in inches.

    b. Using decimals, what "nice" fraction is the ratio in part (a) close to?

    c. The average height of the top ten female volleyball players is 5 ft 9 in. The average height of the top ten male volleyball players is 6 ft 4 in. Write a ratio of the *average women's height to average men's height* in inches.

    d. Using decimals, what "nice" fraction is the ratio in part (c) close to?

    e. How does the ratio in part (b) compare with the ratio in part (d)?

    f. Compare the ratio of *average women's height to women's net height* with the ratio of *average men's height to men's net height*. Describe your findings.

16. **a.** Which line would you use to make predictions about the distance around a person's head or predictions about a person's height? Why?

Distance Around the Head Compared to Height

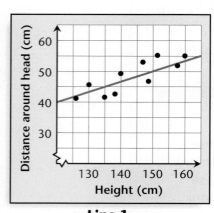

Line 1

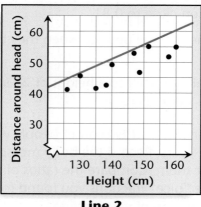

Line 2

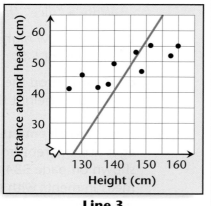

Line 3

b. Use your choice from part (a) to predict each measurement.

• height for a distance around the head of 45 cm

• the distance around your own head

Pages in English	Pages in Spanish
13	14
13	15
15	17
16	18
16	19
18	21
19	21
19	23
20	23
21	23
21	25
23	26
24	28

17. **a.** When English is translated into Spanish it takes up a different amount of space. On graph paper, make a scatter plot with a fitted line that shows the relationship between the number of pages in English and the number of pages in Spanish.

b. Predict the number of pages in Spanish for an article that is 14 pages long in English.

c. Predict the number of pages in English for an article that is 30 pages long in Spanish.

18. **a. Use the data from Labsheet 3A.** On graph paper, make a scatter plot that shows the relationship between the height and the length of the radius.

b. Draw a fitted line on your scatter plot. Copy the table at the right. Then use your fitted line to complete it.

Height (cm)	Radius (cm)
120	?
150	?
180	?
?	24
?	32

19. Nearly 8000 terra-cotta warriors that are $5\frac{1}{2}$ to 6 feet tall have been found near Lintong, China. These figures were found close to the burial site of Qin Shihuangdi, the first emperor of China. Some believe that this army was built to fight the emperor's battles after death.

    a. Use your scatter plot from Exercise 18 to estimate the length of the radius of a 6-foot warrior. (1 ft is about 30.5 cm.)

◄ The warriors are made of terra-cotta, a type of ceramic clay.

    b. **Writing** A 6-foot warrior is 6 in. taller than a $5\frac{1}{2}$-foot warrior. Does this mean that the tibia of a 6-foot warrior is 6 in. longer than the tibia of a $5\frac{1}{2}$-foot warrior? Explain.

Reflecting ◀▶ on the Section

Write your response to Exercise 20 in your journal.

20. Think of some ratios you use in your daily life. Use sketches or descriptions to show what these ratios mean and how you could use them to find unknown values. Include different forms of ratios and explain why each form is used.

Journal

Exercise 20 checks that you understand how ratios are used.

Spiral ◀▶ Review

Find a unit rate for each rate. (Module 6, p. 377)

21. 99 mi on 3 gal   22. $17 for 6 lb   23. $\dfrac{265 \text{ heartbeats}}{5 \text{ min}}$

24. Suppose heads occurred on 14 out of 30 tosses of a coin. Find the experimental probability of tossing heads. (Module 2, p. 80)

Section 3
Extra Skill Practice

You will need: • *graph paper* (Ex. 2)

• *piece of uncooked spaghetti or clear ruler* (Ex. 2)

For Exercises 1 and 2, use the data in the table.

Person	A	B	C	D	E	F	G	H
kneeling height (cm) / Standing height (cm)	$\frac{75}{102}$	$\frac{90}{122}$	$\frac{101}{137}$	$\frac{82}{108}$	$\frac{109}{145}$	$\frac{113}{152}$	$\frac{101}{135}$	$\frac{94}{128}$

1. a. Write each *kneeling height to standing height* ratio as a decimal. Round to the nearest hundredth.

   b. Find the mean of the *kneeling height to standing height* ratios.

   c. Write a "nice" fraction that is close to the mean.

   d. Use your "nice" fraction to estimate the missing entries in the table below.

Kneeling height (cm)	94	?	?	87
Standing height (cm)	?	132	140	?

2. a. Make a scatter plot that shows the relationship between the kneeling height and the standing height of each person in the table.

   b. Use a piece of uncooked spaghetti or a clear ruler to draw a fitted line on your scatter plot.

   c. Use your scatter plot to estimate the missing entries in the table in Exercise 1(d). How do your answers compare?

Standardized Testing ◀▶ Open-Ended

Write a word problem that involves using ratios to make a comparison or prediction.

Solve your word problem. What form of the ratio did you use? Explain why you chose that form.

FOR ASSESSMENT AND PORTFOLIOS

The IDEAL Chair

EXTENDED E2 EXPLORATION

SET UP *You will need: • ruler • string • yardstick*

The Situation

Sometimes it is hard to find a comfortable chair to sit in. Many companies manufacture wooden, polyethylene, and solid plastic classroom chairs in a range of sizes to accommodate the average size student in different grades.

The Problem

Design a chair for your classroom that has the proportions and features that make the chair comfortable not just for sitting, but for learning.

Something to Think About

◆ What size chair would best fit you if your feet are flat on the floor and the chair back supports your back?

◆ What information do you need to consider as you design a chair to fit any student in your classroom?

◆ How will you find and organize your data?

Present your Results

Describe your classroom chair.

◆ Why is it comfortable for sitting and learning?

◆ What other features make your design desirable?

Show the organized information you gathered.

◆ How did you collect the data?

◆ How did you use the information?

Display sketches and/or a model of your chair.

Reflect on Your Design

◆ What did you try that did not work?

◆ What did you do when you were stuck?

◆ What would you change if you were to design another chair?

Section 4 Proportions

IN THIS SECTION

EXPLORATION 1
♦ Exploring Proportions

EXPLORATION 2
♦ Using Proportions

Setting the Stage

Look at the table and graph to see how the world-record long jump for a human compares to the records of several animals.

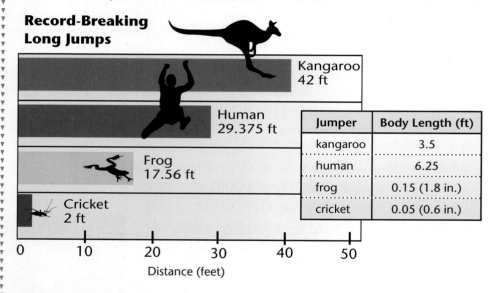

Record-Breaking Long Jumps

Kangaroo 42 ft

Human 29.375 ft

Frog 17.56 ft

Cricket 2 ft

Jumper	Body Length (ft)
kangaroo	3.5
human	6.25
frog	0.15 (1.8 in.)
cricket	0.05 (0.6 in.)

Distance (feet)

Think About It

1 **a.** Which of the four jumped the farthest?

   b. Which of the four can jump more than 10 times its body length?

   c. Which can jump more than 100 times its body length?

   d. Is it fair to compare jumping ability by examining just the distance jumped? Explain.

2 Describe how ratios written in decimal form can be used to identify which jumper traveled the farthest for its size.

GOAL

LEARN HOW TO...
◆ Use cross products to find equivalent ratios
◆ find the missing term in a proportion

AS YOU...
◆ predict how far a jackrabbit can jump

KEY TERMS
◆ proportion
◆ cross products

EXPLORING PROPORTIONS

▸ A black-tailed jackrabbit can jump about as far for its size as the record-breaking kangaroo. You can use this fact to estimate how far a jackrabbit 18 in. long can jump. To find out how, you will explore some properties of equivalent ratios.

3 **Discussion** Tell whether the ratios in each pair are equivalent. Explain how you know.

a. $\frac{10}{12}$ and $\frac{25}{30}$ **b.** $\frac{8}{24}$ and $\frac{4}{20}$ **c.** $\frac{10}{40}$ and $\frac{101}{400}$

d. $\frac{8}{6}$ and $\frac{2}{18}$ **e.** $\frac{12}{36}$ and $\frac{5}{15}$ **f.** $\frac{16}{24}$ and $\frac{27}{36}$

▸ A **proportion** is an equation stating that two ratios are equivalent. One method for determining if two ratios are equivalent is to compare **cross products**.

EXAMPLE

The equation $\frac{16}{10} = \frac{24}{15}$ is a proportion.

One cross product is 16 · 15.

The other cross product is 10 · 24.

$$\frac{16}{10} = \frac{24}{15}$$

---

4 Find the products 16 · 15 and 10 · 24. What do you notice?

5 **a.** Find the cross products for each pair of equivalent ratios in Question 3. What do you notice about them?

b. Find the cross products for the pairs of ratios that are not equivalent in Question 3. What do you notice?

6 Discussion How do you think cross products can be used to tell whether two ratios are equivalent?

✔ QUESTION 7

...checks that you can use cross products to tell whether two ratios are equivalent.

7  **CHECKPOINT** Use cross products to tell whether the ratios are equivalent.

a. $\frac{11}{4}$ and $\frac{15}{6}$ b. $\frac{8}{14}$ and $\frac{24}{32}$ c. $\frac{12}{30}$ and $\frac{30}{75}$

8 Try This as a Class Cathy used cross products to help her find the missing term in the proportion $\frac{9}{12} = \frac{x}{20}$.

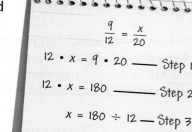

$$\frac{9}{12} = \frac{x}{20}$$

$12 \cdot x = 9 \cdot 20$ —— Step 1

$12 \cdot x = 180$ —— Step 2

$x = 180 \div 12$ — Step 3

$x = 15$ —— Step 4

a. Explain what she did in each step.

b. How can you check whether 15 is the correct value?

c. Can you also use equivalent fractions to find the missing term in the proportion $\frac{9}{12} = \frac{x}{20}$? Explain.

9 📟 Calculator Write a calculator key sequence to find the missing term in the proportion $\frac{12}{16} = \frac{18}{y}$.

✔ QUESTION 10

...checks that you can find a missing term in a proportion.

10 ✔ **CHECKPOINT** Find the missing term in each proportion.

a. $\frac{15}{20} = \frac{9}{y}$ b. $\frac{18}{n} = \frac{12}{8}$ c. $\frac{5}{12} = \frac{12.5}{m}$

11 Now you are ready to estimate how far a jackrabbit can jump.

a. **Discussion** You were told that "A black-tailed jackrabbit can jump about as far for its size as the record-breaking kangaroo." What do you think this means?

b. Use the table on page 396. Why can the proportion below be used to estimate how far a jackrabbit with a body 18 in. long can jump?

$$\frac{42}{3.5} = \frac{d}{1.5}$$

18 in. is equal to 1.5 ft.

c. Find the missing term in the proportion in part (b).

d. Would you expect the jackrabbit to jump exactly the distance you found in part (c)? Explain.

HOMEWORK EXERCISES ▶ See Exs. 1–11 on p. 402.

PRO^{Using}POR_{TIONS}

GOAL

LEARN HOW TO...
◆ write a proportion to solve a problem
◆ use a proportion to make a prediction

AS YOU...
◆ explore the jumping ability of a frog

▶ **Frogs are much better jumpers than humans. To appreciate just how much better, you can use a proportion to explore how far someone with the jumping ability of a frog could jump.**

EXAMPLE

Suppose a 6.25 foot (6 ft 3 in.) tall human has the jumping ability of the record-breaking frog that is 0.15 ft long and can jump 17.56 ft. Write a proportion to find how far this person can jump.

Step 1 Study the situation to find what measures are being compared.

$$\frac{\text{jump distance (ft)}}{\text{body length (ft)}}$$

Jump distance is being compared to body length.

Step 2 Decide what ratios to show in the proportion.

Ratio for the frog   Ratio for the human

$$\frac{\text{jump distance}}{\text{body length}} = \frac{\text{jump distance}}{\text{body length}}$$

Step 3 Fill in the information you know to write the proportion. You know the jump distance and body length of the frog and the body length of the human. Use a variable for the value you do not know.

You want to find the jump distance for the human.

$$\frac{17.56}{0.15} = \frac{d}{6.25}$$

12 Discussion Why was a variable used for the human jump distance?

13 Find the missing term in the proportion. How does the answer compare with the world record for humans given on page 396?

▶ **The super-jumper problem may be a bit unrealistic, but there are many real problem situations where using a proportion is a good method for making predictions.**

14 Suppose a school fundraiser makes a $1.75 profit for every 6 rolls of wrapping paper sold. One class of students sells 256 rolls.

   a. What phrase tells you the measurements that are being compared?

   b. What two words indicate a ratio is being used?

   c. Write a proportion by filling in the values you know. Use a variable for the value you do not know.

Profit ratio for 6 rolls		**Profit ratio for 256 rolls**
$\dfrac{\text{profit}}{\text{number of rolls sold}}$	$=$	$\dfrac{\text{profit}}{\text{number of rolls sold}}$

   d. What is the profit on 256 rolls?

✔ **QUESTION 15**

...checks that you can write a proportion and use it to make a prediction.

15 ✔ **CHECKPOINT** Suppose a car travels 330 mi on 12 gal of gas. Use a proportion to predict how many gallons of gas it will take to travel 500 mi. Show your work.

▶ **In some problem situations, writing a proportion to make a prediction is not appropriate.**

16 **Discussion** The height and the jump distance for the human world-record holder are given on page 396. Do you think it is appropriate to use these measures in a proportion to estimate how far a 5-foot tall person can jump? Explain.

17 **Try This as a Class** If appropriate, use a proportion to solve each problem. If it is not appropriate to use a proportion, explain why not.

   a. While resting, Tani's heart beats 11 times in 10 seconds. How many times will his heart beat during a 2-minute rest?

   b. The ratio of *body weight to daily food intake* for a bird is 10 to 4. How much will a 150-pound person eat in a day?

   c. In 1996, Gail Devers ran 100 m in 11.11 sec to win an Olympic gold medal. How long would it take her to run 1500 m?

▲
On August 30, 1991, Mike Powell set a long jump record of 29 ft $4\frac{1}{2}$ in. The record still stands today.

HOMEWORK EXERCISES ▶ See Exs. 12–18 on pp. 403–404.

Section 4
Key Concepts

▶▶▶▶▶▶▶▶▶▶▶▶▶▶▶▶▶▶▶▶▶▶▶▶▶

Key Terms

Recognizing Proportions (pp. 397–398)

A proportion is an equation stating that two ratios are equivalent.

Example $\frac{4}{6} = \frac{12}{18}$ is a proportion because $\frac{4 \cdot 3}{6 \cdot 3} = \frac{12}{18}$.

proportion

The cross products in a proportion are equal.

Example

$$\frac{4}{6} \overset{\diagdown\diagup}{=} \frac{12}{18}$$

$6 \cdot 12 = 72$

cross products

$4 \cdot 18 = 72$

Finding a Missing Term in a Proportion (p. 398)

You can use cross products to find the missing term in a proportion.

Example Find the missing term in the proportion $\frac{10}{15} = \frac{x}{12}$.

Use cross products to write an equation.

$15 \cdot x = 10 \cdot 12$
$15 \cdot x = 120$
$x = 120 \div 15$
$x = 8$

Then use division to find the value of the variable.

You can check by substituting 8 for x and then checking that the ratios are equivalent.

$\frac{10}{15} \overset{?}{=} \frac{8}{12}$
$10 \cdot 12 \overset{?}{=} 15 \cdot 8$
$120 = 120$

The cross products are equal, so $x = 8$.

Key Concepts Questions

18 Use cross products to tell whether the ratios are equivalent.

a. $\frac{5}{6}$ and $\frac{17}{20}$ **b.** $\frac{48}{36}$ and $\frac{220}{165}$ **c.** $\frac{21}{13}$ and $\frac{189}{117}$

19 Describe two ways to find the missing term in the proportion $\frac{45}{35} = \frac{18}{n}$. Then solve the proportion using both methods. Did you get the same result?

Section 4

Key Concepts

Writing Proportions (pp. 399–400)

When you write a proportion to solve a problem, it is important to set up the proportion correctly.

Example Suppose Miguel's dog eats 2 lb of dog food every 3 days. How many pounds of food will the dog eat in 31 days?

Ratio for 3 days   Ratio for 31 days

pounds of dog food ⟶ $\dfrac{2}{3}$ = $\dfrac{x}{31}$ ⟵ pounds of dog food

number of days ⟶   ⟵ number of days

Key Concepts Questions

20 Use the proportion in the Example above to find how many pounds of food Miguel's dog will eat in 31 days. Would you get the same answer if you used the proportion $\dfrac{3}{2} = \dfrac{31}{x}$? Explain.

21 It is not always appropriate to use a proportion to solve a problem involving ratios. Give an example to illustrate this.

Section 4

Practice & Application Exercises

Find all the equivalent ratios in each list.

1. $\dfrac{15}{60}, \dfrac{24}{32}, \dfrac{75}{300}, \dfrac{21}{28}, \dfrac{3.5}{14}$

2. $\dfrac{6}{7}, \dfrac{10}{12.5}, \dfrac{30}{35}, \dfrac{16}{20}, \dfrac{40}{45}$

In Exercises 3–11, find the missing term in each proportion.

3. $\dfrac{3}{12} = \dfrac{5}{n}$

4. $\dfrac{4}{24} = \dfrac{6}{x}$

5. $\dfrac{5}{15} = \dfrac{y}{24}$

6. $\dfrac{s}{7} = \dfrac{3.5}{1.4}$

7. $\dfrac{20}{8} = \dfrac{4.5}{d}$

8. $\dfrac{5}{m} = \dfrac{2.5}{40}$

9. $16 : 3 = 64 : r$

10. $p : 15 = 4 : 9$

11. $7 : w = 56 : 40$

12. Choose the proportions that have been set up correctly for solving the problem.

The *Water Arc* in Chicago, Illinois, shoots out about 21,000 gal of water over the Chicago River during each 10-minute show. How many gallons of water does it shoot in four minutes?

A. $\dfrac{21,000}{10} = \dfrac{4}{x}$
B. $\dfrac{10}{21,000} = \dfrac{4}{x}$
C. $\dfrac{21,000}{10} = \dfrac{x}{4}$

13. In the movie *Honey I Shrunk the Kids,* an inventor accidentally shrinks his children. They become so small that they are mistakenly thrown out with the trash and must make their way back to the house.

a. **Writing** Nicky explains to the other children, "We are exactly 64 feet from the house, which is the equivalent of 3.2 miles." What does Nicky mean?

b. Nicky can walk one mile in 20 min at his normal height. To predict how long it will take him to walk to the house at his new height, a proportion has been labeled. Fill in the values you know. Use a variable for the value you do not know.

Ratio for 1 mile   Ratio for 3.2 miles

$$\frac{\text{distance}}{\text{time}} = \frac{\text{distance}}{\text{time}}$$

c. Find the missing value in your proportion.

14. Challenge In Exercise 13 Nicky's height was roughly $\frac{1}{4}$ in. Estimate Nicky's normal height. (Remember that 1 mi = 5280 ft.)

15. Probability Connection In 5 out of 24 rolls, a number cube lands on 2.

a. Find the experimental probability of landing on 2.

b. Use your answer to part (a) and a proportion to predict how many times out of 60 rolls a number cube will land on 2.

If appropriate, use a proportion to solve each problem. If it is not appropriate to use a proportion, explain why not.

16. Three year old Mina is 32 in. tall. Mina grew 4 in. in one year. How tall will Mina be in 18 years?

17. For every 4 steps Mina takes, her grandmother takes 3 steps. How many steps will Mina take if her grandmother takes 54 steps?

Oral Report

Exercise 18 checks that you know how to write a proportion to solve a problem.

Reflecting ◀▶ on the Section

Be prepared to report on the following topic in class.

18. a. Write a problem about your everyday life that can be solved using a proportion. Be sure your problem is one in which it is appropriate to use a proportion.

    b. Solve the problem you wrote for part (a). Be sure to include an explanation of how you solved it.

Spiral ◀▶ Review

19. a. For a certain group of people, the mean of the ratios for *distance around the thumb to distance around the neck* is 0.26. Write a "nice" fraction that is close to the mean. (Module 6, p. 389)

    b. Predict the distance around the neck of a person whose thumb measurement is 3.75 in. (Module 6, p. 389)

Draw an example of each type of angle. (Module 2, p. 107)

20. acute   21. obtuse   22. straight   23. right

24. Trace the figure. Then find three ways to divide the figure into eight identical parts. (Module 1, p. 46)

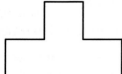

Section 4

Extra Skill Practice

Use cross products to tell whether the ratios are equivalent.

1. $\dfrac{12}{18}$ and $\dfrac{4}{6}$

2. $\dfrac{8}{10}$ and $\dfrac{12}{15}$

3. $\dfrac{3}{50}$ and $\dfrac{6}{75}$

4. $\dfrac{1.5}{3}$ and $\dfrac{10}{20}$

Find the missing term in each proportion.

5. $\dfrac{n}{8} = \dfrac{12}{2}$

6. $\dfrac{8}{12} = \dfrac{12}{g}$

7. $\dfrac{9}{13} = \dfrac{27}{r}$

8. $x : 5 = 27 : 45$

9. $\dfrac{d}{4} = \dfrac{13}{26}$

10. $\dfrac{2}{n} = \dfrac{3}{9}$

11. $\dfrac{2.5}{5} = \dfrac{c}{8}$

12. $3 : 8 = k : 12$

If appropriate, use a proportion to solve each problem. If it is not appropriate to use a proportion, explain why not.

13. Eight newspapers cost $3.60. How much will six newpapers cost?

14. Five white cars drove past Mark's house from 6:00 A.M. to 9:00 A.M. How many will pass his house in twenty-four hours?

15. Janis used four yards of ribbon to make six bows. How many yards of ribbon will she need to make ten more bows?

Standardized Testing ◀▶ Multiple Choice

1. For which values of x and y will the proportion $\dfrac{x}{25} = \dfrac{15}{y}$ be correct?

   I. $x = 20$, $y = 20$ II. $x = 12.5$, $y = 30$ III. $x = 100$, $y = 5$ IV. $x = 5$, $y = 75$

   A I only **B** IV only **C** I and III **D** II and IV

2. For which problems is it appropriate and correct to find the solution using the proportion $\dfrac{x}{75} = \dfrac{10}{45}$?

   I. Darren read 10 pages of a book in 45 minutes. Predict how many pages he can read in 12 minutes.

   II. Sheri bought 10 tapes for the school music library for $45. If the tapes all have the same price, how many can she buy for $75?

   III. Elsa drank 10 oz of water after she finished a 45 min. exercise class. How much do you think she will drink after a 75 min. class?

   A I only **B** II only **C** I and III **D** II and III

Section **5** **Geometry and Proportions**

IN THIS SECTION

EXPLORATION 1
♦ Comparing Shapes

EXPLORATION 2
♦ Models and Scale Drawings

Very SiMiLAR

·-Setting the Stage

Some artists use mathematics to help them design their creations. In M.C. Escher's *Square Limit* below, the fish are arranged so that there are no gaps or overlapping pieces.

Think About It

1 **a.** How are the fish in the middle of the design and the surrounding fish alike?

   b. How are they different?

2 How did Escher create the impression that the design goes on forever inside the square?

Exploration 1

COMPARING SHAPES

GOAL

LEARN HOW TO...
◆ identify similar and congruent figures

AS YOU...
◆ compare pattern block shapes

KEY TERMS
◆ similar figures
◆ corresponding parts
◆ congruent figures

SET UP *Work with a partner. You will need:* • *Labsheet 5A* • *pattern blocks* • *metric ruler* • *tracing paper* • *protractor*

▶ The drawing below shows how Escher used a pattern of squares and triangles to create *Square Limit*. The drawing represents the lower right portion of Escher's work. The two outlined triangles in the drawing are *similar*. **Similar figures** have the same shape but not necessarily the same size.

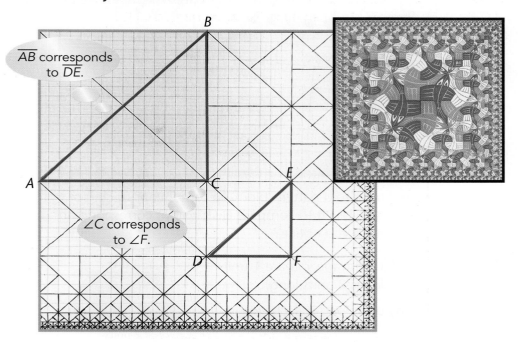

$\overline{AB}$ corresponds to $\overline{DE}$.

∠*C* corresponds to ∠*F*.

▶ When two figures are similar, for each part of one figure there is a **corresponding part** on the other figure.

3 **Discussion** Look at similar triangles *ABC* and *DEF*.

    a. Name another pair of corresponding sides.

    b. Name another pair of corresponding angles.

    c. How many pairs of corresponding angles are there?

    d. How many pairs of corresponding sides are there?

▶ Sometimes it is hard to tell whether two figures are similar just by looking at them. To help determine if two figures are similar, you will use pattern blocks to create similar figures and explore relationships between their corresponding parts.

4 **Try This as a Class** Trapezoid *ABCD* and trapezoid *EFGH* are similar.

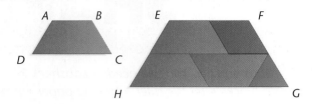

a. Use pattern blocks to build the two trapezoids. Trace around each trapezoid and label it as shown.

b. Copy and complete the tables.

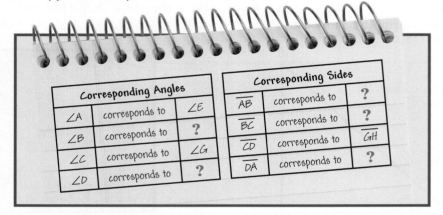

Corresponding Angles

∠A	corresponds to	∠E
∠B	corresponds to	?
∠C	corresponds to	∠G
∠D	corresponds to	?

Corresponding Sides

$\overline{AB}$	corresponds to	?
$\overline{BC}$	corresponds to	?
$\overline{CD}$	corresponds to	$\overline{GH}$
$\overline{DA}$	corresponds to	?

c. Place a red trapezoid pattern block on top of your tracing of trapezoid *EFGH*. Use it to compare each pair of corresponding angles. What do you notice?

5 Three sides of a red trapezoid are 1 unit long and one side is 2 units long.

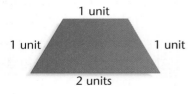

1 unit

1 unit   1 unit

2 units

a. How many units long is each side of trapezoid *EFGH*?

b. Write the ratio of the length of $\overline{AB}$ to the length of $\overline{EF}$ as a fraction.

c. Copy and complete the ratios of the lengths of the other pairs of corresponding sides. Write each ratio as a fraction.

BC means the length of $\overline{BC}$.

$$\frac{BC}{FG} = \frac{?}{?} \qquad \frac{CD}{GH} = \frac{?}{?} \qquad \frac{DA}{HE} = \frac{?}{?}$$

d. What do you notice about the ratios in parts (b) and (c)?

6 **Discussion** Think about your results in Questions 4 and 5.

    a. When two figures are similar, what do you think is true about their corresponding angles?

    b. When two figures are similar, what do you think is true about the ratios of the lengths of their corresponding sides?

7 **Try This as a Class** Use pattern blocks to build the trapezoid below. Is this trapezoid similar to one red trapezoid pattern block? Why or why not?

▶ **Congruent figures** are a special type of similar figures that have the same shape and the same size.

> **EXAMPLE**
>
> △*ABC* is congruent to △*XYZ*. Two figures are congruent even if they have different orientations.
>
> △*ABC* means triangle *ABC*.
>
>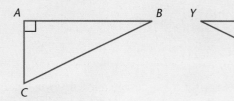

8 **a.** Identify the corresponding angles and corresponding sides of the two triangles in the Example.

    b. Make a tracing of one of the triangles in the Example. Place your tracing over the other triangle so that the corresponding parts match up.

    c. What is the ratio of the lengths of the corresponding sides of two congruent figures? Explain.

9 ✔ **CHECKPOINT** Use Labsheet 5A. Follow the directions on the labsheet to determine which of the *Polygon Pairs* are similar and which are congruent.

✔ **QUESTION 9**

...checks that you can determine if two figures are similar or congruent.

HOMEWORK EXERCISES ▶ See Exs. 1–10 on pp. 414–415.

GOAL

LEARN HOW TO...
◆ use proportions
  to find missing
  lengths

AS YOU...
◆ work with scale
  models and
  drawings

KEY TERM
◆ scale

Exploration 2

Models and SCALE DRAWINGS

SET UP *You will need a customary ruler.*

In South Dakota, a model of the Sioux leader Chief Crazy Horse is being used to construct what may be the world's largest sculpture. When completed, the sculpture will measure 563 ft high by 641 ft long!

▶ **When creating a large piece of art, an artist often makes a model similar to what the completed artwork will be.**

10 a. The Crazy Horse model is similar to the sculpture. What do you know about their corresponding measurements?

b. The height of the model is 16.56 ft. Write and solve a proportion to find the length of the model. Round your answer to the nearest hundredth.

11 Try This as a Class

    a. Did everyone get the same answer for Question 10(b)?

    b. Did everyone use the same proportion?

12 Discussion Explain how you can find the length of the arm on the sculpture when you know that the arm on the model is 7.74 ft long and the height of the model is 16.56 ft.

13 ✔ **CHECKPOINT** Use a proportion to find the missing length in each pair of similar figures.

    a.

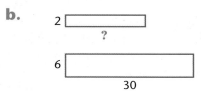

    b.

✔ **QUESTION 13**

...checks that you can use proportions to find missing lengths in similar figures.

▶ The ratio of a measurement on a model or a drawing to the corresponding measurement on the actual object is the **scale**. The floor plan below uses the scale 1 in. : 14 ft.

EXAMPLE

Use the scale to find the length *a* of the actual living room.

Scale: 1 in. : 14 ft

SAMPLE RESPONSE
Measure the length of the living room in the drawing. The length is 1.25 in. Then write and solve a proportion to find the length of the actual living room.

$$\frac{\text{drawing (in.)}}{\text{actual (ft)}} \longrightarrow \frac{1}{14} = \frac{1.25}{a}$$

$$a = 17.5$$

Bath

Living Room

a

Hallway

Kitchen

Dining Room

The actual living room is 17.5 ft long.

14 Try This as a Class Use the floor plan above.

    a. Find the dimensions of the actual kitchen.

    b. Find the dimensions of the actual bath.

▶ The scale for the Crazy Horse model can be found by using the height of the model and the height of the monument.

EXAMPLE

Find the scale for the Crazy Horse model.

SAMPLE RESPONSE

$$\frac{\text{model height (ft)}}{\text{actual height (ft)}} \longrightarrow \frac{16.56}{563} = \frac{16.56 \div 16.56}{563 \div 16.56}$$

$$\approx \frac{1}{33.998}$$

$$\approx \frac{1}{34}$$

The scale is about 1 ft : 34 ft.

15 a. In the Example, why do you think the scale is written as 1 ft : 34 ft instead of 16.56 ft : 563 ft?

   b. Could 5 ft : 170 ft be used to describe the scale of the model? Explain.

✔ **QUESTION 16**

...checks that you can use a scale to find missing measurements in similar figures.

16 ✔ CHECKPOINT

   a. In an architect's drawing, a building is 2.5 ft tall. The actual building is 40 ft tall. What is the scale?

   b. The height of the building's front door is 8 ft. What is the height of the door in the drawing of the building?

HOMEWORK EXERCISES ▶ See Exs. 11–22 on pp. 415–416.

Section 5

Key Concepts

Key Terms

Similar and Congruent Figures (pp. 407–409)

Similar figures have the same shape, but not necessarily the same size. Congruent figures are similar figures that have the same size.

similar figures

Example Quadrilateral ABCD is congruent to quadrilateral EFGH.

congruent figures

$\overline{AB}$ corresponds to $\overline{EF}$.
∠D corresponds to ∠H.

corresponding parts

Properties of Similar Figures (pp. 407–409)

Example △ABC is similar to △DEF.

The corresponding angles have the same measure.

The ratios of the lengths of the corresponding sides are equivalent.

$$m\angle A = m\angle D$$
$$m\angle B = m\angle E$$
$$m\angle C = m\angle F$$

$$\frac{AB}{DE} = \frac{BC}{EF} = \frac{CA}{FD}$$

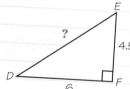

DE means the length of $\overline{DE}$.

Proportions and Scale (pp. 410–412)

scale

You can use proportions to find missing lengths in similar figures. To find DE in △DEF above, solve $\frac{4}{6} = \frac{5}{x}$.

You can use the scale of a drawing or a model to write a proportion to find the measurements of an actual object.

Key Concepts Questions

17 **a.** Solve the proportion $\frac{4}{6} = \frac{5}{x}$ to find DE in the second Example above.

b. Write another proportion that you could use to find DE.

18 Suppose the scale used on a map is 1 in. : 2 mi. How long is a road that is 6 in. long on the map?

YOU WILL NEED

For Ex. 9:
- protractor
- metric or customary ruler

For Exs. 19–22:
- customary ruler

For Ex. 33:
- metric ruler

The figures in each pair are similar. Make a table showing all the pairs of corresponding angles and corresponding sides.

1.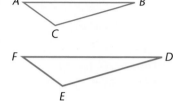

2.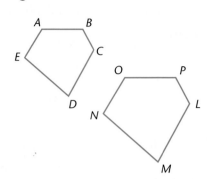

Tell whether the figures in each pair are similar. For the similar figures, tell which are congruent. If they are not similar, explain how you know.

3.

4.

5.

Use the rectangles for Exercises 6–8.

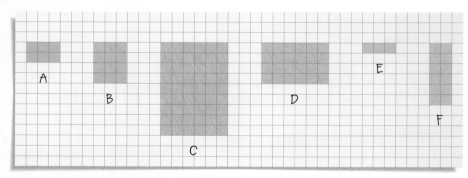

6. a. Name all the rectangles that are similar to rectangle A.

   b. What is the ratio of the lengths of the corresponding sides?

7. a. Name all the rectangles that are similar to rectangle E.

   b. What is the ratio of the lengths of the corresponding sides?

8. Make a sketch of a rectangle that is similar but not congruent to rectangle B. Label the length of each side.

Section 6 Percents and Circle Graphs

Percents and Circle Graphs

IN THIS SECTION

EXPLORATION 1
◆ Writing Percents

EXPLORATION 2
◆ Using Fractions for Percents

EXPLORATION 3
◆ Circle Graphs

Playing the Percentages

Setting the Stage ▸▸▸▸▸▸▸▸▸▸▸▸▸▸▸▸▸▸▸▸▸▸▸▸▸▸▸▸▸▸▸▸▸▸

SET UP *You will need Labsheet 6A.*

Approximately 450 youth, representing all the nations competing in the Olympic Games, participated in the 2004 Olympic Youth Camp in Athens, Greece. The Olympic Youth Camp is a cross-cultural exchange that brings together young people ages 16–18 from around the world. They learn about other cultures, tour historic sites, observe athletes training, and attend the Opening and Closing Ceremonies and four sporting events of their choice.

Use Labsheet 6A. Complete the *Olympic Sporting Events Survey* to find out what sporting events your classmates would most like to attend if selected for an Olympic Youth Camp.

▲
Closing Ceremonies at 2004 Olympic Games

Think About It

1 Suppose your class is similar to the Youth Camp participants. Use the ratios from Question 3 on Labsheet 6A to predict how many of the 450 participants would choose each of the following sporting events as their first choice to attend.

   a. track and field

   b. gymnastics

   c. soccer

   d. a sport other than track and field, gymnastics, or soccer

Exploration 1

Writing Percen%s

SET UP *You will need Labsheet 6B.*

▶ **Describing with Percent** If **62 out of 100 students chose to attend soccer,** then **62** *percent* **of the students chose soccer. Percent means "per hundred" or "out of 100."**

EXAMPLE

You can write **"62 out of 100 students chose to attend soccer"** as:

$\frac{62}{100}$ of the students chose to attend soccer,

0.62 of the students chose to attend soccer, or

62% of the students chose to attend soccer.

% is the symbol for percent.

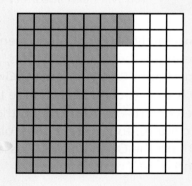

62% can be represented by shading **62** squares on a 100-square grid.

2 **a.** Write the number of unshaded squares in the grid above as a percent.

   b. Write the percent in part (a) as a fraction and as a decimal.

   c. If you combine the shaded and unshaded squares in the grid above, what percent of the grid do you have**?**

   d. Write the percent you found in part (c) as a fraction and as a decimal.

QUESTION 3

...checks that you can write a percent as a decimal and as a fraction.

3 ✔ **CHECKPOINT** Write each percent as a fraction and a decimal.

   a. 40%   **b.** 28%   **c.** 3%

4 Discussion In Class A, 3 out of 20 students were absent when the survey was taken. In Class B, 4 out of 25 students were absent. Why is it hard to tell which class surveyed has a greater fraction of students missing?

▶ Using percents or decimals can help you compare two fractions.

EXAMPLE

Look at Class A from Question 4. Write the fraction of students from Class A that were absent as a percent and as a decimal.

SAMPLE RESPONSE

You can write a fraction as a percent or as a decimal by writing an equivalent fraction in hundredths: $\frac{3}{20} = \frac{?}{100}$.

$$\frac{3}{20} = \frac{3 \cdot 5}{20 \cdot 5} = \frac{15}{100}$$

15 hundredths is **15%** or **0.15**

---

5 a. What is the fraction of students who were absent in Class B?

b. Write the fraction from part (a) as a decimal and as a percent.

c. Which class had the greater percent of absent students?

6 Replace each ? with >, <, or =.

a. 45% ? $\frac{1}{4}$ **b.** 0.7 ? 75%   **c.** 3% ? 0.03

7 ✔ CHECKPOINT Write each fraction or decimal as a percent.

a. $\frac{4}{5}$ **b.** 0.18   **c.** $\frac{1}{50}$ **d.** 0.09

✔ QUESTION 7

...checks that you can write decimals and fractions as percents.

▶ **Recognizing Percents and Decimals** It is helpful to learn the percent and decimal forms for some common fractions.

8 Use Labsheet 6B. Follow the directions to find some *Common Fraction, Decimal, and Percent Equivalents.*

HOMEWORK EXERCISES ▶ See Exs. 1–21 on p. 429.

GOAL

LEARN HOW TO...
♦ use a fraction to find a percent of a number
♦ use a fraction to estimate a percent of a number

AS YOU...
♦ examine data about the U.S. Olympic softball team

Exploration 2

USING Fractions for Percents

SET UP *You will need Labsheet 6C.*

▶ The Olympic Games date back to 776 B.C. when the competition consisted of a single 200-yard foot race. At the 2004 Summer Olympics in Athens, there were 296 events in 28 different sports.

Some of the sports like softball, which became an official medal sport in 1996 at the Atlanta Games, are new Olympic events. In this exploration, you will use percents to examine a variety of facts and figures about players chosen for the 2004 Olympic softball team.

9 In 2004, Lisa Fernandez pitched in her third Olympic Games. While in college, she set a record by winning 93% of her games at UCLA. Lisa won 93 games. How many losses did she have?

10 Amanda Freed was another athlete on the 2004 Olympic softball team. During the 2003 Pan American games, she got a hit 50% of the times she batted.

    a. What fraction in lowest terms is equivalent to 50%?

    b. Amanda batted 14 times in the 2003 Pan American games. Show how to use the fraction you found in part (a) to find how many hits she got.

FOR ◀ HELP

with *equivalent fractions*, see
MODULE 1, p. 61

11 Write each percent as a fraction in lowest terms.

    a. 25%   **b.** 10%   **c.** 20%

✔ QUESTION 12

...checks that you can use a fraction to find a percent of a number.

12 ✔ **CHECKPOINT** In the 2003 Canada Cup, Amanda Freed was at bat 15 times. She had a hit 40% of the times she was at bat. Use a fraction in lowest terms to find how many hits she had.

▶ **Estimating with Percents** You can use a "nice" fraction to estimate a percent or a percent of a number.

> **EXAMPLE**
>
> Natasha Watley was the Most Valuable Player at the 2002 World Championships because she got a hit on 16 out of 31 times at-bat. Use a "nice" fraction to estimate the percent of hits she got.
>
> **SAMPLE RESPONSE**
>
> $\frac{16}{31}$ is close to $\frac{15}{30}$ **or** $\frac{16}{31}$ is close to $\frac{16}{32}$
>
> $\frac{15}{30} = \frac{1}{2} = 50\%$ $\frac{16}{32} = \frac{1}{2} = 50\%$
>
> **Natasha hit about 50% of the time she was at-bat.**

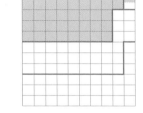

▲ Natasha Watley, 2004 Olympic team shortstop, was Team USA's dominant hitter during the World Championships.

13 During the 2003 Canada Cup, Leah O'Brien-Amico, an outfielder on the 2004 Olympic team, had 9 hits in 22 times at-bat. Use a "nice" fraction to estimate the percent of hits she had.

14 Cat Osterman, the youngest member of the 2004 Olympic team, won 68 out of 82 games while pitching for the University of Texas. Use a "nice" fraction to estimate the percent of games she won.

▶ You know the percent equivalents for many "nice" fractions. In Question 15, you will learn the percent form for $\frac{1}{3}$ and $\frac{2}{3}$.

15 **Use Labsheet 6C.** Use the *Grid for Thirds* to write $\frac{1}{3}$ and $\frac{2}{3}$ as percents.

16 ✔ **CHECKPOINT** In the 2003 Pan American games, Natasha Watley had 7 hits in 24 at-bats. Use a fraction to estimate the percent of hits she got.

17 Suppose a batter got a hit in 32% of her 75 at-bats. Use a "nice" fraction to estimate how many hits she got.

18 **Discussion** Arrange the players in the table in order from least percent of hits to greatest percent of hits. Explain your reasoning.

✔ **QUESTION 16**

...checks that you can use a fraction to estimate a percent.

Player	Hits	At-Bats
A	105	400
B	120	400
C	150	600

HOMEWORK EXERCISES ▶ See Exs. 22–35 on pp. 429–430.

LEARN HOW TO...
+ display data in a circle graph
+ use percents and fractions to estimate angle measures

AS YOU...
+ examine the data from an *Olympic Sporting Events Survey*

KEY TERMS
+ circle graph, pie chart

Exploration 3

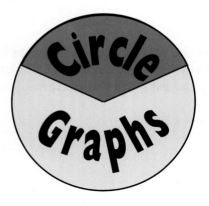

SET UP Work with a partner. You will need: • Labsheet 6A • scissors • tape • colored markers or pencils • protractor • compass • straightedge

▶ To show the part to whole relationship, data are often displayed in a **circle graph** or **pie chart**. In this exploration you will use a circle graph to display some of the data from the *Olympic Sporting Events Survey* in Labsheet 6A.

The results of a survey of 102 students are summarized in the circle graph below. Use the circle graph to answer Questions 19–21.

19 Estimate the fraction of the students that chose soccer.

20 About what percent of the students chose soccer?

21 **a.** Suppose one event on the circle graph was chosen by 24 of the 102 students. Use a "nice" fraction to estimate the percent that chose that event.

b. What event could represent 24 out of 102 on the circle graph?

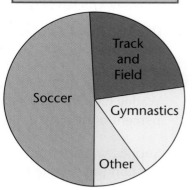

First Choice of Olympic Event to Attend

▶ **Making a Circle Graph** Use Labsheet 6A. Follow the directions in Question 22 to make a circle graph of the results from your class survey.

22   **a.** Cut out the strips of paper on the right side of the labsheet. Use them to make one strip that contains one square for each student surveyed.

b. Color one square for each student that chose track and field. For example, if 5 students chose track and field, then 5 squares should be colored.

c. Repeat part (b) for gymnastics and soccer using a different color for each event.

d. Using a fourth color, color one square for each student who chose a sport other than track and field, gymnastics, or soccer.

Track   Soccer   Gymnastics   Other

e. Tape the ends of your strip together to form a loop with the colored squares on the outside. Do not overlap the ends.

f. Place the loop on a piece of paper.

g. Estimate where the center of the circle created by the loop would be and mark it. Also place a mark where each color begins and ends.

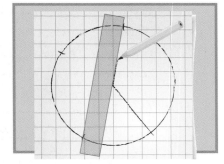

h. Remove the loop. Use a compass to draw a circle around the marks.

i. Use a straightedge to connect the mark where each color begins to the center of the circle.

j. Color and label each section with the name of the sporting event and with the fraction and the percent of the circle it represents.

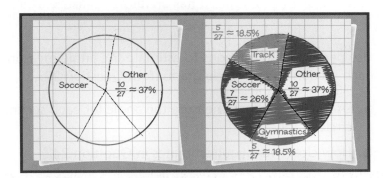

23 Discussion

a. When you add the four fractions on the graph, why is the sum 1?

b. What is the sum of the four percents?

c. Will the sum of the percents always be 100%? Why?

▶ **Using Percents to Construct Circle Graphs** The circle graph shows the part to whole relationship between the number of students that chose each sporting event and the total number of students. The entire 360° circle represents the whole, or 100%. You can use percents to find the angle measure for each section of the circle graph.

EXAMPLE

Use percents and fractions to estimate the angle measure for the soccer section and the track and field section of the circle graph.

SAMPLE RESPONSE

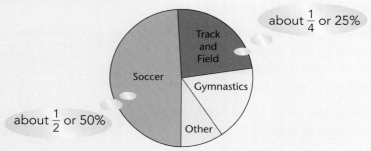

about $\frac{1}{4}$ or 25%

about $\frac{1}{2}$ or 50%

About $\frac{1}{2}$ of the circle represents soccer.

There are 360° in a circle and $\frac{1}{2}$ of 360° = 180°.

The section for soccer has an angle measure of about 180°.

Track and field is about $\frac{1}{4}$ of the circle. $\frac{1}{4}$ of 360° = 90°.

The section for track and field has an angle measure of about 90°.

24 Use percents and fractions to estimate the angle measure for each section in your circle graph from Question 22.

25
a. Use a protractor to measure the angle for each section of your circle graph.

b. How close were your estimates in Question 24?

c. Does the sum of the four angle measures equal 360°? Why or why not?

26 ✔ **CHECKPOINT** **Use Labsheet 6A.** Use the *Olympic Sporting Events Survey* to make a circle graph that displays the data for three sports other than track and field, gymnastics, and soccer. *Note:* Your circle graph should have four sections, one for each of the sports you chose and one for all the other sports.

a. List the sport, the fraction, the percent, and the angle measure for each section in your circle graph.

b. Title your circle graph.

HOMEWORK EXERCISES ▶ See Exs. 36–37 on pp. 430–431.

✔ **QUESTION 26**

...checks that you can use data to make and label a circle graph.

Section 6
Key Concepts ▶▶▶▶▶▶▶▶▶▶▶▶▶▶▶▶▶▶▶▶▶▶▶

Key Terms

Understanding Percent (p. 420)

Fraction Form: $\frac{25}{100}$ or $\frac{1}{4}$

Decimal Form: 0.25

Percent Form: 25%

Percent means "per hundred" or "out of 100."

percent

Using Percents to Compare (p. 421)

Example Which is greater, $\frac{14}{25}$ or $\frac{120}{200}$?

When the denominator is greater than 100, you can divide to find an equivalent fraction with a denominator of 100.

Find equivalent fractions with denominators of 100.

$\frac{14}{25} = \frac{14 \cdot 4}{25 \cdot 4} = \frac{56}{100} = 56\%$ $\frac{120}{200} = \frac{120 \div 2}{200 \div 2} = \frac{60}{100} = 60\%$

So $\frac{120}{200}$ is greater than $\frac{14}{25}$.

Key Concepts Questions

27 **a.** Write 44% as a fraction and as a decimal.

b. Write 0.3 as a fraction and as a percent.

28 Use percents to compare 0.39 and $\frac{7}{20}$.

Section 6 Key Concepts

Key Terms

Using Fractions for Percents (pp. 422–423)

"Nice" fractions like $\frac{2}{5}$ and $\frac{3}{4}$ can be used to find a percent of a number. "Nice" fractions can also be used to estimate a percent or a percent of a number.

Example Use a "nice" fraction to estimate 29% of 40.

29% of 40

$\frac{3}{10}$ of 40

29% is about 30% or $\frac{3}{10}$.

Think: $\frac{1}{10}$ of 40 is 4, so $\frac{3}{10}$ of 40 is 3 • 4 or 12.

Circle Graphs (pp. 424–427)

circle graph, pie chart

A circle graph or pie chart can be used to compare parts of a data set with the whole. You can use percents to find the angle measure for each section of a circle graph.

Example What fraction of gift certificates are redeemed?

Holiday Season Gift Certificates

$85\% = 85$ out of 100
$= \frac{85}{100} = \frac{17}{20}$

15%

85%

□ redeemed ■ not redeemed

Key Concepts Question

29 Calculate the angle measure for the *not redeemed* section in the *Holiday Season Gift Certificates* circle graph.

Section 6

Practice & Application Exercises

YOU WILL NEED

For Ex. 1:
◆ Labsheet 6D

For Ex. 36:
◆ compass or round object
◆ protractor

1. **Use Labsheet 6D.** Follow the directions for *Shading Percents*. Then write a fraction and a decimal for each shaded part.

Write each percent as a fraction and as a decimal.

2. 30%   3. 54%   4. 72%   5. 99%

6. **Writing** In a raffle, Tanisha buys 4 of the 200 tickets sold. In another raffle, her friend Dustin buys 6 of the 300 tickets sold. Who is more likely to win? Why?

Write each decimal as a fraction and as a percent.

7. 0.37   8. 0.4   9. 0.59   10. 0.02

Write each fraction as a decimal and as a percent.

11. $\dfrac{3}{100}$ 12. $\dfrac{9}{25}$ 13. $\dfrac{170}{200}$ 14. $\dfrac{4}{5}$

Replace each ? with >, <, or =.

15. $\dfrac{2}{5}$? 0.45   16. 0.245 ? 23%   17. 56% ? 0.18

18. 72% ? $\dfrac{3}{4}$ 19. 0.9 ? 9%   20. $\dfrac{2}{8}$? 0.18

21. **Visual Thinking** Replace each ? with the number that makes the statement true.

A is ? % of the square.

B is ? % of the square.

C is ? % of the square.

D is ? % of the square.

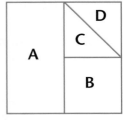

Use a fraction in lowest terms to find each value.

22. 25% of 48   23. 60% of 35   24. 10% of 90

25. 5% of 380   26. 20% of 245   27. 70% of 45

28. Carlos scored in 35% of his 60 soccer games.

   a. Use a "nice" fraction to estimate the number of games in which he scored.

   b. Is your estimate *greater than* or *less than* the actual number of games?

The All American Girls Professional Baseball League (AAGPBL) that existed from 1943 to 1954 inspired the 1992 movie *A League of Their Own*.

29. Teams in the All American Girls Professional Baseball League played games almost every night, with about 120 games a season. How many wins would a team have needed to win 75% of its games?

30. **Mental Math** When dining in a restaurant, some people leave a tip equal to 15% of the bill. Suppose the bill is $40.00.

   a. Use mental math to find 10% of $40.00.

   b. Use mental math to find 5% of $40.00.

   c. Use parts (a) and (b) to find 15% of $40.00.

Estimate a percent for each fraction.

31. $\frac{35}{65}$ 32. $\frac{31}{40}$ 33. $\frac{46}{51}$ 34. $\frac{19}{30}$

35. **Challenge** Kim Maher had 12 hits in 32 at-bats while playing in the Pan American games in 1995. Complete parts (a)–(c) to find the percent of times she got a hit.

   a. Write the fraction $\frac{12}{32}$ in lowest terms.

   b. Find the percent equivalents of $\frac{2}{8}$ and $\frac{4}{8}$.

   c. Show how your answers from part (b) can be used to write $\frac{12}{32}$ as a percent.

36. **Displaying Data** A circle graph can be used to show the part to whole relationship between the area of each continent and the total land area on Earth .

   a. Write each percent in the table as a fraction out of 100.

   b. Use a proportion to find the angle measure in a circle graph for each continent.

World Land Area	
Continent	Percent of total land area*
Asia	30
Africa	20
North America	16
South America	12
Antarctica	10
Europe	7
Australia	5

*Approximate percents

South America
Angle is 43°.

Example

Round to the nearest whole degree.

$$\begin{array}{ccc} & \text{Percent} & \text{Degrees} \\ \text{South America} \longrightarrow & \dfrac{12}{100} & = \dfrac{43.2}{360} \\ \text{Total land area} \longrightarrow & & \end{array}$$

   c. Use a compass or a round object to draw a circle and find its center.

   d. Use a protractor to mark off each angle you found in part (b). Label your graph with the name of each continent and write a title.

   e. How does a circle graph help you compare data?

Reflecting ◀▶ on the Section

37. Use the circle graphs and table for parts (a)–(e).

Participants (in millions)		
Sport	1998	2002
Cross-country skiing	8.8	13.5
Telemark skiing	1.3	3.3
Snowshoeing	2.9	5.9
Alpine skiing	14.8	14.3
Snowboarding	5.5	7.7
Ice Skating	18.5	14.5
Snowmobiling	6.5	4.5
Total Participants	**58.5**	**63.5**

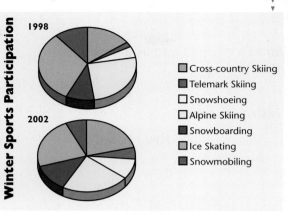

(Winter Sports Participation. 1998 and 2002 circle graphs with legend: Cross-country Skiing, Telemark Skiing, Snowshoeing, Alpine Skiing, Snowboarding, Ice Skating, Snowmobiling)

> **Visual THINKING**
>
> Exercise 37 checks that you can apply ideas about percents.

a. Write a "nice" fraction for the number of participants in each of the following sports in 1998: ice skating, snowshoeing, cross-country skiing.

b. Repeat part (a) for 2002.

c. Use the "nice" fractions from parts (a) and (b) to estimate the percent that participated in ice skating, snowshoeing, and cross-country skiing in 1998 and in 2002.

d. Use the percents from part (c) to estimate the angle measures for ice skating, snowshoeing, and cross-country skiing in each circle graph.

e. What happened to the percent of participants in ice skating from 1998 to 2002? cross-country skiing?

Spiral ◀▶ Review

38. The figures at the right are similar. Name all the pairs of corresponding angles and pairs of corresponding sides. (Module 6, p. 413)

For Exercises 39 and 40, choose the form of the quotient that best answers each question. (Module 1, p. 46)

39. How many 4-inch bows can be made from a 35-inch piece of ribbon?

40. The bill for four people came to $35.00. What is each person's share of the bill?

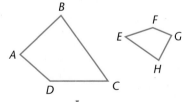

A. 8.75

B. 8

C. 9

D. $8\frac{3}{4}$

Section 6

Extra Skill Practice

Write each decimal as a percent and as a fraction.

1. 0.35
2. 0.28
3. 0.6
4. 0.05

Write each fraction as a decimal and as a percent.

5. $\frac{7}{100}$
6. $\frac{8}{25}$
7. $\frac{9}{10}$
8. $\frac{3}{20}$

Replace each _?_ with >, <, or =.

9. 9% _?_ $\frac{9}{10}$
10. 70% _?_ 0.07
11. 0.5 _?_ 52%
12. 1.1 _?_ 100%
13. 0.75 _?_ $\frac{3}{4}$
14. 20% _?_ $\frac{1}{10}$

Use a fraction in lowest terms to find each value.

15. 25% of 72
16. 80% of 80
17. 10% of 91
18. 90% of 170
19. 5% of 60
20. 75% of 104

Estimate a percent for each fraction.

21. $\frac{19}{61}$
22. $\frac{16}{65}$
23. $\frac{3}{14}$
24. $\frac{5}{49}$

Use a "nice" fraction to estimate each value.

25. 34% of 120
26. 79% of 25
27. 48% of 90

Standardized Testing ◀▶ Multiple Choice

1. Which is the best estimate of 67% of 60?

   A 42   B 40   C 36   D 45

2. For which situation do you save the most money?

   A original price: $25
   discount: 40% off

   B original price: $36
   discount: 25% off

   C original price: $40
   discount: 30% off

   D original price: $22
   discount: 50% off

3. For which situation is the percent you save the greatest?

   A original price: $40
   discount: save $10.20

   B original price: $19.99
   discount: save $1.89

   C original price: $50
   discount: save $9

   D original price: $58.99
   discount: save $20

Module 6   Comparisons and Predictions

The Module Project

Mystery Tracks

Imagine searching for evidence of dinosaurs that lived millions of years ago. Do you picture finding a large bone, or even a whole skeleton? Surprisingly, some dinosaurs and other extinct animals are known only from the tracks they left behind. Footprints can provide several clues about an animal such as its height, weight, age, and running speed.

Measuring and Comparing Lengths Scientists measure dinosaur tracks in several ways. Some ways of measuring the tracks of dinosaurs that walked on two legs are shown below.

SET UP

You will need:
- *metric ruler*
- *protractor*
- *chalk, or large newspaper and marker*

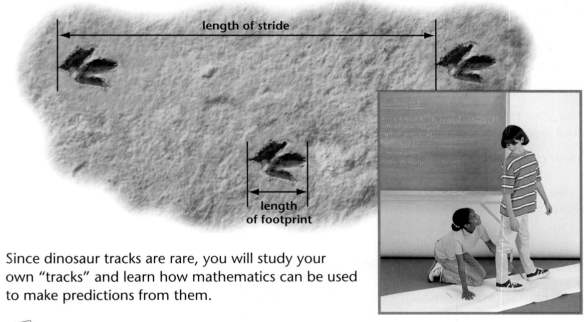

length of stride

length of footprint

Since dinosaur tracks are rare, you will study your own "tracks" and learn how mathematics can be used to make predictions from them.

 Have someone help you find the following measurements for your "tracks." Measure to the nearest centimeter, and be sure to use your normal walking speed.

    a. your height   **b.** your footprint length   **c.** your stride length

 Write the ratio of *your footprint length to your height* in three ways.

Making Predictions Now you will use your "track" data and your classmates' data to predict height.

 3 a. Write your *footprint length to height* ratio as a decimal.

b. Collect the following data from each of your classmates (including yourself):
- height
- stride length
- *footprint length to height* ratio

 4 a. Make a scatter plot that compares stride length to height. If appropriate, fit a line to the data.

b. Use your graph to predict your height from your stride length. How close is the prediction to your actual height?

 5 a. Find the mean of the *footprint length to height* ratio.

b. Write a "nice" fraction that is close to the mean.

c. Use your result from part (b) to predict your height from your foot length.

d. How close is the prediction to your actual height?

 6 Why do you think scientists use footprint length and stride length together to predict the heights of dinosaurs?

Using Angles Now you will look for a method to tell whether a person was walking or running when making tracks.

 7 The diagram shows where to measure a person's step angle. Have someone help you measure your step angle to the nearest degree. Walk at your normal speed.

8 a. How do you think your step angle changes when you run?

b. Have someone help you measure your step angle for a running speed.

c. Does your stride length appear to be shorter or longer when running than when walking?

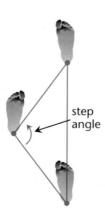

step angle

9 How can you use the measure of the step angle and stride length to tell whether tracks were made by someone walking or running?

Using Your Data Now you will use what you have learned to try to discover who may have made the mystery tracks below.

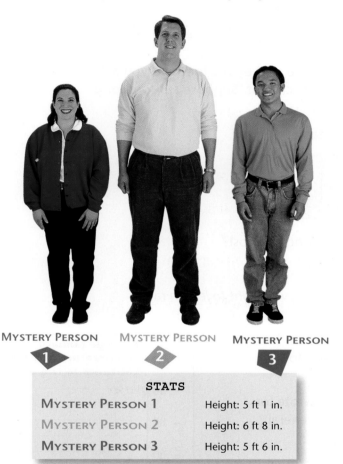

MYSTERY PERSON **1**   MYSTERY PERSON **2**   MYSTERY PERSON **3**

STATS

MYSTERY PERSON 1	Height: 5 ft 1 in.
MYSTERY PERSON 2	Height: 6 ft 8 in.
MYSTERY PERSON 3	Height: 5 ft 6 in.

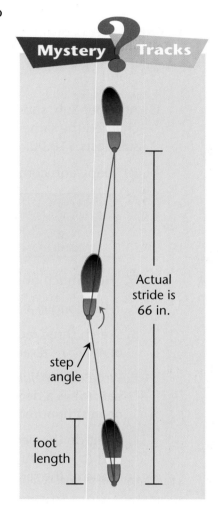

Mystery **?** Tracks

Actual stride is 66 in.

step angle

foot length

10 **a.** Do you think the person was walking or running when making the tracks? Why?

b. Use the scale drawing of the mystery tracks to predict how tall the mystery person is.

c. Who do you think this person may be?

11 Write a report that explains how you made all your predictions. Include your results from Questions 1–9 to support your prediction methods.

Write each ratio three ways. (Sec. 1, Explor. 1)

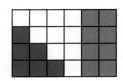

1. the ratio of red squares (■) to blue squares (■)

2. the ratio of blue squares to white squares

Tell whether or not the ratios are equivalent. (Sec. 1, Explor. 1)

3. $\frac{2}{5}$ and $\frac{10}{15}$ 4. 5 : 8 and 15 : 24   5. $\frac{3.3}{2.2}$ and $\frac{12}{8}$

6. At Super Sub, sub sandwiches are sold by the foot and you are charged the same amount for each foot. Suppose a 3-foot-long sub costs $18.00. (Sec. 2, Explor. 1)

   a. Copy and complete the table.

Length (feet)	1	2	3	4
Cost (dollars)	?	?	18	?

   b. How much does a 5-foot-long sub cost?

   c. How long is a $90.00 sub?

7. a. Sketch three rectangles that have *height to length* ratios of 4 : 7, 1 : 4, and 5 : 6. (Sec. 3, Explor. 1)

   b. Write each *height to length* ratio from part (a) as a decimal. Round to the nearest hundredth.

   c. What do the decimals you wrote for part (b) tell you about the general shape of the rectangles?

8. Use the scatter plot to estimate the missing entries in the table. Explain how you found your estimates. (Sec. 3, Explor. 3)

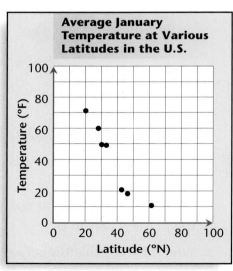

Average January Temperature at Various Latitudes in the U.S.

Latitude (°N)	25	?	44	57
Temperature (°F)	?	37	?	?

Find the missing term in each proportion. (Sec. 4, Explor. 1)

9. $\frac{4}{6} = \frac{10}{x}$ 10. $\frac{3}{2.5} = \frac{y}{5}$ 11. 21 : 3 = z : 18

If appropriate, use a proportion to solve Exercises 12 and 13. If it is not appropriate, explain why not. (Sec. 4, Explor. 2)

12. A model of an airplane has a wingspan of 75 cm and a length of 82.5 cm. The actual airplane is 55 m long. What is its wingspan?

13. Suppose a car's gas mileage is 30 mi/gal at a speed of 30 mi/hr. At what speed will the car get 60 mi/gal?

14. The triangles at the right are similar. Use a proportion to find the missing length. (Sec. 5, Explor. 1)

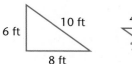

Write each fraction as a decimal and as a percent. (Sec. 6, Explor. 1)

15. $\frac{3}{5}$ 16. $\frac{64}{200}$ 17. $\frac{9}{20}$ 18. $\frac{207}{300}$

For Exercises 19–21, find each value. (Sec. 6, Explor. 2)

19. 25% of 84   20. 50% of 130   21. 10% of 245

22. Raphael answered 45 out of 51 questions on the math test correctly. Use a "nice" fraction to estimate what percent he answered correctly. (Sec. 6, Explor. 2)

23. A total of 70,000 lucky fans will earn a ticket to the Super Bowl. The pie chart below shows the percentages of tickets various organizations receive to distribute. (Sec. 6, Explor. 3)

    a. Write each percent as a "nice" fraction.

    b. About how many of the 70,000 tickets does the NFL office distribute?

    c. Find the angle measure for the 5% section.

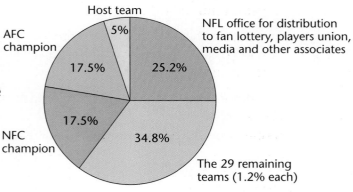

Distribution of Tickets

Reflecting ◀▶ on the Module

24. **Open-ended** Give at least one example of how ratios, proportions, or circle graphs help people make comparisons and predictions.

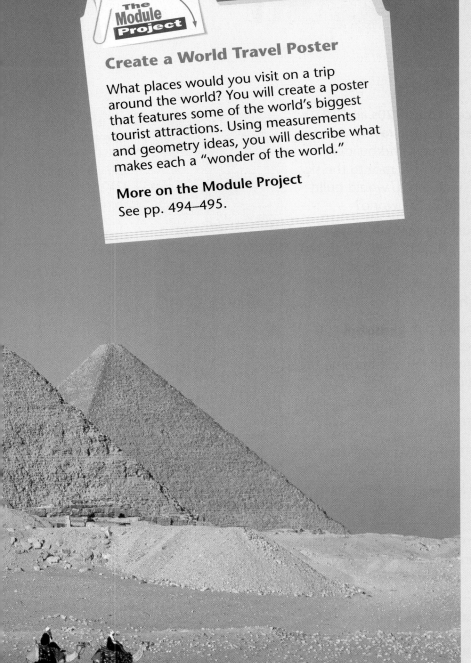

The Module Project

Create a World Travel Poster

What places would you visit on a trip around the world? You will create a poster that features some of the world's biggest tourist attractions. Using measurements and geometry ideas, you will describe what makes each a "wonder of the world."

More on the Module Project
See pp. 494–495.

CONNECTING
MATHEMATICS
The & Theme

MODULE 7 — SECTION OVERVIEW

1 Three-Dimensional Geometry

As you study the Empire State Building:
- Recognize and name prisms
- Draw prisms
- Find volumes of prisms
- Use nets for polyhedra

2 Weight in the Customary System

As you explore the Great Pyramid:
- Measure weight in customary units
- Convert customary units of weight

3 Circles and Circumference

As you explore the Circus Maximus:
- Use a compass to draw a circle
- Identify parts of a circle
- Find circumference

4 Circles and Cylinders

As you learn about Mesa Verde:
- Find areas of circles
- Find volumes of cylinders

5 Temperature, Integers, and Coordinate Graphs

As you learn about Marco Polo:
- Measure temperature in °F and °C
- Compare integers
- Graph ordered pairs of integers

INTERNET
Resources and practice at
classzone.com

439

Race to the SKY

Setting the Stage

The biggest race in the 1920s and 1930s was not happening at the racetrack. In New York City, planners and builders were engaged in a frantic race to the sky. Who, everyone wondered, would build the tallest building in the world?

The Chrysler building seemed to be complete. Then a surprise spire "popped out" of the building's roof. The spire had been secretly assembled inside the building's fire shaft.

To compete, the Empire State Building added six stories and a 200 ft tower to its plans. With these changes, it became the world's tallest building.

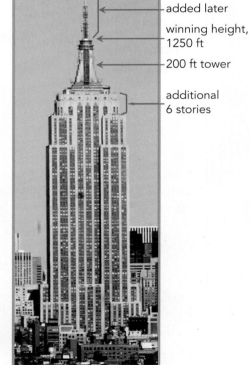

204 ft
TV antenna
added later

winning height,
1250 ft

200 ft tower

additional
6 stories

Empire State Building
Tallest Building,
1931–1972

final height,
1046 ft

first height,
925 ft

Chrysler Building
Tallest Building,
1930–1931

Think About It

1 The Empire State Building has 102 stories, not including the TV antenna. About how high do you think each story is?

2 In the original plan, the Empire State Building contained 36 million cubic feet of space. What do you think a cubic foot is?

▶ **The Empire State Building and the Great Pyramid at Giza are amazing structures. In this module, you will investigate the mathematics related to these and other modern *Wonders of the World*.**

Exploration 1

Figures in Space

SET UP *Work with a partner. You will need: • Labsheet 1A • tape • scissors • index card*

▶ Before the 200-ft tower was added, the Empire State Building was a *polyhedron*. A **polyhedron** is a three-dimensional object made up of flat surfaces, or **faces**, shaped like polygons. For example, a cube is a polyhedron with square faces.

3 **Try This as a Class** Explain whether or not each object is a polyhedron.

a.

a pyramid

b.

a cylinder

▶ Models of some polyhedra can be made from *nets*. A **net** is a flat pattern that can be cut out and folded to form a three-dimensional object. Nets can provide a useful way to model large buildings.

4 **a. Use Labsheet 1A.** Use *Net 1* or *Net 2*. Have your partner use the other net. Follow these steps to fold the nets.

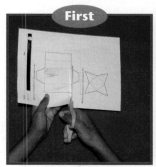

First

Cut on the solid lines.

Next

Fold on the dotted lines.

Then

Tape the faces together.

b. For each polyhedron, describe the shapes of the faces. Are there any pairs of faces that are congruent? If so, which ones?

GOAL

LEARN HOW TO...
◆ recognize prisms
◆ draw prisms
◆ fold a flat pattern to form a polyhedron

AS YOU...
◆ develop spatial visualization skills

KEY TERMS
◆ polyhedron (plural: polyhedra)
◆ face
◆ net
◆ parallel planes
◆ prism
◆ base of a prism
◆ edge
◆ vertex (plural: vertices)
◆ oblique prism
◆ right prism

5 **a.** Set the polyhedron made from *Net 1* on one of its trapezoidal faces. Place an index card on the other trapezoidal face.

   b. Discussion Recall that a plane is a flat surface that extends forever. The index card models a plane. The surface the polyhedron rests on models another plane. The two planes are **parallel planes**. What does it mean for planes to be parallel?

▶ A **prism** is a polyhedron in which two of the faces, the **bases**, are congruent and lie in parallel planes. The other faces are shaped like parallelograms.

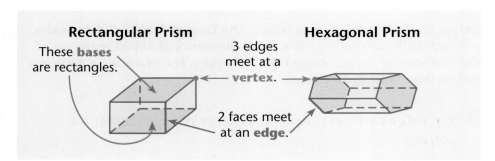

Rectangular Prism

These **bases** are rectangles.

2 faces meet at an **edge**.

Hexagonal Prism

3 edges meet at a **vertex**.

6 **a.** Based on the prisms shown above, how do you think prisms are named?

   b. What kind of prism is shown at the right?

7 **Try This as a Class** Explain whether or not each polyhedron is a prism. If it is, what type of prism is it?

   a. the polyhedron made from *Net 1*

   b. the polyhedron made from *Net 2*

In 1750, Leonhard Euler, a Swiss mathematician, observed a relationship among the number of faces, vertices, and edges of a polyhedron. Question 8 explores this relationship.

8 **a.** Copy and complete the table for the prisms shown above and the polyhedra made from *Nets 1 and 2*.

	Number of Faces	Number of Vertices	Number of Edges
Rectangular Prism	?	?	?
Hexagonal Prism	?	?	?
Polyhedron from Net 1	?	?	?
Polyhedron from Net 2	?	?	?

   b. How does the number of edges of a polyhedron appear to be related to the number of faces and vertices?

   c. Write an equation for the relationship in part (b).

9 **Discussion** The prisms at the right are **oblique prisms**. The prisms on page 442 are **right prisms**. How are oblique prisms and right prisms different?

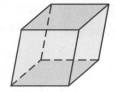

▶ **Drawing Three-dimensional Objects** You may be able to understand drawings of three-dimensional objects better if you learn how to draw them yourself. Here is one way to draw a prism.

Step 1 Draw one base.

Step 2 Copy the base behind and to one side of it. The bases may overlap.

Step 3 Connect pairs of corresponding vertices. Show hidden edges with dashed segments.

 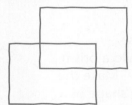 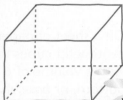

You may need to erase and redraw an edge.

10 **a.** Use the steps above to draw a pentagonal prism.

b. Is the relationship among the number of faces, vertices, and edges you found in Question 8(c) true for a pentagonal prism? Explain.

11 ✔ **CHECKPOINT** Choose the letter of the polyhedron that can be formed from this net.

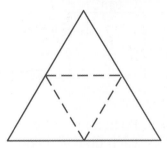

A.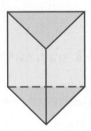

B.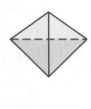

✔ **QUESTION 11**

...checks that you can use a net to visualize a polyhedron.

HOMEWORK EXERCISES ▶ See Exs. 1–14 on pp. 448–449.

Exploration 2

Volumes of Prisms

SET UP *Work with a partner. You will need:* • *Labsheet 1B* • *ruler* • *tape* • *scissors* • *centimeter cubes*

▶ **As the height of the Empire State Building increased, the amount of space it contained, its volume, also increased. Volume is measured in cubic units.**

This is a centimeter cube. Its volume is 1 **cubic centimeter (1 cm³)**.

12 a. On a sheet of paper, use centimeter cubes to build a prism with a volume of 6 cm³. Make the bottom, or *base*, in the shape of a rectangle, and stack identical layers of cubes above it.

b. How many cubes did you use?

c. What is the height of your prism?

d. Trace around the base of your prism. Use your tracing, or *base plan*, to find the area of the base.

13 a. Copy the table. You will fill it in as you build prisms.

Number of layers	Height (cm)	Area of base (cm²)	Volume (cm³)
1	?	6	?
2	?	6	?
3	?	6	?
4	?	6	?

Base Plan

2 cm

3 cm

b. Use the base plan shown at the left. Build a prism by stacking identical layers of centimeter cubes. Each time you add a layer, fill in a row of the table.

c. Use your completed table. How is the volume of your prism related to its height and the area of its base?

14 Discussion The prisms below were made from centimeter cubes. Find the volume of each prism. Explain your method.

a.   b.   c.

Use Labsheet 1B. For Exercises 15–17, use *Net 3*.

15 a. Predict what prism *Net 3* will make.

b. Fold the net. Leave the top open.

c. Did you get the prism you expected? Explain.

d. If you can, use centimeter cubes to find the volume of the prism you made in part (a).

e. Remove any centimeter cubes from the prism and tape down the top.

16 a. Which pairs of faces are parallel and congruent?

b. Which pairs of faces could be bases for the prism?

17 a. How can you find the volume of the prism without using cubes?

b. Use your method to find the volume.

▶ **Prisms that do not have rectangular bases can also be built by beginning with a base plan and stacking identical layers of centimeter cubes.**

18 a. For each base plan below, stack identical layers of centimeter cubes until each prism is the indicated height. Record the number of cubes you used to build each prism.

Prism 1   **Prism 2**

height = 3 cm   height = 2 cm

b. What kind of polygon is used for the base of Prism 2? What do you call this prism?

c. Is the relationship you found in Question 13(c) for rectangular prisms also true for these prisms? Explain.

19 **Use Labsheet 1B.** Repeat Questions 15–17 using *Net 4*.

20 **a.** Set the prism you made from *Net 4* on one of its square faces.

   b. If the square is the base of the prism, what kind of prism did *Net 4* form?

   c. Has the volume of the prism changed from what you found in Question 19? Explain.

   d. What is the area of the base of the prism?

   e. What is the height of the prism?

   f. **Discussion** How did you measure the height of the prism?

   g. How is the volume of the prism related to its height and the area of its base?

21 **Try This as a Class**

   a. What is the height of a prism?

   b. Explain how to find the volume of a prism without using cubes.

▶ **You can find the volume of any prism if you know its height and the area of its base.**

✔ **QUESTION 22**

...checks that you can find the volume of a prism.

22 ✔ **CHECKPOINT** Find the volume of each prism.

   a. right hexagonal prism

   b. right trapezoidal prism

   c. right triangular prism

Area = 9 cm²

4 cm

3.1 cm

Area = 4.2 cm²

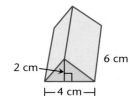

2 cm

6 cm

├─ 4 cm ─┤

23 Although the Empire State Building is not a rectangular prism, it can be approximated by one. Suppose the prism is 1000 ft tall and has a volume of 36 million cubic feet. List three possible pairs of lengths and widths for its base plan.

HOMEWORK EXERCISES ▶ See Exs. 15–32 on pp. 449–450.

Section ① Key Concepts

Parts of a Polyhedron (pp. 441–442)

A polyhedron is a three-dimensional object made up of flat surfaces, or faces, shaped like polygons. Pairs of faces meet in segments called edges. Edges meet in points called vertices.

Prisms (pp. 442–443)

A prism is a polyhedron with two bases that:
- are congruent.
- lie in parallel planes.

The other faces are parallelograms.
A prism is named by the shape of its bases.
The height of a prism is the perpendicular distance between its bases.

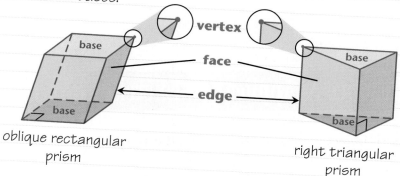

oblique rectangular prism

right triangular prism

The number of faces F, vertices V, and edges E are related by the formula $F + V - 2 = E$.

Drawing and Constructing Polyhedra (pp. 441–443)

One way to draw a prism is to draw the bases first and then connect corresponding vertices.

A net is a flat pattern that can be cut out and folded to form a three-dimensional object.

Key Terms

polyhedron (plural: polyhedra)
face
edge
vertex (plural: vertices)

prism
base of a prism
parallel planes
oblique prism
right prism

net

24 Key Concepts Question

a. Will this net form a prism? If so, what kind of prism? Explain.

b. Describe the shapes of the faces.

c. Show that the number of faces, vertices, and edges of the polyhedron satisfies the formula $F + V - 2 = E$.

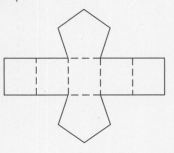

Section ①

Key Terms

volume

cubic unit

cubic centimeter (cm³)

Key Concepts

Volume (pp. 444–446)

The volume of a three-dimensional object is measured in cubic units such as cubic centimeters or cubic feet.

To find the volume (V) of a prism, you can multiply the area of the base (B) by the height of the prism (h): $V = B \cdot h$

25 Key Concepts Question The area of the base of a prism is 6.25 cm². The height of the prism is 2.5 cm. What is the volume of the prism?

Section ①

Practice & Application Exercises

Tell whether each object is shaped like a prism. If it is, name the type of prism.

1.

2.

3.

Choose the letter of the polyhedron that can be formed with each net.

4.
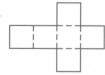

5.

6.

A.

B.

C.

D.

7. Name polyhedra A and C shown above.

8. Is polyhedron D shown above a prism? Why or why not?

9. Is a cube a prism? If so, what type is it? Explain.

10. a. Predict what shape this net will form. Trace the net. Then cut it out and fold it to check your prediction.

    b. Name the polyhedron you made by folding the net.

    c. How many faces, vertices, and edges does the polyhedron have?

    d. Use the methods on page 443 to draw your polyhedron.

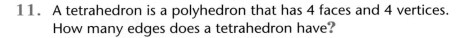

11. A tetrahedron is a polyhedron that has 4 faces and 4 vertices. How many edges does a tetrahedron have?

12. An octahedron has 8 faces and 12 edges. How many vertices does an octahedron have?

13. Polyhedron B shown with Exercises 4–6 on page 448 is a tetrahedron and polyhedron D is an octahedron. Use polyhedra B and D to check your answers to Exercises 11 and 12.

14. **Open-ended** Find an object in your home that is shaped like a prism. Use the methods on page 443 to draw the object.

Find the volume of each prism built with centimeter cubes.

15.

16.

17.

Find the volume of the prism you can build with centimeter cubes using each base plan and indicated height.

18.

    height = 4 cm

19.

    height = 5 cm

20.

    height = 8 cm

Find the volume of each prism.

21. right rectangular

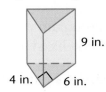

$\frac{1}{2}$ in. $\frac{1}{4}$ in. $\frac{3}{8}$ in.

22. right triangular

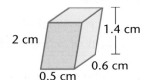

9 in. 4 in. 6 in.

23. oblique rectangular

1.4 cm 2 cm 0.6 cm 0.5 cm

24. Explain the differences among volume, area, and height.

25. For what type of prism is the height equal to the length of an edge joining corresponding vertices of the bases? For what type of prism is this not the case?

Replace each ? with the missing measurement for a prism with base area B, height h, and volume V.

26. $B = 40$ cm^2
   $h = 3$ cm
   $V = \underline{?}$

27. $B = \underline{?}$
   $h = 10$ cm
   $V = 200$ cm^3

28. $B = 18$ cm^2
   $h = \underline{?}$
   $V = 72$ cm^3

12 in.
30 in.
12 in.

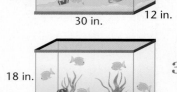
18 in.
30 in.
12 in.

29. It is recommended that pet fish be kept in tanks that hold 25 gal of water or more. Since 1 gal of water takes up 231 in.^{3} of space, you can divide the number of cubic inches by 231 to find the number of gallons. Does each tank at the left hold 25 gal or more?

30. **Visual Thinking** Use the diagram.

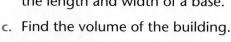
180 ft
72 ft
60 ft
180 ft
15 ft

a. The shape of this building is not a rectangular prism. Why not?

b. Describe one way to separate the building into two rectangular prisms. For each prism, state the height and the length and width of a base.

c. Find the volume of the building.

d. Is the volume of the building still the area of the base times the height? Explain.

31. **Challenge** Create your own net for a prism that has a volume of 32 cm^3.

RESEARCH

Exercise 32 checks that you understand the meaning of volume.

Reflecting ◀▶ on the Section

32. Find information about another skyscraper, including when it was built, its height, and the area of its base. Then estimate its volume. Prepare a report on your findings. Be sure to include your sources of information and the method you used to estimate the volume.

Spiral ◀▶ Review

33. Sketch and label a parallelogram that has a base of 4 cm and a height of 3.5 cm. Then find its area. (Module 5, p. 339)

34. Twelve pens cost $3.84. Use a proportion to find how much five pens cost. (Module 6, p. 401)

Section 1

Extra Skill Practice

For each net, tell whether the polyhedron it will form is a prism. If it is, tell what shape the bases are and name the prism.

1.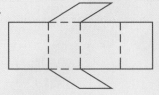

2.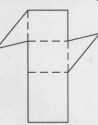

3.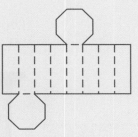

Find the volume of each right prism.

4.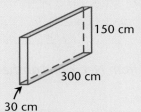
150 cm
300 cm
30 cm

5.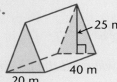
25 m
20 m
40 m

6. Area = 31.7 in.²
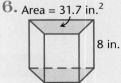
8 in.

Replace each ? with the missing measurement for a prism with a base area B, height h, and volume V.

7. $B = 17$ yd²
$h = $?
$V = 51$ yd³

8. $B = $?
$h = 28$ mm
$V = 1400$ mm³

9. $B = 108$ cm²
$h = 21$ cm
$V = $?

 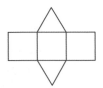

The Great Pyramid

Setting the Stage

KEY TERM
♦ pyramid

SET UP *You will need the polyhedron from Net 2 on Labsheet 1A.*

The ancient Egyptians built huge stone pyramids as tombs for their rulers, or *pharaohs*. Some pyramids contained hidden rooms and secret passages. Many also held gold and other treasures.

After 4500 years, more than eighty Egyptian pyramids are still standing. The largest, the Great Pyramid at Giza, was originally about 480 ft high and has a square base with sides about 755 ft long.

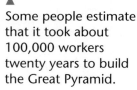
▲
Some people estimate that it took about 100,000 workers twenty years to build the Great Pyramid.

Think About It

1 On a building, one story is about 10 ft high. About how many stories high was the Great Pyramid?

2 a. What is the area of the base of the Great Pyramid?

b. About how many 160 ft by 120 yd football fields would it take to cover the base of the Great Pyramid?

3 The polyhedron you folded from *Net 2* on Labsheet 1A is a **pyramid**. This polyhedron and the Great Pyramid are both square pyramids.

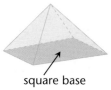
square base

a. Describe the faces of a square pyramid.

b. How is a square pyramid different from a square prism?

Customary
U·n·i·t·s of Weight

GOAL

LEARN HOW TO...
- measure weight in customary units
- convert customary units of weight

AS YOU...
- explore the construction of the Great Pyramid

KEY TERMS
- ounce (oz)
- pound (lb)
- ton

SET UP *You will need: • a scale • a coffee mug • a stapler*

Building the Great Pyramid was an amazing task. The Great Pyramid is made up of two and a half million stone blocks with an average weight of about $2\frac{1}{2}$ tons each. After blocks were dug from a quarry miles away, they needed to be transported to the construction site and moved up to each layer of the pyramid.

4 **a.** Write a numeral for the number of stone blocks used to build the Great Pyramid.

b. The Empire State Building weighs about 365,000 tons. Find the weight of the Great Pyramid in tons and compare it to the weight of the Empire State Building.

▶ To better understand how heavy the blocks were, it is helpful to become familiar with units of weight in the customary system—the **ounce (oz)**, the **pound (lb)**, and the **ton**. The relationships between these units are shown below:

1 lb = 16 oz   **1 ton = 2000 lb**

5 **Discussion** The weight of five quarters is a good benchmark for an ounce. A compact car is a good benchmark for a ton. What can you use as a benchmark for a pound? Explain your reasoning.

6 Choose an appropriate unit (*ounce*, *pound*, or *ton*) for the weight of each item.

a. a box of cereal   **b.** a person   **c.** a truck

d. an orange   **e.** a bicycle   **f.** a pencil

7 Copy the table. Use the benchmarks from Question 5 to estimate the weight of each listed item. Then weigh each item on a scale.

Item	Estimated Weight	Actual Weight
pencil	?	?
coffee mug	?	?
four math books	?	?
stapler	?	?

▶ **Converting Units** Sometimes you need to convert between different units of weight.

8 Complete the steps below to calculate how many pounds a $2\frac{1}{2}$ ton stone block weighs.

> Start with a relationship between tons and pounds.

Step 1: 1 ton = _?_ lb

Step 2: $2\frac{1}{2}$ · 1 ton = $2\frac{1}{2}$ · _?_ lb

Step 3: $2\frac{1}{2}$ tons = _?_ lb

9 Complete the following steps to calculate how many pounds of peanut butter are in a 40-oz jar.

Step 1: Write the conversion fact for changing 1 oz to pounds.
1 oz = _?_ lb

Step 2: Multiply by 40 since you are converting 40 oz to pounds.

Step 3: Complete the multiplication in Step 2.

✔ **QUESTION 10**

...checks that you can convert customary units of weight.

10 ✔ **CHECKPOINT** Convert each measurement to the indicated unit.

a. 1500 lb = _?_ ton(s)   **b.** 36 oz = _?_ lb

c. 5 lb 6 oz = _?_ oz   **d.** $3\frac{1}{4}$ tons = _?_ lb

11 If the average student weighs 100 lb, how many students would weigh as much as an average stone block in the Great Pyramid?

HOMEWORK EXERCISES ▶ See Exs. 1–19 on pp. 456–457.

Section 2
Key Concepts

Pyramids (p. 452)

A pyramid is a polyhedron that has one base.
All the other faces are triangular and meet at a single vertex.
Like a prism, a pyramid is named by the shape of its base.

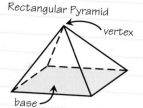

Rectangular Pyramid
vertex
base

pyramid

Customary Units of Weight (pp. 453–454)

Some commonly used units of weight in the customary system are ounce (oz), pound (lb), and ton.

- An ounce is about the weight of 5 quarters.

ounce (oz)

- A pound is about the weight of a loaf of bread.

1 lb = 16 oz

pound (lb)

- A ton is about the weight of a compact car.

1 ton = 2000 lb

ton

Key Concepts Questions

12 Choose the letter of the three-dimensional object that is a pyramid.

A.   B.   C.

13 Name the pyramid in Question 12.

14 Suppose a museum used two and a half million 1-oz blocks to build a scale model of the Great Pyramid at Giza.

a. Should you express the weight of the scale model in *ounces*, *pounds*, or *tons*? Explain your choice.

b. How much will the model weigh in the units from part (a)?

Section 2

Practice & Application Exercises

Choose the best customary unit (*ounce, pound,* or *ton*) to express the weight of each object.

1. airplane

2. postcard

3. ice skates

4. fork

Open-ended Name something that weighs close to each amount.

5. 6 oz

6. 10 lb

Replace each ? with the missing number.

7. 96 oz = ? lb

8. 0.75 lb = ? oz

9. 4000 lb = ? ton(s)

10. 4 oz = ? lb

11. $5\frac{1}{2}$ tons = ? lb

12. 250 lb = ? ton(s)

Give each weight using a combination of pounds and ounces.

13.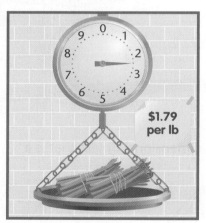

$1.79 per lb

14.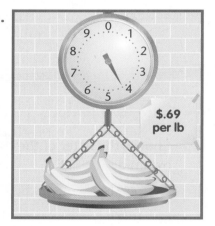

$.69 per lb

15. a. **Estimation** Estimate the cost of each purchase in Exercises 13 and 14. Describe your method.

  b. Calculate the cost of each purchase in Exercises 13 and 14.

16. An apple pie recipe calls for 3 lb of apples. One apple weighs about 7 oz. About how many apples are in this pie?

17. **Archaeology** Tutankhamen was king of Egypt during the period 1347–1339 B.C. Most of the tombs in Egyptian pyramids have had their contents stolen, but the tomb of Tutankhamen was discovered in 1922 with its magnificent treasure still in place.

    a. The solid gold mask found on Tutankhamen's mummy weighs 22 lb. What is the mask's weight in ounces?

    b. Suppose gold sells for $690 per ounce. What is the value of the gold in the mummy's mask?

Use the shipping charge table below for Exercise 18.

18. Ramona wants to send a friend a pair of soccer cleats that weigh 2 lb 3 oz, two shin guards that weigh 6 oz each, and some pictures that weigh 2 oz altogether.

    a. **Estimation** Estimate the shipping charge.

    b. Find the total weight in pounds and ounces of the items Ramona is sending.

    c. What is the shipping charge?

Priority Mail Shipping Charges

Shipping weight	Priority Mail 2-day shipping rate
Up to 2 lb	$3.00
Up to 3 lb	$4.00
Up to 4 lb	$5.00
Up to 5 lb	$6.00

Reflecting ◀▶on the Section

19. Suppose each block used to build this tower weighs 3 oz. What is the weight of the tower in pounds?

Visual THINKING

Exercise 19 checks that you can convert between units of customary weight.

Find the missing measurement for each prism. (Module 7, p. 448)

20. Area of base = 12 cm²

    Volume = 54 cm³

    Height = _?_

21. Height = 6.2 cm

    Volume = 155 cm³

    Area of base = _?_

22. The volume of a rectangular box is 60 cm³. Give two possibilities for the dimensions of the box. (Module 7, p. 448)

23. Suppose *y* represents a length in yards and *f* represents a length in feet. Write a rule in the form of an equation for converting from yards to feet. (Module 1, p. 21; Module 5, p. 302)

Career ▪ Connection

Doctor: Darrell Mease

Darrell Mease monitors the health of children from the time they are born until they become adults. He records the weights of babies because normal growth is a sign of health.

24. A normal birth weight for boys is between 95 oz and 152 oz. Is a 9 lb 7 oz baby boy within the normal range? Explain.

25. From 10 days after birth until 3 months is a time of rapid growth for infants. During this time, doctors like to see an average weight gain of close to 1 oz per day.

    A baby weighs 8 lb 13 oz at her two-week check-up and 11 lb 7 oz at her two-month visit. Is she gaining at about 1 oz per day? Explain.

▲
Pediatrician Darrell Mease works with children in his hometown of Jay, Oklahoma.

Section ②
Extra Skill Practice

Choose the best customary unit (*ounce*, *pound*, or *ton*) to express the weight of each object.

1. softball
2. cow
3. steamship
4. bag of pretzels

5. hammer
6. light bulb
7. desk
8. calculator

Replace each ? with the missing number.

9. 32 oz = ? lb

10. 1600 lb = ? ton(s)

11. 7000 lb = ? ton(s)

12. $3\frac{1}{2}$ lb = ? oz

13. 10 oz = ? lb

14. 16 tons = ? lb

15. 2 tons = ? oz

16. 104 oz = ? lb

17. $4\frac{1}{4}$ lb = ? oz

Replace each ? with <, >, or =.

18. 2.5 lb ? 36 oz

19. 64 oz ? 4 lb

20. 32,000 oz ? 1 ton

21. 0.5 lb ? 6 oz

22. $4\frac{1}{2}$ lb ? 100 oz

23. 1200 lb ? $\frac{1}{2}$ ton

24. $5\frac{1}{4}$ lb ? 84 oz

25. 42 oz ? 3 lb

26. 8500 lb ? 5 tons

Standardized Testing ◀▶ Free Response

1. A circus parade is shown. If each elephant weighs 2.5 tons, the clown car weighs 1 ton, and the people weigh an average of 150 lb each, should they cross the bridge together? Explain.

2. A clown juggles a can of soup (10 oz), a golf ball ($1\frac{1}{2}$ oz), a large apple ($\frac{1}{2}$ lb), and a melon ($2\frac{3}{4}$ lb). When juggling, the clown holds two objects at a time while the rest of the objects are in the air. What is the greatest amount of weight that the clown holds? the least? Explain.

A Weighty Question

The Situation

An old balance scale is on sale at a rummage sale. Only the four weights shown are being sold with the scale. The person selling the balance claims that you can use those weights to find any weight in whole ounces from 1 oz through 40 oz.

The Problem

Prove that the seller's claim is true by showing how to measure each weight from 1 oz through 40 oz.

Something to Think About

◆ How can you organize your work to make sure you do not skip any weights?

◆ Which problem-solving strategies seem helpful for this problem?

Present your Results

Describe what you did to solve the problem. Include any tables, pictures, or charts you made to organize your data. Describe any patterns you noticed while solving the problem.

Section ③ Circles and Circumference

IN THIS SECTION

EXPLORATION 1
◆ Parts of a Circle

EXPLORATION 2
◆ Distance Around a Circle

The Circus Maximus

Setting the Stage ▸▸▸▸▸▸▸▸▸▸▸▸▸▸▸▸▸▸▸▸▸▸▸▸▸▸▸▸▸▸▸▸▸▸▸

One of the wonders of the Roman Empire was the Circus Maximus. This enormous arena was the largest gathering place in ancient Rome, seating 250,000 screaming spectators. As many as 20 four-horse chariots raced around the low wall which ran down the middle of the arena.

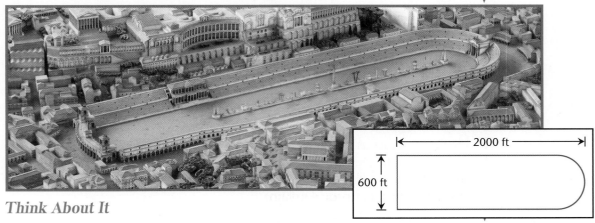

Think About It

1 **a.** How can you estimate the perimeter of the Circus Maximus?

   b. How can you estimate the length of the curved part of the building?

2 The Astrodome in Houston, Texas, holds 60,000 people. About how many times as many people did the Circus Maximus hold?

3 **a.** Estimate the area of the Circus Maximus. Explain how you estimated.

   b. How does the area of the Circus Maximus compare with the area of your classroom?

LEARN HOW TO...
- identify the parts of a circle
- draw a circle

AS YOU...
- explore the Circus Maximus

KEY TERMS
- circle
- center
- radius (plural: radii)
- chord
- diameter

Exploration 1

Parts of a Circle

SET UP You will need: • a piece of string about 30 cm long • two pencils • compass • ruler

The Circus Maximus is shaped like a rectangle with a half *circle* on one end.

▶ To find distances around curved paths, it is helpful to know more about circles. A **circle** is a set of points in a plane that are all the same distance from a given point, the **center**.

4   Think about the definition of a circle. Use it to develop a way to draw a circle using only pencils and string. Then use this method to draw a circle. Label the center of your circle.

5   **Discussion** How did you draw your circle?

▶ A **radius** is a segment from the center of a circle to any point on the circle. A **chord** is a segment that connects two points on a circle.

Point *O* is the center.

$\overline{OA}$ is a radius.

$\overline{BC}$ is a chord.

6   Draw a radius and a chord on your circle.

7   Is a radius a chord? Explain.

✓ QUESTION 8

...checks that you can identify radii and chords of a circle.

8   ✓ **CHECKPOINT** Look at this diagram of segments within a circle.

   a. Name two chords of the circle.

   b. Name two radii of the circle.

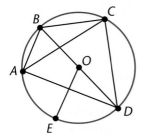

▶ The term *radius* is used for length as well as for segments. Since the length of every radius of a circle is the same, this length is referred to as the *radius* of the circle.

▶ **Drawing Circles** You can use a compass to draw a circle.

First

Open the compass
to the desired radius.

Next

Put the point of the
compass at the center
of the circle.

Then

Draw the circle.
Press down to hold
the compass in place.

The circle
drawn here has
a 3.5 cm radius.

9 **a.** Draw a circle using a compass. Mark its center with a dot.

   b. How does a compass allow you to draw a set of points that
   are all the same distance from a center point?

   c. Draw the longest possible chord. How does the length of
   this chord compare with the length of a radius?

▶ **A diameter of a circle is a chord that passes through the center of
the circle. Every diameter of a circle has the same length. This length
is called the diameter of the circle.**

10 **a.** How is the chord you drew in Question 9(c) related to a
   diameter?

   b. How are the lengths of other chords related to the diameter?

11 ✔ **CHECKPOINT** Use the diagram of the Circus Maximus below.

   a. Use what you know about circles to find the two missing
   dimensions.

   b. Use the scale 1 in. : 200 ft and your ruler and compass to
   make a scale drawing of the Circus Maximus. Label your
   drawing with the actual measurements given and those you
   found in part (a). Save your drawing for use in Exploration 2.

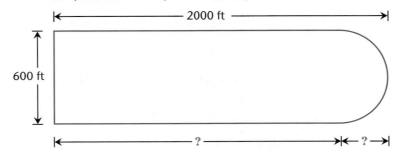

|← ———————— 2000 ft ————————→|

600 ft

|← —————————— ? —————————→|←? →|

✔ **QUESTION 11**

...checks that you
understand the
relationships among
parts of a circle and
that you can draw
a circle.

FOR◀HELP

with *scale
drawings*, see
MODULE 6, p. 413

HOMEWORK EXERCISES ▶ See Exs. 1–7 on p. 467.

GOAL

LEARN HOW TO...
◆ find the circumference of a circle

AS YOU...
◆ investigate Roman chariot wheels and gather data about circles

KEY TERMS
◆ circumference
◆ pi (π)

Distance *around a Circle*

SET UP Work in a group. You will need: • Labsheet 3A • meter stick • 4 circular objects • string • calculator • clear ruler

▶ **Using spoked wheels helped chariot racers gain speed and control. To make the rim and spokes the correct lengths to form a wheel, it was important to know how parts of a circle are related.**

The rim of a Roman chariot ▶ wheel was made by bending a strip of wood to form a circle.

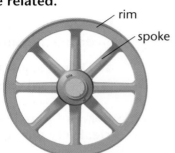

rim
spoke

12 The distance around a circle is its **circumference**. What part of the wheel corresponds to the circumference?

Use Labsheet 3A for Questions 13 and 14.

13 a. Follow the directions for the *Data Table* to find and record the circumference and diameter of circular objects.

b. Make a *Scatter Plot* of the data you collected in part (a).

c. Use your *Scatter Plot* to estimate the circumference of a circle with a diameter of 6 cm.

d. Use your *Scatter Plot* to estimate the diameter of a circle with a circumference of 30 cm.

e. The circumference is about how many times the diameter?

14 Round decimal answers to the nearest hundredth.

a. Add a row to your *Data Table*. Find and record the decimal form of the ratio $\frac{\text{circumference}}{\text{diameter}}$ for each object.

b. What do you notice about the values of the ratios in part (a)?

c. Find the mean of the values of the ratios.

FOR◀HELP

with *scatter plots and fitted lines*, see **MODULE 6, p. 389**

▶ **The Ratio Pi** For any circle, the ratio of the circumference to the diameter is equal to the number represented by the Greek letter π, or **pi**. To estimate pi you can use 3.14 or the ⬛π key on a calculator.

15 a. Press the π key on your calculator. What value appears?

b. Compare the value from part (a) with your result in Question 14(c). How close are the values? How can you explain the difference?

16 Use Labsheet 3A. For each object named in the *Data Table*, find the product $\pi \cdot d$ to the nearest hundredth and compare it with your circumference measurement. What do you notice?

▶ **For any circle, the circumference C equals π times the diameter d.**

$$C = \pi d$$

17 Discussion Find the exact circumference of a circle with the given measurement. (That is, leave your answer in terms of π.)

a. a diameter of 3 ft   **b.** a radius of $\frac{1}{2}$ yd

18 Use 3.14 or the π key on a calculator to estimate the circumference of each circle in Question 17. Round to the nearest hundredth.

▶ **If you know the circumference you can solve for the diameter.**

EXAMPLE

To find the diameter of Earth at the equator, you can use the formula for circumference and substitute the values you know.

$\approx$ means "is about equal to."

$$C = \pi d$$

$40{,}075 \text{ km} \approx 3.14 \cdot d$

$40{,}075 \text{ km} \div 3.14 \approx d$

$12{,}763 \text{ km} \approx d$

The circumference of Earth at the equator is 40,075 km.

The diameter rounded to the nearest kilometer is 12,763 km.

19 ✔ CHECKPOINT Replace each _?_ with the missing length. Round to the hundredths place.

a. $d = \frac{1}{3}$ in., $C \approx$ _?_   **b.** $C = 34.54$ mm, $d \approx$ _?_

20 Use the information from your scale drawing in Question 11. Find the perimeter of the Circus Maximus to the nearest foot.

HOMEWORK EXERCISES ▶ See Exs. 8–18 on pp. 467–468.

✔ **QUESTION 19**

...checks that you can apply the formula for the circumference of a circle.

Section ③ Key Concepts

Key Terms

circle

center

radius (plural: radii)

chord

diameter

circumference

pi (π)

Parts of a Circle (pp. 462–463)

You can use a compass to draw a circle.

In any circle:
- the radius (r) is one half the diameter (d).
- the diameter is the longest chord.
- all radii are the same length.
- all diameters are the same length.

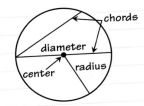

Circumference (pp. 464–465)

The circumference of a circle is the distance around the circle. The ratio of the circumference of any circle to its diameter is pi (π). To find the circumference (C), multiply π by d.

$$\frac{C}{d} = \pi, \text{ so } C = \pi d \text{ or } C = 2\pi r.$$

You can use the value 3.14 or the [π] key on your calculator to estimate π.

Example Find the approximate circumference of a circle that has a radius of 1.5 cm.

≈ means "is about equal to."

$$C = \pi d$$
$$C = \pi \cdot (2r)$$
$$C \approx 3.14 \cdot 2 \cdot 1.5$$
$$C \approx 9.42 \text{ cm}$$

2r = d

The circumference is about 9.42 cm.

21 Key Concepts Question Some Roman chariot wheels had a circumference of about 113 in.

a. How can you estimate the diameter of the wheel?

b. Suppose the rim of the wheel is 3 in. wide and the diameter of the hub is 9 in. About how long is a spoke to the nearest inch?

Note: The length of the spoke is not equal to the radius.

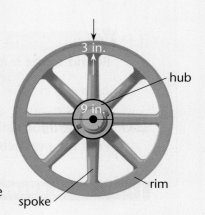

Section 3

Practice & Application Exercises

YOU WILL NEED

For Exs. 4–7:
◆ compass

For Ex. 7:
◆ Labsheet 3B

For Exs. 28–29:
◆ compass
◆ straightedge
◆ drawing paper
◆ colored pencils or markers

Name all the segments of each type shown on the circle with center O.

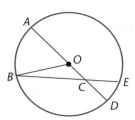

1. radii

2. diameters

3. chords

Use a compass to draw a circle with each radius or diameter.

4. radius = 4 cm   5. diameter = 10 cm   6. radius = $2\frac{1}{4}$ in.

7. **Earthquakes** A seismograph gives information about the strength and location of an earthquake. The *epicenter* of an earthquake is the point on Earth's surface directly over the place where an earthquake occurs.

   a. Readings from the seismograph at Station 1 indicate that an earthquake occurred 100 km away. What do you think the circle drawn around station 1 represents?

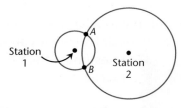

A *seismograph* is an instrument used to record earthquake waves.

   b. A seismograph at Station 2 detected the same quake 300 km away from Station 2. Look at the two circles. Why do you think a scientist is interested in points *A* and *B*, where the two circles intersect?

   c. How do you think scientists can use circles to find the epicenter of an earthquake?

   d. **Use Labsheet 3B.** Use the seismograph locations and the distances in the table on the labsheet. Draw circles on the *Epicenter Map* to find the epicenter of an earthquake that occurred in the South Pacific on March 11, 1997.

Find the approximate circumference of each circle. Round to the nearest hundredth.

8. *d* = 21 in.   9. *d* = 5 cm   10. *r* = 6 ft

For the circle with each given circumference (C), approximate the missing radius or diameter. Replace each __?__ with the missing length. Round to the nearest hundredth.

11. C = 69.08 cm
diameter ≈ __?__

12. C = 28.26 in.
radius ≈ __?__

13. C = 15.7 mm
diameter ≈ __?__

14. **Estimation** The trunk of an African baobab tree can grow up to 30 ft in diameter. About how many people would it take to surround the tree if the people stood with their arms fully extended and their fingertips touching? Explain your thinking.

15. **Algebra Connection** The circumference of a circle is 12.56 cm. What is the ratio of this circumference to the circumference of a circle with a radius twice as long? three times as long?

16. Elia's bicycle wheel has a diameter of 24 in. About how far will it travel in 1 complete turn? in 4 complete turns? Explain.

17. **Challenge** The Colosseum was a large stadium in ancient Rome. Its base was shaped like an oval. Use what you know about circles to estimate the perimeter of the base. Explain how you made your estimate.

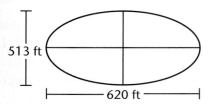

513 ft

620 ft

Journal

Exercise 18 checks that you understand the circumference formula.

Reflecting ◀▶ on the Section

Write your response to Exercise 18 in your journal.

18. The Spanish dollar was minted in Mexico during the eighteenth century. This coin had segments that allowed it to break into 8 equal sections. These bits were used as smaller coins. One-eighth of a Spanish dollar is shown. Use the measurements marked to describe two ways to find the circumference of a whole coin.

Shown larger than actual size.

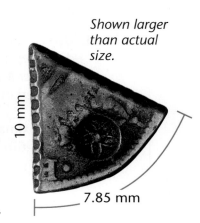

10 mm

7.85 mm

Convert each measurement to pounds. (Module 7, p. 455)

19. 54 oz   **20.** $2\frac{3}{4}$ tons   **21.** 35 oz   **22.** $7\frac{1}{2}$ tons

23. A student's scores on five tests were 84, 86, 38, 85, and 99. Which average best describes the data: the mean, the median, or the mode? Explain. (Module 4, p. 225)

Find the value of *n*. (Module 3, p. 158)

24. $n = 3^2$ **25.** $n = 2^4$ **26.** $n^3 = 1$ **27.** $5^n = 125$

Extension ▶ ▶

Compass Construction

You can make geometric figures called *constructions* using a compass and a straightedge.

28. Follow the steps to draw a circle and make a geometric figure.

Step 1

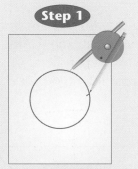

Use a compass to draw a circle. Keep the compass opening the same and put the point of the compass on any point on the circle. Make a small mark on the circle.

Step 2

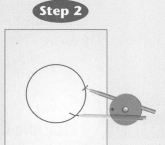

Put the point of the compass on the mark you made and make a second mark. Continue marking around the circle.

Step 3

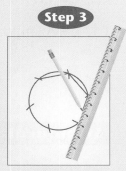

Use a straightedge to connect the marks. Name the geometric figure you made.

29. Draw and mark another circle. Use your straightedge or compass to make a design. Some examples are shown.

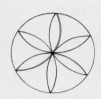
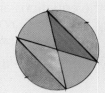
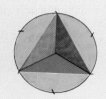

Section 3

Extra Skill Practice

Name all the segments of each type shown on the circle with center O.

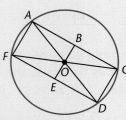

1. diameters

2. chords

3. radii

For each circle in Exercises 4–9, find the approximate circumference. Round to the nearest hundredth.

4. d = 27 in.

5. r = 2.5 cm

6. r = 53 mm

7.
11,300 m

8.
8.125 in.

9.
13.53 ft

Replace each ? with the missing length. Round to the nearest hundredth.

10. d = 5 cm, C ≈ ?

11. C = 11 m, d ≈ ?

12. C = 117.75 ft, r ≈ ?

13. r = 31 in., C ≈ ?

14. C = 55 m, d ≈ ?

15. C = 175.84 cm, r ≈ ?

Section 4 Circles and Cylinders

IN THIS SECTION

EXPLORATION 1
◆ Area of a Circle

EXPLORATION 2
◆ Volume of a Cylinder

The Mystery of Mesa Verde

Setting the Stage ▸

For many years, the ancestors of the Hopi, Zuni, and several other Native American groups lived in stone houses they built in natural caves in the cliffs of Mesa Verde, Colorado. Then something strange happened…

> "…whole villages of people left their homes. It seems that about 650 years ago, they just walked away and left most of their belongings….Why did the ancient ones build stone houses in caves?…And why did they leave?"
>
> **Ruth Shaw Radlauer,** *Mesa Verde National Park*

Although there are many theories, it is still not known for sure why the villages were abandoned.

Think About It

1 Suppose at this moment you and your classmates walked out of your classroom leaving all of your belongings behind. What do you think someone could learn about students and class activities just by looking around the room?

2 The villages contain round rooms called *kivas*. The diameter of one of the kivas is 4.3 m.

a. What is the radius of the kiva?

b. What is the circumference of the floor of the kiva?

c. How do you think the size of the kiva compares with the size of your classroom? Explain.

GOAL

LEARN HOW TO...
- find the area of a circle

AS YOU...
- determine how many people could fit in a kiva

Exploration 1

Area of a Circle

SET UP *You will need Labsheet 4A.*

In her book about Mesa Verde, Ruth Shaw Radlauer discusses the role of the kivas in the lives of people:

> "When children were old enough, they were initiated, or proclaimed adults in a ceremony. Then they could spend some of the winter in a warm kiva. The kiva was a sort of clubhouse for adults and a place for ceremonies."

▶ **To determine how many people could fit inside a kiva, you need to know the area of the floor. The floor of a kiva is shaped like a circle.**

3 Use Labsheet 4A. Follow the directions for *Estimating the Area of a Circle* by finding the areas of the inner and outer squares.

▶ **You can use the method in Question 3 to estimate the area of any circle with radius *r*.**

4 **Try This As A Class** The diagram below can help you see the relationship between the area of the circle and its radius *r*.

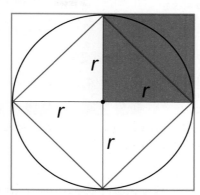

   a. Use the variable *r* to write an expression for the area of the small red square.

   b. How many small red squares fit in the outer square?

   c. Use your answer to part (b) to write an expression for the area of the outer square.

   d. How many of the small red squares fit in the inner square? (*Hint:* Each small red square is made up of two triangles.)

   e. Use your answer to part (d) to write an expression for the area of the inner square.

   f. Use your answers to parts (c) and (e) to write an expression that can be used to estimate the area of the circle.

5 **a.** Use your answer to Question 4(f) to estimate the area of a circle with a radius of 4 cm.

   b. How does your estimate compare to the estimate you found in Question 3?

▶ **Formula for the Area of a Circle** In Question 4, you found an expression that can be used to estimate the area of a circle. To find the actual area *A* of a circle with radius *r*, multiply pi by *r* to the second power.

$$A = \pi r^2$$

You can read r^2 as "*r* squared."

6 **Discussion** How does the formula above compare with the expression you found in Question 4(f)?

EXAMPLE

Find the approximate area of a circle with radius 8.5 cm. Round your answer to the nearest square centimeter.

SAMPLE RESPONSE

$$A = \pi r^2 = \pi \cdot (8.5)^2$$

Method 1	Method 2
To find A, use 3.14 for π.	To find A, use the π key on a calculator.
$3.14 \cdot 8.5^2 = 226.865$	$\boxed{\pi}$ $\boxed{\times}$ 8.5 $\boxed{x^2}$ $\boxed{=}$ 226.98...
The area is about 227 cm².	

This key takes 8.5 to the second power.

7 a. In the Example, why aren't the answers the same?

b. Which answer is more accurate? Why?

8 a. Using 3.14 for π, find the approximate area of a circle with radius 4 cm.

b. How does your answer in part (a) compare to your estimates in Question 3 and Question 5(a)?

✔ QUESTION 9

...checks that you can find the area of a circle.

9 ✔ CHECKPOINT Find the area of each circle to the nearest square centimeter.

a. 3 cm

b.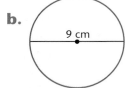
9 cm

▶ The area you find when you use either 3.14 or the π key on a calculator is an estimate. To find the exact area of a circle, you need to write an expression that contains the number π.

For example, to find the exact area of a circle with radius 4 cm, write $\pi \cdot 4^2$. Since $\pi \cdot 4^2 = \pi \cdot 16$, or 16π, the exact area is 16π cm².

10 a. What is the exact area of a kiva floor with diameter 4.3 m?

b. Use 3.14 for π to estimate the area of the kiva floor.

11 Estimate how much floor space an average-sized person needs to stand comfortably. How many people can stand comfortably in the kiva in Question 10?

HOMEWORK EXERCISES ▶ See Exs. 1–13 on pp. 478–479.

Exploration 2

Volume of a Cylinder

GOAL

LEARN HOW TO...
- recognize a cylinder
- find the volume of a cylinder

AS YOU...
- explore the size and shape of a kiva

KEY TERMS
- cylinder
- right cylinder
- oblique cylinder

SET UP *Work in a group of four. You will need:* • *Labsheets 4B–4D* • *scissors* • *tape* • *rice* • *a ruler*

In the summer of 1891, Gustaf Nordenskiöld of Sweden and his team began to uncover the ruins at Mesa Verde. Part of their task was to remove the layers of dust and rubbish that had piled up over the centuries. After digging to a depth of $\frac{1}{2}$ m at one location, they began to see a kiva take shape.

12 How do you think Nordenskiöld could have estimated the amount of dust and rubbish in the kiva without removing it?

A kiva is shaped like a *cylinder*. A 3-dimensional figure that has a curved surface and two congruent parallel bases that are circles is a **cylinder**.

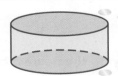

The **bases** are parallel and congruent.

13 **Use Labsheets 4B–4D.** Cut out the nets for the open-topped *Prisms* and *Cylinders*. Fold and tape each net.

14 **Try This as a Class**

a. How are the two cylinders like prisms? How are they different from prisms?

b. Cylinder 1 is a **right cylinder** and Cylinder 2 is an **oblique cylinder**. How are right and oblique cylinders different?

c. How would you measure the height of each cylinder?

d. Which cylinder do you think has the greater volume? Why?

e. Fill Cylinder 2 with rice and then pour the rice into Cylinder 1. Does the rice completely fill Cylinder 1, or is there too much or not enough rice?

f. What can you conclude about the volumes of the cylinders?

15 Which has the greater volume, Prism A or Prism B? Explain.

16

a. Which do you think holds more, Cylinder 1 or Prism A? Why?

b. Which do you think holds more, Cylinder 1 or Prism B? Why?

17

a. Place Cylinder 1 inside the larger prism. Then place the smaller prism inside Cylinder 1.

b. What can you conclude about the volume of Cylinder 1?

c. For each of the prisms and cylinders, find the area of the base and the height. Make a table to record your results.

18

Discussion Add on to the table you completed in Question 17.

a. Find the volumes of Prism A and Prism B. Explain your method.

b. Use the same method you used in part (a) to find the volumes of Cylinder 1 and Cylinder 2.

c. Use your models to decide whether the volume you found for Cylinder 1 is reasonable.

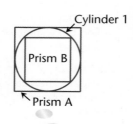

Cylinder 1

Prism B

Prism A

top view

▶ **You can find the volume _V_ of a cylinder with height _h_ and a base with area _B_ in the same way you find the volume of a prism.**

$$V = Bh, \text{ or } V = \pi r^2 h.$$

area of circular base

> ### EXAMPLE
>
> **Find the volume of the right cylinder shown to the nearest cubic centimeter. Use 3.14 for π.**
>
> **SAMPLE RESPONSE**
>
> $$V = \pi r^2 h$$
> $$\approx 3.14 \cdot 4^2 \cdot 5.3 = 266.272$$
>
> **The volume is about 266 cm³.**
>
>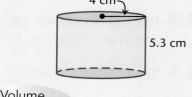
>
> 4 cm
>
> 5.3 cm
>
> Volume is measured in cubic units.

✔ **QUESTION 19**

...checks that you can find the volume of a cylinder.

19 ✔ CHECKPOINT

Find the volume of the right cylinder at the right to the nearest cubic meter. Use 3.14 for π.

10 m

7 m

20

Gustaf Nordenskiöld reported that one of the kivas he uncovered had a diameter of 4.3 m and walls 2 m high. If this kiva was completely full of dust and rubbish, about how much material did Nordenskiöld have to remove?

HOMEWORK EXERCISES ▶ See Exs. 14–22 on p. 479.

Section 4
Key Concepts

▶▶▶▶▶▶▶▶▶▶▶▶▶▶▶▶▶▶▶▶▶▶▶▶▶

Key Terms

Area of a Circle (pp. 472–474)

To find the area (A) of a circle, multiply π by the **radius squared**.

$$A = \pi r^2$$

Using π (pp. 473–474)

- To estimate the answer: Use [π] on a calculator or use 3.14 for π.
- To find the exact answer: Write an expression using the number π.

Cylinders (p. 475)

A 3-dimensional figure that has a curved surface and two congruent parallel bases that are circles is a cylinder.

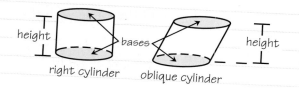

right cylinder   oblique cylinder

cylinder

right cylinder

oblique cylinder

Volume of a Cylinder (pp. 475–476)

To find the volume (V) of a cylinder, multiply the **area of the base** (B) by the **height** (h).

$$V = Bh$$

For a circular base, $B = \pi r^2$.

$$V = \pi r^2 h$$

Example

Find the volume of the right cylinder shown to the nearest cubic inch. Use 3.14 for π.

$$V = \pi r^2 h$$
$$\approx 3.14 \cdot 1.5^2 \cdot 4.5$$
$$\approx 31.793$$

The volume is about 32 in.³

1.5 in.

4.5 in.

Key Concepts Questions

21 Find the volume to the nearest cubic centimeter of a cylinder that has a diameter of 16 cm and a height of 10 cm. Use 3.14 for π.

22 What happens to the volume of the cylinder in Question 21 if the diameter is doubled?

Section 4 Practice & Application Exercises

YOU WILL NEED

For Exs. 30–33:
- graph paper

For Exs. 34–39:
- Labsheet 4E
- scissors
- tape
- rice or dry cereal

Unless you are asked to find exact areas or volumes, use the π key on a calculator or 3.14 for the value of pi. Round to the nearest hundredth.

Find the area of the circle with the given radius (*r*) or diameter (*d*).

1. $r = 2\frac{1}{2}$ in.

2. $d = 6$ ft

3. $d = 4.2$ m

4.
2 cm

5.
3 in.

6.
1.4 mm

Find the exact area of the circle with the given radius (*r*) or diameter (*d*).

7. $r = 25$ mm

8. $d = 3$ in.

9. $r = 4.6$ cm

10. The circumference of a circle is about 28.26 cm. Find the approximate area of the circle.

11. **Archaeology** Gustav Nordenskiöld found a piece of broken pottery at Mesa Verde. The drawing shows a whole bowl based on the broken piece. The top of the bowl is circular with a 14 cm diameter.

    If you made a flat, circular cover for a bowl this size, what would its area be?

broken piece

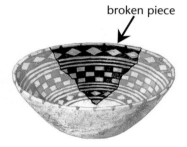

12. **Weather** One of the largest tropical storms ever recorded occurred in the Northwest Pacific on October 12, 1979. This storm, a circular typhoon named Tip, had a radius of 1100 km.

    a. What is the approximate area that Tip covered?

    b. **Estimation** The area of Australia is 7,614,500 km². Suppose Tip had reached Australia. About what fraction of this continent could Tip have covered?

◄ A severe rotating wind storm that forms in the western Pacific Ocean or Indian Ocean is called a typhoon. Similar storms in the Atlantic Ocean or Caribbean Sea are called hurricanes.

13. Challenge Figure *ABCD* is a square. Find the area of the shaded region.

A ___ B

3 in. | 2 in.

D ___ C

Find the volume of each right cylinder. Use 3.14 for π.

14.

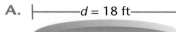

5m

3 m

15.

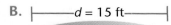

4 m

9 m

16.

20 cm

14 cm

For each right cylinder, replace the ? with the missing measurement.

17. *r* = 2 in.
    h = 6 in.
    V ≈ ?

18. *d* = 3.5 cm
    h ≈ ?
    V = 57.7 cm³

19. *d* = 5.4 m
    h = 8 m
    V ≈ ?

20. Which swimming pool holds more water?

A. |——*d* = 18 ft——|

h = 48 in.

B. |——*d* = 15 ft——|

h = 52 in.

21. Challenge Mugs come in many different shapes and sizes.

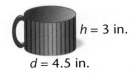

h = 3 in.

d = 4.5 in.

a. What three-dimensional figure are most mugs shaped like?

b. Design a mug that will hold about the same amount of liquid as the one shown, but with different dimensions. Sketch your mug and label its height and diameter.

Reflecting ◀▶ on the Section

22. Make a concept map that pulls together what you have learned about circles, prisms, and cylinders. Include ideas about the following:

• parts of a prism, a circle, and a cylinder

• formulas for area, volume, and circumference

FOR ◀ HELP

with concept maps, see

MODULE 5, p. 344

Visual THINKING

Exercise 22 checks that you can make connections between prisms and cylinders and the methods used to find their volumes.

Spiral ◀▶ Review

Find the circumference of each circle to the nearest hundredth. Use 3.14 for π. (Module 7, p. 466)

23. diameter = 13 ft   **24.** radius = 6 in.   **25.** diameter = 4.5 m

Write each percent as a fraction in lowest terms and as a decimal. (Module 6, p. 427)

26. 40%   **27.** 9%   **28.** 15%   **29.** 63%

Graph each ordered pair on a coordinate grid. (Module 4, p. 256)

30. (5, 4)   **31.** (0, 7)   **32.** (2, 6)   **33.** (7, 3)

Extension ▶ ▶

Volume of a Cone

Home Involvement Use the *Cone and Cylinder Nets* on Labsheet 4E to find the relationship between the volume of a cone and the volume of a cylinder.

34. a. Cut out and fold the nets.

b. How is the cone like a cylinder? like a pyramid?

> The cones you will work with are *circular* cones because their bases are shaped like circles.

c. How is a cone different from a cylinder? from a pyramid?

d. How do the heights of the cone and cylinder compare?

e. How do the shapes and sizes of the bases of the cone and cylinder compare?

35. a. Fill the cone with rice and pour the rice into the cylinder. Repeat until the cylinder is full.

b. How many of the cones filled with rice did it take to fill the cylinder?

36. Write a formula for the volume of a cone.

Find the volume of each cone. Round to the nearest hundredth.

37.

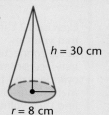

h = 30 cm

r = 8 cm

38.

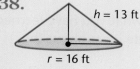

h = 13 ft

r = 16 ft

39.

h = 5 in.

d = 3 in.

Section 4
Extra Skill Practice

Find the area of the circle with the given radius (*r*) or diameter (*d*). Use the π key on a calculator or 3.14 for π. Round to the nearest hundredth.

1. $r = 26.3$ mm

2.
83 in.

3. $r = \frac{1}{2}$ ft

Find the exact area of the circle with the given radius (*r*) or diameter (*d*).

4.
15 cm

5. $d = 49$ yd

6.
18 m

Find the volume of each right cylinder. Round to the nearest hundredth.

7.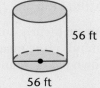
56 ft
56 ft

8.
16 cm
9 cm

9.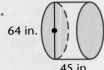
64 in.
45 in.

For each right cylinder, replace the ? with the missing measurement. Round to the nearest tenth in Exercises 10 and 11 and to the nearest whole number in Exercise 12.

10. $r = 4.7$ m
$h \approx \underline{\;?\;}$
$V = 458$ m³

11. $d = 2.5$ ft
$h = 4.5$ ft
$V \approx \underline{\;?\;}$

12. $r = 10$ cm
$h \approx \underline{\;?\;}$
$V = 1885$ cm³

Standardized Testing ◀▶ Performance Task

Suppose Cylinder 1 is full of sand. If you pour the sand from Cylinder 1 into Cylinder 2, can you fill Cylinder 2 to the top? If not, then how much more sand is needed? If so, what volume of sand is left over in Cylinder 1?

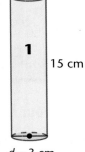
1
15 cm
$d = 3$ cm

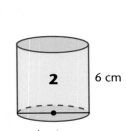
2
6 cm
$d = 6$ cm

Section ⑤ Temperature, Integers, and Coordinate Graphs

World Traveler

Setting the Stage

◀ Marco Polo in a Tartar costume

from *The Great Travelers* by Milton Rugoff

"Of all the travelers the world has known, there is none whose name conjures up [brings to mind] more images of the exotic, of the wonder of unknown places, than that of Marco Polo.

It was in 1271 that the seventeen-year-old Marco set out from Venice with his father and uncle. ...it took the Polos more than three years to reach China and the fabulous court of [its ruler] Kublai Khan... . Eventually [Marco] visited nearly every part of the vast empire... . The Polos finally arrived in Venice after an absence of almost twenty-six years."

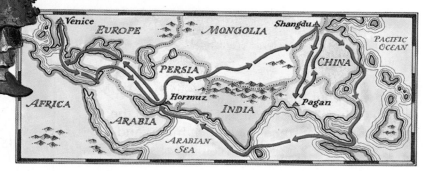

Think About It

1 How many years ago did Marco Polo begin his trip?

2 Use the map of the Polos' route. What different kinds of weather do you think the Polos experienced along the way?

MATHEMATICS
The & Theme

8 SECTION OVERVIEW

Customary and Metric Capacity

As you revisit Patterns and Problem Solving:
- ◆ Convert between customary units of capacity
- ◆ Relate volume and metric capacity
- ◆ Estimate capacity in metric units

② **Estimation and Mental Math**

As you revisit Math Detectives:
- ◆ Use estimation and mental math strategies

③ **Adding and Subtracting Integers**

As you revisit Mind Games:
- ◆ Add and subtract integers

④ **Geometric Probability**

As you revisit Statistical Safari:
- ◆ Find geometric probabilities
- ◆ Use probability to make predictions

⑤ **Transformations**

As you revisit Creating Things:
- ◆ Perform translations, rotations, and reflections

⑥ **Scientific Notation**

As you revisit Comparisons and Predictions:
- ◆ Write large numbers in scientific notation

The Module Project

Play *The Math is Right!*

A quiz game is a fun way to test your knowledge. You will work as a team to create questions that relate to a theme and to the mathematics you have learned this year. Will your questions stump the other teams in your class? Find out when you play *The Math is Right!*

More on the Module Project
See pp. 560–561.

Resources and practice at
classzone.com

499

Section 1 Customary and Metric Capacity

IN THIS SECTION

EXPLORATION 1
• Customary Capacity

EXPLORATION 2
• Metric Capacity

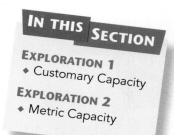

PATTERNS & PROBLEM SOLVING

Setting the Stage

KEY TERMS
• capacity
• gallon (gal)
• quart (qt)
• pint (pt)
• cup (c)
• fluid ounce (fl oz)

SET UP *You will need containers of various sizes.*

The average teen consumes over 7 gallons of soda a month! To compare this to drinking one can, bottle, or fountain drink a day, you need to know the *capacity* of each container. The **capacity** of a container is the amount of liquid it can hold. In the customary system, capacity is measured in **gallons** (**gal**), **quarts** (**qt**), **pints** (**pt**), **cups** (**c**), or **fluid ounces** (**fl oz**).

Milk containers are good benchmarks for estimating capacity. In this activity you will use milk containers to help estimate the capacity of various containers.

ESTIMATING CAPACITY

• Your teacher will hold up an item and ask you to estimate its capacity in either gallons, quarts, pints, cups, or fluid ounces.

• Record the item and your estimate. Then record the actual capacity when your teacher tells it to you.

• Use the previous items and the milk containers to help improve your estimates each time.

Think About It

1 Think about the milk containers and other items to decide whether each statement is reasonable.

    a. I have to fill a cup four times to make a pint.

    b. The maximum capacity of a car's fuel tank is 15 pt.

    c. Some tea kettles can hold about $1\frac{1}{2}$ qt of water.

Adding
+ Integers

GOAL

LEARN HOW TO...
◆ add integers

AS YOU...
◆ analyze the game *Charge-O-Meter*

KEY TERM
◆ opposites

▶ **One strategy for quickly finding how far to move your game piece is to pair positive beans with negative beans. This strategy can also be used to model addition of integers.**

EXAMPLE

Suppose you tossed 5 positive beans and 2 negative beans.

2 positive beans can be paired with 2 negative beans to cancel each other out.

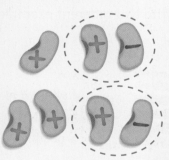

$$+5 \; + \; -2 = \; \underline{?}$$

3 Discussion Look at the addition in the Example.

a. Why do the paired beans cancel each other out?

b. If you tossed the combination of beans shown, how far and in what direction would you move your game piece?

c. What integer is represented by the combination of beans?

d. $+5 + (-2) = \underline{?}$

This is read "5 plus negative 2."

To avoid confusion negative integers can be written in parentheses.

✔ **QUESTION 4**

...checks that you can represent integer addition using a bean model.

4 ✔ **CHECKPOINT**

    a. Suppose you had 24 beans in your cup and you tossed 10 positive beans and 14 negative beans. How would you move your game piece?

    b. Write an integer addition equation for the combination of beans in part (a).

5 Use a bean model to find each sum.

    a. $+1 + (-5)$ **b.** $+6 + (-4)$ **c.** $+3 + (-3)$ **d.** $-5 + (-2)$

Use bean models to help answer Questions 6–8.

6 **Try This as a Class**

    a. Write two different addition equations where both addends (the numbers that are added) are negative.

    b. Is the sum of two negative numbers *positive* or *negative*?

    c. How can you find the sum of two negative numbers without using a bean model?

7 Write two different examples for each case below.

    Case   Examples

    a. one addend is positive, one addend is negative, the sum is a positive integer

    b. one addend is positive, one addend is negative, the sum is a negative integer

    c. one addend is positive, one addend is negative, the sum is zero

8 **Discussion** Explain when the sum of a positive integer and a negative integer will be the given number.

    a. a positive number   **b.** a negative number   **c.** 0

9 Describe a general method for finding the sum of a positive and a negative integer.

10 Try This as a Class The numbers you used to answer Question 8(c) are *opposites*. What do you think it means for two numbers to be **opposites?**

▶ **It is not necessary to label positive integers with a "+" sign. For example, +3 is the same as 3.**

11 ✔ CHECKPOINT Find each sum.

   a. −17 + 25   **b.** 13 + (−7)   **c.** −36 + (−9)

   d. −11 + 11   **e.** −24 + 19   **f.** 12 + (−17)

HOMEWORK EXERCISES ▶ See Exs. 1–21 on pp. 528–529.

✔ QUESTION 11

...checks that you can add integers.

Exploration 2 ▶▶▶▶▶▶▶▶▶▶▶▶▶▶▶▶▶▶▶▶▶

Subtracting — Integers

GOAL

LEARN HOW TO...
- ◆ subtract integers

AS YOU...
- ◆ model thundercloud charges with bean models

SET UP *Work in a group. You will need the 12 beans from Exploration 1.*

Though it is not known for certain how thunderclouds become charged, scientists do know that lightning is the movement of electrical charges from a cloud.

▶ **Integer subtraction can be modeled in a similar way by taking away beans representing positive or negative charges.**

12 What integer is represented by this combination of beans? Explain.

13 **Try This as a Class** Use the bean model for 2 – (–3) shown below.

The combination of beans below represents +2.

3 negative beans are being taken away, making the expression +2 – (–3).

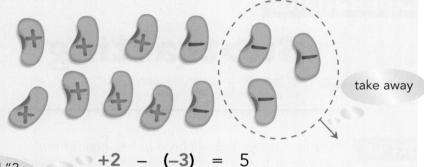

take away

This is read "2 minus negative 3."

+2 – (–3) = 5

a. How is subtracting –3 shown in the model?

b. The difference is 5. How was this found?

14 Write the subtraction equation shown by each bean model.

a.

b.

c.

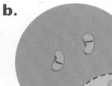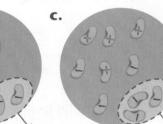

15 Use a bean model to find each difference.

a. –6 – (–3)   **b.** –7 – (–2)   **c.** –4 – (–4)

Algebra Connection For each expression, describe the possible values for *x*.

18. The sum 10 + *x* is a positive integer.

19. The sum –3 + *x* is a negative integer.

20. The sum *x* + 6 is zero.

21. **Challenge** In a magic square, the sum of the numbers in each row, column, and main diagonal is the same. Copy and complete the magic square using –10, –6, –4, 0, 2, 4, and 6.

Magic Square

–8	?	?
?	–2	?
?	?	?

Write the subtraction equation shown by each model.

22.

23.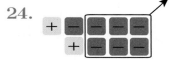

24.

25. Draw a model of 3 that can be used to show the subtraction 3 – (–2).

Write an equivalent addition expression for each subtraction expression. Then find the sum.

26. 18 – (–33)   27. –12 – 9   28. 0 – (–28)

29. **Temperature** The greatest 24-hour temperature change in the United States was recorded in Loma, Montana, on January 14–15, 1972. The temperature rose from –54°F to 49°F.

a. Write a subtraction expression to find the change in temperature.

b. Write an addition expression to find the change in temperature. Use the thermometer above to help explain why this expression gives the same answer as your expression from part (a).

Find the sum or difference.

30. 27 – 55   **31.** 23 + (–18)   **32.** –8 – (–17)

33. –10 – 0   **34.** –29 – (–50)   **35.** –7 + 24

36. –19 – (–19)   **37.** –5 – 8   **38.** 0 – 25

39. –19 + (–19)   **40.** 0 – (–25)   **41.** 26 – (–55)

42. Golf In 1997, twenty-one-year-old Tiger Woods became the youngest winner of the Masters Tournament.

a. *Par* is the number of strokes it should take a very good golfer to get the ball from the tee into the hole. Of the players in the table, who took the most strokes? the fewest?

b. By how many strokes did Tiger Woods beat Tom Kite?

–18 means 18 strokes less than par.

1997 Masters Tournament	
Player	Standings
Tiger Woods	–18
Tom Kite	–6
Tommy Tolles	–5
Tom Watson	–4

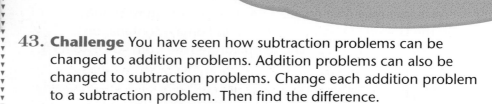

43. Challenge You have seen how subtraction problems can be changed to addition problems. Addition problems can also be changed to subtraction problems. Change each addition problem to a subtraction problem. Then find the difference.

a. –17 + 17   b. 23 + (–8)   c. 14 + (–22)

Oral Report

Exercise 44 checks that you understand integer addition and subtraction.

Reflecting ◀▶ on the Section

Be prepared to report on the following in class.

44. Draw a model and write an equation to show how each situation could occur.

a. adding an integer to a number and getting a sum that is less than the original number

b. subtracting an integer from a number and getting a difference that is greater than the original number

Plot each pair of coordinates on a grid. (Module 7, p. 489)

45. (4, –7)   **46.** (0, 5)   **47.** (–3, –3)   **48.** (–2, 0)

Estimation Estimate each sum or difference. (Module 1, p. 10; Module 5, p. 324; Module 8, p. 516)

49. $5\frac{7}{8} + 7\frac{1}{5}$ **50.** 2763 + 1287   **51.** $9 - 6\frac{8}{11}$

52. $2\frac{2}{7} + 3\frac{1}{8}$ **53.** $16\frac{5}{9} - 4\frac{3}{4}$ **54.** 15.8 + 9.2 + 7.9

Mental Math Use mental math to multiply. (Toolbox, p. 574)

55. 0.137 • 1000   **56.** 4.23 • 100   **57.** 3.59 • 10,000

58. 0.2 • 10   **59.** 2.213 • 1000   **60.** 75 • 100,000

Extension ▶ ▶

Commutative and Associative Properties

Find the sums for each pair of expressions.

61. 2 + (–4)
$\quad$ –4 + 2

62. –3 + (–2)
$\quad$ –2 + (–3)

63. –8 + 15
$\quad$ 15 + (–8)

64. [5 + (–6)] + 2
$\quad$ 5 + (–6 + 2)

65. (–7 + 3) + (–5)
$\quad$ –7 + [3 + (–5)]

66. 13 + [–1 + (–9)]
$\quad$ [13 + (–1)] + (–9)

67. Addition of integers is *commutative*. The order in which the integers are added does not change the result. Explain which pairs of sums in Exercises 61–66 show this property.

68. The addition of integers is also *associative*. The grouping of the integers does not change the result. Explain which pairs of sums in Exercises 61–66 show this property.

Add the integers mentally. Explain the method you used.

69. –21 + 15 + (–9) + 5

70. –8 + 13 + (–3) + (–13)

71. a. Is subtraction of integers commutative?

$\quad$ b. Is subtraction of integers associative?

$\quad$ c. Give examples to support your answers to parts (a) and (b).

Find each sum.

1. $-10 + (-7)$
2. $21 + (-3)$
3. $-34 + (-6)$
4. $7 + (-14)$
5. $-45 + 61$
6. $15 + (-15)$
7. $-21 + (-5)$
8. $16 + (-52)$
9. $-7 + 3$

Find each difference.

10. $6 - (-4)$
11. $-22 - (-13)$
12. $-12 - (-7)$
13. $15 - 19$
14. $-16 - 7$
15. $10 - (-12)$
16. $0 - (-72)$
17. $-51 - 12$
18. $-5 - (-5)$

For each expression, describe the possible values for x.

19. The difference $-4 - x$ is a positive integer.

20. The difference $x - 6$ is a negative integer.

21. The sum $12 + x$ is zero.

Find each sum or difference.

22. $51 - 73$
23. $29 + (-35)$
24. $-96 - (-8)$
25. $0 - (-16)$
26. $-1 - (-5)$
27. $-14 + 62$
28. $-91 + (-35)$
29. $-13 - 18$
30. $12 - 44$

Study Skills ◀▶Listening

Listening to the thoughts and ideas of other people can help clarify your own thoughts. It can also spark new ideas you might not have thought of otherwise.

Look at Discussion Questions 16 and 20 on page 525. Try to remember your class discussion of these questions.

1. What were some of the comments and answers from your classmates?

2. Did any of the ideas from the discussion make you think in a new way? Explain.

Mix It Up

The Situation

Trail mix is a mixture of different types of nuts, dried fruits, and sweets that can be eaten on the go. *Mix It Up* is a new store in town that has several items you can choose from to create your own trail mix.

The Problem

Create several different trail mixes that have one type of nut, one type of fruit, and one type of sweet. Each mix must fill a quart size bag and cost about $5.

Mix It Up

Nuts	Cost/Cup
Almonds	$1.29
Cashews	$1.34
Peanuts	$.81
Fruits	**Cost/Cup**
Apples	$.23
Banana chips	$.37
Raisins	$.43
Sweets	**Cost/Cup**
Chocolate covered cranberries	$2.84
Candy covered chocolate	$2.75
Chocolate chips	$1.38

▲
A mix of raisins and peanuts is a common snack.

Typically, mixes like the one above have extra ingredients to please individual tastes.

Something to Think About

- How many cups are in one quart?
- Fractions of a cup can be used.
- What combinations of three ingredients do you think would taste good?
- What percent of each mix should be nuts? What percent fruits? What percent sweets?

Present Your Results

How many different combinations of nuts, fruits, and sweets are possible?

Name the trail mixes you created.

For each of your trail mixes, list the three ingredients, the amount of each ingredient, the total cost of each ingredient, and the cost of a quart of the trail mix.

Choose one of your trail mixes to be the ***Mix of the Month*** for the *Mix It Up* store. Explain why you chose it.

STATISTICAL

SAFARI

Setting the Stage

In Module 4, you analyzed data about dinosaurs. After dominating the land for 130 million years, dinosaurs disappeared from the face of the Earth at the end of the Cretaceous Period, about 65 million years ago. "Why did the dinosaurs become extinct?" The answer is that nobody knows for sure.

Many scientists believe that a huge asteroid that crashed into the Yucatán Peninsula at a site known as Chicxulub (pronounced CHEEK-shoo-loob) caused the extinction of 70% of the living species, including the dinosaurs, on the planet. The impact blasted a crater 180 km wide and 900 m deep.

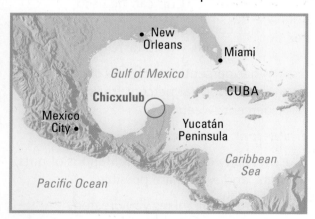

◀ Location of the Chicxulub crater (circle) on Mexico's Yucatán Peninsula

Think About It

1 The Chicxulub crater is about how many times as wide as it is deep?

2 If an asteroid strikes Earth, is it more likely to hit land or water? Why?

Exploration 1

Predicting with Geometric Probability

SET UP *Work as a class. You will need an inflatable globe.*

GOAL

LEARN HOW TO...
- find geometric probabilities
- use probability to make predictions

AS YOU...
- describe the chance of an object falling in a particular area

KEY TERMS
- complementary events
- geometric probability

▶ Since the orbits of most asteroids do not intersect Earth's orbit, it isn't likely that one will strike Earth. However, about 500 meteorites do strike Earth each year. Each meteorite has an equally likely chance of hitting anywhere on Earth. To find the probability that a meteorite will hit land you will conduct an experiment with a globe.

3 Try This as a Class Follow the steps below to simulate a meteorite falling to Earth.

First Make a table like the one below to record the results of your experiment.

Next Carefully toss an inflated globe from one person to another. Each time the globe is caught, make a tally mark to record whether the tip of your left index finger is touching land or touching water before tossing it again. Record the results of 30 tosses.

Then Complete your table by calculating the percent of the tosses that hit land and the percent that hit water.

	Tally	Number of tosses	Percent of tosses
Land			
Water			
Total		30	

FOR ►HELP

with *finding probabilities*, see
MODULE 2, p. 80

4 Discussion Use the results of the globe-tossing experiment.

   a. What percent of Earth do you think is covered by water?

   b. Estimate the probability that a meteorite will hit water.

   c. Estimate the probability that it will hit land.

   d. What is the probability a meteorite will hit either land or water?

▶ When a meteorite strikes Earth, it either hits water or it hits land. The events *a meteorite hits water* and *a meteorite hits land* are **complementary events.** Two events are complementary if one or the other must occur, but they cannot both happen at the same time.

Objects in space travel at great speeds. An aluminum sphere 1 cm in diameter orbiting Earth can cause the same damage to a spacecraft as a 40 lb object traveling 60 mi/hr on Earth!

5 Try This as a Class Use the probabilities you found in Question 4.

   a. If two events are complementary, what must be true about their probabilities?

   b. It is estimated that 500 meteorites hit Earth each year. About how many meteorites would you expect to hit water each year? About how many meteorites would you expect to hit land each year?

▶ In addition to meteoroids, space junk—such as pieces of satellites and rockets—can be harmful to orbiting spacecraft.

6 Try This as a Class Suppose a rectangular sensor is placed in the middle of a rectangular panel on a spacecraft as shown.

   a. If a piece of space junk randomly hits the panel, how can you find the probability that it hits the sensor? Find the probability.

   b. What is the probability that a piece of space junk hits the panel but not the sensor? How did you find the probability?

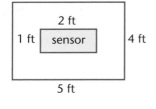

▶ In Question 6, you used areas to find a probability. Probabilities that are based on lengths, areas, or volumes are **geometric probabilities.**

✔ QUESTION 7

...checks that you can find geometric probabilities and use them to make predictions.

7 ✔ CHECKPOINT Suppose an object randomly hits within the circle at the right.

   a. What is the probability that it will hit within the square?

   b. If 200 objects randomly hit within the circle, about how many would you expect to hit within the square?

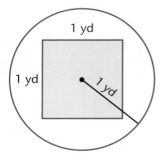

HOMEWORK EXERCISES ▶ See Exs. 1–12 on pp. 538–540.

Section 4
Key Concepts

Geometric Probability (pp. 535–536)

A probability that is based on lengths, areas, or volumes is a geometric probability.

Example

A dart that hits the target is equally likely to hit any point on the target.

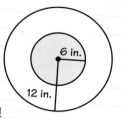

Probability that the dart hits the shaded region = $\dfrac{\text{Area of shaded region}}{\text{Total area of target}}$

$$= \dfrac{\pi \cdot 6^2}{\pi \cdot 12^2} = \dfrac{36\pi}{144\pi} = \dfrac{1}{4}$$

Probability that the dart hits the white region $= 1 - \dfrac{1}{4}$

$$= \dfrac{3}{4}$$

1 minus the probability that the dart hits the shaded region.

Since a dart can hit the white region or the shaded region, but not both, the events *the dart hits the white region* and *the dart hits the shaded region* are complementary events.

You can use the probability $\dfrac{3}{4}$ to predict the number of times a dart will hit the white region when it hits the target 80 times.

$\dfrac{3}{4}$ of the 80 hits are in the white region.

$\dfrac{3}{4}$ of 80 hits = 60 hits

Key Concepts Questions

8 A dart that hits the square target at the right is equally likely to hit any point on the target. What is the probability that the dart hits the shaded region?

9 In the Example above, why does the probability that the dart hits the white region equal 1 minus the probability that the dart hits the shaded region?

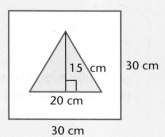

Practice & Application Exercises

Suppose an object falls at random onto each target shown below. For each target, find the probability that the object will land in a shaded region.

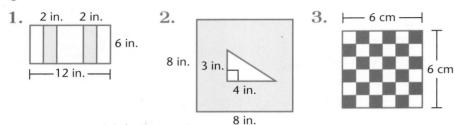

1. 2 in. 2 in. 6 in. 12 in.

2. 8 in. 3 in. 4 in. 8 in.

3. 6 cm 6 cm

Shuffleboard In a game of shuffleboard, players take turns sliding plastic disks onto a scoring area. Players gain or lose the number of points marked on the space their disk is on.

4. If you randomly slide your disk so that it lands somewhere on the green court shown, what is the probability that it will land within the triangle that is outlined in black?

5. If you randomly slide your disk so that it lands within the black triangle, what is the probability that you will score 10 points?

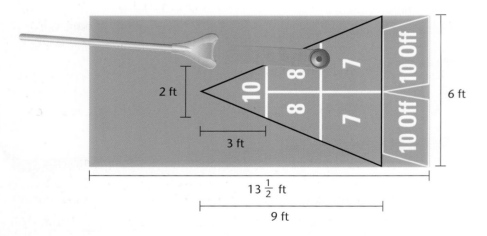

6. At a fair there is a jug filled with water with a small glass at the bottom. To win a prize you must drop a quarter into the jug and have it land in the glass. If the quarter falls randomly to the bottom, what is the probability of winning a prize?

7. **Create Your Own** Draw and shade a target. Include at least two different geometric shapes in your design. Find the probability of a dart hitting a shaded part of your target.

8. **Estimation** Suppose an object falls at random within the rectangle shown.

   a. Estimate the probability the object will land within the shaded circle. Explain how you made your estimate.

   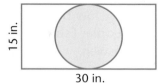
   15 in.
   30 in.

   b. Estimate the probability the object will land within the white area around the circle. How did you make your estimate?

   c. Suppose 250 objects are dropped at random onto the rectangle. About how many objects would you expect to land within the circle?

9. **Ballooning** The balloon festival held in Albuquerque, New Mexico, has a target event where people drop objects from their balloons onto a target area. Suppose an object is randomly dropped onto the target area at the right. What is the probability that the object lands within the 6 in. by 6 in. blue square region?

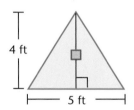
4 ft
5 ft

10. The land area of the United States is about 1.8% of the area of the surface of Earth. If 500 meteorites hit Earth each year, about how many meteorites would you expect to hit the United States each year?

11. a. An object dropped from an airplane is equally likely to land anywhere in the rectangular region below. The area of the rectangular region is approximately 75 mi². The probability that an object will land within the circular region is $\frac{1}{6}$. What is the area of the circular region?

   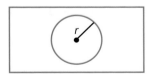
   r

   b. **Challenge** What is the radius of the circular region? Round to the nearest tenth of a mile.

Reflecting ◀▶ on the Section

Write your response to Exercise 12 in your journal.

12. In 1954, Ann Hodges was resting on a sofa when a 4 kg meteorite broke through her roof, ricocheted off a radio, and hit her leg. The probability of a person being hit by a meteorite is actually very low because of the small fraction of Earth that is covered with people. Estimate this probability and explain how you found your answer.

Spiral ◀▶ Review

Convert each measurement to liters. (Module 8, p. 506)

13. 3425 mL

14. 97 kL

15. 250 cm³

16. 0.84 kL

For the circle with each given measurement, replace each ? with the missing diameter or circumference. Round to the nearest hundredth. (Module 7, p. 466)

17. C = 105.6 cm
    d ≈ ?

18. $r = 4\frac{1}{5}$ in.
    C ≈ ?

19. d = 70 ft
    C ≈ ?

20. a. Make a line plot for the data in the table. (Module 4, p. 224)

Month	Jan	Feb	Mar	Apr	May	Jun	Jul	Aug	Sep	Oct	Nov	Dec
Number of days	31	28	31	30	31	30	31	31	30	31	30	31

b. Use your line plot to find the mode and the median for the number of days in the twelve months.

Find each product or quotient. Then use estimation to check that your answer is reasonable. (Module 3, p. 190; Module 4, p. 256)

21. 0.5 • 0.41

22. 10.06 • 0.2

23. 15 ÷ 0.3

Order the numbers from least to greatest. (Module 3, p. 134)

24. 7, 0.7, 0.57, 7.4, 7.29

25. 45.2, 43.5, 45.02, 4.569

26. Find the least common multiple of 15 and 9. (Module 3, p. 168)

Extra Skill Practice

Suppose a dart thrown at random hits each target. What is the probability that it hits the white region?

1.

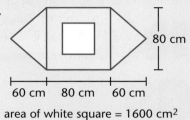

80 cm

60 cm   80 cm   60 cm

area of white square = 1600 cm²

2.

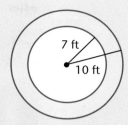

7 ft

10 ft

3.

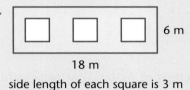

6 m

18 m

side length of each square is 3 m

4.

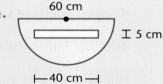

60 cm

5 cm

40 cm

5.

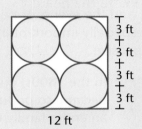

3 ft
3 ft
3 ft
3 ft

12 ft

6.

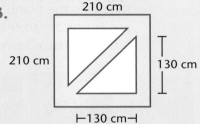

210 cm

210 cm

130 cm

130 cm

Standardized Testing ◀▶ Performance Task

You are designing a dart game where a player will throw darts at a 1 ft by 1 ft board with three to five separate squares drawn on it. Suppose that the squares are all the same size and that a dart thrown at random hits the board.

1. If there are three squares and each has a side length of 2 in., what is the probability that a dart hits a square? Round your answer to the nearest whole percent.

2. Suppose you want players to have about a 30% chance of hitting one of the squares. How many squares would you include and how long would you make each side? Explain.

Section ⑤ Transformations

CREATING THINGS

⊶Setting the Stage

Patchwork quilts are made from scraps of material or old clothing that are cut into shapes and sewn together into a pattern. Ideas for patterns and their names come from people's everyday experiences—the tools they use, the plants or animals they see, and the events or people that are important to them. Patchwork was especially important in colonial times, because fabric was scarce and expensive.

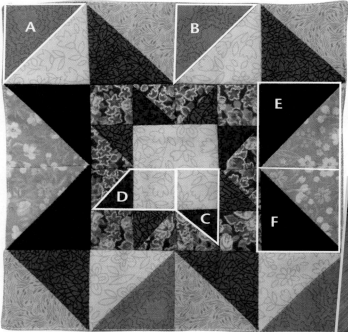

In the 1800s, quilting became so popular that an entire family would often work together to make a quilt.

◀This quilt pattern, called Eight Hands Round, is named for a movement in square dancing.

▶ **A quilter can experiment with patterns by sewing a copy of part of a design and moving it to different positions.**

Think About It ▸▸▸

1 Give directions for *sliding*, *flipping*, or *turning* the outlined quilt patches on page 542 to make each move.

a. Move the triangle labeled A onto the triangle labeled B.

b. Move the group of patches labeled C to D.

c. Move the group of patches labeled E to F.

2 Can any of the moves in Question 1 be done in more than one way? Discuss your ideas.

Exploration 1 ▸▸▸▸▸▸▸▸▸▸▸▸▸▸▸▸▸▸▸▸▸▸▸▸▸▸▸▸▸▸

Translations, Rotations, and Reflections

SET UP *You will need: • Labsheets 5A and 5B • tracing paper • index card or cardboard • scissors • ruler*

3 Follow the steps below to make an isosceles right triangle. Later you will use your triangle to make quilt patch designs.

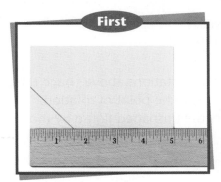

Draw an isosceles right triangle on an index card. The sides forming the right angle should each be $1\frac{1}{2}$ in. long.

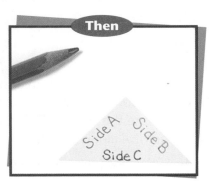

Cut out the triangle and label the sides as shown.

GOAL

LEARN HOW TO...
◆ perform a translation, a rotation, and a reflection

AS YOU...
◆ create quilt patch designs

KEY TERMS
◆ translation
◆ rotation
◆ reflection
◆ transformation

FOR ◂HELP
with *classifying triangles*, see
MODULE 2, pp. 106–107

▶ A **translation** (slide) moves a figure by sliding it. Every point moves the same distance in the same direction in a plane.

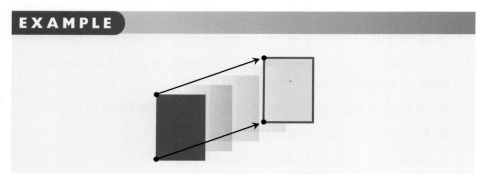

EXAMPLE

4 **a.** Place tracing paper over the Example above and trace the shaded rectangle. Slide your tracing along the arrows until it covers the unshaded rectangle.

b. Did you have to flip or turn the rectangle in part (a)?

c. What do the arrows tell you about the translation?

5 **Use Labsheet 5A.** Follow the directions on the labsheet and use your triangle from Question 3 to create a *Translation Patch.*

▶ A **rotation** (turn) moves a figure by turning it either clockwise or counterclockwise around a fixed point.

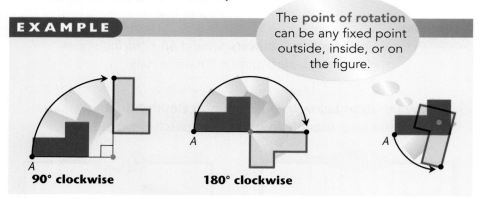

EXAMPLE

The **point of rotation** can be any fixed point outside, inside, or on the figure.

90° clockwise

180° clockwise

6 **a.** Place tracing paper over one of the rotations above. Trace the shaded figure. Put your pencil tip on the point of rotation. Rotate the tracing until it covers the unshaded figure by moving point *A* along the arrow.

b. What does the arrow tell you about the rotation?

c. Could you get the same result by translating the figure?

7 **Use Labsheet 5A.** Follow the directions on the labsheet and use your triangle from Question 3 to create a *Rotation Patch.*

▶ A **reflection** (flip) moves a figure by flipping it across a line.

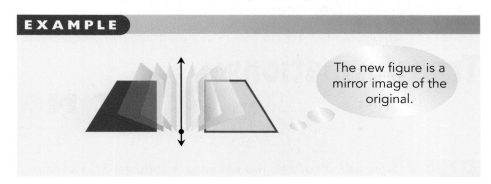

EXAMPLE

The new figure is a mirror image of the original.

8 a. Place tracing paper over the shaded trapezoid in the Example. Trace the shaded figure, the line, and the point on the line. Flip your paper over so that the tracing covers the unshaded figure.

b. How did the line and the point on the line help you to flip the figure?

c. Could you get the same result by translating or rotating the trapezoid?

9 Use Labsheet 5B. Follow the directions on the labsheet and use your triangle from Question 3 to create a *Reflection Patch*.

▶ A **transformation** is a change made to a figure or to its position. Translations, rotations, and reflections are transformations that change the position of a figure but not its size or shape.

10 ✔ CHECKPOINT Name the transformation that will move each shaded trapezoid onto the unshaded trapezoid.

a.   **b.**   **c.**

11 Use Labsheet 5B. Follow the directions on the labsheet and use your triangle from Question 3 to *Create Your Own Patch*.

HOMEWORK EXERCISES ▶ See Exs. 1–10 on pp. 549–550.

✔ **QUESTION 10**

...checks that you can recognize translations, rotations, and reflections.

Exploration 2

Transformations
in QUILTING

SET UP *Work with a partner. You will need: • Labsheet 5C • scissors • clear tape • construction paper • your triangle from Exploration 1*

▶ **This zigzag design is made entirely from isosceles right triangles using two colors of material.**

You will make the section of the design outlined on the quilt.

12 Follow the steps below to make triangles for a zigzag quilt.

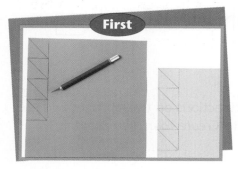

Choose one light and one dark color of construction paper. Use your triangle from Exploration 1 to trace 8 triangles of each color.

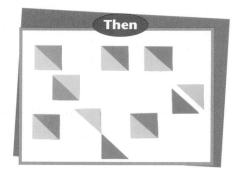

Cut out the triangles. Tape one triangle of each color together to make a square. Make 8 squares.

Use Labsheet 5C for Questions 13–17.

13 **a.** Place a square patch on the square labeled A on the *Zigzag Design*. Match the triangles and the light and dark colors. Tape the patch in place.

b. Place another patch on top of the patch taped over A, matching the triangles and colors. Use a transformation, or a series of transformations, to move the top patch to square B so that it follows the zigzag pattern shown. Tape the patch in place.

c. Describe the transformation or transformations you used in part (b).

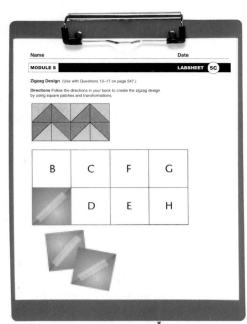

14 **Discussion** Compare answers for Question 13(c). Did everyone use the same transformations? If not, is one way better than another? Why?

15 ✔ CHECKPOINT

a. Place another patch on top of the patch taped over B on the *Zigzag Design*. Match the triangles and colors.

b. Find two different transformations that will move the top patch to C in just one move and continue the zigzag pattern. Tape the patch in place and describe the transformations.

16 **a.** Place a patch on top of the patch taped over C.

b. Use a transformation or a series of transformations to move the top patch to D so that it follows the zigzag pattern. Tape the patch in place. What transformation or series of transformations did you use?

17 **a.** Tape the four remaining patches together to make a separate copy of the large square formed by the patches on A, B, C, and D.

b. Place the copy over the large square so that the patterns match. Use a transformation to move the copy to cover the squares E, F, G, and H, and continue the zigzag pattern. Describe the transformation you used.

✔ **QUESTION 15**

...checks that you can identify and describe transformations.

HOMEWORK EXERCISES ▶ See Exs. 11–20 on pp. 550–551.

Section ⑤
Key Concepts

Key Terms

transformation

translation

rotation

reflection

Transformations (pp. 543–547)

A transformation is a change made to a figure or its position. Translations, rotations, and reflections are transformations that change the position of a figure but not the size or the shape of the figure.

Examples

Translation (slide)

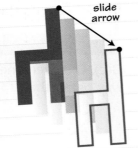

slide arrow

A translation moves every point the same distance in the same direction in a plane. The slide arrow tells the distance and direction to move.

Rotation (turn)

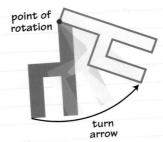

point of rotation

turn arrow

A rotation turns a figure around a fixed point. The turn arrow tells which direction and how many degrees to turn.

Reflection (flip)

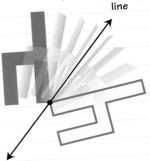

reflecting line

A reflection flips a figure across a line. The new figure is a mirror image of the original.

Key Concepts Questions

18 Use transformations to describe how the figure on the screen changes from view to view.

   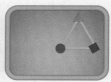

19 Make a simple drawing of an object. Now draw a translation, a rotation, and a reflection of the object. Label each drawing with the transformation you used.

548 Module 8 MATH-Thematical Mix

Section 5

Practice & Application Exercises

Name the transformation shown in each photo.

1.

2.

Name the transformation that will move each shaded figure onto the unshaded figure.

3.

4.

5.

6.

7.

8.

9. **Arts** The Pennsylvania Dutch hex signs below contain several transformations. Dividing the signs into quarters makes it easier to see the transformations.

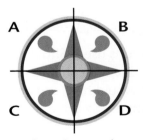

Sun, Star, and
Rain Hex

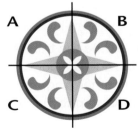

Double Rain Hex
and Luck Symbol

Hex Sign
for Rain

▲
Hex signs are painted
on barns in Pennsylvania.

a. For each hex sign, name the transformation needed to move quarter A to quarter B.

b. For one of the hex signs, you can move quarter A to quarter B in two ways. Name the hex sign and describe the two transformations.

10. Use transformations to describe how the position of the airplane changes from view to view.

11. Use Labsheet 5D. Follow the directions on the labsheet to sketch transformations on the *Grid for Transformations.*

Visual Thinking Sketch the next three terms in each sequence.

12. ⬆, ⬆, ⬆, ⬆ , _?_ , _?_ , _?_ , ...

13. ⬭, ⬭, ⬭, ⬭ , _?_ , _?_ , _?_ , ...

14. ◔, ◷, ◓, ◐ , _?_ , _?_ , _?_ , ...

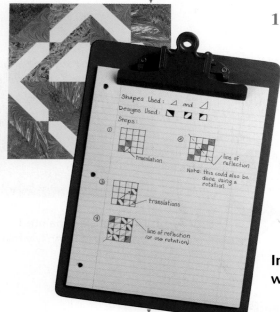

15. a. Create Your Own Make a design that is 40 cm by 40 cm using a combination of at least two transformations. Your original shape or shapes can be no larger than 10 cm by 10 cm. You may cut your shapes from construction paper, wrapping paper, or wallpaper, or you can use computer drawing software.

b. Describe the transformations used. Show a drawing of your original shape or shapes and any other diagrams that would help someone understand what you did.

In Exercises 16 and 17, A changes to B in the same way that C changes to D. Sketch figure D.

16. A   B   C   D

17. A   B   C   D

18. **Home Involvement** Many families treasure quilts that represent their family history and heritage. You can create your own quilt square that displays something about your family's history.

a. To get ideas for your quilt square, discuss the following with your family:

  ◆ where your family originally came from

  ◆ people or places that have been important to your family

  ◆ objects or patterns that are associated with your family or culture

b. Make a sketch of a design for your square.

c. Create your quilt square. Use convenient materials such as colored paper, pieces of fabric, or white paper and fabric crayons.

d. Share your quilt square with your class. Explain how your design relates to your family's heritage.

19. **Challenge** Use the *Double Reflection Grid* on Labsheet 5D.

a. Follow the directions on the labsheet to draw two reflections of a trapezoid.

b. What single transformation has the same result as reflecting the trapezoid across $\overleftrightarrow{AB}$ and then reflecting it across $\overleftrightarrow{AC}$?

Reflecting ◀▶ on the Section

20. Look for examples of company or product logos that use translations, rotations, or reflections. Sketch or copy the designs and describe the transformations.

Logo of the Sarajevo Winter Olympics (1984)

Recycling Logo

RESEARCH

Exercise 20 checks that you can recognize translations, rotations, and reflections.

Spiral ◀▶ Review

Write each fraction in lowest terms. (Module 1, p. 61)

21. $\frac{6}{18}$ 22. $\frac{24}{30}$ 23. $\frac{15}{25}$ 24. $\frac{9}{27}$

Replace each ? with > or <. (Module 7, p. 489)

25. 34 ? 43   26. –3 ? 3   27. –55 ? –56

28. –658 ? 0   29. –7 ? –9   30. 24 ? –2

Name the transformation or transformations that will move each shaded figure onto the unshaded figure.

1.

2.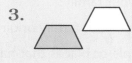

3.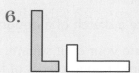

4.

5.

6.

7.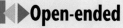

8.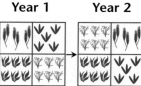

9.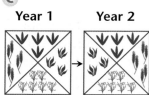

Match each situation with the transformation that best describes it. Choices may be used more than once.

10. Opening a sliding glass door

11. Closing a bureau drawer

12. Flipping a page in a book

13. Turning the minute hand of a clock to adjust the time

   A. rotation   B. reflection   C. translation

Standardized Testing ◀▶ Open-ended

Which farmer really "rotates" the crops? Describe how the other farmers "transform" their fields.

Ⓐ   Year 1   Year 2   Ⓑ   Year 1   Year 2   Ⓒ   Year 1   Year 2

Section **6** Scientific Notation

IN THIS SECTION

EXPLORATION 1
♦ Writing Numbers in Scientific Notation

COMPARISONS and PREDICTIONS

Setting the Stage ▸▸▸▸▸▸▸▸▸▸▸▸▸▸▸▸▸▸▸▸▸▸▸▸▸▸▸▸▸▸▸

SET UP *Work as a class. You will need: • Labsheet 6A • calculator • sticky notes • index cards or planet cutouts • scissors*

In the summer of 2003, NASA launched spacecraft carrying twin robot geologists, the *Mars Exploration Rovers*. Six months later, in January 2004, the rovers landed on Mars and began collecting data in an effort to learn more about the history of Mars.

To better relate to the long trip the rovers took, you will build a model of the planets and compare their distances from the sun.

Use Labsheet 6A. Follow the directions to build the *Planet Distance Model*.

Think About It

1 List the planets in order from least to greatest distance from the sun.

2 Look at the far right column of the table on the labsheet. The distances for Venus, Earth, Jupiter, and Mars were written in a form called *scientific notation*.

   a. What do these numbers have in common?

   b. How do these numbers differ from the other planets' distances that are not written in *scientific notation*?

Exploration 1

Writing Numbers in Scientific Notation

▶ To make reading and writing large numbers easier, they are often written in *scientific notation*. **Scientific notation** uses powers of 10 to express the value of a number. You may have noticed that the numbers you wrote in scientific notation, such as $1.082 \cdot 10^8$ and $7.7833 \cdot 10^8$, have two parts.

> The first part is a number greater than or equal to 1 but less than 10.

$$1.082 \cdot 10^8$$

> The second part is a **power of 10.**

$$7.7833 \cdot 10^8$$

3 Discussion Explain why $7 \cdot 10^3$ is in scientific notation, but $70 \cdot 10^5$ is not.

4 ✔ CHECKPOINT Tell whether each number is written in scientific notation. If a number is not in scientific notation, explain why not.

a. $60 \cdot 10^3$ **b.** $6 \cdot 10^3$ **c.** $0.6 \cdot 10^3$

d. $35 \cdot 10^1$ **e.** $3.5 \cdot 2^3$ **f.** $7.48 \cdot 10^6$

5 Write each number in scientific notation.

a. 54,000,000   **b.** 1,245,000,000   **c.** 99,900

6 Calculator Three of the ways calculators display a number in scientific notation are shown below.

```
   4 E 12        4.e + 12          4 12
```

a. Write the number represented in the displays in standard form.

b. Write the number in scientific notation.

c. How does your calculator display numbers in scientific notation?

7 How would the number 789,000,000 appear in scientific notation on each of the three calculators in Question 6?

▶ So far you have used powers of 10 to write numbers in scientific notation. You can also use powers of 10 to change a number from scientific notation to standard form.

EXAMPLE

Write $8.1 \cdot 10^3$ in standard form.

SAMPLE RESPONSE

$$10^3 = 10 \cdot 10 \cdot 10$$
$$= 1000$$

$$8.1 \cdot 10^3 = 8.1 \cdot 1000 = 8100$$

8 Write each number in standard form.

a. $2.38 \cdot 10^1$ **b.** $2.38 \cdot 10^2$ **c.** $2.38 \cdot 10^3$

d. $2.38 \cdot 10^4$ **e.** $2.38 \cdot 10^5$ **f.** $2.38 \cdot 10^6$

9 **Discussion** Look for a pattern in the problems and answers from Question 8.

a. What happened to the decimal point in the product when 2.38 was multiplied by 10^3? by 10^2? by 10^4?

b. What happens to the decimal point of a number when it is multiplied by 10^9? Test your prediction by writing $2.38 \cdot 10^9$ in standard form.

c. How can you use the exponent on the power of 10 to change a number from scientific notation to standard form?

d. What is the exponent on the power of 10 when 23,800,000 is written in scientific notation?

10 a. **Use Labsheet 6A.** Write the distance from the sun for Mercury, Neptune, Saturn, and Uranus in scientific notation.

b. Using scientific notation, list all 8 planets in order from greatest distance to least distance from the sun.

c. How did you use scientific notation to put the planets in order?

d. If you lay the sticky notes for Mars and Earth on top of each other, by how many notes do they differ? How many kilometers does this represent?

HOMEWORK EXERCISES ▶ See Exs. 1–20 on pp. 556–558.

Section 6

Key Concepts

Scientific Notation (pp. 554–555)

To write a number in scientific notation, write it as a number greater than or equal to 1 but less than 10, times a power of ten.

Make the first part a number greater than or equal to 1 but less than 10.

$$9,800,000,000 = 9.8 \cdot 1,000,000,000 = 9.8 \cdot 10^9$$

To change a number in scientific notation to standard form, multiply by the power of ten.

The second part is a power of 10.

$$5.32 \cdot 10^7 = 5.32 \cdot 10,000,000 = 53,200,000$$

11 Key Concepts Question When $5.32 \cdot 10^7$ is written in standard form there are eight digits in the answer. Why is the 10 raised to only the 7th power?

Section 6

Practice & Application Exercises

Write each number in scientific notation.

1. 157,000
2. 7000
3. 56,000,000
4. 10.2
5. 5600
6. 9 billion

Write each number in standard form.

7. $5.9 \cdot 10^4$
8. $1 \cdot 10^2$
9. $9.82 \cdot 10^5$
10. $8.1 \cdot 10^7$
11. $6 \cdot 10^1$
12. $3.5 \cdot 10^8$

Use scientific notation to express each fact.

13. The temperature of volcanic lava can reach 1500°F.

14. The temperature on the surface of the sun is about 10,000°F.

15. Lightning reaches temperatures of up to 50,000°F.

16. Write the world population for each year in standard form.

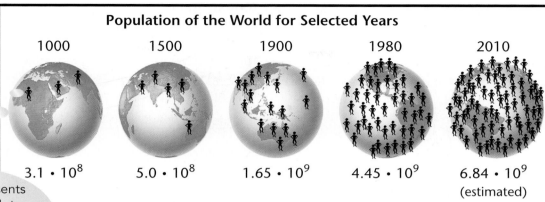

Population of the World for Selected Years

1000	1500	1900	1980	2010
$3.1 \cdot 10^8$	$5.0 \cdot 10^8$	$1.65 \cdot 10^9$	$4.45 \cdot 10^9$	$6.84 \cdot 10^9$ (estimated)

1 figure represents 10^8 people. (Note: Numbers have been rounded to show only whole figures.)

17. The largest volcano on Mars is Olympus Mons. It is $3.74 \cdot 10^2$ mi in diameter and $1.6 \cdot 10^1$ mi high. The largest volcano on Earth is Mauna Loa in Hawaii. It is 75 mi in diameter and 6.3 mi high.

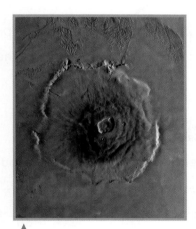

▲ Aerial view of Olympus Mons on Mars

  a. Compare the heights of the two volcanoes. Which is taller, and by how many miles?

  b. Compare the diameters. Which volcano is wider, and by how many miles?

18. In 2005, a group of scientists discovered an object in our solar system that was estimated to be about one-and-a-half times the size of Pluto. The object, nicknamed Xena, is approximately 9 billion miles from the sun.

  a. Write the distance of Xena from the sun in scientific notation.

  b. Earth is approximately $9.3 \cdot 10^7$ mi from the sun. Write this distance in standard form.

  c. Xena is about how many miles farther from the sun than Earth is from the sun?

19. a. Without changing the numbers to standard form, tell whether the tons of plastic collected in the United States *increased* or *decreased* from 2004 to 2005.

Recyclable Materials Collected in the United States

Material	Amount collected for recycling in 2004	Amount collected for recycling in 2005
plastic	$2.73 \cdot 10^6$ tons	$2.76 \cdot 10^6$ tons
glass	$1.6 \cdot 10^6$ tons	$1.65 \cdot 10^6$ tons

b. How did the number of tons of glass collected from 2004 to 2005 change? Explain.

RESEARCH

Exercise 20 checks that you understand how to write numbers in both scientific notation and standard form.

Reflecting ◀▶ on the Section

20. a. Look in magazines or newspapers to find three examples of articles including numbers greater than 100,000.

b. Tell what each number represents.

c. For each example, write the number in both standard form and scientific notation.

Spiral ◀▶ Review

Find each sum or difference. (Module 8, p. 527)

21. $-18 + 7$ **22.** $-26 + (-17)$ **23.** $15 + (-8)$

24. $25 - (-18)$ **25.** $-36 - 13$ **26.** $-12 - (-3)$

27. A dart thrown at random hits the square target shown at the right. Find the probability that it hits the shaded area. (Module 8, p. 537)

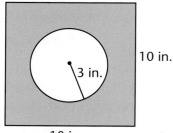

10 in.

3 in.

10 in.

Find each product or quotient. (Module 3, p. 178; Module 5, p. 352)

28. $5 \cdot 2\frac{1}{3}$ **29.** $6\frac{3}{5} \div 4$ **30.** $\frac{5}{12} \cdot 2\frac{3}{8}$

31. $8 \div 2\frac{1}{4}$ **32.** $3\frac{2}{7} \cdot 5\frac{1}{2}$ **33.** $10\frac{2}{5} \div 4\frac{1}{4}$

Section

Extra Skill Practice

Write each number in scientific notation.

1. 49,800,000
2. 16.34
3. 32 billion
4. 958
5. 2,500,000
6. 326,000
7. 76,300
8. 2 million
9. 24

Write each number in standard form.

10. $1.1 \cdot 10^3$
11. $6.08 \cdot 10^1$
12. $5.03 \cdot 10^6$
13. $4.14 \cdot 10^3$
14. $2 \cdot 10^9$
15. $4.1 \cdot 10^2$
16. $3.041 \cdot 10^5$
17. $1.9 \cdot 10^9$
18. $9.9 \cdot 10^4$

Without changing the numbers to standard form, order the numbers from least to greatest.

19. $2 \cdot 10^2$, $3.5 \cdot 10^1$, $1.3 \cdot 10^3$

20. $4.53 \cdot 10^6$, $4.3 \cdot 10^7$, $4.682 \cdot 10^5$

21. $5.5 \cdot 10^3$, $5.5 \cdot 10^6$, $5.5 \cdot 10^2$

Standardized Testing ▶Multiple Choice

Write: Ⓐ if the amount in column A is greater.

Ⓑ if the amount in column B is greater.

Ⓒ if the amounts in column A and column B are equal.

Ⓓ if there is no way to tell which amount is greater.

	Column A	Column B
1.	$1.735 \cdot 10^6$	$17.35 \cdot 10^5$
2.	120	$1.2 \cdot 10^1$
3.	$1.8 \cdot 10^4$	$1.7 \cdot 10^5$

The Math is Right!

Have you ever watched a quiz show on TV? A quiz game can be a fun way to test your knowledge. You will work as a team to create questions for a math quiz game. Will your questions stump the other teams in your class? You'll find out when you play *The Math is Right!*

Getting Started Your team is responsible for writing a set of eight questions. The set should include at least one question related to each of the first seven module themes and use mathematics you have studied this year.

1 Decide for which module themes each team member will write questions.

2 Choose a mathematical concept for each question.

Game Format In *The Math is Right!*, your team's questions will be read aloud or shown on an overhead projector. Each of the other teams will work together to agree on an answer. No team is allowed to answer its own questions!

3 Write each question so it relates to the module theme and uses mathematical concepts you studied this year.

4 Make sure your questions are clear and ask for specific answers.

Revising Your Questions Now that you have written your questions, you can test them out on your teammates.

5 Take turns reading your quiz questions to your teammates. Make sure that everyone understands each question and agrees on an answer.

6 Rewrite any questions that are not clear.

7 Write each question on an index card or overhead transparency. Write your team number at the top of the card and the answer on the bottom.

SET UP

Work in a team of four.

You will need:
- *8 index cards or 8 overhead transparencies*
- *markers*

Module Themes

1. Patterns and Problem Solving
2. Math Detectives
3. Mind Games
4. Statistical Safari
5. Creating Things
6. Comparing and Predicting
7. Wonders of the World

8 Review your team's questions and decide which one you think is the most challenging. Mark this question with a star. This will be used as a bonus question in *The Math is Right!*

Play *The Math is Right!*

Get Ready

Your teacher should have each team's questions in separate, shuffled piles.

* Sit in a group with your team.

* Make sure each player has paper and pencil.

Play the Game

* Your teacher picks a card from Team 1's pile, reads it out loud, and then sets a timer for two minutes.

* Team 1 is not allowed to answer the question.

* When time is up the teams put their pencils down and then show their answers. All answers must be written down.

* Each team gets 10 points for a correct answer.

* The next question read is from Team 2's pile and Team 2 is not allowed to answer.

* Continue reading questions in this manner.

Bonus Question

If a bonus question is drawn, teams answering the question decide how many points they want to risk on the question before it is read.

* Each team writes the point value on a piece of paper and turns it over. A team without any points can risk up to 10 points.

* Each team gets the number of points it risked for a correct answer to a bonus question.

* Teams with incorrect answers to bonus questions lose the number of points they risked.

Winning the Game

The team with the most points when all the questions have been read or the class period ends wins.

You will need: • *tracing paper* (Exs. 19–22)

1. A recipe calls for $\frac{1}{2}$ c of cooking oil. Choose the letter of each amount that will supply enough oil for the recipe. (Sec. 1, Explor. 1)

   A. $\frac{1}{4}$ pt   B. $\frac{1}{3}$ c   C. 5 fl oz   D. $\frac{1}{16}$ gal

2. To make 1 chicken loaf you need $1\frac{1}{3}$ c of chicken broth. Suppose you want to make 7 loaves to freeze. (Sec. 1, Explor. 1)

   a. How many cups of broth do you need?

   b. How many pints do you need?

   c. How many fluid ounces do you need?

3. It is recommended that people drink about 4 L of water a day. Give the dimensions of a rectangular container that has a capacity of exactly 4 L. (Sec. 1, Explor. 2)

Mental Math Explain how to use trading off to find each sum. (Sec. 2, Explor. 1)

4. 23 + 79   5. 1.06 + 4.98   6. 0.75 + 0.24 + 0.86

Explain how to use front-end estimation to estimate each sum. (Sec. 2, Explor. 1)

7. 146 + 609 + 234   8. $15.13 + $24.49   9. 3.3 + 8.15 + 6.65

Find each sum or difference. (Sec. 3, Explors. 1 and 2)

10. −19 + 25   11. −36 − 3   12. 0 − (−18)

13. −12 + (−12)   14. 42 − 68   15. −21 + 15

For each target, a dart that hits the target is equally likely to hit any point on the target. Find the probability that the dart hits the shaded area. (Sec. 4, Explor. 1)

16.

area of rectangle = 5 cm²
diameter of circle = 7 cm

17.

The four small triangles are all the same size.

18.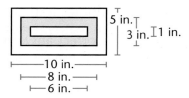

Sketch each flower and show how one part of the flower is a reflection or a rotation of another part. (Sec. 5, Explors. 1 and 2)

19.

20.

21.

22.

Write each number in standard form. (Sec. 6, Explor. 1)

23. $5.67 \cdot 10^3$

24. $1.002 \cdot 10^5$

25. $7 \cdot 10^8$

26. $2.3 \cdot 10^1$

27. $9.11 \cdot 10^2$

28. $1.833 \cdot 10^4$

Write each number in scientific notation. (Sec. 6, Explor. 1)

29. 4,400,000

30. 7700

31. 789

32. 62,000

33. 5,000,000,000

34. 377,125

Reflecting ◀▶ on the Module

35. Each section in this module connects to the theme of a previous module. For example, Section 5 connects to *Creating Things*, the theme of Module 5. Choose one section in this module and explain how the mathematics connects to the mathematics in the module with the same theme.

CONTENTS

STUDENT RESOURCES

STUDENT RESOURCES

TOOLBOX

Whole Number Place Value

Each digit in a number has a place. To find the value of a digit, multiply the digit by the value of the place.

Millions			Thousands			Ones		
Hundreds	Tens	Ones	Hundreds	Tens	Ones	Hundreds	Tens	Ones
	8	3	2	9	5	0	4	1

The places are grouped into periods.

Period: millions
Place: one millions
Value: **3,000,000**

83,295,041 ← standard form

In expanded form 83,295,041 is written as:
80,000,000 + 3,000,000 + 200,000 + 90,000 + 5,000 + 40 + 1

In words, 83,295,041 is expressed as:
eighty-three million, two hundred ninety-five thousand, forty-one

---

EXAMPLE

Write the place and the value of each underlined digit.

	1,248,630	225,000	85,699

SOLUTION

place: **one millions**   place: **ten thousands**   place: **tens**

value: **1,000,000**   value: **20,000**   value: **90**

Write the place and the value of each underlined digit.

1. 841,670   2. 335,928   3. 56,831,000

4. 28   5. 993,671   6. 403,200

Give the following information about the number 469,224.

7. the place of the 6   8. the value of the digit in the tens place

Write each number in standard form.

9. fifteen million, nine hundred forty-six thousand, six hundred nineteen

10. two hundred twenty thousand, nine

Write each number in words.

11. 518   12. 23,400   13. 70,000,624   14. 450,672

Comparing Whole Numbers

The symbols below are used to compare numbers:

> (is greater than)   < (is less than)   = (is equal to)

Thinking about place value will help you compare two numbers and put a list of numbers in order.

EXAMPLE

To compare 23,760 and 23,748, first line up the digits of each number by place value. Then compare the digits in each place, starting at the left. If the digits are equal, compare the digits in the next place to the right, and so on until you come to different digits.

23,760 is greater than 23,748 because it has a greater digit in the first place that is different, the tens place.

Compare digits from left to right since the leftmost place has the greatest value.

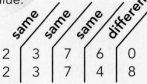

same	same	same	different: 6 > 4	
2	3	7	6	0
2	3	7	4	8

EXAMPLE

Write the list of numbers in order from greatest to least.

2,227   21,237   20,080   1,919   450,900   34,888

SOLUTION   Compare the digits in each place starting with the greatest place value.

		2	2	2	7
	2	1	2	3	7
	2	0	0	8	0
		1	9	1	9
4	5	0	9	0	0
	3	4	8	8	8

hundred thousands: The only number with a digit in the hundred thousands place is 450,900, so 450,900 is the greatest number.

ten thousands: 3 > 2 so 34,888 is greater than both 21,237 and 20,080. Check the next digit of 21,237 and 20,080. 1 > 0 so 21,237 > 20,080.

thousands: 2 > 1 so 2,227 > 1,919.

450,900 > 34,888 > 21,237 > 20,080 > 2,227 > 1,919

Replace each ? with >, <, or =.

1. 2224 ? 1810
2. 20,111 ? 19,991
3. 3,201,999 ? 419,963
4. 37,011 ? 370,110
5. 897,500 ? 190,001
6. 5,402,320 ? 5,410,320
7. 198,999 ? 199,000
8. 891,450 ? 340,232
9. 50,777,760 ? 51,666,700

Write each list of numbers in order from greatest to least.

10. 239,400; 47,777; 24,000; 79,899
11. 6,150,762; 892,570; 7,902,500; 937,400

Rounding Whole Numbers and Money

To round a number to a given place, look at the digit to the right of that place to decide whether the number is greater or less than the halfway point.

If the digit in the place to the right is less than 5 (0, 1, 2, 3, or 4), round down.

If the digit in the place to the right is 5 or greater (5, 6, 7, 8, or 9), round up.

EXAMPLE

Round 5839 to the nearest hundred.

SOLUTION   5839 is between 5800 and 5900.

Look at the digit to the right of the hundreds place: the 3 in the tens place. 3 is less than 5, so 39 is less than half of 100. Round down to the nearest hundred, 5800.

5839

5839 rounded to the nearest hundred is 5800.

The halfway number.

5839

←—————— 5839

5800   5850   5900

EXAMPLE

Round $42.61 to the nearest one dollar.

SOLUTION $42.61 is between $42 and $43.

6 is the digit to the right of the dollars place. 6 is greater than 5, so 61 cents is greater than half of a dollar. Round up to the nearest dollar, $43.

$42.61

$42.61 rounded to the nearest one dollar is $43.

Round each number to the given place.

1. 888 (nearest ten)

2. 94,575 (nearest hundred)

3. 85,920 (nearest thousand)

4. 27,380,573 (nearest million)

5. 602 (nearest hundred)

6. 43 (nearest ten)

7. 298,722 (nearest ten thousand)

8. 68,274 (nearest hundred)

Round each amount to the given place.

9. $949.50 (nearest dollar)

10. $4369.75 (nearest ten dollars)

11. $52.05 (nearest dollar)

12. $644.00 (nearest hundred dollars)

Adding Whole Numbers and Money

To add whole numbers, add place by place. First add the ones, then the tens, then the hundreds, then the thousands, and so on.

EXAMPLE

Find 206 + 58.

SOLUTION   Rewrite the numbers, lining up the ones, the tens, and the hundreds.

Add the ones and trade if needed.

Add the tens and trade if needed.

Add the hundreds.

Trade 14 ones for 1 ten and 4 ones.

$$\begin{array}{r} {\scriptstyle 1} \\ 206 \\ + 58 \\ \hline 4 \end{array}$$

$$\begin{array}{r} {\scriptstyle 1} \\ 206 \\ + 58 \\ \hline 64 \end{array}$$

$$\begin{array}{r} {\scriptstyle 1} \\ 206 \\ + 58 \\ \hline 264 \end{array}$$

206 + 58 = 264

Money amounts can be expressed in dollars using a dollar sign ($) and a dot. The dot separates the whole dollars and the parts of a dollar. Money amounts can also be expressed in cents using a cents sign (¢) and no dot. No matter which way the number is written, you add money place by place. First add the pennies, then the dimes, then the one dollars, then the ten dollars, and so on.

EXAMPLE

$.75 means 75 cents, or 7 dimes and 5 pennies.

Find $3.80 + $9.44 + $.75.

SOLUTION   Line up the pennies, the dimes, and the dollars.

Add the pennies, dimes, and dollars separately. Trade as needed.

Trade 19 dimes for 1 dollar and 9 dimes.

$$\begin{array}{r} {\scriptstyle 1} \\ \$3.80 \\ \$9.44 \\ + \$.75 \\ \hline \$13.99 \end{array}$$

Add.

1. 2767 + 465
2. 8219 + 4499
3. 66,405 + 35,511
4. 2,082 + 58,875
5. 35,294 + 62,472
6. 77,996 + 5,687 + 5,434
7. $8.14 + $3.97
8. $20.87 + $18.17
9. $27.40 + $16.75
10. $54.25 + $66.65
11. $31.24 + $11.83
12. $26.50 + $88.95

Mental Math

When you want to use mental math to add, it helps to break numbers into parts.

To add two-digit numbers, you can break up at least one of the numbers you are adding into tens and ones and add on these parts separately.

EXAMPLE

Find 38 + 15.

SOLUTION   Break 15 into tens and ones: 15 = 10 + 5

$$38 + 10 = 48 \quad \leftarrow \text{Add the tens to 38.}$$
$$48 + 5 = 53 \quad \leftarrow \text{Add the ones to the result.}$$
$$38 + 15 = 53$$

Sometimes it is helpful to add enough to reach a number that ends in 0 and then add the rest.

EXAMPLE

Find $5.75 + $1.50.

SOLUTION   You need $.25 to get $5.75 to reach $6.00, so break $1.50 into $.25 + $1.25.

$$\$5.75 + \$.25 = \$6.00 \quad \leftarrow \text{Add the \$.25 to the \$5.75.}$$
$$\$6.00 + \$1.25 = \$7.25 \quad \leftarrow \text{Add the remaining \$1.25 to the result.}$$
$$\$5.75 + \$1.50 = \$7.25$$

Use mental math to find each sum.

1. 56 + 67
2. 35 + 47
3. 452 + 29
4. 253 + 68
5. 49 + 322
6. 796 + 35
7. 428 + 67
8. 634 + 157
9. 181 + 494
10. $6.90 + $5.35
11. $4.20 + $14.37
12. $6.28 + $4.10
13. $8.35 + $5.00
14. $2.45 + $11.95
15. $3.99 + $4.98
16. $15.50 + $4.75
17. $9.84 + $3.56
18. $17.69 + $5.36

Subtracting Whole Numbers and Money

To subtract whole numbers, subtract the ones, then the tens, then the hundreds, and so on. Trade before each step if necessary.

EXAMPLE

Find 3001 – 1953.

SOLUTION Rewrite the numbers, lining up the ones, the tens, and so on.

Since there are no tens or hundreds, trade 1 thousand for 9 hundreds, 9 tens, and 10 ones to get more ones.

You need to trade to get more ones.

Now you can subtract.

```
  2 9 9 11              2 9 9 11
  3 0 0 1               3 0 0 1
- 1 9 5 3             - 1 9 5 3
                        1 0 4 8  ← difference
```

3001 – 1953 = 1048

Check your answer with addition. The difference plus the number subtracted should equal the number you started with: 1048 + 1953 = 3001.

When you subtract money, first subtract the pennies, then the dimes, then the one dollars, then the ten dollars, and so on.

EXAMPLE

Find $5.45 – $2.86.

SOLUTION Line up the dollars and cents.

Subtract the pennies. Trade first if needed.

Subtract the dimes. Trade first if needed.

Subtract the dollars.

```
    3 15            4 13 15          4 13 15
  $5.45            $5.45            $5.45
- $2.86          - $2.86          - $2.86
      9               59            $2.59
```

Put in a dot to separate dollars and cents.

$5.45 – $2.86 = $2.59

Your answer can be checked with addition.
$2.59 + $2.86 = $5.45

Subtract.

1. 8712 – 134   2. 506 – 318   3. 9501 – 4688   4. 2500 – 379
5. 7211 – 709   6. 6040 – 2199   7. $46.26 – $17.18 8. $401.40 – $13.00
9. $183.50 – $119.42   10. $333.25 – $299.86   11. $501.00 – $180.67

Multiplying Whole Numbers and Money

To multiply whole numbers, begin by lining up the numbers you are multiplying. Multiply the entire first number by the ones of the second number, by the tens of the second number, and so on.

EXAMPLE

Find 583 × 304.

SOLUTION Rewrite the numbers, lining up the ones, the tens, and the hundreds.

0 tens × 583 = 0, so no product is written.

$$
\begin{array}{r}
583 \\
\times\, 304 \\
\hline
2332 \\
+\, 174900 \\
\hline
177{,}232
\end{array}
$$

← 4 × 583 ← Multiply by **4** ones.
← 300 × 583 ← Multiply by **3** hundreds.
product → ← 304 × 583

Zeros are used to hold the ones and tens place.

When multiplying with money, you can think of dollars and cents as just cents and multiply as you do with whole numbers.

EXAMPLE

Find 7 × $3.25.

SOLUTION $3.25 is equal to 325 cents.

$$
\begin{array}{r}
325¢ \\
\times\, 7 \\
\hline
2275¢
\end{array}
$$

← Multiply 325 by 7.

Think of 2275 cents as 22 hundred cents and another 75 cents. Each hundred cents is worth one dollar so you have 22 dollars and 75 cents.

7 × $3.25 = $22.75

Multiply.

1. 25 × 38
2. 96 × 504
3. 146 × 260
4. 655 × 337
5. 158 × 29
6. 14 × 2048
7. 6 × $38.18
8. 22 × $16.01
9. 41 × $2.72
10. 60 × $31.50
11. 2 × $54.82
12. 303 × $9.95

Dividing Whole Numbers

Dividing whole numbers is the same as finding how many times the divisor goes into the dividend.

Sometimes when you divide there will be a remainder. The remainder is a number that is leftover after the divisor goes into the dividend as many times as possible.

$$9 \leftarrow \text{quotient}$$
$$\text{divisor} \rightarrow 5\overline{)45} \leftarrow \text{dividend}$$

EXAMPLE

Find $968 \div 27$.

SOLUTION   Rewrite the division in columns to organize your work. Try to divide 27 into each place or combination of places in 968, starting at the left.

You will need to multiply and subtract each time you write a digit in the quotient. Be careful to keep columns lined up.

hundreds place	tens place	ones place
27 does not go into 9.	Divide 27 into 96. It goes in 3 times.	Divide 27 into 158. It goes in 5 times.

$$27\overline{)968}$$

$$\begin{array}{r} 3 \\ 27\overline{)968} \\ -81 \\ \hline 15 \end{array}$$

$$\begin{array}{r} 35 \text{ R}23 \\ 27\overline{)968} \\ -81 \downarrow \\ \hline 158 \\ -135 \\ \hline 23 \end{array}$$

$27 \times 3 = 81$
Subtracting 81 from 96 gives a remainder of **15**.

Combine the **15** tens remaining and the **8** ones from the dividend to get **158**.

$27 \times 5 = 135$
Subtracting 135 from 158 gives a remainder of **23**.

$968 \div 27 = 35$ R23 (35 remainder 23)

To check the answer, multiply the quotient by the divisor and add the remainder. The result should equal the dividend.

$$35 \times 27 = 945 \qquad 945 + 23 = 968$$

Divide.

1. $3205 \div 8$
2. $500 \div 64$
3. $9875 \div 4$
4. $269 \div 21$
5. $7852 \div 26$
6. $8080 \div 15$
7. $741 \div 36$
8. $520 \div 45$
9. $6800 \div 42$
10. $350 \div 102$
11. $1208 \div 34$
12. $344 \div 26$

Number Fact Families

The following is an example of a number fact family for addition and subtraction:

$$7 + 9 = 16 \qquad 9 + 7 = 16 \qquad 16 - 7 = 9 \qquad 16 - 9 = 7$$

You can use a number fact family to find missing numbers. For example, suppose you want to find the missing number in $7 + \underline{?} = 16$. If you know that $16 - 7$ will give you the same number, you can subtract to find the missing number.

A number fact family for multiplication and division is given below:

$$6 \times 2 = 12 \qquad 2 \times 6 = 12 \qquad 12 \div 6 = 2 \qquad 12 \div 2 = 6$$

You can use this family to complete the number sentence $12 \div \underline{?} = 2$.

EXAMPLE   addends—↘   ↙—sum

Complete the number fact family for $3 + 5 = 8$.

SOLUTION   You can write the other addition fact in the family by switching the order of the addends. You can write the related subtraction facts by starting with the sum and taking away each addend.

$$3 + 5 = 8 \qquad\qquad 5 + 3 = 8 \qquad\qquad 8 - 3 = 5 \qquad\qquad 8 - 5 = 3$$

EXAMPLE

Find the missing number: $18 \div \underline{?} = 2$

SOLUTION   You know from the multiplication and division number fact families that the missing number is the same for $18 \div \underline{?} = 2$ as for $18 \div 2 = \underline{?}$.

$$18 \div 2 = 9. \text{ Therefore } 18 \div 9 = 2.$$

Complete each number fact family.

1. $6 + 3 = 9$ $3 + \underline{?} = 9$ $9 - \underline{?} = 6$ $9 - \underline{?} = \underline{?}$

2. $16 \div 2 = \underline{?}$ $\underline{?} \div \underline{?} = 2$ $\underline{?} \times 8 = 16$ $\underline{?} \times \underline{?} = 16$

Find each missing number.

3. $23 + \underline{?} = 35$

4. $344 - \underline{?} = 320$

5. $\underline{?} + 12 = 65$

6. $62 - \underline{?} = 37$

7. $\underline{?} - 4 = 77$

8. $\underline{?} + 51 = 83$

9. $\underline{?} - 8 = 95$

10. $\underline{?} \times 4 = 52$

11. $\underline{?} \div 7 = 9$

12. $7 \times \underline{?} = 56$

13. $\underline{?} \div 3 = 13$

14. $6 \times \underline{?} = 72$

15. $\underline{?} \div 4 = 12$

16. $28 \div \underline{?} = 7$

17. $\underline{?} \times 3 = 42$

Multiplying and Dividing by Tens

You can use mental math to multiply by 10, 100, 1000, and so on, by thinking about place value.

EXAMPLE

To find 100×23, think: 1 hundred taken 23 times is 23 hundreds.

$100 \times 23 = 2300$

You can use what you know about multiplying by 10, 100, or 1000 to multiply other numbers that end in one or more zeros.

EXAMPLE

To find 200×80, first multiply the non-zero digits and then put on the extra zeros.

$200 \times 80 = 2 \times 100 \times 8 \times 10 = 16 \times 1000 = 16{,}000$

$2 \times 8 = 16$

$100 \times 10 = 1000$, so you need 3 zeros at the end.

The mental math strategies shown for multiplying numbers ending in zeros can also help you to divide numbers ending in zeros. Think about the relationship between division and multiplication.

EXAMPLE

To find $670{,}000 \div 1000$, think: $\underline{?} \times 1000 = 670{,}000$.

$670{,}000 \div 1000 = 670$

To find $48{,}000 \div 60$, think about the zeros and the non-zero digits separately.

$48{,}000 \div 60 = 800$

Think: $\underline{?} \times 6 = 48$

Think: $\underline{?} \times 10 = 1000$

Multiply or divide.

1. 100×500
2. 200×30
3. 5000×300
4. 400×4000
5. 3000×200
6. 5000×100
7. $200 \times 60{,}000$
8. $10{,}000 \times 2{,}000$
9. $8{,}000 \times 40{,}000$
10. $800{,}000 \div 2$
11. $10{,}000 \div 1{,}000$
12. $10{,}000 \div 200$
13. $3900 \div 30$
14. $20{,}000 \div 400$
15. $250{,}000 \div 50$

Perimeter and Using a Ruler

The perimeter (*P*) of a figure is the distance around it. You can find the perimeter by adding the lengths of the sides together.

EXAMPLE

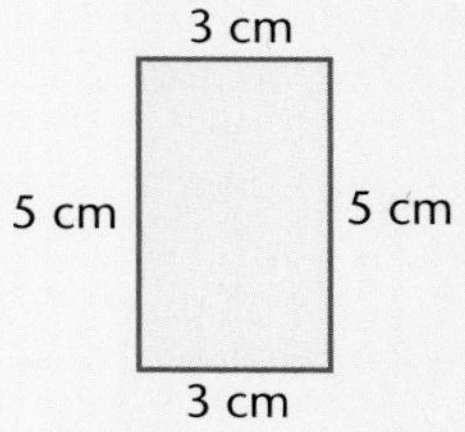
3 cm
5 cm
5 cm
3 cm

$3 + 5 + 3 + 5 = 16$
$\mathbf{P = 16}$ **cm**

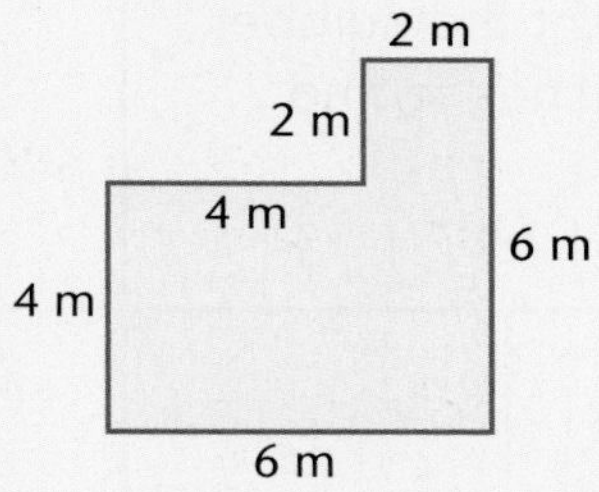
2 m
2 m
4 m
6 m
4 m
6 m

$4 + 2 + 2 + 6 + 6 + 4 = 24$
$\mathbf{P = 24}$ **m**

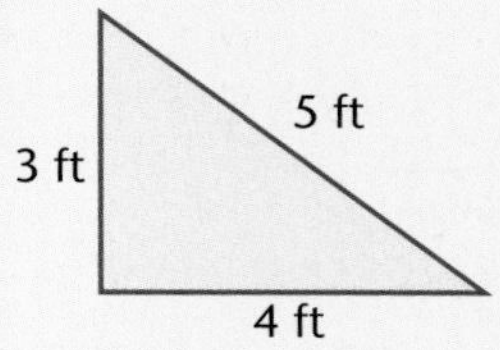
5 ft
3 ft
4 ft

$3 + 5 + 4 = 12$
$\mathbf{P = 12}$ **ft**

A ruler is a tool that is used to measure length. A United States customary ruler shows measurements in inches.

The other end of the pencil is between 3 in. and 4 in. It does not reach the halfway mark, so round down.

EXAMPLE

Use a ruler to measure the pencil to the nearest inch.

Line up one end of the pencil with the 0 mark on the ruler.

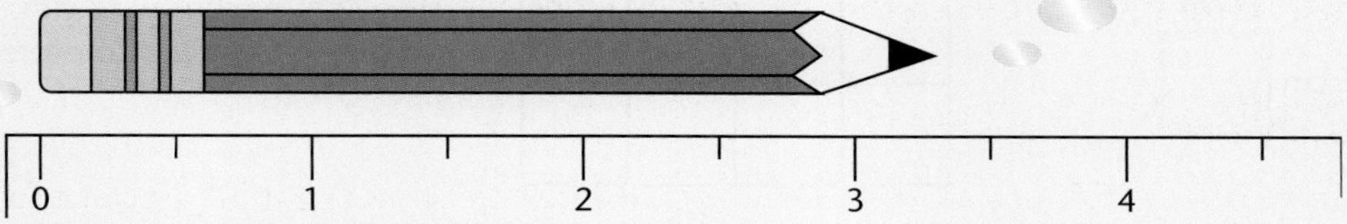
0
1
2
3
4

The pencil is about 3 in. long.

For Exercises 1–5, find the perimeter of each figure.

1.
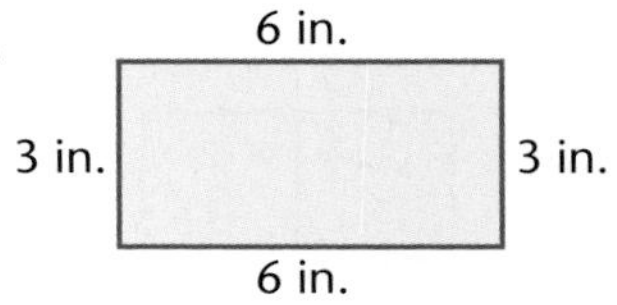
6 in.
3 in.
3 in.
6 in.

2.
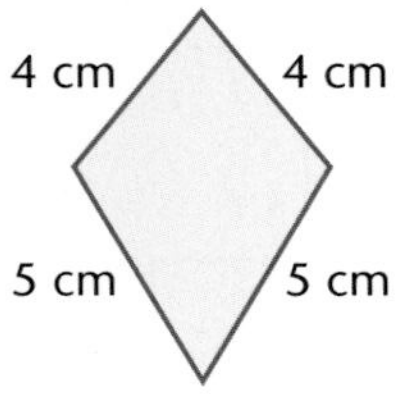
4 cm
4 cm
5 cm
5 cm

3.
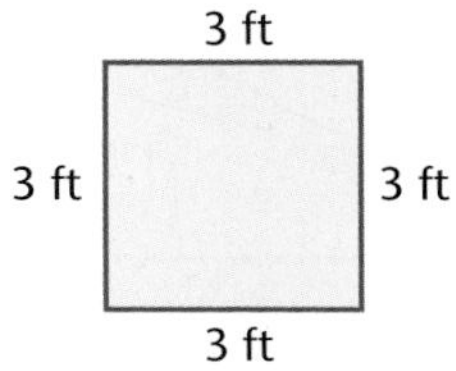
3 ft
3 ft
3 ft
3 ft

4. a square with sides 5 cm long

5. a triangle with sides 3 in., 5 in., and 6 in. long

Use a ruler to measure each nail to the nearest inch.

6.
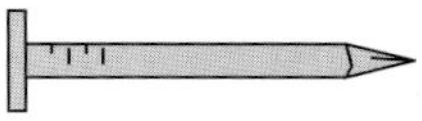

7.
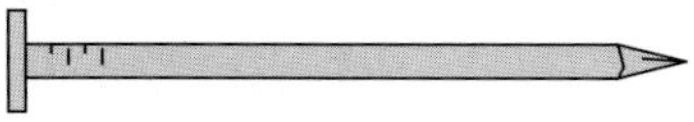

Area

The area of a figure is the amount of surface it covers. Area is measured in square units. The square units used may be square inches, square centimeters, square feet, or squares of any other size.

EXAMPLE

This square is a square inch.

1 in.

1 in.

You can count the number of square inches to find the area.

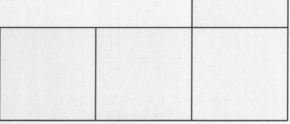

The area of the figure on the right is 4 square inches.

EXAMPLE

The square on the left is a square centimeter.

1 cm

1 cm

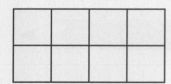

Add 4 square centimeters in each row to get 8 square centimeters.

The area of the figure on the right is 8 square centimeters.

Find the area of each figure. Each small square is 1 centimeter by 1 centimeter.

1.

2.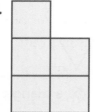

3.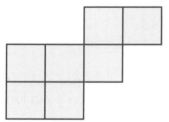

Time Conversions and Elapsed Time

The chart below can help you convert time measurements. You can also use these relationships when you subtract to find elapsed time.

60 seconds (sec) = 1 minute (min)
60 minutes (min) = 1 hour (hr)
24 hours (hr) = 1 day
7 days = 1 week

EXAMPLE

Find the missing number: 20 min = _?_ seconds

SOLUTION   Every 1 min equals 60 seconds.
20 min = 20 × 60 seconds = **1200 seconds**

EXAMPLE

How much time has elapsed between 8:30 A.M. and 10:15 A.M.?

SOLUTION

$$\begin{array}{r} 9 \quad 75 \\ 10:15 \text{ A.M.} \rightarrow \quad \cancel{10} \text{ hr } \cancel{15} \text{ min} \\ - \quad 8:30 \text{ A.M.} \rightarrow \quad - \quad 8 \text{ hr } 30 \text{ min} \\ \hline 1 \text{ hr } 45 \text{ min} \end{array}$$

Trade 1 hr for 60 min. Then combine the 60 min with the 15 min already there.

EXAMPLE

How much time has elapsed between 3:00 P.M. and 1:30 A.M.?

SOLUTION

$$\begin{array}{r} 1:30 \text{ A.M.} \rightarrow \quad 13 \text{ hr } 30 \text{ min} \\ - \quad 3:00 \text{ P.M.} \rightarrow \quad - \quad 3 \text{ hr } 00 \text{ min} \\ \hline 10 \text{ hr } 30 \text{ min} \end{array}$$

To get to 1:30 A.M. you need to go another hour and a half past 12:00 midnight. Add 1 hr 30 min to 12 hr to get 13 hr 30 min.

Change each time measurement to the given unit of time.

1. 8 hr to minutes
2. 72 hr to days
3. 180 seconds to minutes

Find how much time has elapsed between the given times.

4. 12:40 P.M. and 5:35 P.M.
5. 9:30 A.M. and 11:23 P.M.
6. 6:10 P.M. and 9:06 P.M.
7. 10:45 P.M. and 12:20 A.M.

Reading a Graph

A graph is a visual display of data. Different types of graphs are used depending on the type of data and the relationship you are showing.

EXAMPLE

To read a bar graph, find the bar that represents the information you are looking for. Think of extending a line from the end of the bar to the numbers on the scale.

To see what each point represents on a line graph, think of drawing a line across or down to each of the scales.

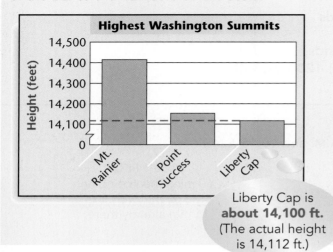

Liberty Cap is **about 14,100 ft.** (The actual height is 14,112 ft.)

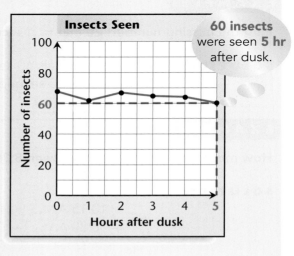

60 insects were seen **5 hr** after dusk.

Use the graph to estimate each value.

1. By the end of 1998, how many World Cup tourneys had Brazil played? had France played?

2. What was the population of Birmingham, Alabama, in 1990? in 1994?

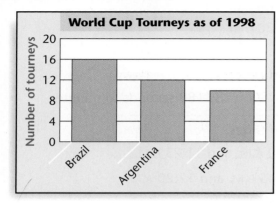

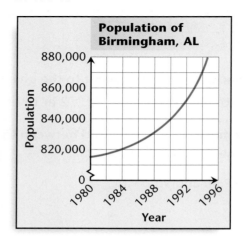

Making a Pictograph

A pictograph can be used to display data. Usually a symbol is used to represent a given number of items.

EXAMPLE

Make a pictograph to represent the number of campers each summer.

Year	1993	1994	1995	1996	1997	1998
Campers	600	640	690	655	700	750

SOLUTION You can use 1 triangle for each 100 campers. You can also use part of a triangle to show part of 100.

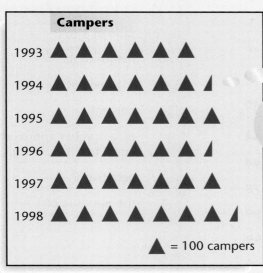

There are 6 hundreds in 600, so use 6 full triangles to show 600 campers. There are 40 campers left and 40 is almost half of 100, so you can show half of another triangle.

▲ = 100 campers

1. Make a pictograph to represent the students studying music in each grade.

Grade	6th	7th	8th
Students studying music	71	90	85

2. Make a pictograph to represent the money spent on advertising in 1994. The dollar amounts have been rounded to the nearest billion.

Advertising medium	newspapers	magazines	television	radio	direct mail
Billions of dollars	34	8	34	10	29

TABLE OF SYMBOLS

SYMBOL		Page	SYMBOL		Page
$+$	plus	**3**	2^3	3rd power of 2	**156**
$-$	minus	**3**	$\frac{3}{4}$	3 divided by 4	**222**
$\times$	times	**3**	$\geq$	is greater than or equal to	**225**
$\cdot$	times	**3**	$\approx$	is about equal to	**225**
$\div$	divided by	**3**	(x, y)	ordered pair of numbers	**254**
$=$	equals	**3**	$1:2$	ratio of 1 to 2	**366**
$(\ )$	parentheses—grouping symbol	**4**	AB	length of $\overline{AB}$	**408**
$\ldots$	and so on	**16**	$\triangle ABC$	triangle ABC	**409**
$\frac{3}{4}$	3 parts of 4	**40**	$\%$	percent	**420**
$\overline{)}$	divided into	**44**	π	pi, a number approximately equal to 3.14	**464**
R	remainder	**44**	-1	negative 1	**483**
$\{\ \}$	braces, enclose objects of a set	**78**	-1	the opposite of 1	**527**
$\overleftrightarrow{AB}$	line AB	**99**			
$\overline{AB}$	segment AB	**99**			
$\overrightarrow{AB}$	ray AB	**99**			
$\|$	is parallel to	**100**			
$\perp$	is perpendicular to	**100**			
$\llcorner$	right angle	**100**			
$\angle A$	angle A	**103**			
$\degree$	degree(s)	**103**			
1.2	decimal point, separates whole numbers from parts of a whole number	**131**			
$<$	is less than	**133**			
$>$	is greater than	**133**			

TABLE OF MEASURES

Time

60 seconds (sec)	= 1 minute (min)
60 minutes	= 1 hour (hr)
24 hours	= 1 day
7 days	= 1 week
4 weeks (approx.)	= 1 month

$$\left.\begin{array}{c} 365 \text{ days} \\ 52 \text{ weeks (approx.)} \\ 12 \text{ months} \end{array}\right\} = 1 \text{ year}$$

10 years = 1 decade
100 years = 1 century

METRIC

Length

10 millimeters (mm) = 1 centimeter (cm)

$$\left.\begin{array}{c} 100 \text{ cm} \\ 1000 \text{ mm} \end{array}\right\} = 1 \text{ meter (m)}$$

1000 m = 1 kilometer (km)

Area

100 square millimeters = 1 square centimeter
(mm^2) (cm^2)
10,000 cm^2 = 1 square meter (m^2)
10,000 m^2 = 1 hectare (ha)

Volume

1000 cubic millimeters = 1 cubic centimeter
(mm^3) (cm^3)
1,000,000 cm^3 = 1 cubic meter (m^3)

Liquid Capacity

1000 milliliters (mL) = 1 liter (L)
1000 L = 1 kiloliter (kL)

Mass

1000 milligrams (mg) = 1 gram (g)
1000 g = 1 kilogram (kg)
1000 kg = 1 metric ton (t)

Temperature — Degrees Celsius (°C)

0°C = freezing point of water
37°C = normal body temperature
100°C = boiling point of water

UNITED STATES CUSTOMARY

Length

12 inches (in.) = 1 foot (ft)

$$\left.\begin{array}{c} 36 \text{ in.} \\ 3 \text{ ft} \end{array}\right\} = 1 \text{ yard (yd)}$$

$$\left.\begin{array}{c} 5280 \text{ ft} \\ 1760 \text{ yd} \end{array}\right\} = 1 \text{ mile (mi)}$$

Area

144 square inches (in.^{2}) = 1 square foot (ft^2)
9 ft^2 = 1 square yard (yd^2)

$$\left.\begin{array}{c} 43,560 \text{ ft}^2 \\ 4840 \text{ yd}^2 \end{array}\right\} = 1 \text{ acre (A)}$$

Volume

1728 cubic inches (in.^{3}) = 1 cubic foot (ft^3)
27 ft^3 = 1 cubic yard (yd^3)

Liquid Capacity

8 fluid ounces (fl oz) = 1 cup (c)
2 c = 1 pint (pt)
2 pt = 1 quart (qt)
4 qt = 1 gallon (gal)

Weight

16 ounces (oz) = 1 pound (lb)
2000 lb = 1 ton (t)

Temperature — Degrees Fahrenheit (°F)

32°F = freezing point of water
98.6°F = normal body temperature
212°F = boiling point of water

GLOSSARY

A ▶▶▶▶▶▶▶▶▶▶▶▶▶▶▶▶▶▶▶▶▶▶▶▶▶▶▶▶▶

acute angle (p. 104) An angle with a measure greater than 0° but less than 90°. *See also* angle.

acute triangle (p. 104) A triangle with three acute angles.

angle (p. 103) A figure formed by two rays that have a common endpoint.

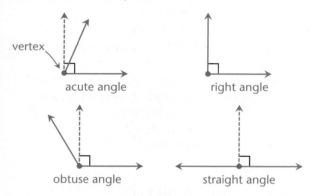

vertex

acute angle   right angle

obtuse angle   straight angle

area (p. 331) The number of square units of surface a figure covers.

average (p. 218) A single number used to describe what is typical of a set of data. *See* mean, median, *and* mode.

axes (p. 255) *See* coordinate grid.

B ▶▶▶▶▶▶▶▶▶▶▶▶▶▶▶▶▶▶▶▶▶▶▶▶▶▶▶▶▶

back-to-back stem-and-leaf plot (p. 262) A stem-and-leaf plot that compares two related sets of data.

bar graph (p. 578) A graph used to compare data by comparing the lengths of bars.

base (p. 156) *See* power.

base of a polygon (pp. 334, 335) *See* parallelogram *and* triangle.

base of a 3-dimensional figure (pp. 442, 452, 475) *See* prism, pyramid, *and* cylinder.

benchmark (p. 203) An item whose measure you know that can be used to estimate lengths. For example, you could use your height to estimate the height of a doorway.

C ▶▶▶▶▶▶▶▶▶▶▶▶▶▶▶▶▶▶▶▶▶▶▶▶▶▶▶▶▶

capacity (p. 500) The amount of liquid a container can hold.

center (p. 462) *See* circle.

certain event (p. 79) An event that must happen. It has a probability of 1.

chord (p. 462) A segment that connects two points on a circle. *See also* circle.

circle (p. 462) The set of points in a plane that are all the same distance from a given point, the center.

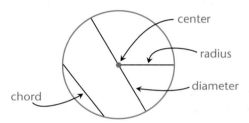

center

radius

diameter

chord

circle graph (p. 424) A circular-shaped graph that shows the part to whole relationship between data. A whole circle represents 100%. Also called a *pie chart*.

circumference (p. 464) The distance around a circle.

cluster (p. 217) A group of numerical data items that are bunched closely together.

common denominator (p. 287) A common multiple of the denominators of two or more fractions.

compatible numbers (p. 8) Numbers that have sums, products, or quotients that are easy to find and compute with.

complementary events (p. 536) Two events are complementary if one or the other must occur, but they cannot both happen at the same time.

composite number (p. 153) A whole number greater than 1 that has more than two factors.

congruent (p. 409) Having the same size and shape.

congruent figures (p. 409) Figures that have the same shape and the same size.

connections (p. 90) Similarities that relate two patterns, problems, ideas, or applications.

coordinate grid (p. 255) A grid formed using two number lines as axes. The axes intersect at the point (0, 0) called the *origin*.

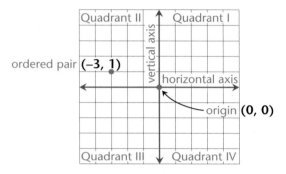

corresponding parts (p. 407) A pair of sides or angles that have the same relative position in two similar or congruent figures.

cross products (p. 397) Equal products formed from a pair of equivalent ratios by multiplying the numerator of each fraction by the denominator of the other fraction.

proportion   cross products

$$\frac{2}{3} = \frac{4}{6} \qquad \begin{array}{c} 2 \cdot 6 \\ 3 \cdot 4 \end{array}$$

cubic unit (p. 444) A unit for measuring volume.

cylinder (p. 475) A 3-dimensional figure that has a curved surface and two parallel, congruent bases that are circles.

cylinder

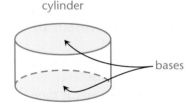

bases

D ▸

decimal system (p. 131) A system of numbers based on 10.

degree (p. 103) A unit of measurement for angles. The symbol for degrees is °.

denominator (p. 40) The bottom number in a fraction that tells how many equal-sized parts the whole is divided into.

diameter (p. 463) A chord that passes through the center of a circle and the length of such a chord. *See also* circle.

difference (p. 570) The result when two numbers are subtracted.

distributive property (p. 176) Each addend inside a set of parentheses can be multiplied by a factor outside the parentheses. For example, $3 \cdot (4 + 2) = 3 \cdot 4 + 3 \cdot 2$.

divisible (p. 149) When a number can be evenly divided by another number, it is divisible by that number.

dot plot (p. 216) *See* line plot.

E ▸

edge (p. 442) A segment on a polyhedron where two faces meet. *See also* prism.

empty set (p. 202) A set with no objects in it.

equally likely (p. 76) Outcomes are equally likely if they have the same chance of occurring.

equation (p. 19) A mathematical sentence that uses the symbol "=" between two expressions to show that they have the same value.

equilateral triangle (p. 101) A triangle with three sides of equal length.

equivalent decimals (p. 133) Two decimals that represent the same amount.

equivalent fractions (p. 55) Fractions that name the same part of a whole.

equivalent ratios (p. 367) Ratios that can be written as equivalent fractions.

estimate (p. 5) An answer that is not exact.

evaluate an expression (p. 19) To substitute a number for each variable, then carry out any operations in the expression.

event (p. 78) A set of outcomes for a particular experiment.

experiment (p. 75) An activity whose results can be observed and recorded.

experimental probability (p. 75) The experimental probability of an outcome is the ratio of the number of times the outcome happened to the number of times the experiment was repeated.

exponent (p. 156) A raised number that tells how many times a base is used as a factor. *See also* power.

expression (p. 2) A mathematical phrase that can contain numbers, variables, and operations.

F ▶▶▶▶▶▶▶▶▶▶▶▶▶▶▶▶▶▶▶▶▶▶▶▶▶▶▶▶▶

face (p. 441) A flat surface of a polyhedron. *See also* prism.

factor (p. 150) When a whole number is divisible by a second whole number, the second number is a factor of the first.

factor tree (p. 153) *See* prime factorization.

fitted line (p. 387) A line that passes near to most of the data points in a scatter plot, so that close to half of the data points fall above the line and close to half fall below the line.

fraction (p. 40) A number that compares a part with a whole.

front-end estimation (p. 514) A method of estimation that focuses on the leftmost digits, since they have the greatest value.

G ▶▶▶▶▶▶▶▶▶▶▶▶▶▶▶▶▶▶▶▶▶▶▶▶▶▶▶▶

gap (p. 217) When numerical data are plotted on a number line (as in a line plot), a large interval in which there are no data items is a *gap* in the data.

general case (p. 91) When you solve a problem for one situation and extend it to any such situation, you are extending the solution to the general case.

geometric probability (p. 536) A probability that is based on length, area, or volume.

greatest common factor (GCF) (p. 151) The greatest number that is a factor of each of two or more numbers.

H ▶▶▶▶▶▶▶▶▶▶▶▶▶▶▶▶▶▶▶▶▶▶▶▶▶▶▶▶

height of a polygon (pp. 334, 335) *See* parallelogram, triangle.

I ▶▶▶▶▶▶▶▶▶▶▶▶▶▶▶▶▶▶▶▶▶▶▶▶▶▶▶▶

impossible event (p. 79) An event that cannot happen. It has a probability of 0.

inequality (p. 285) A mathematical sentence that uses symbols such as > (greater than) or < (less than) to compare values.

integer (p. 484) Any number in the set {..., –3, –2, –1, 0, 1, 2, 3, ...}.

intersect (p. 334) Two segments or figures that meet at a common point intersect.

inverse operations (p. 238) Operations that "undo" each other. For example, addition and subtraction are inverse operations.

isosceles triangle (p. 101) A triangle with two or more sides of equal length.

L ▶▶▶▶▶▶▶▶▶▶▶▶▶▶▶▶▶▶▶▶▶▶▶▶▶▶▶▶

least common denominator (p. 287) The least common multiple of the denominators of two or more fractions.

least common multiple (LCM) (p. 167) For two or more whole numbers, the least number in the list of their common multiples.

line (p. 99) A straight arrangement of points that extends forever in opposite directions.

line graph (p. 265) A graph on which the plotted points are connected with line segments. It may show changes that take place over time.

line plot (p. 216) A plot displaying data above the appropriate points along a scale. The scale must include the greatest and least values of the data. Also called a *dot plot*.

lowest terms (p. 58) A fraction is in lowest terms when 1 is the greatest whole number that will divide both the numerator and the denominator evenly.

M ▶▶▶▶▶▶▶▶▶▶▶▶▶▶▶▶▶▶▶▶▶▶▶▶▶▶▶▶

mean (p. 220) The sum of a set of numerical data divided by the number of data items.

median (p. 219) The middle data item in a set of data in numerical order. If there is no single middle item, the number halfway between the two data items closest to the middle.

mixed number (p. 42) The sum of a whole number and a nonzero fraction.

mode (p. 218) The data item or items that occur most often in a set of data.

multiple (p. 166) A multiple of a whole number is the product of that number and any nonzero whole number.

N ▶▶▶▶▶▶▶▶▶▶▶▶▶▶▶▶▶▶▶▶▶▶▶▶▶▶▶▶

negative (p. 483) Less than zero.

net (p. 441) A flat pattern that can be cut out and folded to form a 3-dimensional object.

"nice" fraction (p. 385) A fraction like $\frac{1}{3}$, $\frac{1}{4}$, or $\frac{2}{5}$ that can be used to estimate a ratio or percent, making computation easier.

numerator (p. 40) The top number in a fraction that tells how many parts of the whole to consider.

O ▸

oblique cylinder (p. 475) A cylinder whose curved surface is not perpendicular to the bases.

oblique prism (p. 443) A prism such that each edge joining a vertex of one base and a vertex of the other base is not perpendicular to the bases.

obtuse angle (p. 104) An angle with a measure greater than 90° but less than 180°. *See also* angle.

obtuse triangle (p. 104) A triangle with one obtuse angle.

opposites (p. 521) Two numbers whose sum is equal to 0; one addend is positive, one addend is negative.

order of operations (p. 3) The order to follow when performing operations: simplify inside parentheses, multiply or divide left to right, and finally add or subtract left to right.

ordered pair (p. 254) The numbers that give the location of a point on a coordinate grid. The first number gives the horizontal position and the second number gives the vertical position. *See also* coordinate grid.

origin (p. 255) *See* coordinate grid.

outcome (p. 75) The result of an experiment.

P ▸

parallel lines (p. 100) Lines on a flat surface that do not meet.

parallel planes (p. 442) Planes that do not intersect.

parallelogram (p. 115) A quadrilateral with two pairs of parallel sides.

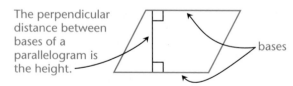

The perpendicular distance between bases of a parallelogram is the height. — bases

percent (p. 420) "per hundred" or "out of 100."

perimeter (p. 575) The distance around a figure.

perpendicular (p. 100) The relationship between lines or segments that meet at a right angle.

pi (π) (p. 464) The ratio of circumference to diameter for any circle. The value of π is approximately equal to 3.14.

pie chart (p. 424) *See* circle graph.

place value (p. 131) The numerical value assigned to the different positions of digits in a number that is written in decimal form.

plane (p. 100) A flat surface that extends forever.

point (p. 99) A specific location in space.

polygon (p. 112) A closed plane figure made from segments, called sides, that do not cross.

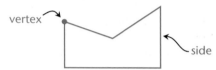

vertex — side

A polygon can have 3 or more sides. Some types of polygons are:

pentagon (5 sides)   hexagon (6 sides)
octagon (8 sides)   decagon (10 sides)

polyhedron (plural: polyhedra) (p. 441) A 3-dimensional object made up of flat surfaces, called faces, shaped like polygons.

population (p. 59) A whole set of objects being studied.

positive (p. 483) Greater than zero.

power (p. 156) An expression that represents repeated multiplication of the same factor.

8 is a power of 2

standard form $8 = 2 \cdot 2 \cdot 2 = 2^3$
exponent
power
base

prime factorization (p. 153) A number written as the product of prime factors. A factor tree helps to find the prime factorization.

factor tree

12
3   4
    2   2

The prime factorization of 12 is $2 \cdot 2 \cdot 3$.

prime number (p. 153) A whole number greater than 1 that has exactly two factors, 1 and the number itself.

prism (p. 442) A polyhedron with two congruent bases that lie in parallel planes, and whose other faces are parallelograms.

rectangular prism

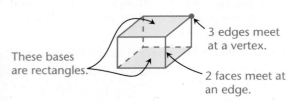

These bases are rectangles.

3 edges meet at a vertex.

2 faces meet at an edge.

probability (p. 75) A number from 0 to 1 that tells you how likely something is to happen.

product (p. 571) The result when two or more numbers are multiplied.

proportion (p. 397) An equation stating that two ratios are equivalent.

protractor (p. 117) A tool used to measure an angle.

pyramid (p. 452) A space figure that has one polygon-shaped base. All the other faces are triangles that meet at a single vertex.

rectangular pyramid

vertex

base

Q ▸

quadrant (p. 487) The four parts of a coordinate grid divided by the axes. *See also* coordinate grid.

quadrilateral (p. 114) A polygon with four sides.

quotient (p. 572) The result when two numbers are divided.

R ▸

radius (plural: radii) (p. 462) A segment from the center of a circle to any point on the circle and the length of such a segment. *See also* circle.

range (p. 216) The difference between the greatest and the least values of a set of numerical data.

rate (p. 374) A ratio that compares two quantities measured in different units. Rates describe how one measure depends on another measure.

ratio (p. 366) A type of comparison of two numbers or measures. Ratios can be written several ways. For example, the ratio of 8 and 12 can be expressed as 8 to 12, 8 : 12, or $\frac{8}{12}$.

ray (p. 99) A part of a line that starts at a point and extends forever in one direction.

endpoint ➔

reciprocals (p. 346) Two numbers whose product is equal to 1.

reflection (p. 545) A change made to a figure by flipping it across a line.

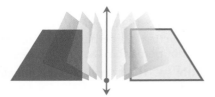

regular polygon (p. 113) A polygon that has sides that are all of equal length and angles that are all of equal measure.

representations (p. 89) Diagrams, tables, graphs, and other visual means to help you solve problems and explain your solutions.

rhombus (p. 115) A parallelogram with all sides the same length.

right angle (p. 104) An angle with a measure of 90°. *See also* angle.

right cylinder (p. 475) A cylinder whose curved surface is perpendicular to the bases.

right prism (p. 443) A prism such that each edge joining a vertex of one base and a vertex of the other base is perpendicular to the bases.

right triangle (p. 104) A triangle that has one right angle.

rotation (p. 544) A change made to a figure by turning it around a fixed point. The point of rotation can be any fixed point outside, inside, or on the figure.

A

round (p. 5) To approximate a number to a given place. For example, 28 rounded to the nearest ten is 30.

rule (p. 16) An explanation of how to create or extend a pattern.

S ▸▸▸▸▸▸▸▸▸▸▸▸▸▸▸▸▸▸▸▸▸▸▸▸▸▸▸▸

sample (p. 59) Part of a whole set of objects being studied.

scale (p. 411) The ratio of a measurement on a model or a drawing to the corresponding measurement on the actual object.

scalene triangle (p. 101) A triangle with no sides of equal length.

scatter plot (p. 388) A graph that shows the relationship between two sets of data. The data are represented by points, and a fitted line can be drawn based on the pattern in the points.

scientific notation (p. 554) A form of writing a number using a number greater than or equal to 1 but less than 10 and a power of 10.

segment (p. 99) Two points on a line and all points between them.

endpoints

sequence (p. 15) An ordered list of numbers or objects.

set (p. 78) Any collection of objects.

similar figures (p. 407) Figures that have the same shape but not necessarily the same size.

solution of an equation (p. 236) A value of a variable that makes an equation true.

solving an equation (p. 236) The process of finding solutions of an equation.

standard form (p. 153) A number written without using exponents. *See also* power.

stem-and-leaf plot (p. 249) A display of data where each number is represented by a *stem* (the leftmost digits) and a *leaf* (the rightmost digits).

straight angle (p. 104) An angle with a measure of 180°. *See also* angle.

sum (p. 569) The result when two or more numbers are added.

T ▸▸▸▸▸▸▸▸▸▸▸▸▸▸▸▸▸▸▸▸▸▸▸▸▸▸▸▸

term of a sequence (p. 17) An individual number or object in a sequence.

term number (p. 17) Indicates the order or position of a term in a sequence.

theoretical probability (p. 78) The ratio of the number of outcomes in the event to the total number of possible outcomes.

trading off (p. 513) A method that involves taking away from one number and adding the same amount to another number, to have numbers that are easier to add using mental math.

transformation (p. 545) A change made to a figure or its position.

translation (p. 544) A change made to a figure by sliding every point of it the same distance in the same direction.

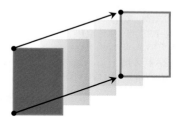

trapezoid (p. 115) A quadrilateral with exactly one pair of parallel sides.

triangle (pp. 101, 112) A polygon with three sides.

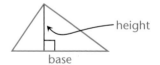
height
base

U ▸▸▸▸▸▸▸▸▸▸▸▸▸▸▸▸▸▸▸▸▸▸▸▸▸▸▸▸

unit rate (p. 376) A form of a rate that gives an amount per one unit.

V ▸▸▸▸▸▸▸▸▸▸▸▸▸▸▸▸▸▸▸▸▸▸▸▸▸▸▸▸

variable (p. 19) A letter or symbol that represents a quantity that is unknown or that can change.

Venn diagram (p. 115) A diagram that uses a drawing to show how sets are related.

vertex of an angle (p. 103) The endpoint of the rays of an angle. *See also* angle.

vertex (plural: vertices) of a polygon (p. 112) Each endpoint of a side of a polygon. *See also* polygon.

vertex of a prism (p. 442) A point where three edges meet. *See also* prism.

volume (p. 444) The amount of space an object contains.

INDEX

of mixed numbers, 177–178,
181–183
by whole numbers, 176–178,
180–183
with money, 571
order of operations and, 3–4,
10
properties, 176–177, 178
by tens, 574
of whole numbers, 571

CREDITS

ACKNOWLEDGMENTS
108 Graphic and text from *Puzzles and Brain Twisters* by Fred Walls. Copyright © 1970 by Franklin Watts, Inc. Reprinted by permission of Franklin Watts, an imprint of Scholastic Library Publishing, Inc. **181** Excerpt and illustration from *Justin and the Best Biscuits in the World* by Mildred Pitts Walter. Text copyright © 1986 by Mildred Pitts Walter. Illustrations copyright © 1986 by Catherine Stock. Used by permission of HarperCollins Publishers. **214** Excerpts and illustrations from *The Phantom Tollbooth* by Norton Juster and illustrated by Jules Feiffer, copyright © 1961 and renewed by Norton Juster, illustrations copyright © 1961 and renewed 1989 by Jules Feiffer. Used by permission of Random House Children's Books, a division of Random House, Inc. **282** Excerpt and illustration from *Sadako and the Thousand Paper Cranes* by Eleanor Coerr, illustrated by Ronald Himler, text copyright © 1977 by Eleanor Coerr, copyright © 1977 by Ronald Himler, illustrations. Used by permission of G.P. Putnam's Sons, A Division of Penguin Young Readers Group, A Member of Penguin Group (USA) Inc., 345 Hudson Street, New York, NY 10014. All rights reserved. **364** "One Inch Tall," from *Where the Sidewalk Ends* by Shel Silverstein. Copyright © 2004 by Evil Eye Music, Inc. Reprinted with permission from the Estate of Shel Silverstein and HarperCollins Children's Books. **373** Excerpt from "The Great Flood of 1993" by Barbara Brownell, *National Geographic World,* October 1993. Copyright © 1993 National Geographic Society. Reprinted by permission of National Geographic Society.

PHOTOGRAPHY
See copyright page for additional acknowledgments.
1 © Settimio Cipriani/Grand Tour/Corbis; **15** © Araldo de Luca/Corbis; **22** *all* © Kent Wood/Photo Researchers, Inc.; **27, 28, 30** *all* RMIP/Richard Haynes/McDougal Littell/Houghton Mifflin Co.; **34** © Royalty-Free/Corbis; **35** © Tami Dawson/Alamy; **38** © Fridmar Damm/zefa/Corbis; **39** *all* HeritageAuctions.com; **40** *top* Courtesy of William Eckberg; *bottom* © Dinodia/The Image Works; **53** © Alessandro D'Amico/AAD Worldwide Travel Images/Alamy; **54** *all* RMIP/Richard Haynes/McDougal Littell/Houghton Mifflin Co.; **62** © Walter Bibikow/Index Stock Photography; **63** *all* © PhotoDisc; **65** © Peter Menzel/Stock Boston; **68, 69** *all* © Artville; **72–73** © Skyscan Photolibrary/Alamy; **74** *left* © David Young-Wolff/PhotoEdit; *right* Courtesy of The American Numismatic Association; **83** RMIP/Richard Haynes/McDougal Littell/Houghton Mifflin Co.; **85** *top* © Artville; *bottom* © Paul C. Chauncey/Corbis;

86 © Stephanie Reix/For Picture/Corbis; **89** Ken Karp/McDougal Littell/Houghton Mifflin Co.; **94** RMIP/Richard Haynes/McDougal Littell/Houghton Mifflin Co.; **95** *top* © Karl Kinne/zefa/Corbis; *center* © Atlantide Phototravel/Corbis; *bottom* © Anders Blomqvist/Getty Images; **97** RMIP/Richard Haynes/McDougal Littell/Houghton Mifflin Co.; **100** © Royalty-Free/Corbis; **103** *left* © David Sanger/Getty Images; *right* © Momatiuk-Eastcott/Corbis; **116** © Don Hammond/Design Pics/Corbis; **117** *all* RMIP/Richard Haynes/McDougal Littell/Houghton Mifflin Co.; **124, 125** *all* Bonnie Spence/McDougal Littell/Houghton Mifflin Co.; **128–129** © Phil Schermeister/Corbis; **130** Tracey Wheeler McDougal Littell/Houghton Mifflin Co.; **135** © Ariadne Van Zandbergen/Getty Images; **144** *all* RMIP/Richard Haynes/McDougal Littell/Houghton Mifflin Co.; **160** © Peter Johnson/Corbis; **164** *top* © Artville; *bottom* © Michael Newman/PhotoEdit; **165** RMIP/Richard Haynes/McDougal Littell/Houghton Mifflin Co.; **169** © Paul A. Souders/Corbis; **170** *top* © National Portrait Gallery, Smithsonian Institution/Art Resource, NY; *bottom* Courtesy of Emiko Tokunaga; **189** RMIP/Richard Haynes/McDougal Littell/Houghton Mifflin Co.; **198–199** © Frans Lanting/Minden Pictures; **200** *left* © DLILLC/Corbis; *center* © David Hosking/Photo Researchers, Inc.; *right* © franzfoto.com/Alamy; **203** © Douglas Hill/Beatworks/Corbis; **204** © Joe McDonald/Corbis; **206** *left* © Peter Burian/Corbis; *right* © Colin Seddon/Alamy; **212** © Kevin Schafer/Getty Images; **215** Lyle Andersen/McDougal Littell/Houghton Mifflin Co.; **218** © altrendo nature/Getty Images; **220** © Digital Vision/Getty Images; **223** © Tom Brakefield/Getty Images; **226** © Chris Birck/NBAE/Getty Images; **227** School Division/Houghton Mifflin Co.; **228** © AFP/Getty Images; **231** *left* © John Bracegirdle/Getty Images; *center* © George D. Lepp/Corbis; *right* © Joseph Van Os/Getty Images; **232** © Konrad Wothe/Getty Images; **235** © Gerard Lacz/Animals Animals; **241** © Don S. Montgomery/Corbis; **242** *top left* © Bettmann/Corbis; *right* © AP Images; *bottom left* © Ed Clark/Time Life Pictures/Getty Images; **254** RMIP/Richard Haynes/McDougal Littell/Houghton Mifflin Co.; **259** © Justin Lane/epa/Corbis; **260** © Jeremy Spiegel **265** © Dani/Jeske/Animals Animals; **267** © DLILLC/Corbis; **273** © David M. Dennis/Animals Animals; **274, 276** *all* RMIP/Richard Haynes/McDougal Littell/Houghton Mifflin Co.; **280–281** © Jim West/The Image Works; **282** School Division/Houghton Mifflin Co.; **283** *all* Bonnie Spence/McDougal Littell/Houghton Mifflin Co.; **284, 286** *all* RMIP/Richard Haynes/McDougal Littell/Houghton Mifflin Co.; **295** © D.E.

Cox/Stone/Getty Images; **296** School Division/ Houghton Mifflin Co.; **299** © Dean Conger/Corbis; **300** © Charles E. Rotkin/Corbis; **303** RMIP/Richard Haynes/McDougal Littell/Houghton Mifflin Co.; **304** © Amos Nachoum/Corbis; **307, 308** *all* Bonnie Spence/ McDougal Littell/Houghton Mifflin Co.; **310** RMIP/ Richard Haynes/McDougal Littell/Houghton Mifflin Co.; **318** © Charles Bennett/AP Images; **319** School Division/ Houghton Mifflin Co.; **321** *left* RMIP/Richard Haynes/ McDougal Littell/Houghton Mifflin Co.; *center* School Division/Houghton Mifflin Co.; *right* © Lowe Art Museum/SuperStock; **325** Allan Penn/McDougal Littell/ Houghton Mifflin Co.; **327** © AP Images/Rusty Kennedy; **330** © Riccardo Spila/Grand Tour/Corbis; **333** © Walter Bibikow/The Image Bank/Getty Images; **334** RMIP/ Richard Haynes/McDougal Littell/Houghton Mifflin Co.; **335** © Photosindia/Getty Images; **345** © Peter Guttman/Corbis; **346** RMIP/Richard Haynes/McDougal Littell/Houghton Mifflin Co.; **354** *left* © William Leaman/ Alamy; *right* © Roger Tidman/Corbis; **359** © Goro Uno/ HAGA/The Image Works; **362–363** © Louie Psihoyos/ Corbis; **365** © Andrew Bain/Lonely Planet Images; **366** *left, center right* Bonnie Spence/McDougal Littell/ Houghton Mifflin Co.; *center left, right* © Artville; **369** *top right* © FAN travelstock/Alamy; *dogs* © PhotoDisc; **370** *grass* © D. Hurst/Alamy; *person* © Comstock; *basset hound* © Comstock; *bottom* © Bettmann/Corbis; **373** © Elaine Thompson/AP Images; **374** RMIP/Richard Haynes/ McDougal Littell/Houghton Mifflin Co.; **378** © Brand X Pictures; **382** *all* RMIP/Richard Haynes/McDougal Littell/ Houghton Mifflin Co.; **384** *top* RMIP/Richard Haynes/ McDougal Littell/Houghton Mifflin Co.; *bottom* Allan Penn/McDougal Littell/Houghton Mifflin Co.; **386** © Popperfoto/Alamy; **387** *all* RMIP/Richard Haynes/ McDougal Littell/Houghton Mifflin Co.; **391** © Tony Gutierrez/AP Images; **393** © O. Louis Mazzatenta/ National Geographic Image Collection; **395** © Barry Rosenthal/Getty Images; **400** © AFB/Stringer/Getty Images; **403** © Kim Karpeles/Alamy; **404** © Jack Hollingsworth/Corbis; **406, 407** M.C. Escher's *Square Limit* © 2007 The M.C. Escher Company-Holland. All rights reserved. www.mcescher.com; **410** © Nik Wheeler/Corbis; **412** © Rhoda Sidney/PhotoEdit; **415** © PhotoDisc; **417** *all* Courtesy of Marcia McNutt; **419** © Andreas Rentz/Bongarts/Getty Images; **422** © AFP/Getty Images; **423** © Getty Images; **430** © Bettman/Corbis; **433, 435** *all* RMIP/Richard Haynes/McDougal Littell/ Houghton Mifflin Co.; **438–439** © Jose Fuste Raga/ Corbis; **440** *left* © Simon McBride/AA World Travel/ Topfoto/The Image Works; *right* © Reuters/Corbis; **441** *all* Bala Mullur/McDougal Littell/Houghton Mifflin Co.; **442** © mediacolor's/Alamy; **444, 445, 448, 449** *all* School Division/Houghton Mifflin Co.; **452** © Rick Strange/AA World Travel/Topfoto/The Image Works; **453** © Richard T. Nowitz/Corbis; **457** *all* School Division/Houghton Mifflin Co.; **458** Courtesy of Dr. Darrell Mease; **461** © Scala/Art Resource, NY; **463** *all* RMIP/Richard Haynes/McDougal Littell/Houghton

Mifflin Co.; **465** School Division/Houghton Mifflin Company Co.; **467** © Reuters/Corbis; **468** *top* © Atlantide Phototravel/Corbis; *center* © Charles E. Rotkin/ Corbis; *bottom* Courtesy of the American Numismatic Society; **472** © Richard Broadwell/Corbis; **475** © Craig Lovell/Eagle Visions Photography/Alamy; **478** © NOAA/ AP Images; **482** *top* © PhotoDisc; *bottom* © Roger-Viollet/The Image Works; **488** RMIP/Richard Haynes/ McDougal Littell/Houghton Mifflin Co.; **494** *pyramids, Taj Mahal* © Goodshoot/Corbis; *bottom* RMIP/Richard Haynes/McDougal Littell/Houghton Mifflin Co.; **498–499** © Chuck Place/Alamy; **503** Bonnie Spence/ McDougal Littell/Houghton Mifflin Co.; **504** *all* RMIP/ Richard Haynes/McDougal Littell/Houghton Mifflin Co.; **505** *all* School Division/Houghton Mifflin Co.; **507** *bottom left* RMIP/Richard Haynes/McDougal Littell/ Houghton Mifflin Co.; *right* School Division/Houghton Mifflin Co.; **508** © Ron Wurzer/AP Images; **510** © Jim Cooper/AP Images; **520** *left* © Paul A. Souders/Corbis; *right* School Division/Houghton Mifflin Co.; **523** © Aaron Horowitz/Corbis; **528** *all* © Jupiterimages; **530** © Leo Mason/Corbis; **533** © Purestock/Getty Images; **535** *all* RMIP/Richard Haynes/McDougal Littell/ Houghton Mifflin Co.; **536** NASA Johnson Space Center (NASA-JSC); **539** © Vince Streano/Corbis; **542** *left* School Division/Houghton Mifflin Co.; *right* © Peter Hvizdak/The Image Works; **543, 546** *all* School Division/ Houghton Mifflin Co.; **549** *top left* © Bruno Barbier/ Robert Harding World Imagery/Corbis; *top right* © Duomo/Corbis; *bottom* © Superstock, Inc./Superstock; **551** © Bob Daemmrich/The Image Works; **553, 557** NASA Jet Propulsion Laboratory (NASA-JPL); NASA Jet Propulsion Laboratory (NASA-JPL); **560** RMIP/Richard Haynes/McDougal Littell/Houghton Mifflin Co.; **563** *all* © PhotoDisc.

ILLUSTRATION
15, 63 Robin Storesund/McDougal Littell/Houghton Mifflin Co.; **63** Robin Storesund/McDougal Littell/ Houghton Mifflin Co.; **172, 295** David Ballard; **332** Chris Costello; **367** Jeremy Spiegel/McDougal Littell/Houghton Mifflin Co.; **381, 390** Hannah Bonner; **396** Robin Storesund/McDougal Littell/Houghton Mifflin Co.; **472** Chris Costello; **478** Matthew Pippin; **482** Chris Costello; **508, 529** Robin Storesund/McDougal Littell/ Houghton Mifflin Co.

All other illustrations by McDougal Littell/Houghton Mifflin Co. or School Division/Houghton Mifflin Co.

SELECTED ANSWERS

MODULE 1

Section 1, Practice and Application (p. 11)

1. a. 355; The answer is not reasonable because the first hurdle would be at 45 m and, since 45 m + 355 m = 400 m, the second hurdle would be at the finish line.
b. (400 − 40 − 45) ÷ 9 **c.** 35 meters **3.** 36 **5.** 10 **7.** 7
9. 3 **11.** (11 + 5) ÷ 4 **13.** 50 − (4 • 6) **17.** about 14,000; not possible to tell whether estimate is greater than or less than exact product **19.** about 200; less than **21.** about 9,700; less than **23.** 40 **25.** 120
27. 600 **29. a.** 4,941 **b.** 240 **c.** 364 **d.** 580
31. 26 • 200 is 26 • 2 = 52 greater than the exact answer. 25 • 200 is 198 − 25 • 2 = 148 less than the exact answer. So 26 • 200 is closer.
33. 25 • 400 = 10,000

Spiral Review (p. 13)
36. < **37.** > **38.** 3,000 **39.** 180

Extra Skill Practice (p. 14)
1. 26 **3.** 13 **5.** 15 **7.** 5 **9.** 37 **11.** 14 **13.** about 300, greater than **15.** about 100, less than **17.** about 1800, not possible to tell **19.** about 280, not possible to tell **21.** about 2,600, greater than **23.** about 4,500, greater than **25.** 40 **27.** 90 **29.** 1,200 **31.** 1,800

Standardized Testing (p. 14)
1. A **2.** C

Section 2, Practice and Application (p. 22)
1.
Start with △ and add shapes in this order
▽, ▱, △ to continue pattern.
3. 63, 54, 45, 36; Start with 99 and subtract 9 from each term to get the next term. **5.** end of August
7. a.

Term Number	1	2	3	4
Term	1	2	4	8

b. Each term is twice the preceding term. **c.** 32 cells

11. $t = 3 \cdot n$
13. a.

Term Number	5	6	7	8
Term	60	72	84	96

b. The term is 12 times the term number. **c.** $t = 12 \cdot n$
d. $t = 12 \cdot 30 = 360$
15. a.

b.

Term Number	1	2	3	4	5	6
Term	2	5	8	11	14	17

c. Make rectangle 10 squares tall and 3 squares wide. Remove the square from the top right corner.
d. Start with 2 and add 3 to each term to get the next term. Multiply the term number by 3 and subtract 1.
e. $t = 3n − 1$; $t = $ term; $n = $ term number
f. $t = 3 \cdot 25 − 1 = 74$

Spiral Review (p. 25)
20. three thousand six hundred seventy-two
21. six hundred seventy-one thousand five hundred ninety-eight **22.** twenty-three thousand eight hundred fifty-six **23.** 1216 **24.** 135 **25.** 8129 **26.** 4875
27. 23,328 **28.** 502
29.
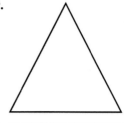

30.
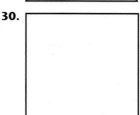

31.

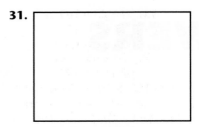

Extra Skill Practice (p. 26)
1. 125, 150, 175, 200, 225; Multiply the term number by 25. Or, start with 25 and add 25 to each term to get the next term. **3.** 96, 84, 72, 60, 48; Multiply the term number by 12 and subtract the product from 156. Or, start with 144 and subtract 12 from each term to get the next term. **5.** 81, 243, 729, 2187, 6561; Multiply each term by 3 to get the next term.
7. a.

Term Number	14	15	16	17
Term	140	150	160	170

b. $t = 10n$ **c.** $t = 10 \cdot 40 = 400$

Study Skills (p. 26)
1. Answers will vary. **2.** Toolbox, Tables, Glossary, Index, Selected Answers **3.** page 567

Section 3, Practice and Application (p. 34)
1. a. Which of two monthly service contracts for 8 to 10 hours a month on-line is a better buy? **b.** the monthly fee, number of included hours, and hourly rate for hours beyond the number included **c.** whether there are limits on the total number of hours or available times, and whether either has cheaper telephone access
3. a. How many times does a given event occur?
b. the time periods over which the tour runs, and the frequency and length of the trips **c.** whether there is more than one double-hulled canoe (If not, the times given could not be exact. There would need to be time to load and unload.) **5.** too much information; Jon had $25.00 **7.** If you are online 8 hr, the standard contract is cheaper. For 9 hr the costs are the same. For 10 hr the frequent user contract is cheaper. **9.** Try a simpler problem, make a table, look for a pattern; Draw chains with 1, 2, 3, and 4 triangles. Find the perimeters. Enter the values in a table. Make a prediction. **11.** 25 times
13. No later than 6:45 AM

Spiral Review (p. 36)
16. 5,600 **17.** $40 **18.** $7 **19.** 35,000 **20.** 900
21. 45,000 **22.** 10,000 **23.** 100,000 **24.** 6,000
25. 560 **26.** 21,000 **27.** 72,600 **28.** 32,000
29. 1,000,000 **30.** 63,000,000 **31.** 12 **32.** 1600
33. 70

34.

Term Number	1	2	3	4	5	6
Term	4	8	12	16	20	24

$t = 4n$ where n is the term number and t is the term

Extra Skill Practice (p. 37)
1. too much; the cost of markers and pens **3.** not enough; Jose's age, ticket price **5.** 4 mi; make a picture or diagram **7.** $83.50; work backward

Standardized Testing (p. 37)
Answers will vary.

Section 4, Practice and Application (p. 47)
1. $\frac{1}{2}$ **3.** $\frac{4}{12}$ **5. a.** $\frac{3}{8}$ **b.** $\frac{5}{8}$ **c.** 1; the two fractions together represent the whole. **7.** $\frac{4}{3}$, $1\frac{1}{3}$ **9.** $\frac{5}{2}$, $2\frac{1}{2}$ **11.** $\frac{3}{4}$, $\frac{5}{9}$, $\frac{7}{16}$, $\frac{9}{25}$, $\frac{11}{36}$ **13. c.** $\frac{1}{2}$ **d.** Answers will vary. Sample Responses:

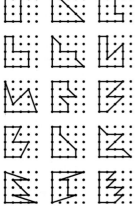

15. The figures are congruent because they have the same size and shape. **17.** The figures are congruent because they have the same size and shape.
21. $1\frac{7}{8}$ **23.** $4\frac{2}{3}$ **25.** $\frac{19}{12}$ **27.** $\frac{8}{3}$ **29.** $\frac{25}{8}$ **31.** $\frac{108}{11}$
32–35.

37. $7\frac{3}{7}$ **39. a.** Let t = the term and n = the term number; $t = \frac{3 \cdot n}{6}$ **b.** $\frac{3}{6}$, 1, $1\frac{3}{6}$, 2, $2\frac{3}{6}$ **c.** 5 more turns
41. b (1.50); Half of a dollar is $0.50.

Spiral Review (p. 51)
44. Add 3 and 2, then multiply the sum by 4.
45. Divide 10 by 2, then add the quotient to 7.
46. Multiply 3 by 2, then subtract the product from 8.
47. $1.55 **48.** 11 postcards and 19 letters **49.** 340
50. 15,900 **51.** 43,890,000

Extra Skill Practice (p. 52)
1. False; The two parts of the triangle are not the same size. **3.** True **5.** $\frac{5}{2}$, $2\frac{1}{2}$ **7.** $3\frac{1}{3}$ **9.** $4\frac{1}{4}$ **11.** $10\frac{1}{2}$ **13.** $\frac{49}{9}$

15. $\frac{24}{7}$ **17.** $2\frac{1}{5}$ **19.** $4\frac{2}{4}$ **21.** $4.50

Standardized Testing (p. 52)

1. a. 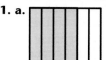 **b.** **c.**

2. $1\frac{3}{9}$, $2\frac{6}{9}$, $3\frac{1}{9}$, $4\frac{4}{9}$; Sample Response: To get the next term, add 4 to the numerator of the previous term and use the same denominator. Then rewrite any improper fractions to mixed numbers or whole numbers.

Section 5, Practice and Application (p. 62)

1. a. $\frac{1}{2}$ **b.** $\frac{4}{8}$ **3.** $\frac{2}{5}$, $\frac{4}{10}$ **5.** $\frac{2}{3}$, $\frac{4}{6}$ **7.** $\frac{1}{3}$, $\frac{2}{6}$ **9. a.** Samples: $\frac{4}{16}$, $\frac{2}{8}$, $\frac{1}{4}$. **b.** 208¢ **c.** $\frac{52}{208}$ **d.** It is equivalent because each stamp has the same value. **11.** 21 **13.** 2 **15.** 9
17. $\frac{10}{15}$, $\frac{12}{18}$, $\frac{14}{21}$ **19.** $\frac{3}{20}$ **21.** $\frac{4}{9}$ **23.** $\frac{2}{3}$ **25.** $\frac{1}{12}$
27. a. $\frac{18}{24}$ **b.** $\frac{9}{12}$; divided both numerator and denominator by 2. **c.** $\frac{3}{4}$; divided the numerator and denominator of $\frac{9}{12}$ by 3. **d.** $\frac{3}{4}$; the fraction is in lowest terms.
29. a. No **b.** Yes **c.** Yes **31.** 15 **33.** 9 **35.** 6 **37.** 15
39. 8 triangles **41.** 14 triangles **43.** pine: 216 grains; grass: 162 grains; oak: 135 grains; cactus: 27 grains
45. about 4

Spiral Review (p. 66)

50. 350, greater than **51.** 14,000, not possible to tell **52.** 1600, not possible to tell **53.** 400, greater than **54.** 4, less than **55.** 7800, less than **56.** 58
57. 480 **58.** 280 **59.** 1200 **60.** The term is 7 times the term number. **61.** 420 **62.** No, the circle is not divided into 4 equal parts. **63.** 135 **64.** 8,497 **65.** 1,293

Extra Skill Practice (p. 67)

1. $\frac{2}{10}$, $\frac{1}{5}$ **3.** $\frac{4}{8}$, $\frac{1}{2}$ **5.** $\frac{8}{18}$, $\frac{12}{27}$, $\frac{16}{36}$ **7.** $\frac{6}{16}$, $\frac{9}{24}$, $\frac{12}{32}$
9. $\frac{2}{12}$, $\frac{3}{18}$, $\frac{4}{24}$ **11.** $\frac{1}{8}$, $\frac{2}{16}$, $\frac{3}{24}$ **13.** $\frac{2}{5}$, $\frac{12}{30}$, $\frac{18}{45}$ **15.** 42
17. 12 **19.** 1 **21.** 120 **23.** $\frac{1}{6}$ **25.** $\frac{1}{5}$ **27.** $\frac{7}{16}$ **29.** $\frac{4}{15}$
31. $\frac{3}{8}$ **33.** 12 **35.** 6 **37.** 24 **39.** 15

Standardized Testing (p. 67)

1. B **2.** B

Review & Assessment (pp. 70–71)

1. 45 **2.** 47 **3.** 6 **4.** 21 **5.** 12 **6.** 19 **7.** about $40 \cdot 70 = 2,800$ **8.** about $250 - 190 = 60$ **9.** about $3,100 + 900 = 4,000$ **10.** about $260 + 30 + 90 = 380$ **11.** about $200 \cdot 10 = 2,000$ **12.** about $3,500 - 2,100 = 1,400$
13. greater than; He rounded $47.98 up and $22.31 down, so he increased the difference.

14. $67 + 143 = 210$
$19 + 31 = 50$
$210 + 50 = 260$
16. $5 \cdot 2 = 10$
$10 \cdot 46 = 460$

15. $4 \cdot 25 = 100$
$7 \cdot 5 = 35$
$100 \cdot 35 = 3,500$
17. $34 + 66 = 100$
$100 + 158 = 258$

18. 176, 173, 170; Start with 188. Subtract 3 from each term to get the next term, or subtract 3 times the term number from 191 to find the term. **19.** 75, 90, 105; The term is 15 times the term number, or start with 15 and add 15 to each term to get the next term.
20.

Term No.	5	6	7
Term	9	10	11

$t = n + 4$ where t = term and n = term number
$t = 50 + 4 = 54$

21.

Term No.	5	6	7
Term	20	24	28

$t = 4n$ where t = term and n = term number
$t = 4(50) = 200$

22.

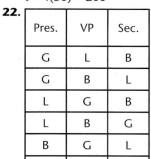

Pres.	VP	Sec.
G	L	B
G	B	L
L	G	B
L	B	G
B	G	L
B	L	G

G = Gail
B = Ben
L = Lita

23. page 130; $130 \cdot 131 = 17,030$ **24.** False; The square is not divided into two equal-sized parts.
25. False; The circle is divided into 4 equal-sized pieces, so $\frac{1}{4}$ of the circle is shaded. **26.** True **27.** 33 **28.** 3
29. 7 **30.** 7 **31.** Answers will vary. $\frac{1}{5}$, $\frac{4}{20}$, $\frac{2}{10}$
32. b and c. Multiplying or dividing both the numerator and denominator of a fraction by the same number yields an equivalent fraction. **33.** $\frac{1}{4}$ **34.** $\frac{3}{4}$ **35.** $\frac{5}{6}$
36. $\frac{3}{8}$ **37.** $\frac{7}{8}$ **38.** 9 **39.** 20 **40.** 50 **41.** 49

Section 1, Practice and Application (p. 81)

1. $\frac{25}{60}$ or $\frac{5}{12}$ **3. a.**

Experimental Probability of Heads
$\frac{4}{10}$ or $\frac{2}{5}$
$\frac{44}{100}$ or $\frac{11}{25}$
$\frac{502}{1000}$ or $\frac{251}{500}$
$\frac{5067}{10000}$

b. 4,933 tails **c.** $\frac{4933}{10000}$ **5. a.** $\frac{8}{25}$ **b.** 17; $\frac{17}{25}$ **c.** The probabilities have a sum of $\frac{8}{25} + \frac{17}{25} = \frac{25}{25}$, or 1. **d.** about 32 $(25 \times 4 = 100, \text{ so } 8 \times 4 = 32)$; about 68 $(100 - 32)$ **7.** Yes, all outcomes have the same chance of occurring because each specific numbered card or face card does not appear more than once. **9. a.** $\frac{11}{66}$ or $\frac{1}{6}$; $\frac{5}{66}$

Spiral Review (p. 83)

12. six ways

Quarters	Dimes	Nickels
1	1	0
1	0	2
0	3	1
0	2	3
0	1	5
0	0	7

13. 25, 29 **14.** 20, 27 **15.** Exercise 13: Begin with 9 as the first term. Add 4 to the previous term to get the next term; Exercise 14: Begin with 2 as the first term, then add 3, then 4, then 5, increasing the amount you add to the previous term by one each time.

Extra Skill Practice (p. 84)

1. $\frac{15}{80}$ or $\frac{3}{16}$ **3.** $\frac{50}{80}$ or $\frac{5}{8}$ **5. a.** {A, I, E, G, D, C, F, H}
b. Yes, each outcome has the same chance of occurring because the circle is divided into equal partitions and each outcome appears on the spinner once.

7. $\frac{0}{8}$ or 0 **9.** $\frac{3}{8}$ **11.** "The spinner stops on B" is impossible since there is no B on the spinner. None are certain.

Study Skills (p. 84)

1–2. Answers will vary.

Section 2, Practice and Application (p. 93)

1. Student scores will vary. 8 days since on the 8th day the snail advances 3 ft and is out of the well before night

when he usually slips back. **3. a.** $C = 2$, $E = 5$, $D = 7$, $G = 1$, $K = 3$ **b.** Multiply 257 by 13 and check your solution. **5. a.** Not correct. This line divides the square into one right triangle and one pentagon. **b.** Correct. The square figure is broken into two three sided polygons that each have a right angle, since the line only affected two of the four right angles in the square. **c.** Not correct. Although there are two right triangles, the figure is not a square. **7.** Answers vary. Sample Response: How many ways can the lower star reach the upper star through left and up moves only? **9. a.** least is 5 games; greatest is 11 games; Explanations will vary. This problem is similar to the first round of the World Cup Problem. **b.** Scores will vary.

Spiral Review (p. 95)

11. 43 **12.** 45 **13.** 36
14.

Term Number	1	2	3	4	5	6
Term in the sequence	5	9	13	17	21	**25**

Begin the first term with 5, then add 4 to obtain each succeeding term.

Extra Skill Practice (p. 96)

1. 2 blocks north; 6 blocks west

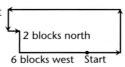
2 blocks north
6 blocks west   Start

3. Sue is the president.

	Pres	VP	Sec	Treas
John	No	Yes	No	No
Sue	Yes	No	No	No
Lisa	No	No	No	Yes
Fernando	No	No	Yes	No

5.

Tables of 4	Tables of 2
7	0
6	2
5	4
4	6
3	8
2	10
1	12
0	14

Standardized Testing (p. 96)

Yes; Each person can carry 31 lb. There are a number of ways to divide the weight. Sample: Caroline carries clothing 10 lb, food 14 lb, first-aid kit 1 lb, camping stove 6 lb. Juanita carries the tent 7 lb, lantern 3 lb, water 15 lb, two sleeping bags 6 lb.

Review & Assessment (pp. 196–197)
1. six and fifty-six hundredths **2.** seven ten-thousandths **3.** one thousand two hundred eight and three tenths **4.** thirty-five and one tenth **5.** one hundred twenty-three thousandths **6.** twenty-five thousand one and five hundredths **7.** five hundred twenty-one and sixty-three hundredths **8.** one and twenty-two thousandths **9.** six hundred and seven hundredths **10.** < **11.** < **12.** = **13.** > **14.** < **15.** = **16.** 500.92 **17.** 11 **18.** 6.103 **19.** 15.17 **20.** 2.212 **21.** 5.217 **22. a.** Max $3.85, Rachel $1.51, Alisha $2.98 **b.** $8.34 **23.** 0, 2, 4, 6, 8 **24.** 0, 5 **25.** 0, 3, 6, 9 **26.** 3 **27.** No; he missed 6 × 18; Sample Response: I tried all the factors from 1 to 11 and checked for each matching factor so that the pairs produce a product of 108. **28.** 12 **29.** 1 **30.** 26 **31.** composite **32.** composite **33.** prime **34.** composite **35.** >; 32 > 25 **36.** =; 4 • 4 • 4 = (2 • 2) • (2 • 2) • (2 • 2) = 64 **37.** <; $3^3 < 3^4$ **38.** 2^5 **39.** 97 **40.** $2^2 \cdot 3 \cdot 5^2$ **41.** 3 • 7 • 11 **42.** Sunday **43.** $\frac{1}{10}$ **44.** $\frac{10}{21}$ **45.** $\frac{5}{18}$ **46.** $\frac{3}{8}$ **47.** $\frac{45}{4}$ or $11\frac{1}{4}$ **48.** $\frac{50}{6}$ or $8\frac{1}{3}$ **49.** $\frac{13}{24}$ **50.** $\frac{29}{10}$ or $2\frac{9}{10}$ **51.** 7 **52.** 34 **53.** 16 **54.** 26 **55.** 0.128 **56.** 1851.3 **57.** 0.0282

MODULE 4

Section 1, Practice and Application (p. 209)
1. a. The bear is an omnivore. **b.** The bear eats both meat and plants. **c.** If a bear is an omnivore and eats both meat and plants, then an omnivore eats both meat and plants. **3.** Horse and pronghorn antelope; Set F **5. a.** Cheetah, Lion, Gray wolf, Coyote, Jaguar **b.** The animals in Set D are carnivores that have a maximum speed greater than or equal to 60 km/hr. **7. a.** meat **b.** Answers will vary. Sample Response: Yes. Carnivores use speed to catch other animals. **9.** Nearest millimeter; measuring to the smaller unit provides a more exact measurement. **11.** millimeter **13.** 7 m **15.** 1 mm **17.** gram or kilogram **19.** 15 kg **21.** 0.5 g **23. a.** 25–30 mm **b.** 2.5–3.0 cm **29.** 0.0034 **31.** 0.07 **33.** 0.0001 **35.** 650 **37.** 2.54 or 2.540 **39.** 720 **41.** Spectacled Bear; Thomson's Gazelle (It is possible for human infants to survive at birth weights as low as those of an infant lion or gorilla.) **43.** > **45.** >

Spiral Review (p. 212)
47. a. 8 **b.** 7 **c.** 20 **48.** 7 **49.** 12 **50.** They were found in both Alberta and Colorado. **51. a.** inside rectangles, but outside rhombuses **b.** inside rhombuses, but outside rectangles **c.** inside the overlap area of rectangles and rhombuses **d.** outside of rectangles and rhombuses, but inside quadrilaterals

Extra Skill Practice (p. 213)
1. Vampire Bat, Pika, Koala, Gorilla, Guinea Pig, Orangutan; Set C **3.** 3 **5.** Set C; chimpanzees live on land and do not have tails **7.** 0.0025 **9.** 348 **11.** 2.93 or 2.930 **13.** 400

Study Skills (p. 213)
1. The example on page 204 shows how to use decimals to record measurements. The example on page 207 shows how to convert a measurement from millimeters to meters. **2. a.** empty set, benchmark, kilometer, meter, centimeter, millimeter, metric ton, kilogram, gram, milligram **b.** Answers will vary. Sample Response: A set with no objects is an empty set.

Section 2, Practice and Application (p. 226)
1. Range: 90 – 72 = 18 **3.** 79 in. and 80 in. **5. a.** Range = 5 **b.**

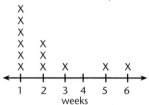

7. Yes; 6 years **9.** Answers vary. Sample Response: They are spread out over a wide range. **11.** Mean = 7; Median = 5; Modes = 5 and 12 **13.** Mean =20; Median = 20; No mode **19. a.** The mode **b.** No; The mode implies Thom will probably get an A. The mean (about 82) and the median (80) are better descriptions of his scores. The teacher will probably use the mean. **21.** 0.73 **23.** 0.83 **25.** 1.13 **27.** 1.75 **29.**

31. 0.396 **33.** 4.3 **35.** 102.34

Spiral Review (p. 229)
38. Royal Albatross; arctic tern **39.** about 225 cm **40.** about 20 cm **41.** $\frac{1}{2}$ **42.** $\frac{19}{10}$ **43.** $\frac{3}{4}$ **44.** $\frac{1}{25}$ **45.** 5 **46.** 53 **47.** 57

Extra Skill Practice (p. 230)
1.   **Average Lifespans of Selected Animals**

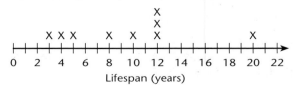

3. 5 **5.** Sample Response: Median, because that is about the center of where the data are clustered and the mean is affected by the extreme (20). **7.** Mean = 4; Median = 4; Mode = 4 **9.** Mean = 345; Median = 283.5; no mode

11. 12.46 **13.** 367.13 **15.** 0.19 **17.** 1.33 **19.** 0.81

Answers will vary. Sample Response: 2 2 3 6 7

Section 3, Practice and Application (p. 241)
1. incorrect; 800 ÷ 4 = 200; 195.8 **3.** incorrect; 21 ÷ 7
= 3; 3.02 **5.** 0.08; 0.6 ÷ 6 = 0.1 **7.** 1.09; 12 ÷ 12 = 1
9. 9.325; 36 ÷ 4 = 9 **11.** 1.3075 cm **13.** 0.875
15. 1.8 **17.** $x + 4 = 8$
21.

$x = 2$
23.

$x = 6$
25. $1973 + y = 1979$ **27.** $m + 2 = 20$; m = number of
existing members **29.** $m + 3 = 17$; m = number of
medals Alice had before **31.** $B - 5.75 = 4.25$;
B = amount of money John had originally **33.** $a = 28$
35. $q = 63$ **37.** $b = 43$ **39.** $x = 1.74$ **41.** $n = 4.5$
43. $n = 3.94$ **45.** no, 0.2 + 6 = 6.2, not 8 **47.** $B - 165 =$
357.49; B = balance before the withdrawal; $522.49
49. $1450.24 + I = 1453.95$; I = interest; $3.71
51. $a = 44.8$; paper and pencil **53.** $y = 291$; paper and
pencil **55.** $s = 5$; mental math

Spiral Review (p. 244)
58. 64 **59.** 13.40 **60.** 3.0 **61.** 0.361 **62.** 2 + 6 > 7; yes
63. 5 + 3 = 8; no **64.** 2 + 13 < 35; no **65.** 0.4 + 0.7
> 1; yes **66.** 21 **67.** 72 **68.** 21 **69.** $\frac{21}{45} = \frac{7}{15}$
70. $\frac{3}{2} = 1\frac{1}{2}$ **71.** $\frac{99}{32} = 3\frac{3}{32}$ **72.** 3, 5 **73.** 2, 3, 5, 9, 10
74. none **75.** 5 **76.** 16 **77.** 11.5 **78. a.** 12 hours
b. Answers will vary; Sample Response: make a table,
guess and check

Extension (p. 245)
79. Remove one [+] tile from each side of the
equation. **81.** Remove two [+] tiles from each side
of the equation. **83.** $n = 1$, check $1 + 1 \overset{?}{=} 2 \cdot 1$, 2 = 2;
$n = 4$, check $4 + 6 \overset{?}{=} 2 + 2 \cdot 4$, 10 = 10; $n = 3$, check
$2 \cdot 3 + 3 \overset{?}{=} 3 \cdot 3$, 9 = 9; $n = 2$, check $2 + 5 \overset{?}{=} 3 + 2 \cdot 2$,
7 = 7

Extra Skill Practice (p. 246)
1. 0.09; 0.5 ÷ 5 = 0.1 **3.** 3.115; 12 ÷ 4 = 3 **5.** 3.454;
27 ÷ 9 = 3 **7.** no, 7.22 **9.** correct **11.** $6 = 1 + n$
13. $53 + b = 85$; b = number of apples Jill's brother
picked **15.** $q = 50$

Standardized Testing (p. 246)
1. B **2.** D

Section 4, Practice and Application (p. 257)
1. 62; 100 **3.** Mean = 84, Median = 86, Mode = 86
5. They represent the integers in the tens place between
the least value and the greatest value in the table. The
0 is included to represent the digit in the tens place of a
one-digit number.
7.   Meat Consumption by Small and
          Medium-Sized Predatory Dinosaurs

0	4
1	9
2	1 1 6 7
3	
4	6 7 8

4 | 8 means 4.8 kg per day

9. 30 years; Answers may vary. Sample Response: The
bar graph because it is easy to see the tallest bar
11. Gray Wolf; Sample Response: The bar graph
because the stem-and-leaf plot doesn't identify individual animals **13.** 15.9 years; Sample Response: The
stem-and-leaf plot because the numbers would have to
be estimated from the bar graph **15.** 60 **17.** 2.8
19. 18.75 **21.** 285.5 **23.** 0.902 **25. a.** 36 × 0.12 =
4.32; yes it is correct **b.** 1.2 × 0.05 = 0.06; it is incorrect
c. 50 × 0.003 = 0.15; it is incorrect **27.** 6.25 lb
29. 5.4 min **31.** (1, 5) **33.** (8, 26)
35–42.

43. a–b.

c. 7, 6 **d.** (2, 2), (5, 8), (7, 12), (8, 14); Sample
Response: For every increase of 1 in the input, the output increases by 2. To find the output for $4\frac{1}{2}$, notice that
$4\frac{1}{2} - 2 = 2\frac{1}{2}$ and $2\frac{1}{2} \cdot 2 = 5$; 2 + 5 = 7.
45. a–b.

c. square

47. a. $2 \cdot t$ **b.** $3 \cdot p$ **c.** $4 \cdot q$ **d.** $2 \cdot t + 3 \cdot p + 4 \cdot q$
49. a. Sample Response:

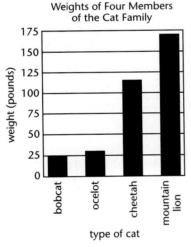

Length of a side (cm)	Area (cm²)	Perimeter (cm)
1	1	4
2	4	8
3	9	12
4	16	16

b. Let s = the length of a side and A = the area. $A = s^2$
c. Let s = the length of a side and P = the perimeter.
$P = 4 \cdot s$

Spiral Review (p. 262)
52. 0.09 **53.** 5.27184 **54.** 9.423 **55.** 3 quarters and
4 dimes **56.** $\frac{13}{8}$; $1\frac{5}{8}$

57. range: 145

Weights of Four Members of the Cat Family

(bar graph: weight (pounds) vs type of cat — bobcat ≈25, ocelot ≈30, cheetah ≈117, mountain lion ≈170)

Extension (p. 262)
59. men: mean: 10.1; median: 10.0; modes: 9.9, 10.0,
and 10.1; women: mean: 11.1, median: 11.1; mode:
11.1 **61.** Sample Response: Because the plots line up
according to stems, you can easily compare the data.
For example, it is clear that the median for the men's
winning times is lower than the median for the women's
winning times and that more men than women had
winning times between 10 sec and 11 sec.

Extra Skill Practice (p. 263)
1. 77 **3.** 2 tests **5.** 70 **7.** 3.4 **9.** 29.35 **11.** 5.7
13. G **15.** A **17.** (5, 0) **19. a.** $t = 18 \cdot x$ where
t = number of T-shirts made and x = hours a machine
runs **b.** 4 hr: 72 T-shirts; 20 hr: 360 T-shirts

Standardized Testing (p. 263)
Sample Response: The product of the divisor and the
quotient equals the dividend. Because the divisor is
between 0 and 1, the product of the divisor and the
quotient is less than the quotient, and therefore the
quotient is greater than the dividend. For example,
$12 \div 0.5 = 24$, and you can see that the quotient, 24, is
greater than the dividend, 12.

Section 5, Practice and Application (p. 271)
1. a.

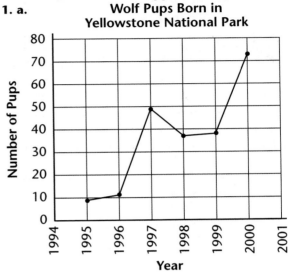

Wolf Pups Born in Yellowstone National Park

b. Sample Response: The number of pups born
increased slightly from 1995 to 1996 and then made
a big jump from 1996 to 1997. From 1997 to 1998,
the number of pups born decreased by about 12 pups
and then increased slightly the next year. The number
increased rapidly from 1999 to 2000. **3. a.** Florida
b. Estimates will vary. Sample responses are given.
Alaska: about 26, California: about 45, Florida: about
47, Kentucky: about 40, Vermont: about 30; Florida
5. Sample responses are given. **a.** No, graph 1 appears
to show this relationship, but in graph 2 the bar for public transit and carpoolers is about one-fifth of the bar for
those that drive alone. **c.** Graph 1; The bars for commuters who carpool or use public transit are longer than the
corresponding bars in graph 2 and in comparison to the
bars for commuters who drive alone. **d.** On graph 1, the
vertical scale goes from 0 to 100 in increments of 10. On
graph 2, the vertical scale goes from 20 to 70 in increments of 5. **7.** Stem-and-leaf plot (A bar graph would
get too crowded for more than 10 contestants)
9. Bar graph; a double bar graph can show the difference between male and female numbers. **11.** Sample
Response: The median; There is no mode and the mean
will be affected by extreme data values. **13.** Sample
Response: The median; The mean is affected by the
extreme values 52 and 61. The mode could be used, but
the mode usually is only used with categorical data.

15. mode; The data are categorical. **17.** mean; The mode has to be a whole number. The median has to be a whole number or the mean of two whole numbers, which would have a 5 in the tenths place.

Spiral Review (p. 274)
19. $\overline{WT}, \overline{TW}$ **20.** $\overrightarrow{CA}$, A ray must be named with its endpoint first. **21.** ∠PAY, ∠YAP, or ∠A **22. a.** $\frac{2}{6}$ or $\frac{1}{3}$ **b.** $\frac{0}{6}$ or 0 **c.** $\frac{4}{6}$ or $\frac{2}{3}$ **d.** $\frac{5}{6}$ **23.** 2 · 2 · 3 · 7

Extra Skill Practice (p. 275)
1. The number of grizzlies being removed was on the rise in the late 60's and early 70's. Then the number dropped drastically after 1972. **3.** Answers will vary. **5.** Answers will vary. Before 1972: mean = 6.25, mode = 3, and median = 5.5; After 1972 the mean, mode and median are all 2.

Standardized Testing (p. 275)
1. median; It is 200 and fairly represents four of the five data values. There is no mode and the mean is affected by the large number of elephants in Laos. **2.** mean; The extreme data value for Laos gives a mean of about 341 elephants. Without that data value the mean for the four countries is about 189.

Review & Assessment (pp. 278–279)
1. 8000 **2.** 23 **3.** 1.3 **4.** 2300 **5.** 500 **6.** 4000 **7.** 42
8. Maximum Speed of Some Yellowstone Park Mammals

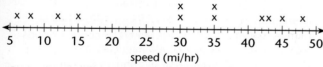
speed (mi/hr)

9. 4 animals **10.** yes, clusters appear from 6 to 15 mi/hr, 30 to 35 mi/hr, and 42 to 48 mi/hr. There is a large gap from 16 to 29. **11. a.** approximately 30–35 mi/hr **b.** approximately 6–15 mi/hr
12. modes = 30 and 35, median = 32.5, mean ≈ 29.1
13. Answers will vary. Sample Response: The median since the data are grouped in three clusters and the median falls in the middle of the middle cluster. There is a large gap between the lower cluster and the rest of the data, and this affects the mean. Since there are two modes, the mode is not an appropriate average to use for the data. **14.** 3.505 **15.** 19.705 **16.** 0.7
17. Sample: b + 45 = 315; b = number of baseball cards Jon had before the purchase. **18.** d = 51 **19.** f = 22
20. k = 4.7 **21.** s = 5.55 **22.** x = 7.9 **23.** w = 21
24. 1181.1 **25.** 0.97888 **26.** 1.224 **27.** 91 cm
28. 30 cm **29.** median: 79.5 cm; modes: 77 cm and 86 cm

30. a–b.
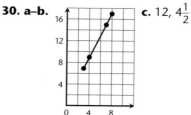
c. 12, $4\frac{1}{2}$

31. Graph 2 is easier to read. It clearly shows that there were two years (1983 and 1988) when cereal production was less than 1.8 billion metric tons and two years (1985 and 1986) when production was greater than 1.8 billion metric tons. So the median is the mean of the production in 1984 and 1987 which appears to be about 1.8 billion metric tons. **32.** Graph 1; The line appears almost flat, indicating very little change.
33. The scale on the vertical axis was changed so it started at 1600 (instead of 0) and was divided into increments of 50 (instead of 350).

MODULE 5

Section 1, Practice and Application (p. 291)
1. No; The sections of the strip are not equal in length. **3.** $\frac{2}{4} = \frac{1}{2}$ **5.** $\frac{5}{12} < \frac{1}{2}$ **7.** $\frac{2}{3}, \frac{9}{10}, \frac{49}{50}, \frac{99}{100}$ **9.** >
11. > **13.** > **17.** < **19.** > **21.** = **23.** > **25.** > **27.** >
29. Trinja

Spiral Review (p. 293)
33. $5\frac{1}{2}$ **34.** $2\frac{3}{12}$ **35.** $4\frac{3}{7}$ **36.** $4\frac{1}{3}$
37.   Daily High Temperatures
          in a Midwest City in July

```
 5 | 6 9
 6 | 1 4 8 9 9
 7 | 1 2 2 7 7 8 8 8 8
 8 | 0 2 2 2 4 5 5 7 7 9
 9 | 0 1 1 8
10 | 1
```

          7 | 1 means 71 degrees Fahrenheit

Extension (p. 293)
39. $\frac{1}{2}$ **41.** $\frac{1}{2}$

Extra Skill Practice (p. 294)
1. > **3.** > **5.** > **7.** > **9.** < **11.** > **13.** < **15.** > **17.** <
19. < **21.** <

Study Skills (p. 294)
1. Pages 287–288

Section 2, Practice and Application (p. 302)
1. Sample Response: about 6 in. **3.** Sample Response: about 2 ft **5.** Sample Response: an unsharpened pencil

7. Sample Response: the length of my living room
9. feet **11.** inches **13. a.** $1\frac{1}{2}$ in. **b.** $1\frac{2}{4}$ in. **c.** $1\frac{3}{8}$ in.

15. 198 **17.** $4\frac{1}{2}$ **19.** 99 **21.** $\frac{2}{3}$ yd **23.** $\frac{18}{36}$ yd or $\frac{1}{2}$ yd

25. 6 yd 2 ft 1 in. **27.** 1 mi 1198 yd **29.** 1 yd 1 ft 10 in.
31. 7 yd 1 ft

Spiral Review (p. 305)
34. < **35.** < **36.** > **37.** 10 ways. (2 quarters; 1 quarter
2 dimes 1 nickel; 1 quarter 1 dime 3 nickels; 1 quarter
5 nickels; 5 dimes; 4 dimes 2 nickels; 3 dimes 4 nickels;
2 dimes 6 nickels; 1 dime 8 nickels; 10 nickels)

Extra Skill Practice (p. 306)
1. 2 in. **3.** $1\frac{3}{4}$ in. **5.** 27 **7.** $4\frac{1}{6}$ **9.** $\frac{1}{2}$ **11.** $11\frac{1}{4}$
13. 180 **15.** $\frac{2}{3}$ **17.** 5 yd 1 ft 7 in. **19.** 2 ft **21.** 11 yd
2 ft **23.** 1 mi 71 yd **25.** 2 yd 1 in.

Standardized Testing (p. 306)
Sample Response: To measure 1 in., place the longest
strip on top of the midsize strip with the left ends meet-
ing. Mark the right end of the midsize strip on the longest strip. The mark will be 2 in. from the end. Fold the
2 in. strip in half. You now have a 1 in. measure. You can
use it to mark off a 3 in. piece or any combination that
adds to 3 in. to overlap the strips. The total length will
be 3 ft 2 in. + 2 ft 9 in. + 3 ft 4 in. − 3 in. = 3 yd.

Section 3, Practice and Application (p. 313)
1. $\frac{7}{9}$ **3.** $\frac{21}{20} = 1\frac{1}{20}$ **5.** $\frac{7}{9}$ **7.** $\frac{4}{7}$ **9.** $\frac{1}{8}$ **11.** $\frac{7}{45}$ **13. a.** $\frac{3}{2}$ or
$1\frac{1}{2}$ **b.** $\frac{5}{16}$ **c.** $\frac{11}{24}$ **15. a.** Subtract $\frac{1}{3}$ from each side of the
equation. To do this you would need to rewrite $\frac{1}{3}$ as $\frac{7}{21}$
and $\frac{5}{7}$ as $\frac{15}{21}$. **b.** $\frac{8}{21}$

Spiral Review (p. 315)
20. $1\frac{3}{4}$ **21.** 3520 **22.** $5\frac{1}{3}$ **23.** 2 yd 1 ft 6 in.
24. 3 mi 1320 yd 2 ft **25.** 2 yd 2 ft 7 in. **26. a.** 4 **b.** 8
c. 3 **d.** 9 **e.** 1 **27.** 35 **28.** 85 **29.** 49 **30.** 83 **31.** 9
32. 12 **33.** 37 **34.** 153 **35.** 15 **36.** 23

Extra Skill Practice (p. 316)
1. $\frac{7}{15}$ **3.** $\frac{17}{18}$ **5.** $\frac{35}{33} = 1\frac{2}{33}$ **7.** $\frac{11}{13}$ **9.** $\frac{2}{5}$ **11.** $\frac{9}{28}$
13. $\frac{37}{30} = 1\frac{7}{30}$ **15.** $\frac{11}{12}$ **17.** $\frac{7}{6} = 1\frac{1}{6}$ **19.** $\frac{27}{20} = 1\frac{7}{20}$
21. $\frac{139}{126} = 1\frac{13}{126}$ **23.** $\frac{59}{90}$ **25.** $\frac{13}{8} = 1\frac{5}{8}$ **27.** $\frac{7}{12}$

Standardized Testing (p. 316)
1–2. Answers will vary.

Section 4, Practice and Application (p. 325)
1. about 10 **3.** about 5 **5.** $10\frac{1}{6}$ **7.** $8\frac{23}{24}$ **9.** $5\frac{13}{18}$
11. $8\frac{4}{5} + 1\frac{1}{5} = 10$ and $4\frac{3}{8} + 2\frac{5}{8} = 7$; $10 + 7 + 6\frac{1}{3} = 23\frac{1}{3}$

13. a. $3\frac{3}{8}$ is closer to $3\frac{1}{2}$ than to 3. **b.** high; Both numbers were rounded up. **c.** $8\frac{7}{40}$; The sum is lower than the
estimate. **15.** $1\frac{3}{20}$ **17.** $\frac{3}{8}$ **19.** $7\frac{6}{11}$ **21.** $3\frac{2}{3}$; $3\frac{1}{3} + \frac{2}{3} = 4$,
so $3\frac{1}{3} + 3\frac{2}{3} = 7$ **23.** $1\frac{3}{4}$; $1\frac{1}{4} + \frac{3}{4} = 2$, so $1\frac{1}{4} + 1\frac{3}{4} = 3$
25. a. Sharon; $\frac{1}{4}$ in. **b.** $3\frac{1}{8}$ in. **27.** $2\frac{1}{4}$ ft **29.** $1\frac{1}{4}$ in.

Spiral Review (p. 328)
32. $\frac{9}{25}$ **33.** $\frac{1}{12}$ **34.** $\frac{41}{30}$ or $1\frac{11}{30}$ **35.** 0.52 **36.** 0.57
37. 0.63 **38.** $2 \times 3^2 \times 7$ **39.** 2×7^2 **40.** $3^2 \times 17$
41. neither **42.** impossible **43.** certain **44.** 9 **45.** 6
46. 40

Extension (p. 328)
47. a. $4{:}16 - 1{:}37 = 3{:}76 - 1{:}37 = 2{:}39$; 2 hr 39 min
b. Sample Response: The regrouping is the same
because I had to change a whole (1 hour) into parts
(60 minutes). The regrouping is different because the
parts (minutes) can be represented by whole numbers.

Extra Skill Practice (p. 329)
1. $8\frac{1}{4}$ **3.** $10\frac{1}{10}$ **5.** $4\frac{7}{60}$ **7.** $2\frac{1}{18}$ **9.** $4\frac{17}{28}$ **11.** $8\frac{11}{18}$
13. $3\frac{1}{4}$ **15.** $2\frac{5}{16}$ **17.** $18\frac{1}{2}$ **19.** $16\frac{5}{6}$ **21.** $\frac{17}{20}$ **23.** $2\frac{43}{45}$

Standardized Testing (p. 329)
1. D **2.** E

Section 5, Practice and Application (p. 340)
1. Answers will vary. **3.** 9 **5.** 2394 **7.** 1,000,000;
1 km = 1000 m, so 1 km^2 = 1 km • 1 km =
1000 m • 1000 m = 1,000,000 m^2 **9.** 20 cm^2
11. 2600 yd^2 **13.** Answers will vary. E: 12.5 cm^2;
F: 3.38 cm^2; G: 5.2 cm^2; H: 5.46 cm^2 **15. d.** Yes; They
represent the area of the same figure. **17.** 120 cm^2
19. $24 = \frac{1}{2} \cdot 8 \cdot h$; 6 ft **21.** $14 = 2 + 3 + 3 + 2 + x$; 4
in. **23.** 4 **25.** 32
27. Sample Response:

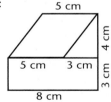

Spiral Review (p. 342)
30. 17.7 **31.** $\frac{5}{24}$ **32.** 4.2
33. a.

Input	2	5	6	10
Output	1	7	9	17

b. (2, 1), (5, 7), (6, 9), (10, 17)

33. c.

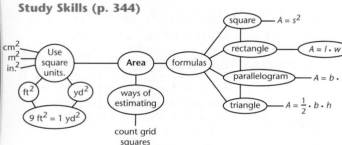

d. 2.5

Extension (p. 343)
37. a. 16 cm²; Sample Response: I estimated the average width at about 2 cm and the length at about 8 cm and multiplied. **b.** 40,000 km² **c.** about 64,000 km²

Extra Skill Practice (p. 344)
1. 24,192 **3.** $\frac{2}{3}$ **5.** $40\frac{1}{2}$ **7.** 916.8 mm² **9.** $22\frac{3}{4}$ cm²

11. 80 cm² **13.** $148 = 34 + 34 + 58 + x$; $x = 22$ in.
15. $12.5 = 2.5 \cdot h$; $h = 5$ ft

Study Skills (p. 344)

square — $A = s^2$

cm²
m²
in.² — Use square units.

ft²   yd²

$9\ ft^2 = 1\ yd^2$

Area — formulas

rectangle — $A = l \cdot w$

parallelogram — $A = b \cdot h$

triangle — $A = \frac{1}{2} \cdot b \cdot h$

ways of estimating

count grid squares

Section 6, Practice and Application (p. 353)
1. $\frac{1}{10}$ **3.** $\frac{3}{2}$ **5.** 3 **7.** 2 **9.** $13\frac{1}{3}$ **11.** 3 **13.** $1\frac{1}{8}$ **15. a.** 13 pieces **b.** Yes, $\frac{1}{3}$ of a piece **17.** $2\frac{2}{9}$ **19.** $2\frac{1}{6}$ **21.** $1\frac{1}{4}$

23. 9 **25.** 1 **27. a.** $-\frac{15}{16}$ **b.** Monday - 96; Tuesday - 105

29. a. less than; Sample Response: $2 \cdot 6 = 12$ and $\frac{3}{4} > \frac{1}{2}$, so $2 \cdot 6\frac{3}{4} > 13$ **b.** $1\frac{23}{27}$

Spiral Review (p. 355)
32. 21 **33.** $20\frac{2}{5}$ **34.** $1\frac{1}{6}$ **35.** (4, 6) **36.** (1, 3) **37.** (6, 0)
38. 14 **39.** 15 **40.** 5

Extra Skill Practice (p. 356)
1. 6 **3.** $\frac{1}{32}$ **5.** 6 **7.** 9 **9.** $4\frac{1}{2}$ **11.** $3\frac{1}{7}$ **13.** $4\frac{5}{32}$ **15.** $3\frac{3}{5}$

17. $1\frac{1}{2}$ **19.** $9\frac{1}{3}$ **21.** $2\frac{1}{4}$ **23.** $\frac{12}{23}$ **25.** $\frac{1}{20}$ **27.** 16

29. $\frac{9}{16}$

Standardized Testing (p. 356)
C

Review & Assessment (pp. 360–361)
1. $\frac{3}{100}$, $\frac{4}{7}$, $\frac{2}{3}$, $\frac{5}{3}$ **2.** $\frac{4}{5}$, $\frac{9}{10}$, $\frac{19}{20}$, $\frac{99}{100}$ **3.** $\frac{1}{7}$, $\frac{1}{4}$, $\frac{4}{5}$, $\frac{7}{8}$
4. $\frac{1}{4}$, $\frac{1}{2}$, $\frac{2}{3}$, $\frac{5}{6}$ **5.** $\frac{5}{8} > \frac{7}{12}$ **6.** $\frac{4}{9} > \frac{6}{15}$ **7.** $\frac{11}{16} < \frac{3}{4}$ **8.** $\frac{8}{13} < \frac{2}{3}$
9. $0.73 > 0.69$ **10.** $0.56 < 0.66$ **11.** $0.47 > 0.43$

12. 126 **13.** $2\frac{5}{6}$ **14.** $1\frac{3}{22}$ **15.** $8\frac{2}{3}$ **16.** 63 **17.** 6030

18. $\frac{3}{2}$ or $1\frac{1}{2}$ **19.** $\frac{19}{21}$ **20.** $3\frac{7}{15}$ or $\frac{52}{15}$ **21.** $7\frac{7}{24}$ or $\frac{175}{24}$

22. $9\frac{33}{40}$ or $\frac{393}{40}$ **23.** $6\frac{1}{2}$ or $\frac{13}{2}$ **24.** $\frac{3}{8}$ **25.** $6\frac{1}{15}$ or $\frac{91}{15}$

26. $2\frac{3}{5}$ or $\frac{13}{5}$ **27.** $\frac{13}{24}$ **28.** $2\frac{1}{12}$ or $\frac{25}{12}$ **29.** $\frac{39}{40}$

30. $23\frac{1}{6}$ hours **31.** $6\frac{1}{4}$ **32.** $8\frac{1}{2}$ **33.** $5\frac{15}{16}$ **34.** $1\frac{1}{4}$

35. $1\frac{1}{6}$ mi **36.** rectangle; triangle; parallelogram

37. Answers will vary.
rectangle: base = 4.2 cm
      height = 2.5 cm
      area ≈ 10.5 cm²
triangle: base = 9.2 cm
      height = 2.4 cm
      area ≈ 11.0 cm²
parallelogram: base = 5.3 cm
      height = 3.4 cm
      area ≈ 18.0 cm²

38. $9h = 54$; $h = 6$ ft **39.** $\frac{1}{2} \cdot 5b = 19$; $b = 7.6$ cm

40. $x = 12$ **41.** $m = 18$ **42.** $x = 48$ **43.** $\frac{14}{9}$ or $1\frac{5}{9}$ **44.** 24

45. $\frac{7}{5}$ or $1\frac{2}{5}$ **46.** $\frac{19}{24}$ **47.** $\frac{9}{8}$ or $1\frac{1}{8}$ **48.** $\frac{4}{9}$ **49.** $1\frac{43}{56}$ **50.** $\frac{13}{24}$

51. 10 pieces; $8 \div \frac{3}{4} = \frac{32}{3} = 10\frac{2}{3}$.

MODULE 6

Section 1, Practice and Application (p. 369)
1. yes **3.** no **5.** no **7.** Team B **9. a.** 24 **b.** 6

11. a. 3 to 30 **b.** 20 to 6 **13. a.** 3:1, 3 to 1, $\frac{3}{1}$

b. 27 steps **c.** 4 steps **15.** Sample Response: If you were only one inch tall, you couldn't ride a bike. And climbing into your bed would be a terrifying hike. You never could play basketball, Or safely stroll around the mall. A summer walk would take till fall, If you were one inch tall.

Spiral Review (p. 371)
18. $\frac{48}{5}$ or $9\frac{3}{5}$ **19.** $\frac{7}{6}$ or $1\frac{1}{6}$ **20.** $\frac{112}{5}$ or $22\frac{2}{5}$ **21.** 0.8

22. 0.0524 **23.** 87.2 **24.** 0.027 **25.** 9 **26.** 0.608
27. 3 **28.** 5 **29.** 20

Extra Skill Practice (p. 372)

1. 256 to 120, 256:120, $\frac{256}{120}$ **3.** 37 to 183, 37:183, $\frac{37}{183}$
5. 4 forks, 8 spoons **7.** yes **9.** no **11.** no

Study Skills (p. 372)

1. A ratio is a type of comparison of two numbers or measures. **2.** "8:12" is read "the ratio of 8 to 12." **3.** 1 m equals 100 cm or 1000 mm. **4.** The book covers both customary and metric measurement, including length, area, volume, and capacity.

Section 2, Practice and Application (p. 377)

1. Yes **3.** Yes **5.** No **7.** Yes **9.** $3/hr **11.** 1.5 ft per step **13.** $3\frac{2}{5}$ pages per min **15.** $3.80 for 10 pens; Those pens cost $.38 apiece, while the other pens cost $.44 apiece. **17.** 900 mi; 54,000 mi **19.** $20

Spiral Review (p. 379)

22. 0.83 **23.** 0.52 **24.** 0.73 **25.** 0.72 **26.** mean: 80; median: 80; modes: 80 and 86 **27.** mean: $58\frac{5}{6}$; median: 50; mode: 48

Extra Skill Practice (p. 380)

1. Yes **3.** Yes **5.** 8 km/hr **7.** $7.50 per book **9.** 28 mi/gal **11.** $5.76 for 12 oranges **13. a.** about 360 mi **b.** about 21,600 mi

Standardized Testing (p. 380)

1. a. warm air **b.** 82 ft/sec **2.** 16,530 ft

Section 3, Practice and Application (p. 390)

1. a. thumb: about 10 cm; neck: about 40 cm; waist: about 80 cm **b.** Collar could be 41 cm and wrist 21 cm. Students should note that shirt openings equal to the measures of Gulliver's neck (40 cm) and wrist (20 cm) would be uncomfortably tight.

41 cm

21 cm

3. 0.78 **5.** 0.29 **7. a.** about 162 cm **b.** about 184 cm **c.** No; The estimated heights vary too greatly.
9. $\frac{3}{10}$ **11.** $\frac{3}{5}$ **13. a.** $\frac{4}{5}$ **b.** about 4 ft **c.** about 35 in.
15. a. 88 : 96 **b.** $\frac{9}{10}$ **c.** 69 : 76 **d.** $\frac{9}{10}$ **e.** They are close. The nice fractions are the same. **f.** 69 : 88 ≈ 0.78, 76 : 96 ≈ 0.79; The ratios are very close.

17. a. Sample graph:
b. about 16 pages
c. about 25 pages

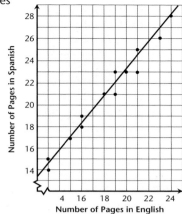

Number of Pages in English Compared to Number of Pages in Spanish

Number of Pages in English (x-axis), *Number of Pages in Spanish* (y-axis)

19. a. about 1 ft

Spiral Review (p. 393)

21. 33 mi/gal **22.** about $2.83 per lb **23.** 53 heartbeats per min **24.** $\frac{14}{30} = \frac{7}{15}$

Extra Skill Practice (p. 394)

1. a. A: 0.74, B: 0.74, C: 0.74, D: 0.76, E: 0.75, F: 0.74, G: 0.75, H: 0.73 **b.** about 0.74 **c.** $\frac{3}{4}$
d.

Kneeling height (cm)	94	**99**	**105**	87
Standing height (cm)	**125**	132	140	**116**

Standardized Testing (p. 394)

Answers will vary.

Section 4, Practice and Application (p. 402)

1. $\frac{15}{60}$, $\frac{75}{300}$, and $\frac{3.5}{14}$; $\frac{24}{32}$ and $\frac{21}{28}$ **3.** 20 **5.** 8 **7.** 1.8
9. 12 **11.** 5 **13. b.** $\frac{1 \text{ mi}}{20 \text{ min}} = \frac{3.2 \text{ mi}}{x}$ **c.** 64 min
15. a. $\frac{5}{24}$ **b.** about 13 times **17.** 72 steps

Spiral Review (p. 404)

19. a. $\frac{1}{4}$ **b.** about 15 in. **20.**

21. **22.** **23.**

24.

Extra Skill Practice (p. 405)

1. Yes **3.** No **5.** 48 **7.** 39 **9.** 2 **11.** 4 **13.** $2.70
15. $6\frac{2}{3}$ yd

1. D. II and IV **2.** B. II only

Section 5, Practice and Application (p. 414)

1.

$\overline{AC}$	corresponds to	$\overline{FE}$
$\overline{AB}$	corresponds to	$\overline{FD}$
$\overline{CB}$	corresponds to	$\overline{ED}$
$\angle A$	corresponds to	$\angle F$
$\angle B$	corresponds to	$\angle D$
$\angle C$	corresponds to	$\angle E$

3. similar and congruent; Corresponding angles have the same measure and corresponding sides have the same length. **5.** similar but not congruent; Corresponding angles have the same measure and the ratios of the lengths of corresponding sides are equivalent but not 1:1. **7. a.** F **b.** 6:2 or 3:1
9. Sample Responses:
a.

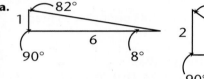 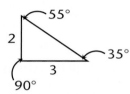

b. These two right triangles only have one pair of congruent angles, the right angles; the ratio of the lengths of the shorter legs is 1:2 and the ratio of the lengths of the longer legs is 2:1. Since the corresponding angles of the triangles are not congruent and the ratios of the lengths of the corresponding sides are not equivalent, the triangles are not similar. **11.** $DE = 2.5$, $DF = 2$
13. 60 ft **15.** 4.5 ft **17. a.** about 1 ft: 16.3 ft
b. about 3.7 ft long and about 2.5 ft wide **19.** 400 mi
21. 240 mi

Spiral Review (p. 417)

23. no **24.** yes **25.** yes **26.** $3\frac{3}{5}$ **27.** 288 **28.** $8\frac{5}{6}$
29. 0.4 **30.** 0.3 **31.** 0.75 **32.** 0.5

Career Connection (p. 417)
33. a. 1 cm = 132 km **b.** about 66 km

Extra Skill Practice (p. 418)
1. similar **3.** 32.4 cm **5.** 48 in. **7.** 80 ft

Standardized Testing (p. 418)
1. The ratio of lengths along the bottoms of the parallelograms is 2 to 4 (or 1 to 2), yet along the sides the ratio is 1 to 3.

2. Sample responses:

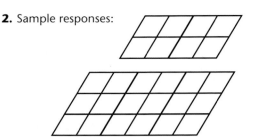

Section 6, Practice and Application (p. 429)
1. a. 1% 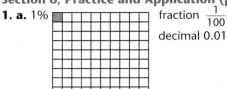 fraction $\frac{1}{100}$ decimal 0.01

b. 10% 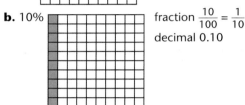 fraction $\frac{10}{100} = \frac{1}{10}$ decimal 0.10

c. 25% 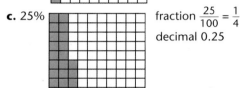 fraction $\frac{25}{100} = \frac{1}{4}$ decimal 0.25

d. 46% 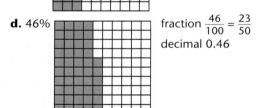 fraction $\frac{46}{100} = \frac{23}{50}$ decimal 0.46

e. 67% 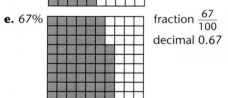 fraction $\frac{67}{100}$ decimal 0.67

f. 100% 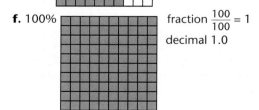 fraction $\frac{100}{100} = 1$ decimal 1.0

3. $\frac{54}{100}$ or $\frac{27}{50}$; 0.54 **5.** $\frac{99}{100}$; 0.99 **7.** $\frac{37}{100}$; 37%
9. $\frac{59}{100}$; 59% **11.** 0.03, 3% **13.** 0.85, 85% **15.** < **17.** >
19. > **21.** 50, 25, 12.5, 12.5 **23.** 21 **25.** 19

27. 31.5 **29.** 90 wins **31.** about 50% **33.** about 90%

Spiral Review (p. 431)
38. ∠A and ∠G, ∠D and ∠F, ∠C and ∠E, ∠B and ∠H;
$\overline{AD}$ and $\overline{GF}$, $\overline{DC}$ and $\overline{FE}$, $\overline{CB}$ and $\overline{EH}$, $\overline{BA}$ and $\overline{HG}$ **39.** B
40. A

Extra Skill Practice (p. 432)
1. 35%, $\frac{35}{100}$ or $\frac{7}{20}$ **3.** 60%, $\frac{60}{100}$ or $\frac{3}{5}$ **5.** 0.07, 7%
7. 0.9, 90% **9.** < **11.** < **13.** = **15.** 18 **17.** 9.1 **19.** 3
21. about $33\frac{1}{3}$% **23.** about 20% **25.** about 40
27. about 45

Standardized Testing (p. 432)
1. B **2.** C **3.** D

Review & Assessment (pp. 436–437)
1. 8 to 6, 8:6, $\frac{8}{6}$ **2.** 6 to 10, 6:10, $\frac{6}{10}$ **3.** no **4.** yes
5. yes
6. a.

Length (feet)	1	2	3	4
Cost (dollars)	6	12	18	24

b. $30
c. 15 ft

7. a.
4 m / 7 m ; 4 m / 1 m ; 5 m / 6 m
b. $\frac{4}{7} \approx 0.57$, $\frac{1}{4} = 0.25$, $\frac{5}{6} \approx 0.83$ **c.** Sample Response: The
closer the decimal is to 1, the closer the rectangle is to a
square. **8.** I drew a fitted line for the scatter plot, and I
used the line to make my estimates.

Latitude (°N)	25	40	44	57
Temperature (°F)	65	37	25	5

9. x = 15 **10.** y = 6 **11.** z = 126 **12.** 50 m **13.** Not
appropriate; It is not reasonable to assume that the ratio
of a car's mileage to its speed is always the same.
14. 5 ft **15.** 0.6, 60% **16.** 0.32, 32% **17.** 0.45, 45%
18. 0.69, 69% **19.** 21 **20.** 65 **21.** 24.5 **22.** about 90%
23. a. 25.2% $\approx \frac{1}{4}$, 17.5% $\approx \frac{1}{5}$, 5% $= \frac{1}{20}$, 34.8% $\approx \frac{7}{20}$
b. 17,500 tickets **c.** 18°

MODULE 7

Section 1, Practice and Application (p. 448)
1. No, there are no parallel faces. **3.** Yes; right triangular
prism **5.** B **7.** A: right hexagonal prism; C: right square
prism (or cube) **9.** Yes; It is a square or rectangular
prism. **11.** 6 edges **15.** 12 cm³ **17.** 60 cm³
19. 30 cm³ **21.** $\frac{3}{64}$ in.³ **23.** 0.42 cm³ **25.** The height
of a right prism is equal to the length of an edge joining
corresponding vertices of the bases; When the prism is
oblique. **27.** 20 cm² **29.** top tank holds about 18.7 gal,
no; bottom tank holds about 28.1 gal, yes

Spiral Review (p. 450)
33. Area = 14 cm² **34.** $1.60

Extra Skill Practice (p. 451)
1. Yes; Possible responses: rectangles; oblique rectangular prism parallelograms; a right prism with parallelogram shaped bases **3.** Yes; octagons; right octagonal
prism **5.** 10,000 m³ **7.** 3 yd **9.** 2268 cm³

Standardized Testing (p. 451)
D

Section 2, Practice and Application (p. 456)
1. ton **3.** pound **5.** Sample: 30 quarters **7.** 6 **9.** 2
11. 11,000 **13.** 2 lb 8 oz **15. a.** (Ex 13) about $4.50,
since 2 lb 8 oz = $2\frac{1}{2}$ lb and $2\frac{1}{2} \cdot 1.8 = 4.50$;
(Ex 14) about $3.00, since 4 lb 4 oz = $4\frac{1}{4}$ lb and
$4\frac{1}{4} \cdot 0.70 \approx 3.00$ **b.** (Ex 13) actual cost: $4.48; (Ex 14)
actual cost: $2.93 **17. a.** 352 oz **b.** $242,880

Spiral Review (p. 458)
20. 4.5 cm **21.** 25 cm² **22.** Sample Response:
2 cm × 15 cm × 2 cm; 6 cm × 2 cm × 5 cm
23. f = 3 · y

Career Connection (p. 458)
25. Yes; She has gained 42 oz in about 42 days.

Extra Skill Practice (p. 459)
1. ounce **3.** ton **5.** ounce or pound **7.** pound **9.** 2
11. 3.5 **13.** $\frac{5}{8}$ **15.** 64,000 **17.** 68 **19.** = **21.** > **23.** >
25. <

Standardized Testing (p. 459)
1. Yes; The total weight is 13,800 lb which is less than
7 tons (14,000 lb). **2.** greatest: 54 oz; least: 9.5 oz; The
melon and the soup can weigh 54 oz together. The golf
ball and apple weigh 9.5 oz together.

Section 3, Practice and Application (p. 467)
1. $\overline{OA}$, $\overline{OB}$, $\overline{OD}$ **3.** $\overline{AD}$, $\overline{BE}$ **7. a.** a circle with a radius of
100 km (All of the points 100 km from Station 1.)
b. These are the points that are 100 km from Station 1
and 300 km from Station 2, so they are the possible
locations for the epicenter. **c.** Use the distance of the
epicenter from a third reporting station to draw a third
circle. The point of intersection of all 3 circles is the position of the epicenter. **d.** The epicenter of the earthquake
was located in the Philippine Islands at approximately
8° N, 127° E. (See Labsheet 3B.) **9.** 15.7 cm **11.** 22 cm
13. 5 mm **15.** $\frac{1}{2}$, $\frac{1}{3}$

Spiral Review (p. 469)

19. $3\frac{3}{8}$ lb **20.** 5500 lb **21.** $2\frac{3}{16}$ lb **22.** 15,000 lb
23. the median; The mean is affected by the score of 38 which is unusually low in comparison to the other scores. There is no mode. **24.** $n = 9$ **25.** $n = 16$
26. $n = 1$ **27.** $n = 3$

Extension (p. 469)
29. Answers will vary.

Extra Skill Practice (p. 470)
1. $\overline{AD}$, $\overline{FC}$ **3.** $\overline{OA}$, $\overline{OF}$, $\overline{OD}$, $\overline{OC}$ **5.** 15.7 cm **7.** 35,482 m
9. 84.97 ft **11.** 3.50 m **13.** 194.68 in. **15.** 28 cm

Standardized Testing (p. 470)
1. C **2.** A

Section 4, Practice and Application (p. 478)
1. 19.63 in.² **3.** 13.85 m² **5.** 7.07 in.² **7.** 625π mm²
9. 21.16π cm² **11.** about 153.86 cm²
15. 452.16 m³ **17.** 75.36 in.³ **19.** 183.12 m³

Spiral Review (p. 480)
23. 40.82 ft **24.** 37.68 in. **25.** 14.13 m **26.** $\frac{2}{5}$, 0.4
27. $\frac{9}{100}$, 0.09 **28.** $\frac{3}{20}$, 0.15 **29.** $\frac{63}{100}$, 0.63
30–33.

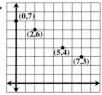

Extension (p. 480)
35. b. 3 cones of rice **37.** 2009.60 cm³ **39.** 11.78 in.³

Extra Skill Practice (p. 481)
1. 2171.91 mm² **3.** 0.79 ft² **5.** 600.25π yd²
7. 137,858.56 ft³ **9.** 144,691.2 in.³ **11.** 22.1 ft³

Standardized Testing (p. 481)
No; about 63.59 cm³ more sand is needed.

Section 5, Practice and Application (p. 490)
1. Sample Response: light weight clothing such as long pants and a shirt; tennis, jogging, hiking; It is warm but not hot. **3.** Sample Response: heavy clothing such as a winter coat, hat, scarf, gloves, boots; ice skating, skiing; It is quite cold. **5.** Sample Response: –60°F or –50°C
7. a. The number of degrees is the same. **b.** One is negative and one is positive. **9.** 25°F; 12°F; 30°F
11. –349 **13.** 10 **15.** <. **17.** >
19. Sample Response:

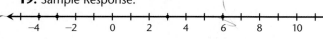

21. –60 **25. b.** Answers will vary.

Spiral Review (p. 492)
28. 28.26 in.² **29.** 200.96 cm² **30.** 9.62 m²
35. Sample Response: I would use estimation. I could round $2.29 up to $2.50 and 1.7 up to 2. Then 2 · $2.50 = $5. Since both numbers are rounded up, I know the estimate is higher than the actual cost and I have enough money.

Extra Skill Practice (p. 493)
1. Sample Response: 41°F or 5°C **3.** Sample Response: 59°F or 15°C **5.** < **7.** < **9.** > **11.** H
12–19.

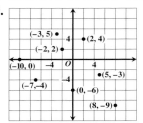

Standardized Testing (p. 493)
1. Sample Response: I would prefer 32°C because it is hot enough to go swimming. **2.** Sample Responses: $x < 0$, $x > –10$

Review & Assessment (pp. 496–497)
1. a. Answers will vary. an oblique pentagonal prism
2. a. two of the faces are pentagons, five are parallelograms of which one is a rectangle **b.** an oblique pentagonal prism **3.** 7 faces, 10 vertices, 15 edges
4. a. area of the pentagonal base = 20 mm · 18 mm + $\frac{1}{2}$ (20 mm · 17 mm) = 530 mm², height of the prism = 37 mm **b.** 19,610 mm³ **5.** The exact volume is 643.5 in.³ **6. a.** $.71 per pound **b.** about 9 apples **7.** 48
8. 5 **9.** $1\frac{3}{4}$ **10. a.** O **b.** any two of $\overline{OE}$, $\overline{OB}$, and $\overline{OD}$
c. $\overline{AE}$, $\overline{BE}$ **d.** $\overline{BE}$ **11.** 2.5 cm **12. a.** about 15.7 cm
b. about 19.6 cm² **13.** 10,597.5 ft³ **14.** warmer; 83°F; The difference between 33° below 0 and 50° above 0 on the Fahrenheit scale is 83 degrees. **15.** < **16.** < **17.** >
18. a–b.

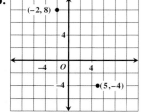

MODULE 8

Section 1, Practice and Application (p. 507)
1. D **3.** C **5.** E **7.** 22 **9.** 5 **11.** 3 **13. a.** 200,000 glasses **b.** 100,000 lb **c.** It would double the number of

glasses to 400,000 and the number of pounds the boat can support to 200,000. **15.** It has grown by more than $1\frac{1}{2}$ cups of soda. **17.** 20 mL, 0.02 L **19.** 1045.5 mL, 1.0455 L **21.** 1.8 **23.** 0.892 **25.** 2500 **27.** 30 L **29.** 250 mL **31.** about 21,000,000,000,000 kL; I estimated the volume in cubic meters by converting the surface area from km^2 to m^2 and then multiplying the surface area by the depth. Then I used the fact that a container with volume 1 m^3 has a capacity of 1 kL.

Spiral Review (p. 510)
34. 18.4 **35.** 14.7 **36.** 1.08 **37.** 28 **38.** 5.6
39. $2\frac{5}{24}$ **40.** $\frac{29}{50}$, $\frac{21}{50}$ **41.** about 863.5 $in.^3$ **42.** about 47.1 cm^3

Career Connection (p. 510)
43. a. $\frac{3}{4}$ c flour, $\frac{3}{4}$ c whole wheat flour, $\frac{1}{6}$ c butter, $\frac{1}{3}$ c shortening, $\frac{1}{8}$ c water, $\frac{1}{8}$ c cider **b.** $7\frac{1}{4}$ cups

Extra Skill Practice (p. 511)
1. 16 **3.** $\frac{1}{2}$ **5.** $3\frac{1}{2}$ **7.** $1\frac{3}{4}$ **9.** 8 **11.** 4.2 **13.** 0.75 **15.** 0.628 **17.** 6 fl oz **19.** 2 L **21.** 700 mL

Standardized Testing (p. 511)
greater than 0.01 L

Section 2, Practice and Application (p. 517)
1. 84 **3.** 115 **5.** 78 **7. a.** Sample Response: (832 − 1) + (999 + 1) = 831 + 1000 = 1831 **c.** Add 1000 and subtract 1. (That way you have added 999 to the first volunteer's number.) **9.** about 54 **11.** about 220 **13. a.** $750 **b.** $400 **c.** $1200; $400 · 3 = $1200.

Spiral Review (p. 518)
15. 14.4 **16.** 8 **17.** 28 **18.** $6\frac{1}{4}$ **19.** 6 **20.** $\frac{1}{4}$
21. 3000 **22.** 70 **23.** 2.3 **24.** 115,552 cm^3
25. 66,442.4 cm^3 **26.** $1\frac{2}{3}$ **27.** $2\frac{4}{9}$ **28.** $\frac{1}{16}$

Extra Skill Practice (p. 519)
1. about 5000 **3.** about 30 **5.** about 11 **7.** about 450 **9.** 92 **11.** 305 **13.** 152 **15.** 186 **17.** 65.3 **19.** 110

Standardized Testing (p. 519)
1. Sample responses are given. **a.** $3.95 + $4.91 + $5.83 **b.** $3.65 + $4.61 + $5.73 **c.** $3.15 + $4.01 + $5.83 **2. a.** $3.86 + $4.97 + $5.88 **b.** $3.42 + $4.71 + $5.83 **c.** $3.74 + $4.01 + $5.26

Section 3, Practice and Application (p. 528)
1. − 2 **3.** 3 **5.**

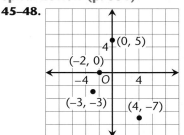

7. No; 5 of the tiles would have to total 0 and that is not possible. **9.** − 44 **11.** −15 **13.** −10 **15.** −32

17. a. 1300, 450, 1575 **b.** −300, −1150, −25
19. integers less than 3 **23.** 7 − (−3) = 10
25. **27.** −12 + (−9) = −21

29. a. 49 − (−54) = 103 **b.** 49 + 54 = 103; The thermometer shows that there are 49 degrees between 49°F and 0°F and there are 54 degrees between 0° and −54°F, for a total of 103 degrees. **31.** 5 **33.** −10 **35.** 17 **37.** −13 **39.** −38 **41.** 81

Spiral Review (p. 531)
45–48.

49. about 13 **50.** about 4000 **51.** about 2 **52.** about 5 **53.** about 12 **54.** about 33 **55.** 137 **56.** 423 **57.** 35,900 **58.** 2 **59.** 2,213 **60.** 7,500,000

Extension (p. 531)
61. −2, −2 **63.** 7, 7 **65.** −9, −9 **67.** Exercises 61–63 include a pair of expressions in which the same addends are added in different orders and the answers are the same. **69.** −10; group −21 with (−9) and 15 with 5 to get −30 + 20 = −10 **71. a.** no **b.** no **c.** Sample Response: part (a): 5 − 7 = −2 and 7 − 5 = 2; part (b): 10 − (8 − 3) = 5 and (10 − 8) − 3 = −1

Extra Skill Practice (p. 532)
1. −17 **3.** −40 **5.** 16 **7.** −26 **9.** −4 **11.** −9 **13.** −4 **15.** 22 **17.** −63 **19.** integers less than −4 **21.** −12 **23.** −6 **25.** 16 **27.** 48 **29.** −31

Study Skills (p. 532)
1–2. Answers will vary.

Section 4, Practice and Application (p. 538)
1. $\frac{1}{3}$ **3.** $\frac{1}{2}$ **5.** $\frac{1}{9}$ **9.** $\frac{1}{40}$ **11. a.** 12.5 mi^2

Spiral Review (p. 540)
13. 3.425 L **14.** 97,000 L **15.** 0.25 L **16.** 840 L **17.** 33.63 cm **18.** 26.38 in. **19.** 219.80 ft
20. a. **b.** 31; 31

21. 0.205; half of 0.4 = 0.2 **22.** 2.012; 0.2 · 10 = 2

23. 50; $1 \div 0.3 \approx 3$, so $15 \cdot 3 = 45$ **24.** 0.57, 0.7, 7, 7.29, 7.4 **25.** 4.569, 43.5, 45.02, 45.2 **26.** 45

Extra Skill Practice (p. 541)
1. $\frac{1}{7}$ **3.** $\frac{1}{4}$ **5.** about 0.22

Standardized Testing (p. 541)
1. about 8% **2.** Answers will vary. Sample Response: The combined area of the squares should be about 44 in.^{2} For example: 4 squares, each 3.3 in. on a side.

Section 5, Practice and Application (p. 549)
1. reflection **3.** translation **5.** translation **7.** reflection **9. a.** reflection; rotation or reflection; rotation
b. Quarter A can be moved to Quarter B in the middle Hex symbol by rotation or reflection.

11.

13.  **17.**

Spiral Review (p. 551)
21. $\frac{1}{3}$ **22.** $\frac{4}{5}$ **23.** $\frac{3}{5}$ **24.** $\frac{1}{3}$ **25.** < **26.** < **27.** > **28.** <
29. > **30.** >

Extra Skill Practice (p. 552)
1. reflection **3.** translation **5.** translation **7.** rotation **9.** translation **11.** C **13.** A

Standardized Testing (p. 552)
A; B: The crops in the two upper sections are rotated one section clockwise. The lower left crop is replanted in the same section, while the lower right crop is moved to the upper left; C: reflection across a vertical line dividing the field

Section 6, Practice and Application (p. 556)
1. $1.57 \cdot 10^5$ **3.** $5.6 \cdot 10^7$ **5.** $5.6 \cdot 10^3$ **7.** 59,000
9. 982,000 **11.** 60 **13.** $1.5 \cdot 10^3$ **15.** $5 \cdot 10^4$
17. a. Olympus Mons is 9.7 mi higher. **b.** Olympus Mons is 299 mi wider in diameter. **19. a.** increased
b. The tons of glass collected increased. It was previously $1.6 \cdot 10^6$ and then changed to 1.65 times the same power of 10.

Spiral Review (p. 558)
21. –11 **22.** –43 **23.** 7 **24.** 43 **25.** –49 **26.** –9
27. about 72% **28.** $11\frac{2}{3}$ **29.** $1\frac{13}{20}$ **30.** $\frac{95}{96}$ **31.** $3\frac{5}{9}$
32. $18\frac{1}{14}$ **33.** $2\frac{38}{85}$

Extra Skill Practice (p. 559)
1. $4.98 \cdot 10^7$ **3.** $3.2 \cdot 10^{10}$ **5.** $2.5 \cdot 10^6$ **7.** $7.63 \cdot 10^{4}$
9. $2.4 \cdot 10^1$ **11.** 60.8 **13.** 4140 **15.** 410
17. 1,900,000,000 **19.** $3.5 \cdot 10^1, 2 \cdot 10^2, 1.3 \cdot 10^3$
21. $5.5 \cdot 10^2, 5.5 \cdot 10^3, 5.5 \cdot 10^6$

Standardized Testing (p. 559)
1. C **2.** A **3.** B

Review & Assessment (pp. 562–563)
1. A, C, D **2. a.** $9\frac{1}{3}$ c **b.** $4\frac{2}{3}$ pt **c.** $74\frac{2}{3}$ fl oz **3.** Sample answer: 10 cm by 10 cm by 40 cm **4.** $22 + 80 = 102$
5. $1.04 + 5.00 = 6.04$ **6.** $0.75 + 0.25 + 0.85 = 1.85$
7. 900 + 100; about 1000 **8.** $15 + $25; about $40.00
9. 17 + 1; about 18 **10.** 6 **11.** –39 **12.** 18 **13.** –24
14. –26 **15.** –6 **16.** about 87% **17.** $\frac{1}{4}$ **18.** $\frac{9}{25}$
19. reflection **20.** reflection or rotation **21.** reflection or rotation **22.** reflection **23.** 5,670 **24.** 100,200
25. 700,000,000 **26.** 23 **27.** 911 **28.** 18,330
29. $4.4 \cdot 10^6$ **30.** $7.7 \cdot 10^3$ **31.** $7.89 \cdot 10^2$
32. $6.2 \cdot 10^4$ **33.** $5 \cdot 10^9$ **34.** $3.77125 \cdot 10^5$

TOOLBOX ANSWERS

NUMBERS AND OPERATIONS

Whole Number Place Value (p. 565)
1. place: one hundred thousands; value: 800,000
2. place: one thousands; value: 5,000 **3.** place: ten millions; value: 50,000,000 **4.** place: ones; value: 8
5. place: ten thousands; value: 90,000 **6.** place: hundreds; value: 200 **7.** ten thousands **8.** 20
9. 15,946,619 **10.** 220,009 **11.** five hundred eighteen **12.** twenty-three thousand, four hundred
13. seventy million, six hundred twenty-four **14.** four hundred fifty thousand, six hundred seventy-two

Comparing Whole Numbers (p. 566)
1. > **2.** > **3.** > **4.** < **5.** > **6.** < **7.** < **8.** > **9.** <
10. 239,400; 79,899; 47,777; 24,000 **11.** 7,902,500; 6,150,762; 937,400; 892,570

Rounding Whole Numbers and Money (p. 567)
1. 890 **2.** 94,600 **3.** 86,000 **4.** 27,000,000 **5.** 600
6. 40 **7.** 300,000 **8.** 68,300 **9.** $950.00
10. $4370.00 **11.** $52.00 **12.** $600.00

Adding Whole Numbers and Money (p. 568)
1. 3232 **2.** 12,718 **3.** 101,916 **4.** 60,957
5. 97,766 **6.** 89,117 **7.** $12.11 **8.** $39.04 **9.** $44.15
10. $120.90 **11.** $43.07 **12.** $115.45

Mental Math (p. 569)
1. 123 **2.** 82 **3.** 481 **4.** 321 **5.** 371 **6.** 831 **7.** 495
8. 791 **9.** 675 **10.** $12.25 **11.** $18.57 **12.** $10.38
13. $13.35 **14.** $14.40 **15.** $8.97 **16.** $20.25
17. $13.40 **18.** $23.05

Subtracting Whole Numbers and Money (p. 570)
1. 8578 **2.** 188 **3.** 4813 **4.** 2121 **5.** 6502 **6.** 3841
7. $29.08 **8.** $388.40 **9.** $64.08 **10.** $33.39
11. $320.33

Multiplying Whole Numbers and Money (p. 571)
1. 950 **2.** 48,384 **3.** 37,960 **4.** 220,735 **5.** 4582
6. 28,672 **7.** $229.08 **8.** $352.22 **9.** $111.52
10. $1890.00 **11.** $109.64 **12.** $3014.85

Dividing Whole Numbers (p. 572)
1. 400 R5 **2.** 7 R52 **3.** 2468 R3 **4.** 12 R17 **5.** 302
6. 538 R10 **7.** 20 R21 **8.** 11 R25 **9.** 161 R38 **10.** 3 R44
11. 35 R18 **12.** 13 R6

Number Fact Families (p. 573)
1. 6; 3; 6, 3 **2.** 8; 16, 8; 2; 8, 2 **3.** 12 **4.** 24 **5.** 53
6. 25 **7.** 81 **8.** 32 **9.** 103 **10.** 13 **11.** 63 **12.** 8
13. 39 **14.** 12 **15.** 48 **16.** 4 **17.** 14

Multiplying and Dividing by Tens (p. 574)
1. 50,000 **2.** 6000 **3.** 1,500,000 **4.** 1,600,000
5. 600,000 **6.** 500,000 **7.** 12,000,000
8. 20,000,000 **9.** 320,000,000 **10.** 400,000 **11.** 10
12. 50 **13.** 130 **14.** 50 **15.** 5000

MEASUREMENT

Perimeter and Using a Ruler (p. 575)
1. 18 in. **2.** 18 cm **3.** 12 ft **4.** 20 cm **5.** 14 in. **6.** 1 in.
7. 2 in.

Area (p. 576)
1. 6 cm^2 **2.** 5 cm^2 **3.** 7 cm^2

Time Conversions and Elapsed Time (p. 577)
1. 480 min **2.** 3 days **3.** 3 min **4.** 4 hr 55 min
5. 13 hr 53 min **6.** 2 hr 56 min **7.** 1 hr 35 min

DATA DISPLAYS

Reading a Graph (p. 578)
1. 16 tourneys, 10 tourneys **2.** about 840,000 people, about 870,000 people

Making a Pictograph (p. 579)
1.
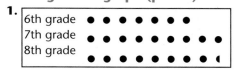

2.